Dana Facaros and Michael Pauls

P9-ARX-068

Italian Riviera

Cadogan Guides
West End House, 11 Hills Place, London W1R 1AH
email *guides@morrispub.co.uk*

The Globe Pequot Press
6 Business Park Road, PO Box 833, Old Saybrook,
Connecticut 06475–0833

Copyright © Dana Facaros and Michael Pauls, 1999
Illustrations © Horatio Monteverde, 1994 and 1997

Book and cover design by Animage

Front cover photograph © The Travel Library/Philip Enticknap
Back cover photograph ©The Travel Library/Stuart Black
Inside back cover photograph courtesy of the Italian State Tourist Board
(ENIT) London
Maps © Cadogan Guides, drawn by Map Creation Ltd

Editorial Director: Vicki Ingle
Series Editor: Linda McQueen

Editor: Kate Paice
Proofreading: Linda McQueen
Indexing: Isobel McLean

Production: Book Production Services

A catalogue record for this book is available from the
British Library

ISBN 1-86011-955-7

Printed and bound in Great Britain by Cromwell Press Ltd.

The author and publishers have made every effort to ensure the accuracy of the information in the book at the time of going to press. However, they cannot accept any responsibility for any loss, injury or inconvenience resulting from the use of information contained in this guide.

About the Authors

Dana Facaros and Michael Pauls have now written more than 20 Cadogan Guides. For three years they and their two children, Jackson and Lily, lived in a tiny Umbrian hilltop village, then an equally remote French village in the Lot. They now live in Ireland.

Authors' Acknowledgements

Thanks to Joe Fullman for his updating work, and especially for trying out all the hotels and restaurants. Also thanks to the provincial tourist offices, who took the time to answer questions. And to Kate, who diligently and gracefully edited it and tried all the recipes.

The publishers would like to thank the Italian Tourist Board in London for their help with fact checking and for permission to use their library photograph of the Villa Durazzo-Pallavicini in Pegli.

Please help us keep this guide up to date

We have done our best to ensure that the information in this guide is correct at the time of going to press. But places and facilities are constantly changing, and standards and prices in hotels and restaurants fluctuate. We would be delighted to receive any comments concerning existing entries or omissions, as well as suggestions for new features. Authors of the best letters will be offered a copy of the Cadogan Guide of their choice.

Contents

Riviera in Italian simply means shore, but in Liguria the shore is *the* Riviera, a rugged, rock-bound rainbow of coast linking France to Tuscany, dotted with the mellowed names of holiday legend—Portofino, Rapallo, the Cinque Terre, San Remo, Portovenere, the Gulf of Poets, Bordighera, Alassio, the rivieras of flowers, of palms, of olives.

One of nature's most perfect suntraps, like the glittering French Côte d'Azur just the other side of the border, the Riviera is endowed with a climate similar to that of the Bay of Naples, a singular fact that attracted the first wealthy chilblained Britons over 150 years ago. Some of these pioneering Victorians even dared to get wet, tempted by what is surprisingly one of the rarer Italian commodities—beautiful beaches.

Introduction

Not the large, buxom beaches required by mass tourism, but rather refined, slender strands in magical settings, beneath cliffs and natural hanging gardens, backed by old fishing towns squeezed between the sea and the rocks.

People prone to vertigo should approach the Riviera with caution. The scent alone can be heady; wherever they find a bit of horizontal ground or a nook to drill a root, lemons, vines, herbs and flowers grow with luxuriant abandon amid the maritime pines and cypresses. Rank upon rank of silvery olives, Liguria's totem tree and source of its pale green ichor, march up the drywall terraces. Drenched in a warm light, the colours along the coast are dazzling and rich: the reds, blues and yellows glisten as if newly born for the occasion. In contrast, a short drive up the dizzying hairpins into the hinterland or *entroterra* leads into another world, framed by mountains that mean business, where stone-walled villages seem to grow organically out of the hilltops, over lush green woodlands: even Italians are surprised to learn that Liguria is the most densely forested region in Italy.

But there's more. In the centuries before trains and tourism, Liguria was fairly isolated from the rest of Italy, giving it a distinct identity and language (fortunately everyone also speaks the more conventional brand of Italian, not to mention a bit of English). It may be beautiful, but the truth is the Riviera is poor in resources, bony under its pretty frock of olives and flowers, but with a marrow that on more than one occasion made this coast a key world-player. After the first millennium, the Republic of Genoa became a Mediterranean seapower and wheeler-dealer rivalled only by Venice, an experience that helped to form the Ligurian character—feisty, shrewd, adventurous, avaricious, indepen-dent-minded and, above all, tenacious. The word 'no' only makes a Ligurian try harder. Look at Columbus. Look at the vineyards on the sheer sea-plunging slopes of the medieval Cinque Terre, a reflection of the Ligurian character at its best.

But there was to be another chapter to the story. In the mid-1500s, just when most of Italy was sinking into an arty backwater, the Republic of Genoa became the financial centre of Europe, vacuuming up the profits of Spain's treasure fleet as soon as it docked in Seville. Side by side with the tall medieval houses and striped Romanesque and Gothic churches of the old seagoing Republic blossomed the baroque and rococo hothouse architecture of the bankers' republic: urban palaces, suburban villas and churches—nothing too intellectual, mind you, but lavishly and festively decorative, with interiors of sublime excess that mirror Liguria's extravagant nature. Expect more vertigo, especially in Genoa, where many of these sumptuous residences are now museums and galleries. In the 'Genoese Century' (late 16th century to late 17th century) nearly every fishing village along the Riveria found the wherewithal to finance a baroque fantasy by the sea, or a sanctuary to the Madonna on a hill; the best are like big pink *semifreddo* concoctions, good enough to eat.

Liguria led the fight for Italian unification in the mid-19th century, but after that the region seemed to doze off a bit; the bombardments of the Second World War left much of it shattered and discouraged, especially Genoa. The Columbian demi-millennial in 1992 seems to have been a turning point: a plethora of new attractions confirms the big city as a 'must stop' instead of an obstacle between the eastern and western Rivieras. For visitors, it's only an added bonus to the beloved charms of the coast—the beauty, the beaches, the exquisite cuisine, the popular festivals and the sense of well-being that seems to come naturally—that is, when you aren't feeling dizzy.

Ligurian Landmarks: A Guide to the Guide

If you're approaching from the west and the haughty French Riviera or Côte d'Azur, the Italian Riviera comes as a pleasant surprise: laid back, genteel, as comfortable as an old pair of shoes—no one cares if your socks don't quite match, or you've brought the children along. This western part of the coast under the Maritime Alps is the **Riviera di Ponente**, the sunset shore, voluptuous and luxuriant. The elongated metropolis of Genoa divides it from the wilder **Riviera di Levante**, the coast of the rising sun, where the Apennines in places stand right next to the sea. To the east, the Riviera rainbow touches down in a Tuscan pot of gold, or rather marble, in the Apuan Alps by Carrara.

The **Via Aurelia** (SS1), successor to the ancient Roman Via Julia Augusta, runs along the coast offering the finest scenery, side by side with the railway, which rather unfortunately for aesthetics hugs much of the coast—the problem is that there's simply no other place to put it. The best thing to do on the Riviera is to base yourself somewhere along it, in one or two places, and explore from there, at least once venturing into lush woodlands of the mountainous *entroterra*, where a car may come in handy. Otherwise public transport, especially along the coast, is good enough for most purposes and spares you the stress of trying to find a place to park. East of Genoa, the ideal way to see the most stunning scenery—the Monte di Portofino and the Cinque Terre—is by boat and on foot.

This book follows the long curl of Liguria from west to east. The landmarks along the way begin smack on the French frontier: the prehistoric caves of **Balzi Rossi** and the stunning botanical gardens at **Villa Hanbury**, and the **Val di Roja**, with the ancient Ligurian rock engravings at Monte Bégo and frescoes by the delightful Giovanni Canevesio, all near **Ventimiglia**, a fine town in its own right. The Riviera's original capitals of sun and fun, **Bordighera** and **San Remo**, still make splendid bases for exploring, especially for excursions to the medieval hill villages of **Dolceacqua** and **Taggia**.

The best olive oil in Italy, or so they claim, comes from the groves behind the provincial capital of **Imperia**; beyond it lies the delightful coral fishers' village of **Cervo**, the wide beach at **Alassio**, and the fascinating palaeochristian and medieval survivals to be found in **Albenga**, near the Riviera's most beautiful caves at **Toirano** and golf course at **Garlenda**. Towards **Savona**, long Genoa's sea-going rival, is the lovely beach at **Finale**, the charming seaside village of **Varigotti** and the once independent maritime republic of **Noli**, with a beautiful Romanesque church. Beyond Savona, you find Liguria's ceramics capital **Albissola**, the regional park of Béigua, and, lying in the embrace of the Genoese metropolitan area, **Pegli**, with its museums and villas, and the fascinating Romantic gardens of Villa Durazzo-Pallovincini.

Genoa, La Superba and Italy's busiest port, shares the vertical geography of its Rivieras. There's more to see and do than you might expect: noble palaces and churches full of art, an evocative medieval quarter and a 13th-century lighthouse, La Lanterna, a great oriental museum, crockery from the Last Supper, one of the world's most extraordinary cemeteries, and all the new attractions of the Porto Antico, ranging from the biggest aquarium in Europe to a new museum of the Antarctic. Or you could take in an opera at the Teatro Carlo Felice, with its new super-duper acoustics; or just wander about munching a slice of warm *focaccia* or *farinata* from one of Genoa's snack kings.

East of Genoa there are more villas and gardens at **Nervi**, followed by the **Gulf of Paradise**, framed by the magnificent promontory of the **Monte di Portofino**. Here are a number of places straight out of picture postcards—the fishing village of **Camogli**, the ancient abbey of **San Fruttuoso**, the resorts of **Santa Margherita Ligure** and **Rapallo**, and ultra-chic **Portofino**. Beyond, in the *entroterra*, are lovely drives into the Apennines. Down the coast is the picturesque beach at **Sestri Levante**, followed by the unique **Cinque Terre**, five medieval villages tucked under sheer mountains striped with stone-walled terraces, immersed in vineyards and laced together by a stunning seaside footpath (and now a road).

La Spezia at the head of the **Gulf of Poets** (famous residents included Shelley and Byron) has another good set of museums, of the sea, art, and archaeology. Beautiful old **Portovenere**, on one end of the gulf, is almost as chic as Portofino these days, while on the east side **Lérici** and the high coast over the Val di Magra close off the region; here too are the ruins of ancient Roman **Luni**, its medieval successor **Sarzana**, and the Lunigiana, the border region with Tuscany, where the castle of **Pontrémoli** has a remarkable collection of statue steles made by the ancient Ligurians.

Travel

By Air
from the UK and Ireland

Flying is obviously the quickest and most painless way of getting to Italy from the UK. The most convenient airport serving Liguria is Cristoforo Colombo in Genoa, ✆ 010 651 2727, with direct flights from the UK, although these cater mainly for business travellers and so are often a bit pricey. There is a second airport on the Riviera di Ponente, at Villanova di Albenga, which now takes a few international flights on smaller airlines (call ✆ 0182 582 919). You may find that you can get cheaper fares by flying to Nice, the second busiest airport in France, which is only a short train ride from Ventimiglia or San Remo. Alternatively, another possible way to save money is by flying to Milan, which is linked up to half a dozen British airports, and connected to Genoa by fast and frequent trains. Nor is Pisa airport far from Liguria, especially if you plan to visit the Riviera di Levante. Scheduled services are, in the main, more expensive than charters although there are a couple of low-cost airlines whose scheduled flight prices can compete with the very lowest charter fares (*see* below).

Most scheduled flights are operated either by the Italian state airline **Alitalia**, ✆ (020) 7602 7111, or **British Airways**, ✆ (0345) 222 111. A few services are operated by **KLM UK**, ✆ (0870) 507 4074. Return fares vary greatly, depending on the season. The best-value deals are usually **Apex** or **SuperApex** fares, though you must book at least seven, and sometimes fourteen, days ahead, and stay a Saturday night in Italy—no alterations or refunds are possible without high penalties. Return scheduled fares typically range from around £200 off-season; midsummer fares will probably be well over £250. **Sabena**, ✆ (020) 8780 1444, and **Lufthansa**, ✆ (0345) 737 747, can offer cheaper fares to Milan (around £180 return), but these often have quite rigid restrictions and involve flying via another European destination such as Brussels.

There are, however, two companies currently offering extremely cheap scheduled flights: **Go** airlines, ✆ (0845) 605 4321, a branch of British Airways, operates flights between London Stansted and Milan (21 times a week), which, if booked in advance, can cost as little as £100 return, although on a heavily booked flight this can rise to around £300. The starting prices for **Ryanair** (✆ (0541) 569 569) flights from Stansted to Pisa and Genoa are around £80 and most prices are below £150. They also sometimes run special offers when a return flight to one of these destinations can cost as little as £30.

Early birds get the best seats in the airline business, so think well ahead when booking. If you're prepared to be flexible (and philosophical), last-minute stand-bys can be a snip. Children, young people or bona fide students, and senior citizens may travel for reduced fares.

From Ireland, **Alitalia** ✆ (01) 844 6035 and **Aer Lingus**, Dublin ✆ (01) 705 3333 or Belfast ✆ (0645) 737 747, operate direct flights to Rome and Milan. The frequency depends on the time of year.

charter flights

Many inexpensive charter flights are available to popular Italian destinations in summer, though you are unlikely to find the sort of rock-bottom bargains as you get to, say, Spain. One of the biggest UK operators is **Italy Sky Shuttle**, which uses a variety of carriers. You may find cheaper fares by combing the small ads in the travel pages, or from a specialist agent. Use a reputable ABTA-registered one, such as **Trailfinders**, ✆ (020) 7937 5400, or **Campus Travel** (*see* below). All these companies offer particularly good student and youth rates too. The main problems with cheaper flights tend to be inconvenient or unreliable flight schedules, and booking restrictions, i.e. you may have to make reservations far ahead, accept given dates and, if you miss your flight, there's no redress. Take good travel insurance, however cheap your ticket is.

discount agencies

Italy Sky Shuttle, 227 Shepherd's Bush Road, London W6 7AS, ✆ (020) 8748 1333.

Italflights, 125 High Holborn, London WC1V 6QA, ✆ (020) 7405 6771.

Italia Nel Mondo, 6 Palace Street, London SW1E 5HY, ✆ (020) 7828 9171.

Budget Travel, 134 Lower Baggot Street, Dublin 2, ✆ (01) 661 1866.

students and youth travel

Besides saving 25 per cent on regular flights, young people under 26 have the choice of flying on special discount charters.

Campus Travel, 52 Grosvenor Gardens, SW1W 0AG, or 174 Kensington High Street, London W8 7RG, ✆ (020) 7730 3402, with branches at most UK universities, including Bristol, ✆ (0117) 929 2494; Manchester, ✆ (0161) 833 2046; Edinburgh, ✆ (0131) 668 3303; Birmingham, ✆ (0121) 414 1848; Oxford, ✆ (01865) 242 067; Cambridge, ✆ (01223) 324 283; or find their website at *www.campustravel.co.uk.*

STA, 74 and 86 Old Brompton Road, London SW7, or 117 Euston Road, London NW1, ✆ (020) 7361 6161; Bristol, ✆ (0117) 929 4399; Leeds, ✆ (0113) 244 9212; Manchester, ✆ (0161) 834 0668; Oxford, ✆ (01865) 792 800; Cambridge, ✆ (01223) 366 966; Edinburgh, ✆ (0131) 226 7747.

USIT, Aston Quay, Dublin 2, ✆ (01) 679 8833; Cork, ✆ (021) 270 900; Belfast, ✆ (01232) 324 073; Galway, ✆ (091) 565 177; Limerick, ✆ (061) 415 064; Waterford, ✆ (051) 872 601: **Ireland**'s largest student travel agents.

from mainland Europe

Air travel between Italy and other parts of Europe can be relatively expensive, especially for short hops, so check overland options unless you're in a great hurry. You may need to shop around a little for the best deals, and perhaps choose a less prestigious carrier. Some airlines (**Alitalia, Qantas, Air France**, etc.) offer excellent rates on the European stages of intercontinental flights, and Rome is an important touchdown for many long-haul services to the Middle or Far East. Many of these may have inconvenient departure times and booking restrictions. Amsterdam, Paris and Athens are good centres for finding cheap flights: a Rome–Paris fare with Air India or Kenya Airways could cost you under £150 return.

from the USA and Canada

The main Italian air gateways for direct flights from North America are Rome and Milan, though, if you're doing a grand tour, check fares to other European destinations (Paris or Amsterdam, for example) which may well be cheaper. **Alitalia**, ✆ (800) 223 5730, Canada ✆ (800) 563 5954, is the major carrier, but **TWA**, ✆ (800) 892 4141, **British Airways**, ✆ (800) 247 9297, and **Delta**, ✆ (800) 221 1212, also fly from a number of cities. From Canada, **Air Canada**, ✆ (800) 776 3000, and **KLM**, ✆ (800) 361 5330, operate from Toronto and Montreal. Summer round-trip fares from New York cost around US$800–1000. However, British Airways sometimes run World Offers when prices may well drop under the $700 mark. Otherwise, it may well be worth your while to catch a cheap flight to London (New York–London fares are always very competitive) and then fly on from there. Prices are rather more from Canada, so you may prefer to fly from the States. As elsewhere, fares are very seasonal and much cheaper in winter, especially mid-week. From Rome you can pick up a flight to Genoa (or catch a train).

charters, discounts and special deals

From North America, standard scheduled flights on well-known airlines are expensive, but reassuringly reliable and convenient: older travellers or families may prefer to pay extra for such a long journey (9–15 hours' flying time). Resilient, flexible and/or youthful travellers may be willing to shop around for budget deals on consolidated charters, stand-bys or perhaps even courier flights (remember, you can usually only take hand luggage with you on the last). In the USA, **Airhitch** and **Council Charter** are leading reputable cheap-flight specialists. Check the *Yellow Pages* for courier companies: **Now Voyager** is one of the largest USA ones, ✆ (212) 431 1616. For discounted flights, try the small ads in newspaper travel pages (e.g. *New York Times*, *Chicago Tribune*, *Toronto Globe & Mail*). Firms like **STA** or Canada-based **Travel Cuts** are worth contacting for student fares. Numerous travel clubs and agencies also specialize in discount fares, but may require an annual membership fee; for the complete dope, pick up a copy of Michael McColl's *Worldwide Guide to Cheap Airfares*.

discount agencies

Airhitch, 2641 Broadway, 3rd Floor, New York, NY 10025, ✆ (212) 864 2000.

Council Travel, 205 E 42nd Street, New York, NY 10017, ✆ (1 800) 743 1823.

Last Minute Travel Club, 132 Brookline Avenue, Boston, MA 02215, ✆ (800) 527 8646.

Now Voyager, 74 Varick Street, Suite 307, New York, NY 10013, ✆ (212) 431 1616.

STA, 48 East 11th Street, New York, NY 10003, ✆ (1 800) 777 0112.

Travel CUTS, 187 College Street, Toronto, Ontario M5T 1P7, ✆ (416) 979 2406.

STA Travel, New York City, ✆ (212) 627 3111, or toll-free, ✆ (1 800) 777 0112.

Council Travel, 205 E 42nd Street, New York, NY 10017, ✆ (1 800) 743 1823. Major specialists in student and charter flights; branches all over the USA.

Travel CUTS, 187 College Street, Toronto, Ontario M5T 1P7, ✆ (416) 979 2406. Canada's largest student travel specialists; branches in most provinces.

By Rail

from the UK and Europe

A train journey from London to Genoa used to be something of a nightmare, involving ferries and station changes and taking around 16 hours. This experience can still be repeated, should you so desire it. There is, however, following the opening of the Channel Tunnel and the construction of new fast rail networks throughout Europe, an alternative. Take a Eurostar to Paris and a TGV to Nice, then a local train to Ventimiglia, San Remo or Genoa, and your journey time could be reduced by as much as four hours depending on your destination in Liguria (11 hours from London Waterloo to Nice). Unfortunately the price for this journey is around £129, plus up to £14 for the four-hour trip to Genoa. Train travel, at whatever speed, has its benefits—the opportunity it gives travellers to watch the changing scenery, to acclimatize themselves to new surroundings and take time to prepare for their arrival in a new country—but in an age of low-cost airlines, it is not much of an economy. For more information, contact either **Rail Europe Travel Centre**, 179 Piccadilly, London, W1, ✆ (0990) 848 848, or **Eurostar**, EPS House, Waterloo Station, London, SE1, ✆ (0345) 881 881; unfortunately, at the time of writing Eurostar do not arrange train packages to Italy.

If you are just planning to see Liguria, inclusive rail passes are a waste of money. Fares on FS (*Ferrovie dello Stato*), the Italian State Railway, are among the lowest, kilometre for kilometre, in Europe. If you plan more extensive rail travel around Europe, **Interail** (UK) or **Eurail** passes (USA/Canada) give unlimited travel for under-26s throughout Europe for one or two months. Various other cheap youth fares (BIJ tickets etc.) are also available; organize these before you leave home. Useful addresses for rail travel include **Eurotrain**, 52 Grosvenor Gardens, London SW1, ✆ (020) 7730 8518; **Wasteels Travel**, adjacent to Platform 2, Victoria Station, London SW1, ✆ (020) 7834 7066; any branch of **Thomas Cook**, or **CIT** (*see* addresses below). A month's full Interail pass costs £259 for under-26s, £349 for those over 26, though you can now buy cheaper zonal passes covering three or four countries only. If you intend travelling extensively by train just within Italy, one of the special Italian tourist passes may be a better bet (*see* 'Getting Around').

A convenient pocket-sized **timetable** detailing all the main and secondary Italian railway lines is available in the UK, costing £9 (plus 90p postage). Contact **Italwings**, Travel & Accommodation, The Linen Hall, Suite 217, 162–8 Regent Street, London W1R 5TB. If you wait until you arrive in Italy, however, you can pick up the Italian timetable (in two volumes) at any station for about L4,500 each.

From the USA and Canada, contact **Rail Europe**, 226–230 Westchester Ave, White Plains, NY 10604, ✆ (914) 682 2999 or ✆ (800) 438 7245. **Wasteels** also have a USA office at 5728 Major Boulevard, Suite 308, Orlando, 32819 Florida, ✆ (407) 351 2537.

CIT offices outside Italy

UK: Marco Polo House, 3–5 Lansdowne Road, Croydon, Surrey, ✆ (0891) 715 151 (50p a minute), ✉ (020) 8681 1712.

USA: 15 West 44th Street, 10th Floor, New York, NY 10036, ✆ (800) 248 7245, ✉ (888) FAX CIT.

Canada: 1450 City Councillors Street, Suite 750, Montreal H3A 2E6, ✆ (514) 845 4310.

By Road

by bus and coach

Eurolines is the main international bus operator in Europe, with representatives in Italy and many other countries. In the UK, they can be found at Victoria Coach Station, London SW1, ✆ (0990) 80 80 80, and are booked through National Express. There are regular services running to Genoa. Needless to say, the journey is very long, 26½ hours, and the relatively small savings on price (a return ticket from London to Genoa costs £119; single £83) make it a masochistic choice in comparison with a discounted air fare, or even rail travel.

by car

Driving to Liguria from London is a rather lengthy and expensive proposition. If you're only staying for a short period, check costs against airline fly-drive schemes. It's the best part of 20 hours' driving time from the UK, even if you stick to fast toll roads. There are two main routes, depending on personal preference: the Calais–Genoa route via Lausanne and the Great Bernard Pass (or tunnel) is a scenic and and fairly hassle-free route via the Alps, but, if you pass through Switzerland, expect to pay for the privilege (around £14 or 30SFr for motorway use). In winter the passes may be closed and you will have to stick to the expensive tunnels (one-way tolls range from about L37,000 for a small car). The other route is barrel straight through France down the A1, take the *péripherique* around Paris to the A6 to Lyon and the A7 to Marseille, then continue east into Italy, taking the A8 along the French Riviera. You can avoid some of the driving by putting your car on the train, though this is scarcely a cheap option. **Express Sleeper Cars** run to Milan from Paris or Boulogne (infrequently in winter). Foreign-plated cars are no longer entitled to free breakdown assistance from the **Italian Auto Club** (ACI), but their prices are fair. Phone ACI on ✆ (06) 49 981 to find out the current rates.

To bring a GB-registered car into Italy, you need a **vehicle registration document, full driving licence** (and international driving permit if you have one of the old-fashioned licences) and **insurance papers**—these must be carried at all times when driving. Non-EU citizens should preferably have an **international driving licence** which has an

Italian translation incorporated. Your vehicle should display a nationality plate indicating its country of registration. Before travelling, check everything is in perfect order. Minor infringements like worn tyres or burnt-out sidelights can cost you dear in any country. A **red triangular hazard sign** is obligatory; also recommended are a spare set of bulbs, a first-aid kit and a fire extinguisher. Spare parts for non-Italian cars can be difficult to find, especially Japanese models. Before crossing the border, fill her up; *benzina* is very expensive in Italy.

For more information on driving in Italy, *see* 'Getting Around By Car', p.15, or contact the motoring organizations **AA**, ✆ (0990) 500 600, or **RAC**, ✆ (0800) 550 550, in the UK, and **AAA**, ✆ (813) 289 5000, in the USA.

Entry Formalities

EU nationals with a valid passport can enter Italy freely and stay as long as they like. Citizens of the USA, Canada, Australia and New Zealand need only a valid passport to stay up to three months in Italy, unless they get a visa in advance from an Italian embassy or consulate. By law you should register with the police within eight days of your arrival in Italy. In practice this is done automatically for most visitors when they check in at their first hotel. Don't be alarmed if the owner of your self-catering property proposes to 'denounce' you to the police when you arrive—it's just a formality.

Tour Operators and Special Interest Holidays

Dozens of general and specialist companies offer holidays on the Riviera. Some of the major ones are listed below.

UK general

Bladon Lines, 56–8 Putney High Street, London, SW15 1SF, ✆ (020) 8785 3131.

Cosmos, Tourama House, 17 Holmesdale Road, Bromley, Kent, BR2 9LX, ✆ (020) 8464 3444.

First Choice Plc, First Choice House, London Road, Crawley, West Sussex, RH10 2GX, ✆ (0161) 745 7000.

Inghams, 10–18 Putney Hill, London, SW15 6AX, ✆ (020) 8780 4450.

Magic of Italy, 227 Shepherds Bush Road, London, W6 7AS, ✆ (020) 8748 7575.

Sunvil, Sunvil House, 7–8 Upper Square, Old Isleworth, Middlesex TW7 7BJ, ✆ (020) 8568 4499.

UK special interest

Abercrombie & Kent (city breaks, country retreats and island-hopping cruises), Sloane Square House, Holbein Place, London, SW1W 8NS, ✆ (020) 7730 9600.

Alternative Travel (walking and cycling tours), 69–71 Banbury Road, Oxford, OX2 6PE, ✆ (01865) 315 685.

Arblaster & Clarke Wine Tours, Clark House, Farnham Road, West Liss, Hants, GU33 6JQ, ✆ (01730) 893 344.

Brompton Travel (tailor-made), Brompton House, 64 Richmond Road, Kingston-upon-Thames, Surrey, KT2 5EH, ✆ (020) 8549 3334.

Citalia (opera), Marco Polo House, 3–5 Lansdowne Road, Croydon, CR9 1LL, ✆ (020) 8686 5533.

Italia 2000 (sporting holidays: golf, sailing, mountain biking), 8 Timperley Way, Up Hatherley, Cheltenham, Gloucestershire, GL51 5RH, ✆ (01242) 234 215.

Italiatour (football tickets, equestrian holidays, cooking classes, agriturism) 4–5 Dawson Street, Dublin 2, ✆ (01) 671 7821.

Kirker (Portofino-based tours), 3 New Concordia Wharf, Mill Street, London, SE1 2BB, ✆ (020) 7231 3333.

Liaisons Abroad (authorized agents for Genoa's Teatro Carlo Felice, for opera and ballet tickets), Chenil House, 181–3 Kings Road, London, SW3 5EP, ✆ (020) 7376 4020.

Martin Randall Travel (cultural tours to Genoa), 10 Barley Mow Passage, Chiswick, London W4 4PH, ✆ (020) 8742 3355.

Ramblers (walking tours), Box 43, Welwyn Garden City, Hertfordshire, AL8 6PQ, ✆ (01707) 331 133.

Solo's (singles), 54–8 High Street, Edgware, Middlesex, HA8 7EJ, ✆ (020) 8951 2800.

Special Tours (escorted cultural tours: art, architecture, gardens), 81a Elizabeth Street, London, SW1W 9PG, ✆ (020) 7730 2297.

in the USA/Canada

American Express Vacations (prepacked or tailor-made tours), 300 Pinnacle Way, Norcross, GA 30093, ✆ (800) 241 1700.

CIT Tours (general and skiing) 342 Madison Avenue, Suite 3207, New York, NY 10173, ✆ (212) 697 2100.

Connaissance & Cie (wine tours), 790 Madison Avenue, New York, NY 10021, ✆ (212) 472 5772.

Esplanade Tours (art and architecture tours), 581 Boyston Street, Boston, MA 02116, ✆ (617) 266 7465.

Italiatour (fly-drive in conjunction with Alitalia), 666 5th Avenue, New York, NY 10103, ✆ (212) 765 2183.

Maupintour, 1515 St Andrew's Drive, Lawrence, Kansas, KA 66047, ✆ (913) 843 1211.

Olson Travelworld, 970 West 190th Street, Suite 425, Torrance, California, CA 90502, ✆ (310) 354 2600.

Travel Concepts (wine and food tours), 62 Commonwealth Avenue, Suite 3, Boston, MA 02116, ✆ (617) 266 8450

Getting Around

Italy has an excellent network of airports, railways, highways and byways and you'll find getting around fairly easy—until one union or another takes it into its head to go on strike (to be fair they rarely do it during the high holiday season). There's plenty of talk about passing a law to regulate strikes, but it won't happen soon, if ever. Instead, learn to recognize the word in Italian: *sciopero* (SHO-per-o), and do as the Romans do—quiver with resignation. There's always a day or two's notice, and strikes usually last only a day, just long enough to throw a spanner in the works if you have to catch a plane. Keep your ears open and watch for notices posted in the stations.

By Air

Air traffic within Italy is intense, with up to ten flights a day on popular routes. Domestic flights are handled by Alitalia, ATI (its internal arm) or Avianova. Air travel makes most sense when hopping between north and south. Shorter journeys are often just as quick (and much less expensive) by train or even bus if you take check-in and airport travelling times into account.

Domestic flight costs are comparable to those in other European countries: a full-price return fare from Rome to Genoa (an hour's journey) costs about L400–500,000 (one-way tickets are half price). A complex array of discounts are available for night flights, weekend travel, senior (60 plus) and youth fares (12–26-year-olds; half-price or less for younger children). Family reductions are also available (up to 50%). Each airport has a bus terminal in the city; ask about schedules as you purchase your ticket to avoid hefty taxi fares. Baggage allowances vary between airlines. Tickets can be bought at CIT offices and other large travel agencies.

By Rail

FS information from anywhere in Italy, © 1478 88088, open 7am–9pm www.fs-on-line.com

Italy's national railway, the **FS** (*Ferrovie dello Stato*), is well run, inexpensive (despite recent price rises) and often a pleasure to ride. There are also several private rail lines that may not accept Interail or Eurail passes. On the FS, some of the trains are sleek and high-tech, but much of the rolling stock hasn't been changed for fifty years. Possible unpleasantnesses you may encounter, besides a strike, are delays, crowding (especially at weekends and in the summer), and crime on overnight trains, where someone rifles your bags while you sleep. The crowding, at least, becomes much less of a problem if you reserve a seat in advance (*fare una prenotazione*); the fee is small and can save you hours standing in some train corridor. On the more expensive trains, **reservations** are mandatory. Do check that the date on your ticket is correct; tickets are only valid the day they're purchased unless you specify otherwise. Sleepers and couchettes on overnight trains must also be reserved in advance. At sleepy rural train stations without information boards, the imminent presence of a train is signalled by a platform bell.

Tickets may be purchased not only in the stations, but at many travel agents in the city centres. Fares are strictly determined by the kilometres travelled. The system is computerized and runs smoothly, at least until you try to get a reimbursement for an unused ticket (usually not worth the trouble). Be sure you ask which platform (*binario*) your train arrives at; the big permanent boards in the stations are not always correct. Always remember to stamp your ticket (*convalidare*) in the not-very obvious yellow machines at the head of the platform before boarding the train. Failure to do so could result in a fine. If you get on a train without a ticket you can buy one from the conductor, with an added 20% penalty. You can also pay a conductor to move up to first class or get a couchette, if there are places available.

There is a fairly straightforward **hierarchy of trains**. At the bottom of the pyramid is the humble *Locale* (euphemistically known sometimes as an *Accelerato*) which often stops even where there's no station in sight; it can be excruciatingly slow. When you're checking the schedules, beware of what may look like the first train to your destination—if it's a *Locale*, it will be the last to arrive. A *Diretto* stops far less, an *Expresso* just at the main towns. *Intercity* trains whoosh between the big cities and rarely deign to stop. *Eurocity* trains link Italian cities with major European centres. Both of these services require a supplement—some 30% more than a regular fare. Lording it above these are the *ETR 500 pendolino* trains, similar to the French TGV service, which can travel at up to 186mph. Reservations are free, but must be made at least five hours before the trip, and on some trains there are only first-class coaches. Sitting on the pinnacle are the true Kings of the Rails, the super-swish and super-fast *Eurostars*. These make very few stops, have both first and second class carriages, and carry a supplement which includes an obligatory seat reservation. So, the faster the train, the more you pay.

The FS offers several **passes**. A flexible option is the 'Flexi Card' (marketed as a 'Freedom Pass' in the UK) which allows unlimited travel for four days within a month (L206,000), 8 days within a month (L287,000), 12 days within a month (L368,000) plus seat reservations and supplements on Eurostars. Another ticket, the *Kilometrico*, gives you 3000 kilometres of travel, made on a maximum of 20 journeys, and is valid for two months (second class L206,000, first class L338,000); one advantage is that it can be used by up to five people at the same time. However, supplements are payable on *Intercity* trains. Other discounts, only available once you're in Italy, are 15 per cent on same-day return tickets and three-day returns (depending on the distance involved), and discounts for families of at least four travelling together. Senior citizens (men 65 and over, women 60) can also get a *Carta d'Argento* ('silver card') for L44,000, entitling them to a 20 per cent reduction in fares. A *Carta Verde* bestows a 20% discount on people under 26 and also costs L44,000.

Refreshments on routes of any great distance are provided by bar cars or trolleys; you can usually get sandwiches and coffee from vendors along the tracks at intermediary stops. Station bars often have a good variety of take-away travellers' fare; consider at least investing in a plastic bottle of mineral water, since there's no drinking water on the trains.

Besides trains and bars, Italy's stations offer other **facilities**. Most have a *Deposito*, where you can leave your bags for hours or days for a small fee. The larger ones have porters (who charge L1500–2000 per piece) and some even have luggage trolleys; major stations have an *Albergo Diurno* ('Day Hotel', where you take a shower, get a shave and have a haircut), information offices, currency exchanges open at weekends (not at the most advantageous rates, however), hotel-finding and reservation services, kiosks with foreign papers, restaurants, etc. You can also arrange to have a rental car awaiting you at your destination—Avis, Hertz, Aurotrans and Maggiore are the most widespread firms in Italy.

Beyond that, some words need to be said about riding the rails on the most serendipitous national line in Europe. The FS may have its strikes and delays, its petty crime and bureaucratic inconveniences, but when you catch it on its better side it will treat you to a dose of the real Italy before you even reach your destination. If there's a choice, try for one of the older cars, depressingly grey outside but fitted with comfortably upholstered seats, Art Deco lamps and old pictures of the towns and villages of the country. The washrooms are invariably clean and pleasant. Best of all, the FS is relatively reliable, and even if there has been some delay you'll have an amenable station full of clocks to wait in; some of the station bars have astonishingly good food (some do not), but at any of them you may accept a well-brewed cappuccino and look blasé until the train comes in. Try to avoid travel on Friday evenings, when the major lines out of the big cities are packed.

By Coach and Bus

Inter-city coach travel is sometimes quicker than train travel, but also a bit more expensive. The Italians aren't dumb: you will find regular coach connections only where there is no train to offer competition; in Liguria they are especially useful for getting up into the mountain valleys. Coaches almost always depart from the vicinity of the train station, and tickets usually need to be purchased before you get on. In many regions they are the only means of public transport and well used, with frequent schedules. If you can't get a ticket before the coach leaves, get on anyway and pretend you can't speak a word of Italian; the worst that can happen is that someone will make you pay for a ticket. The base for all **country bus** lines is the provincial capitals.

City buses are the traveller's friend. Most cities (at least in the north) label routes well; all charge flat fees for rides within the city limits and immediate suburbs, at the time of writing around L1500. Bus tickets must always be purchased before you get on, either at a tobacconist's, a newspaper kiosk, in bars, or from ticket machines near the main stops. Once you get on, you must 'obliterate' your ticket in the machines in the front or back of the bus; controllers stage random checks to make sure you've punched your ticket. Fines for cheaters are about L50,000, and the odds are about 12 to 1 against a check, so many passengers take a chance. If you're good-hearted, you'll buy a ticket and help some over-burdened municipal transit line meet its annual deficit.

By Car

The advantages of driving in Italy generally outweigh the disadvantages, but, before you bring your own car or hire one, consider the kind of holiday you're planning. If you're sticking to the Riviera and Genoa, both well served by trains and buses, you may be better off not driving at all: parking and traffic are impossible, and one-way street systems, signals and signs can seem like an exercise in obfuscation to the uninitiated.

Third-party **insurance** is a minimum requirement in Italy (and you should be a lot more than minimally insured, as many of the locals have none whatever!). Obtain a Green Card from your insurer, which gives proof that you are fully covered. Also get hold of a **European Accident Statement** form, which may simplify things if you are unlucky enough to have an accident. Always insist on a full translation of any statement you are asked to sign. Breakdown assistance insurance is a sensible investment (eg AA's Five Star or RAC's Eurocover Motoring Assistance).

Petrol (*benzina*; unleaded is *benzina senza piombo*, and diesel *gasolio*) is still very expensive in Italy (around L1800 per litre). Many petrol stations close for lunch in the afternoon, and few stay open late at night, though you may find a 'self-service' where you feed a machine nice smooth L10,000 notes. Motorway (*autostrada*) tolls are quite high. Rest stops and petrol stations along the motorways stay open 24 hours. Other roads— *superstrade* on down through the Italian grading system—are free of charge.

Italians are famously anarchic behind a wheel. The only way to beat the locals is to join them by adopting an assertive and constantly alert driving style. Bear in mind the maxim that he/she who hesitates is lost (especially at traffic lights, where the danger of crashing into someone at the front is less great than that of being rammed from behind). All drivers from boy racers to elderly nuns seem to tempt providence by overtaking at the most dangerous bend, and no matter how fast you are hammering along the *autostrada*, plenty will whizz past at supersonic rates. North Americans used to leisurely speeds and gentler road manners may find the Italian interpretation of the highway code stressful. Speed limits (generally ignored) are 130kph on motorways, 110kph on main highways, 90kph on secondary roads, and 50kph in built-up areas. Speeding fines may be as much as L500,000, or L100,000 for jumping a red light (a popular Italian sport).

If you are undeterred, you may actually enjoy driving in Italy, at least away from the congested tourist centres. Signposting is generally good, and roads are well maintained. Some are feats of engineering that the Romans themselves would have admired—bravura projects suspended on cliffs, crossing valleys on vast stilts and winding up hairpins.

Buy a good road map (the Italian Touring Club series is excellent). The **Automobile Club of Italy** (ACI) is a good friend to the foreign motorist. Besides having bushels of useful information and tips, they can be reached from anywhere by dialling ✆ **116**—also use this number if you have to find the nearest service station. If you need major repairs, the ACI can make sure the prices charged are according to their guidelines. ACI regional headquarters in Genoa are Viale delle Brigate Partigiane 1/a, ✆ 010 53941, ✉ 010 592 829, and they have branches throughout the city.

Hiring a Car

Hiring a car, *autonoleggio*, is simple but not particularly cheap—Italy has some of the highest car hire rates in Europe. A small car (Fiat Punto or similar) with unlimited mileage and collision damage waiver will set you back around L70,000–90,000 per day, including tax, although if you hire for the car for over three days, this will decrease slightly pro rata. Take into account that some hire companies require a deposit amounting to the estimated cost of the hire. The minimum age limit is usually 25 (sometimes 23) and the driver must have held their license for over a year—this will have to be produced, along with the driver's passport, when hiring the car. Note that unless you specify (and pay a lot more) the car will be a manual stick shift. Most major rental companies have offices in airports or main stations, though it may be worthwhile checking prices of local firms.

Taking all things into account, it makes sense to arrange your car hire with a domestic firm before making your trip and, in particular, to check out fly-drive discounts. This is usually the cheaper option. Prices tend towards the L70,000 per day mark, often with large discounts for a second week of hire. The deposit is also usually waived.

Car Rental Agencies

UK and Ireland

Avis, ✆ (0990) 900 500.

Hertz, ✆ (0990) 996 699.

National Car Rental, ✆ (0990) 365 365.

Car Rental Direct, ✆ (020) 7604 4688.

Hertz, Dublin, ✆ (01) 660 2255.

USA and Canada

Avis, ✆ (800) 331 1084.

Hertz, ✆ (800) 654 3131.

Hertz, Canada ✆ (800) 263 0600.

Hitchhiking

It is illegal to hitch on the *autostrade*, though you may pick up a lift near one of the toll booths. Don't hitch from the city centres, head for suburban exit routes. For the best chances of getting a lift, travel light, look respectable and take your sunglasses off. Hold a sign indicating your destination if you can. Never hitch at points where you may cause an accident or obstruction: Italian traffic conditions are bad enough as it is. Women should try never to hitch alone.

Mopeds, Vespas and scooters are the vehicles of choice for a great many Italians. You will see them everywhere. In the traffic-congested towns this is a ubiquity born of necessity; when driving space is limited, two wheels are always better than four. However, in Italy, riding a two-wheeler often seems to be as much a form of cultural and social expression as it does a means of getting from A to B. Stand watching the traffic on a busy town corner for any length of time and certain trends will begin to become apparent. For one thing, there is a clear generational control at work over an individual's choice of machine. Italian youths tend to prefer chic Italian lines, Vespas, Lambrettas and the like, which they parade self-consciously through the town's main drags; while older members of society, more often than not, plump for mopeds: the type you can actually pedal, should you feel so inclined. Choosing your machine, however, is only the first stage of this cultural process; it then becomes necessary to master the Italian way of riding. This almost invariably means dispensing with a crash helmet, despite the fact that they are compulsory, so as to be better able to perfect the method of riding in as laid-back a style as possible whilst still achieving an alarming rate of speed: riding sidesaddle, while on the phone, while smoking, while holding a dog or child under one arm—all of these methods have their determined and expert adherents. Despite the obvious dangers of this means of transport (especially if you choose to do it Italian-style), there are clear benefits to moped riding in Italy. For one thing it is cheaper than car hire—costs for a *motorino* range from about L30,000 per day, scooters somewhat more (up to L50,000)—and can prove an excellent way of covering a town's sites in a limited space of time. Furthermore, because Italy is such a scooter-friendly place, car drivers are more conditioned to their presence and so are less likely to hurtle into them when taking corners. Nonetheless, you should only consider hiring a moped if you have ridden one before (Italy's hills and alarming traffic are no place to learn) and, despite local examples, you should always wear a helmet (you should also be over 14). Also, be warned, some travel insurance policies exclude claims resulting from scooter or motorbike accidents.

Italians are keen cyclists, racing drivers up the steepest hills; if you're not training for the Tour de France, consider Liguria's very rugged and steep topography and busy roads well before planning a bicycling tour, especially in the hot summer. Prices range from about L20,000 per day, which may make buying one interesting if you plan to spend much time in the saddle: L190,000–L300,000, either in a bike shop or through the classified ads. Alternatively, if you bring your own bike, do check the airlines to see what their policies are on transporting them. Bikes can be transported by train in Italy, either with you or within a couple of days of your arrival—apply at the baggage office (*ufficio bagagli*).

Practical A–Z

Protected from nasty winds and cold by the mountains, the Italian Riviera enjoys the mildest **winter** climate on the peninsula. The warmest towns are the most sheltered: Alassio and Bordighera. While the coast gets fairly moderate rains in the winter (*see* chart, below), the mountains just behind get buckets of water and more than a dusting of snow; in a couple of places you can even ski. This is a good time to visit Genoa, with its musical and opera seasons in full swing. In January, mimosa blooms along the coast as a harbinger of spring.

Spring, especially the period between April and June, is a lovely time to visit, and coincides with Easter celebrations and other traditional festivities. The mountain meadows are covered with wildflowers. It's usually warm enough to swim or at least sunbathe by May, often with snow-topped mountains for a backdrop behind the palms.

Summer, shunned by the Grand Tourists and Victorians because of the excessive heat and sun, is now the high season, and both Rivieras are packed. The Italians themselves hit the beaches in August. Accommodation is at a premium, and the traffic on the few roads, especially the Via Aurelia, tends to get bottled up fairly quickly.

Autumn can be lovely. The weather is mild, places aren't crowded and the light, even in November and December, has a fine warm quality to it. In recent years, however, perhaps as a result of global warming, the area has been subject to tempestuous autumn rains. In October 1998 San Remo endured its worst floods since 1875. There are no crowds, but note that by December mountain villages only ten miles from the sea as the crow flies can be snowed in.

Average Temperatures in °C (°F)

	January	April	July	October
Genoa	8.4 (47)	14.5 (58)	24.6 (76)	18.1 (64)
San Remo	9.7 (49)	14.4 (58)	23.4 (73)	17.9 (64)
Alassio	11.9 (53)	15.4 (60)	25.7 (78)	15.8 (61)
Chiavari	9.9 (50)	14.0 (57)	22.9 (72)	12.8 (54)

Average Monthly Rainfall in Millimetres (inches)

	January	April	July	October
Genoa	109 (4)	82 (3)	35 (1½)	135 (5)
San Remo	67 (2½)	56 (2)	14 (½)	88 (3½)
Alassio	67 (2½)	53 (2)	10 (½)	17 (1)
Chiavari	136 (5)	138 (5)	14 (½)	46 (2)

Crime

There is relatively little petty crime in Liguria, by Italian standards—fewer than average purse-snatchings, less pickpocketing and minor thievery of the white collar kind (always check your change) and a smaller risk of car break-ins and theft. Nearly all mishaps can be avoided with adequate precautions. Scooter-borne purse-snatchers can be foiled if you stay on the inside of the pavement and keep a firm hold on your property (sling your bag-strap across your body, don't dangle it from one shoulder). Pickpockets strike in crowded buses or trams and gatherings; don't carry too much cash, and split it so you won't lose the lot at once. In cities and popular tourist sites, beware groups of scruffy-looking women or children with placards, apparently begging for money. They use distraction techniques to perfection. The smallest and most innocent-looking child is generally the most skilful pickpocket. If you are targeted, the best technique is to grab sharply hold of any vulnerable possessions or pockets and shout furiously (Italian passers-by will often come to your assistance if they realize what is happening). Be extra careful in train stations, don't leave valuables in hotel rooms, and always park your car in garages, guarded lots or on well-lit streets, with portable temptations well out of sight. Purchasing small quantities of soft drugs for personal consumption is technically legal in Italy, though what constitutes a small quantity is unspecified, and if the police don't like you to begin with, it will probably be enough to get you into big trouble.

Political terrorism, once the scourge of Italy, has declined greatly in recent years, mainly thanks to special quasi-military squads of black-uniformed national police, the *carabinieri*. Local matters are usually in the hands of the *Polizia Urbana*; the nattily dressed *Vigili Urbani* concern themselves with directing traffic, and handing out parking fines. If you need to summon any of them, dial ✆ 113.

Disabled Travellers

Italy has been relatively slow off the mark in its provision for disabled visitors. Cobblestones, uneven or non-existent pavements, the appalling traffic conditions, crowded public transport and endless flights of steps in many public places are all disincentives; the geography of Liguria will always make much of it inaccessible, although you should be alright on the coast and in most of Genoa. A national support organization in your own country may well have specific information on facilities in Italy, or will at least be able to provide general advice. The Italian tourist office or CIT (travel agency) can also advise on hotels, museums with ramps and so on. If you book rail travel through CIT, you can request assistance. Once in Italy, a disabled cooperative, ✆ 167 179 179, offers advice on accommodation and travel.

In the UK, contact the **Royal Association for Disability & Rehabilitation** (RADAR), and ask for their guide *Holidays & Travel Abroad: A Guide for Disabled People* (£3.50). They are based at 25 Mortimer St, London W1N 8AB, ✆ (020) 7637 5400. Americans should contact the **Society for the Advancement of Travel for the Handicapped** (SATH), 347 Fifth Avenue, Suite 610, New York 10016, ✆ (2112) 447 7284. Another useful organization, which provides help on both sides of the Atlantic, is **Mobility International**, at 228 Borough High Street, London SE1, ✆ (020) 7403 5688, or PO Box 3551, Eugene, Oregon 97403, USA, ✆ (503) 343 1284. Australians could try **Australian Council for the Rehabilitation of the Disabled** (ACROD), 55 Charles Street, Ryde, New South Wales, ✆ (02) 9809 4488. If you need help while you are in Italy, contact the local tourist offices.

Embassies and Consulates

UK

Milan: Via San Paulo 7, ✆ 02 723 001.
Rome: Via XX Settembre 80/a, ✆ 06 482 5441.

Ireland

Rome: Largo Nazareno 3, ✆ 06 678 2541.

USA

Milan: Largo Donegani 1, ✆ 02 2900 1841.
Rome: Via V. Veneto 119/a, ✆ 06 46741.

Canada

Milan: Via Vittorio Pisani 19, ✆ 02 669 7451.
Rome: Via Zara 30, ✆ 06 440 3028.

Australia

Milan: Via Borgagna 2, ✆ 02 7601 1330.
Rome: Via Alessandria 215, ✆ 06 852 721.

New Zealand

Rome: Via Zara 28, ✆ 06 440 2928.

Festivals

Liguria puts on some of Italy's most attractive festivals, including some of ancient origin. Every *comune* has at least one or two honouring patron saints, at which the presiding Madonna is paraded through the streets decked in fairy lights and gaudy flowers. Shrovetide and Holy Week are great focuses of activity. *Carnival*, after being suppressed and ignored for decades, has been revived in many places, displaying the gorgeous music and pageantry of the *commedia dell'arte* with Harlequin and his motley crew. Other festivals are purely secular affairs sponsored by political parties (especially the ex-Communists and Socialists), where everyone goes to meet friends. Relaxed village *festas* can be just as enjoyable as (or more so than) the big national crowd-pullers. Outsiders are nearly always welcome. Whatever the occasion, eating is a primary pastime at all Italian jamborees, and all kinds of regional specialities are prepared. Check at the local tourist office for precise dates, which alter from year to year, and often slide into the nearest weekend.

Jan–July	Opera and ballet season in **Genoa**
5–6 Jan	Child-oriented Epiphany celebrations throughout Italy honour the good stocking-filling witch La Befana
20 Jan	San Sebastiano, ancient processions at **Dolceacqua**
Late Jan	Festival of Italian Popular Song, **San Remo**; also parade of floats covered with flowers in *San Remo in fiore*
Early Feb	Festa dei Fùrgari, in honour of San Benedetto Revelli in **Taggia**, celebrating the town's near-miraculous escape from the Saracen invaders. The celebrations feature firework displays and bonfires and there is also a parade of historical costumes. Mimosa festival, **Pieve Ligure**
Feb	Shrovetide Carnivals all over Italy; masked balls in the historic palaces along Via Garibaldi, **Genoa**
March/April	Holy Week celebrations, with processions of the various *confraternities*, especially in **Genoa** and **Savona**, where on Good Friday the marchers bear heavy floats of sculptured figures of the Passion dating from the 17th century. The *Calata dalla Croce* in **Ceriana** is a medieval revival of Holy Week celebrations in the town, and includes a procession of the Dead Christ
Easter Week	Antique market in the streets, **Sarzana**
19 March	San Giuseppe street fair, **La Spezia**
30 April	Historic procession in honour of St Catherine of Siena, **Varazze**
May	*Città della Donne*, women's month-long festival, with sports, theatre, culture and more dedicated to women, **Varazze**
May (2nd Sun)	*Sagra del Pesce*, fish festival at **Camogli**, including an enormous fry-up in a giant frying pan, served to all comers
May (4th Sun)	*Focaccia* festival, **Recco**
Pentecost	Festa della Barca, **Baiardo**
June	Historical Regatta of the Four Ancient Maritime Republics (boat race between the rival sea-towns of Pisa, Venice, Amalfi and **Genoa**—location alternates). Genoa's turn will next come in 2000. Battle of Flowers, **Ventimiglia**. Festival of ethnic music, **Alassio**
23–4 June	St John's Day celebrations in **Genoa**, **Celle Ligure** and **Laigueglia**, with an enormous bonfire and lights on the sea
29 June	Festival of the Sea, **Alassio**, including a procession of boats decked with flowers
Corpus Christi	*Infiorate*—patterns in the streets made with flowers, at **Diano Marina**, **Montegrosso** and **Sassello**

July	Ballet festival, **Nervi**. International harp festival, **Isolabona**. Sagra delle Rose, **Pogli** (Ortoverto, near Albenga). Festa del Marchesato, **Finale**. Mediterranean festival, Porto Antico, **Genoa**. Jazz festival, in the towns of the **Golfo di Paradiso**
July and Aug	International Chamber Music Festival, **Cervo**. Arts festival, **Villa Faraldi** (above San Bartolomeo del Mare). Cabaret, **Loano**. Classical music concerts, **San Fruttuoso**
Early July	Garlic festival, **Vessálico**. Historical re-enactment of a pirate attack, with music, flowers and dancing, **Ceriale**
2 July	Procession of the Madonna, **Loano**
July (3rd Sun)	Festival of Mary Magdalen, complete with a Dance of Death, **Taggia**
July (last Sun)	Festivals of lights on the sea, **Arma di Taggia**. Landing of the Saracens, **Laigueglia**
August	*Agosto medievale*, **Ventimiglia**, with costumes, medieval music and other events. Bathtub races, **Diano Marino**. Election of Miss Muretto, **Alassio**. Festival of classical ballet in the caves, **Toirano**. International piano competitions, **Finale Ligure**
August (1st Sat)	Festival of little fish, wine and bread, all in abundance, **Ospedaletti**
August (1st Sun)	Festival of the Sea, **La Spezia**. Stella Maris nautical procession, **Camogli**
August (2nd Sun)	Historical regatta, **Ventimiglia**. Palio del Golfo rowing regatta, **La Spezia**
14 August	*Torta dei Fieschi*, **Lavagna**: historical re-enactment of a sumptuous 13th-century wedding, featuring a massive cake made by local bakers
15 August	Sea festival, **Diano Marina**. Big traditional festival at the Madonna della Costa, **San Remo**. Huge fireworks show over the bay, **Alassio**
September	Antique yacht and sailboat regatta, every other year, **Imperia**. Regatta dei Rioni, **Noli**. Humour festival, **Bordighera**. National Truffle Fair, **Millesimo**
7–8 September	Fire festival, **Recco**
October	The Rassegna Tenco, international festival of songwriters who sing, **San Remo**
October (1st Sun)	Wine festival, **Pornassio**
November	*Cantar da Costa*, festival of Brazilian music and culture, **Genoa**

December	*Rassagna della ceramica*—big ceramics exhibition, at **Albisola**. National pianists' competition, **Albenga**
13 December	Santa Lucia, **Savona**
Mid-December	Ligurian handicrafts fair, **Genoa**
24 December	*Ceremonia del Confuoco*, the lighting of new fires, **Savona**

Food and Drink

There are those who eat to live and those who live to eat, and then there are the Italians, for whom food has an almost religious significance, unfathomably linked with love, La Mamma and tradition. In this singular country, where millions of otherwise sane people spend much of their waking hours worrying about their digestion, standards both at home and in the restaurants are understandably high. Few Italians are gluttons, but all are experts on what is what in the kitchen; to serve a meal that is not properly prepared and more than a little complex is tantamount to an insult.

For the visitor this national culinary obsession comes as an extra bonus to the senses— along with the Riviera's remarkable sights and the warm sun on your back, you can enjoy some of the best tastes and smells the world can offer, prepared daily in Italy's kitchens and fermented in its countless wine cellars. Eating *all'Italiana* is not only delicious and wholesome, but now undeniably trendy. Foreigners flock here to learn the secrets of Italian cuisine and the even more elusive secret of how the Italians can live surrounded by such delights and still fit into their sleek Armani trousers.

Breakfast (*colazione*), however, is no lingering affair, but an early morning wake-up shot to the brain: a *cappuccino* (espresso with hot foamy milk, often sprinkled with chocolate—incidentally, first thing in the morning is the only time of day at which any self-respecting Italian will touch the stuff), a *caffè latte* (foamed white coffee) or a *caffè lungo* (a generous portion of espresso), accompanied by a croissant-type roll called a *cornetto* or *briosce*, or a fancy pastry. This repast can be consumed in any bar and repeated during the morning as often as necessary. Breakfast in most Italian hotels seldom represents great value, although many now put on buffets ranging from very discreet to fabulous.

Lunch (*pranzo*), generally served around 1pm, is the most important meal of the day for the Italians, with a minimum of a first course (*primo piatto*—any kind of pasta dish, broth or soup, rice dish or pizza), a second course (*secondo piatto*—a meat dish, accompanied by a *contorno* or side dish—usually a vegetable, salad, or potatoes), followed by fruit or dessert and coffee. You can, however, begin with a platter of *antipasti*—the appetizers that Italians do so brilliantly, ranging from warm seafood delicacies, salami in any of a hundred varieties, lovely vegetables, savoury toasts, olives, pâté and many, many more. There are restaurants that specialize in *antipasti*, and they usually don't take it amiss if you decide to forget the pasta and meat and just nibble on these scrumptious hors-d'œuvres (though in the end it will probably cost you more than a full meal would). Most Italians accompany their meal with wine and mineral water—*acqua minerale*, with or without bubbles (*con* or *senza gas*), which supposedly aids digestion—concluding their meals with a *digestivo* liqueur.

Cena, the **evening meal**, is usually eaten around 8pm, or later in the summer. This is much the same as *pranzo* although lighter, usually without the pasta; a pizza and beer, eggs or a fish dish. In restaurants, however, they offer all the courses, so if you have only a sandwich for lunch you have a full meal in the evening.

In Italy the various terms for types of **restaurants**—*ristorante*, *trattoria* or *osteria*—have been confused. These days a *trattoria* or *osteria* can be just as elaborate as a restaurant, though rarely is a *ristorante* as informal as a traditional *trattoria*. Unfortunately the old habit of posting menus and prices in the windows has fallen from fashion, so it's often difficult to judge variety or prices, but as a rule, the fancier the fittings, the fancier the **bill**, although neither of these points has anything at all to do with the quality of the food. If you're uncertain, do as you would at home—look for lots of locals. When you dine out, mentally add to the bill (*conto*) the bread and cover charge (*pane e coperto*, between L2000 and L4000), and a 15% service charge. This is often included in the bill (*servizio compreso*); if not, it will say *servizio non compreso*, and you'll have to do your own arithmetic. Additional tipping is at your own discretion.

People who haven't visited Italy for years will be amazed at how much **prices** have risen; though in some respects eating out in Italy is still a bargain, especially when you figure out how much all that wine would have cost you at home. In many places you'll often find restaurants offering a *menu turistico*—full, set meals of usually meagre inspiration for L20,000–30,000. More imaginative chefs often offer a *menu degustazione*, a set-price gourmet meal that allows you to taste their daily specialities and seasonal dishes. Both of these are cheaper than if you had ordered the same food à la carte.

We have divided restaurants into the following price categories, although of course price depends very much on what you order:

very expensive	over L80,000
expensive	L50,000–80,000
moderate	L30,000–50,000
cheap	below L30,000

When you leave a restaurant you will be given a receipt (*scontrino* or *ricevuto fiscale*) which according to Italian law you must take with you out of the door and carry for at least 60 metres. If you aren't given one, it means the restaurant is probably fudging on its taxes and thus offering you lower prices. There is a slim chance the tax police (*Guardia di Fianza*) may have their eye on you and the restaurant, and if you don't have a receipt they could slap you with a heavy fine.

As the pace of modern urban life militates against traditional lengthy home-cooked repasts with the family, followed by a siesta, alternatives to sit-down meals have mushroomed. Many office workers now behave much as their counterparts elsewhere in Europe and consume a rapid snack at lunchtime, returning home after a busy day to throw together some pasta and salad in the evenings. Even the original Italian fast food alternative, a buffet known as the 'hot table' (*tavola calda*), is becoming harder and harder to find among the international and made-in-Italy fast food franchises of various descriptions; bars often double as *panicotecas* (which make hot or cold sandwiches to order, or serve *tramezzini*, little sandwiches on plain, square white bread that are always much better than they look); outlets selling pizza or *focaccia* by the slice (*al taglio*) are common in city centres. At any grocer's (*alimentari*) or market (*mercato*) you can buy the materials for countryside or hotel-room picnics; some will make the sandwiches for you.

What comes as a surprise to many visitors is the tremendous regional diversity at the table; often next to nothing on the menu looks familiar, and dishes are disguised by a local or dialect name. Expect further mystification, as many Italian chefs have wholeheartedly embraced the concept of *nouvelle cuisine*, or rather *nuova cucina*, and are constantly inventing dishes with even more names. If your waiter fails to elucidate, the menu decoder at the back of this book may help.

Ligurian Cuisine, or the Marriage of Popeye and Olive Oyl

Liguria, with its wonderful seafood, its fresh, sun-ripened vegetables (including Popeye's favourite spinach and its cousin chard) and its delicious pale green olive oil (*see* p.111), has one of the healthiest of all Italian cuisines, the one that nearly perfectly matches all the criteria of the much vaunted Mediterranean diet: olive oil as its main source of fat, lots of greens, legumes, pulses and fresh vegetables, but very little meat; little milk, butter or cream, but a discreet amount of cheese, and wine in moderation. Italians call it *cucina povera*, 'poor cuisine'.

Although it's now the prize item on restaurant menus, seafood used to play a surprisingly small role in the traditional diet of the Riviera; after all, one's garden, especially in this delicious climate, was always much more reliable, especially in the centuries of pirates and constant warfare. Locally grown vegetables here still taste the way vegetables should, with an emphasis on fragrance and freshness; this, after all, is the land that gave the world **pesto**, that tangy, rich, and thoroughly addictive sauce of basil, pine nuts, garlic, olive oil and cheese, traditionally ground with a mortar and pestle (which gave it its name) and spooned on top of pasta or mixed in with minestrone. Forget those jars you can buy in your local supermarket—try the real McCoy, with basil grown in Prà (just west of Genoa).

The special **pasta** forms of Liguria are *trenette* (like linguine) and *trofie*, simple twists made of wheat or chestnut flour, prepared with traditional recipes that combine fresh vegetables and herbs and wild mushrooms in season. More elaborate forms include *pansotti*, filled with spinach and herbs, served with a delicious walnut sauce; and ravioli, invented in Nice (back when it was still *Nizza*). On the Riviera it comes in a hundred varieties, including the popular *ravioli di magro*, 'lean ravioli' filled with chard or herbs (especially borage), egg, *grana padano* cheese and marjoram, and served with melted butter and fresh thyme. For feast days, you would get ravioli with *tuccu*, a thick meat sauce. Lasagne, not with tomato and mince but deliciously baked with vegetables or seafood, is another favourite.

Minestrone and other vegetable **soups** on the Riviera often comes with *bigareli*, tiny pieces of homemade pasta, rubbed between the fingers. Around La Spezia the classics are *lattughe ripiene in brodo* (stuffed lettuce in broth) and *mesciùa*, made of spelt (an old form of wheat), cannellini beans and chick peas, from a recipe handed down by the Romans at Luni. The Ligurians aren't big eaters of rice and *risotti*, as it was for a long time an expensive import, but in Genoa you may find *riso arrosto alla genovese*—rice baked in a mould with sausage, mushrooms, artichoke hearts and cheese.

Genoa is the birthplace of some of Italy's most elaborate **cold dishes**—*cima alla genovese*, breast of veal stuffed with minced sweetbreads, pistachios, veal, egg, dried mushrooms, artichoke hearts, peas and various herbs (*see* p.146). Another, *cappon magro*, may sound like lean capon but in fact is a salad of cold fish, shellfish, hard-boiled eggs and vegetables, served with a garlicky sauce made with anchovies, oil and vinegar. During Easter (and at other times) don't pass up a chance to try *torta pasqualina*, the king of pies, traditionally made of 33 sheets of pasta, one for each year that Jesus lived, filled with ricotta, artichoke hearts, spinach, chard, courgettes, onions and hard-boiled eggs.

For all that, in most Riviera restaurants **seafood** is lord and master in every course save dessert, which is great if you love fish and not so great if you don't. Anchovies, long one of Liguria's chief exports, are a common *antipasto* up and down the coast; sometimes you may even see *cottolette di acciughe*, anchovy 'cutlets' (stuffed and fried anchovies). Seafood stars in a wide variety of mixed salads, pasta dishes, fish soups and stews, including *burridà* (in Genoa and the Riviera di Ponente), a soup made of white fish served with garlic sauce, not unlike Provençal *bourride*, although *burridà* may include cuttlefish and peas. *Zimino* is another favourite, a stew made of a mixture of fish, with fennel, onion, celery, tomatoes, olive oil and parsley. *Ciuppin* (from the Riveria di Levante) and *buddego* are other fish stews, while *rascasse* is a lighter fish soup.

The now rare *datteri del mare* (Litophaga litophaga) are a speciality of the Ligurian coast: date-shaped and very tasty little mussel-like shellfish with such a long life cycle that a particularly elderly person is described as 'older than a date clam'. Fishermen attempting to shorten their span resorted even to explosives to blow up their favourite rocky shelters; now their fishing is strictly regulated, and you'll be very lucky to find the legendary *zuppa di datteri*, which is like *moules marinière*, only much finer. The more common *mitili*, the local mussels, are often stuffed and baked, as are *arselle* (clams). Cockles (*tartufi di mare*) are another common shellfish, while octopus (*polpo*) is a favourite in the Gulf of Poets (in salads, or boiled and placed in a mould, and served in slices as an *antipasto*). Squid (*totani*) is often stuffed with a mix of breadcrumbs, parmesan, mortadella and tomatoes. Then there are oysters, and scampi, and scampi's 'poor' cousin, the mantis shrimp or squill (*cicale*), eaten fresh from the sea.

More expensive offerings from the sea (usually priced by weight on the menu) include Mediterranean lobster (*aragosta*), sea bass (known either as *branzino*, *spigola*, or *lupo di mare*), and *orata* or *dorata* (varieties of sea bream). For special occasions, there's *triglie all'imperatrice*, a rich dish of red mullet cooked with tomatoes, cream, onions, capers, white wine and cognac. It may seem a bit odd for a coastal region, but salt and the more prestigious wind-dried cod (*bacalà* and *stoccofisso*, respectively) are also big favourites, introduced by medieval English merchants, although rest assured that any cod dish in Liguria will be utterly unrecognizable compared to the codfish fingers in your freezer. The Genoese like to eat either one in the form of light fritters, while a prize dish in many seafood restaurants is *bacalà mantecado* (puréed and flavoured with garlic).

Among the few **land food** specialities you'll find stewed rabbit (*coniglio in umido*), often stuffed and roasted, and snails, either *bagioi*, in a mint-flavoured tomato sauce, or *lumache alla genovese*, served with anchovies, garlic, oil, basil and dry white wine. Guinea fowl and chicken *fricassea* are traditional dishes, as is *fritto alla stecco*, a mix of sweetbreads and mushrooms, dipped in egg and breadcrumbs and fried on a skewer. Lamb (often fried in a fricassee with artichokes) prevails over beef and pork, although you may find *brasato di manzo alla genovese*, braised beef with vegetables and mushrooms in red wine. Look for steak (or prawns) prepared *s'a ciappa*, grilled on a slab of slate. The occasional French influence has seeped over the border to the Riviera di Ponente, where you'll find dishes such as *brandacüyun* (dried cod with potatoes, like *brandade*). Other dishes are more idiosyncratic, like *ü marò*, a sauce of ground fava beans and anchovies, invented by sailors to prevent scurvy and now used to accompany boiled meats; and the *gran pistau* from Pigna, grain boiled with bacon then fried with leeks and garlic, which food historians date back to the Middle Ages because it uses animal fat instead of olive oil (olive cultivation only began in earnest under the Benedictines). In higher altitudes, the chestnut was long just as important as the olive, supplying the flour for bread (*pattona*) and pasta from its dried nuts; *porcini* mushrooms grow in chestnut forests and hold a prime place on autumn restaurant menus, served with pasta or polenta.

Liguria is a specialist in **finger food** and other snacks. *Focaccia,* a soft kind of pizza dough, crispy golden on the outside, has crossed international boundaries, and can be bought in stands along the street like slices of pizza: it may come with cheese or onions or olives, spinach, cheese and ham, or simply sprinkled with rosemary and salt. The Riviera has its own pizzas: *pasta cu-a pumata*, soft and crispy and topped with tomatoes, and *sardenària*, topped with tomato sauce, anchovies, basil, salted olives, capers, garlic and oregano. Even simpler, and also sold in streetside stands or pizzerias, are *farinata* and *panissa*, both made of chick-pea meal and olive oil, the former baked in a hot wood oven, the latter fried. On the Riviera di Levante, you may also find *sgabei*, bread dough rolled out, cut into small rhomboids and fried in hot olive oil; and *testaroli* (or *panigacci*), introduced by the Saracens and similar to pitta, cooked over a very hot fire and served with olive oil and parmesan or with pesto.

The villages in the Maritime Alps and Apennines produce a few speciality **cheeses** that make it down to some of the posher restaurants on the coast; any local sheep cheese is bound to be excellent. Each town in Liguria seems to have its special **pastry or sweet**: the best-known cake is the Genoese *pandolce*, filled with raisins, pine nuts and candied fruits. In Ventimiglia, you'll find *castagnola*, a traditional pastry made of chestnuts, sugar, cinnamon and cloves; there are also *crostoli*, airy anise-flavoured fritters served with warm *zabaglione*; *millesimi al rhum*, the delicious chocolates from Millesimo; *gobelletti* (or *cobbelletti*), shortcrust biscuits made in Genoa, often with cherry, pear or fig jam; the *torta di riso dolce*, a sweet rice-pudding cake from the Lunigiana in the far east; the *spongata* or *spungata*, a pastry filled with jam and topped with sugar; *buccellato*, a festive cake, often with pine nuts, raisins or nuts; and *castagnaccio*, a flat cake made of chestnut flour, covered with pine nuts, scented with rosemary, and eaten with creamy fresh ricotta.

Wine and Spirits

Italy is a country where everyday wine is cheaper than Coca-Cola or milk, and where nearly every family owns some vineyards or has some relatives who supply most of their daily needs—which are not great. Even though they live in one of the world's greatest wine-growing countries, Italians imbibe relatively little, and usually only at meals.

If Italy has an infinite variety of regional dishes, there is an equally bewildering array of **regional wines**, many of which are rarely exported because they are best drunk young. Even wines that are well known and often derided clichés abroad, like Chianti or Lambrusco, can be wonderful new experiences when tasted on their home turf. Unless you're dining at a restaurant with an exceptional cellar, do as the Italians do and order a carafe of the local wine (*vino locale* or *vino della casa*). You won't often be wrong. Most Italian wines are named after the grape and the district they come from. If the label says DOC (*Denominazione di Origine Controllata*) it means that the wine comes from a specially defined area and was produced according to a certain traditional method. DOCG (*Denominazione di Origine Controllata e Garantia*) is allegedly a more rigorous classification, indicating that the wines not only conform to DOC standards, but are tested by government-appointed inspectors. At present few wines have been granted this status, but the plan is to increase the number steadily. *Classico* means that a wine comes from the oldest part of the zone of production, though it is not necessarily better than a non-Classico. *Riserva*, *superiore* or *speciale* denotes a wine that has been aged longer and is more alcoholic; *Recioto* is a wine made from the outer clusters of grapes, with a higher sugar and therefore alcohol content. Other Italian wine words are *spumante* (sparkling), *frizzante* (pétillant), *amabile* (semi-sweet), *abbocato* (medium dry) and *passito* (strong sweet wine made from raisins). *Rosso* is red, *bianco* white; between the two extremes lie *rubiato* (ruby), *rosato*, *chiaretto* or *cerasuolo* (rosé). *Secco* is dry, *dolce* sweet, *liquoroso* fortified and sweet. *Vendemmia* means vintage, a *cantina* is a cellar, and an *enoteca* is a wine shop or museum where you can taste and buy wines.

Liguria, like every other self-respecting Italian region, produces wine, although very little, owing to its topography. Most are whites—good ones to try include **Pigato** from Albenga, named for its grape, which produces a fine, full-flavoured straw-coloured wine with a slightly bitter almond taste that can quickly make you tipsy, but compares very favourably with **DOC Cinqueterre**, made in that lovely zone (where it tastes best), which is also fresh and dry. Another white wine, which many people consider Liguria's best, is straw-yellow **Vementino**, a crisp dry fruity wine made from the local malvasia grape produced around Diano Castello just east of Imperia; **Vermentino dei Colli di Luni**, grown on the Tuscan frontiers of the Riviera, has recently been accorded DOC status. The Cinque Terre also produce a famous sweet white wine called **Sciacchetrà**, made from grapes that grow by the sea, formerly used only as a medicine, or to celebrate a wedding or birth, but now a prized dessert wine.

Liguria's best red wine is **DOC Rossese di Dolceacqua**, which is vinified either to be drunk young and ruby red or to take a few years' ageing, when it becomes a fine structured deep garnet wine, aromatic and soft, perfect with chicken or rabbit dishes. Other good ones are **Rossese di Albenga** and **Dolcetto.**

Italy turns its grape harvest to other uses too, producing Sicilian **Marsala**, a famous fortified wine fermented in wooden casks, ranging from very dry to flavoured and sweet, and **vin santo**, a sweet Tuscan speciality often served with almond biscuits. **Vermouth** is an idea from Turin, made of wine flavoured with Alpine herbs and spices. Italians are fond of post-prandial brandies (to aid digestion)—**Stock** or **Vecchia Romagna** appear on the best-known Italian brandy bottles. **Grappa** is a rough, schnapps-like spirit drunk in black coffee after a meal (a *caffè corretto*). Other drinks you'll see in any Italian bar include **Campari**, a red bitter drunk on its own or in cocktails; **Fernet Branca, Cynar** and **Averno**, popular aperitif/digestifs; and a host of liqueurs like **Strega**, the witch potion from Benevento, apricot-flavoured **Amaretto**, cherry **Maraschino**, aniseed **Sambuca** or herby **Millefiori**.

Spirits like whisky or gin are reasonably priced in Italy; locals rarely drink them, despite intensive advertising, and if you are ordering in a remote village, the bartender may let you say 'when' as he pours.

Health and Emergencies

You can insure yourself against almost any mishap—cancelled flights, stolen or lost baggage and ill health. Check any current policies you hold to see if they cover you while abroad, and under what circumstances, and judge whether you need a special **traveller's insurance** policy for the journey. Travel agencies sell them, as well as insurance companies.

Citizens of EU countries are entitled to **reciprocal health care** on Italy's National Health Service and a 90% discount on prescriptions (bring **Form E111** with you). The E111 does not cover all medical expenses (no repatriation costs, for example, and no private treatment), and it is advisable to take out separate travel insurance for full cover. Citizens of non-EU countries should check carefully that they have adequate insurance for any medical expenses and the cost of returning home. Australia has a reciprocal health care scheme with Italy, but New Zealand, Canada and the USA do not. If you already have health insurance, a student card or a credit card, you may be entitled to some medical cover abroad.

In an **emergency**, dial *©* **115** for fire and *©* **113** for an ambulance (*ambulanza*) or to find the nearest hospital (*ospedale*). Less serious problems can be treated at a *Pronto Soccorso* (casualty/first aid department) at any hospital clinic (*ambulatorio*), or at a local health unit (*Unita Sanitarial Locale*—USL). Airports and main railway stations also have **first-aid posts**. If you have to pay for health treatment, make sure you get a receipt so that you can make any claims for reimbursement later.

Dispensing **chemists** (*farmacia*) are generally open from 8.30am to 1pm and from 4 to 8pm. Pharmacists are trained to give advice for minor ills. Any large town will have a *farmacia* that stays open 24 hours; others take turns to stay open (the address rota is posted in the window).

No specific **vaccinations** are required or advised for citizens of most countries before visiting Italy; the main health risks are the usual travellers' woes of upset stomachs or the effects of too much sun. Take a supply of **medicaments** with you (insect repellent, anti-diarrhœal medicine, sun lotion and antiseptic cream), and any drugs you need regularly.

Most Italian doctors speak at least rudimentary English, but if you can't find one, contact your embassy or consulate for a list of English-speaking doctors. Standards of health care in the north are generally higher than in the deep south.

Maps and Publications

The maps in this guide are for orientation only and, to explore in any detail, invest in a good, up-to-date regional map before or after arriving. The green Touring Club Italiano map (1:200,000) is excellent and up to date.

For an excellent range of maps in the UK, try **Stanford's**, 12–14 Long Acre, London WC2 9LP, ✆ (020) 7836 1321, or **The Travel Bookshop**, 13 Blenheim Crescent, London W11 2EE, ✆ (020) 7229 5260. In the USA, try **The Complete Traveller**, 199 Madison Ave, New York, NY 10016, ✆ (212) 685 9007. Italian tourist offices can often supply good area maps and town plans.

Money

It's a good idea to order a wad of lire from your home bank to have on hand when you arrive in Italy, the land of strikes, unforeseen delays and quirky banking hours (*see* below). Take great care how you carry it, however, and don't keep it in one place. Traveller's cheques are a good idea. When you change money, expect much queueing and form-filling (and bring your passport). Banks and exchange bureaux licensed by the Bank of Italy give the best exchange rates for currency or traveller's cheques. Hotels, private exchanges in resorts and FS-run exchanges at railway stations usually have less advantageous rates, but are open outside normal banking hours. In addition, there are exchange offices at most airports. Remember that Italians indicate decimals with commas and thousands with full points.

Most British banks have an arrangement with their Italian counterparts, whereby you can, for a significant commission, use your bank card to take money out of Italian ATMs (Bancomats), but check with your bank first. Bancomats also take Eurocheque cards and credit cards, as long as you know the PIN number. Banks will advance you cash on a credit card or Eurocheque with a Eurocheque card. Visa, American Express and Diner's are more widely accepted than MasterCard (Access). Large hotels, resort area restaurants, shops and car hire firms will accept plastic as well; smaller places may not.

If you have a credit limit on your card, you may want to have your bank enlarge it before you go. Italy is an expensive country, and you may find yourself spending more than you intended to. If your credit card stops working and you've run out of traveller's cheques, you can have money transferred to you through an Italian bank, but be warned that this process may take over a week, even if it's sent urgent, *espressissimo* (wiring it through the post office may be faster). You will need your passport as identification when you collect it. Sending cheques by post is inadvisable.

On 1 January 1999, Italy joined the first wave of European Monetary Union whereupon the Euro became the official currency of Italy and the lira a denomination thereof. In the short term, however, the introduction of the new currency is unlikely to have much of an effect on the lives of ordinary Italians. There are, after all, no Euro coins or notes as yet—these are not scheduled to be introduced until the second wave of monetary union gets under way in January 2002. Italian notes and coins will continue to be used during the three-year transitional period. However, you can, should you so wish, have your credit card bills charged in Euros.

Opening Hours and Museums

In Liguria most shops close down at 1pm until 3 or 4pm to eat and properly digest the main meal of the day. Afternoon hours are from 4 to 7, often from 5 to 8 in the hot summer months. Bars are often the only places open during the early afternoon. City offices, shops and restaurants may close down completely during August when locals go on holiday. In any case, don't be surprised if you find anywhere in Italy unexpectedly closed (or open for that matter), whatever its official stated hours.

banks

Banking hours vary, but core times are Monday to Friday 8.30am–1pm and 3–4pm, closed weekends and on local and national holidays (*see* below), as well as the afternoon before a holiday. Outside normal hours though, you will usually be able to find somewhere to change money (albeit at disadvantageous rates).

shops

Shops usually open Monday to Saturday from 8am to 1pm and 3.30pm to 7.30pm, although hours vary according to season and are shorter in smaller centres. In some large cities hours are longer. Some supermarkets and department stores stay open throughout the day.

offices

Government-run dispensers of red tape (e.g. visa departments) often stay open for quite limited periods, usually during the mornings, Monday to Friday. It pays to get there as soon as they open (or before) to spare your nerves in an interminable queue. Anyway, take something to read, or write your memoirs.

museums and galleries

Many of Italy's museums are magnificent, many are run with shameful neglect, and many have been closed for years for 'restoration' with slim prospects of reopening in the foreseeable future. With two works of art per inhabitant, Italy has a hard time financing the preservation of its national heritage; enquire at the tourist office to find out exactly what is open and when before setting off on a wild-goose chase.

churches

Italy's churches have always been a prime target for art thieves and as a consequence are usually locked when there isn't a sacristan or caretaker to keep an eye on things. All churches, except for the really important cathedrals and basilicas, close in the afternoon at the same hours as the shops, and the little ones tend to stay closed. Always have a pocketful of coins for the light machines in churches, or whatever work of art you came to inspect will remain clouded in ecclesiastical gloom. Don't do your visiting during services, and don't come to see paintings and statues in churches the week preceding Easter—you will probably find them covered with mourning shrouds.

In general, Sunday afternoons and Mondays are dead periods for the sightseer—you may want to make them your travelling days. Places without specified opening hours can usually be visited on request, but it is best to go before 1pm. We have listed the hours of important sights and museums, and specified which ones charge admission. Entrance charges vary widely; major sights are fairly steep (L10,000 plus), but others may be completely free. EU citizens under 18 and over 65 get free admission to state museums, at least in theory.

National Holidays

Most museums, as well as banks and shops, are closed on the following national holidays.

1 January (New Year's Day)

6 January (Epiphany)

Easter Monday

25 April (Liberation Day)

1 May (Labour Day)

15 August (Assumption, also known as *Ferragosto*, the official start of the Italian holiday season)

1 November (All Saints' Day)

8 December (Immaculate Conception)

25 December (Christmas Day)

26 December (*Santo Stefano*, St Stephen's Day)

In addition to these general holidays, many towns also take their patron saint's day off.

Packing

You simply cannot overdress in Italy; whatever grand strides Italian designers have made on the international fashion merry-go-round, most of their clothes are purchased domestically, prices be damned. Now whether or not you want to try to keep up with the natives is your own affair and your own heavy suitcase—you may do well to compromise and just bring a couple of smart outfits for big nights out. It's not that the Italians are very formal; they simply like to dress up with a gorgeousness that adorns their cities just as much as those old Renaissance churches and palaces. The few places with dress codes are the major churches and basilicas (no shorts, sleeveless shirts or strappy sundresses—women should tuck a light silk scarf in a bag to throw over the shoulders), casinos and a few posh restaurants.

After agonizing over fashion, remember to pack small and light: trans-Atlantic airlines limit baggage by size (two pieces up to 1.5m in height and width are free; in second-class you're allowed one of 1.5m and another up to 110cm). Within Europe limits are by weight; 20kg (44lb) in second class, 30kg (66lb) in first. You may well be penalized for anything larger. If you're travelling mainly by train, you'll want to keep bags to a minimum: jamming big suitcases on overhead racks in a crowded compartment isn't much fun for anyone.

Never take more than you can carry; but do bring the following: any prescription medicine you need, an extra pair of glasses or contact lenses if you wear them; a pocket knife and corkscrew (for picnics), a flashlight (for dark frescoed churches, caves and crypts), a travel alarm (for those early trains) and a pocket Italian-English dictionary (for flirting and other emergencies; outside the main tourist centres you may well have trouble finding someone who speaks English). If you're a light sleeper, consider earplugs.

Your laptop or other electric appliances will work in Italy if you adapt and/or convert them to run on 220 AC with two round prongs on the plug.

Photography

Films and developing are much more expensive than they are in either the UK or the USA, though there are plenty of outlets where you can obtain them. You are not allowed to take pictures in most museums and in some churches. Most cities now offer one-hour processing if you need your pics in a hurry.

Post Offices

Dealing with *la posta italiana* has always been a risky, frustrating, time-consuming affair. It is one of the most expensive and slowest postal services in Europe. Even buying the right stamps requires dedicated research and saintly patience. One of the scandals that mesmerized Italy in recent years involved the minister of the post office, who disposed of literally tons of backlog mail by tossing it in the Tiber. When the news broke, he was replaced—the new minister, having learned his lesson, burned all the mail the post office was incapable of delivering. Not surprisingly, fed-up Italians view the invention of the fax machine as a gift from the Madonna.

Post offices in Italy are usually open from 8am until 1pm (Monday to Saturday), or until 6 or 7pm in a large city. To have your mail sent *poste restante* (general delivery), have it addressed to the central post office (*Fermo Posta*) and expect to wait around three to four weeks for it to arrive. Make sure your surname is very clearly written in block capitals. To pick up your mail you will have to present your passport and pay a nominal charge. Stamps (*francoboli*) may be purchased in post offices or at tobacconists (*tabacchi*, identified by their blue signs with a white T). Prices fluctuate. The rates for letters and postcards (depending how many words you write!) vary according to the whim of the tobacconist or postal clerk.

You can also have money telegraphed to you through the post office; if all goes well, this can happen in a mere three days, but expect a fair proportion of it to go into commission.

Shopping and Markets

'Made in Italy' has become a byword for style and quality, especially in fashion and leather, but also in home design, ceramics (in Liguria the biggest centre is Albisola), kitchenware, jewellery, lace and linens, glassware and crystal, chocolates, bells, Christmas decorations, hats, straw work, art books, engravings, handmade stationery, gold and silver-ware, bicycles, sports cars, woodworking, a hundred kinds of liqueurs, aperitifs, coffee machines, gastronomic specialities such as olive oil, *pumate séche* (sundried tomatoes with basil), artichoke cream and dried porcini mushrooms, and antiques (both reproductions, and the real thing). You'll find the best variety of goods in Genoa and San Remo, and lots of designer boutiques in the resorts—in other words, where the money is. For less expensive clothes and household items you can nearly always do better at home.

Non-EU citizens should save all receipts for customs on the way home; however, if you spend over a certain amount in a shop you can get a tax rebate at the airport; participating shops have details. If you are looking for antiques, be sure to demand a certificate of authenticity—reproductions can be very, very good. To get your antique or modern art purchases home, you will have to apply to the Export Department of the Italian Ministry of Education and pay an export tax as well; your seller should know the details.

Liguria has some colourful **markets**: most towns have weekly food markets, open from 8am to 1pm, and San Remo has the largest flower market in Europe. Many towns have antique and bric-à-brac markets that run once or twice a month, all usually combined with organic food stands (*mercantino biologico*).

Every Saturday: Ventimiglia

First Saturday and Sunday: Finaleborgo, Savona (Piazza Chabrol), Genoa (Palazzo Ducale)

First Sunday: Olivetta San Michele

Second Saturday and Sunday: Chiávari

Second Sunday: Vallecrosia Alta

Third Saturday and Sunday: Taggia, Arma di Taggia and Pietra Ligure

Third Sunday: Noli, San Lorenzo al Mare, Recco

Fourth Saturday and Sunday: Pietra Ligure

Fourth Sunday: Dolceacqua, Pieve di Teco, Bogliasco

Sports and Activities

You can find almost any conceivable summer sport on the Riviera, from the obvious water sports to bungee jumping (above Triora) and parachuting (at Albenga's airport). The most exhaustive source on all sporting facilities available in Liguria is the regional sports committee, CONI, Via Ippolito d'Aste 3/4, Genoa, © 010 570 5633.

As on the French side of the Riviera, *bocce* (the same as *boules*) is a very popular game: it doesn't take up much space, doesn't require much energy, takes about five minutes to learn (if a lifetime to perfect) and you can bet on it. In some resorts you'll even find indoor all-weather *boccidromes*.

Pallone elastico, 'rubber ball', on the other hand, is a kind of rustic outdoors handball unique to the mountain valleys of Liguria and southern Piemonte, where space to play other sports is even more limited by the vertical geography. You can play *pallone elastico* against any old wall (next to a bar is always good), whacking it with your fist and chasing after it. You can bet on it, too, and there are championship matches, which are covered assiduously in the local press.

cycling

About three-quarters of Italy is hilly or mountainous, and all of Liguria is, so a cycling holiday is no soft option. Although a few hotels hire out bikes for pedalling around the resorts (a good idea, as parking is often at a premium) it's rare to find one good enough for longer forays, for which it is best to bring your own bike (a mountain bike if possible) and spare parts. Most airlines and rail companies will transport bikes quite cheaply. You can buy a good bike in Italy for L200,000–300,000. For something special go to Celle Ligure where they make Olmo racing bikes; there's a shop at Via Poggi 22 (*www.immagine. com/olmo/celle.htm*).

fishing

You don't need a permit for sea-fishing (without an aqualung), but Italy's coastal waters, polluted and over-exploited, may disappoint. Commercial fishing has depleted marine life to such an extent that the government has begun to declare two- and three-month moratoria on all fishing to give the fish a break. Many mountain streams are stocked, but to fish in fresh water you need to purchase a year's membership card (currently L189,000) from the **Federazione Italiana della Pesca Sportiva**, which has an office in every province; they will inform you about local conditions and restrictions. Bait and equipment are readily available.

football

Soccer (*il calcio*) is a national obsession. For many Italians its importance far outweighs tedious issues like the state of the nation, the government of the day, or any momentous international event—not least because of the weekly chance (slim but real) of becoming an instant lira billionaire in the Lotteria Sportiva. All major cities, and most minor ones, have at least one team of some sort. The sport was actually introduced by the English, but a Renaissance game, something like a cross between football and rugby, has existed in Italy for centuries.

Modern Italian teams are known for their grace, precision, and coordination; rivalries are intense, scandals, especially involving bribery and cheating, are rife. The tempting rewards offered by such big-time entertainment attract all manner of corrupt practices, yet crowd violence is minimal. Big-league matches are played on Sunday afternoons from September to May. Genoa has two teams: the first division Sampdoria, and older and less successful Genoa, stuck in the second division. For information, contact the Federazione Italiana Giuoco Calcio, Via G Allegri 14, 00198 Rome, ✆ 06 84911.

golf

Italians have been slower than some nationalities to appreciate the delights of biffing a small white ball into a hole in the ground, but they're catching on fast. There are now four courses, spread across Liguria: **Arenzano**, near Genoa, **Garlenda**, at Garlenda (above Albenga), **Marigola**, at Lerici, and **Rapallo**, at Rapallo, Ulivi (near San Remo). These are often beautifully placed among the olive groves. You will need to book a tee-off time, especially in season.

mountains and skiing

What? In Liguria? Well, *certamente*; perhaps not enough mountains to base a holiday around, but some good escape hatches into cool green nature if the coast starts to drive you crazy. In the steep crescent that forms the border with Piemonte, you'll find trails (including the 440km Alta Via dei Monti Liguri from Ventimiglia to Ceparana which includes sections of the European E1 and E7), as well as Alpine refuges in the 'Little Dolomites' by Buggio and above Mónesi, both on the French border, with a funicular to make the ascent up 2200m. Walking in higher altitudes is generally practicable between May and October, after most of the snow has melted; all the necessary gear—boots, packs, tents, etc—are readily available in Italy but for more money than you'd pay at home. Mountain refuges are run by the Italian Alpine Club (CAI), represented in every province.

On the French border, by Monte Saccarello, Mónesi has a ski resort, and there's another, mostly for cross-country, at Santo Stefano d'Aveto (1017m) in the Apennines. If you prefer your mountains even more vertical, the cliffs at Finale Ligure attract free climbers from around Europe.

riding holidays

Riding holidays are on offer in the hills, often associated with *agriturismo* holidays (*see* 'Where to Stay: Rural Self-Catering', below); most cities and resorts also have riding stables. For more information, contact the local **Agriturist** office, or the **Associazione Nazionale per il Turismo Equestre**, Via A Borelli 5, 00161 Rome, ✆ 06 444 1179. One possibility, the **Maneggio Molino Martino**, at Dolcedo, ✆ 0368 331 6358, can arrange one- or two-week rides along the old salt roads of the Maritime Alps.

tennis

If soccer is Italy's most popular spectator sport, tennis is probably the game most people actually play. Every *comune* has public courts for hourly hire, especially resorts. Private clubs may offer temporary membership to passing visitors, and hotel courts can often be used by non-residents for a reasonable fee. Contact local tourist offices for information.

The **beaches** along the Riviera are often very beautiful, although a good many are pebbly. Most of the desirable sand is plagued (or blessed, according to your point of view) by that peculiarly Italian phenomenon, the concessionaire, who parks ugly lines of sunbeds and brollies all the way along the best stretches of coast, and charges all comers handsomely for the privilege. During the winter you can see what happens when the beaches miss out on their manicures: many get depressingly rubbish-strewn. No one bats an eye at topless bathing, though nudism requires more discretion.

The Italian Riviera is one of the prettiest regions for **sailing**, and the larger resorts, especially on the Riviera di Ponente, are well equipped with **windsurf** rentals (although the sport is fairly tame in these sheltered parts), **waterskiing** facilities and so on. A few areas make for excellent **diving**: Ventimiglia with its coral and fish, and Alassio and its Isola Gallinaria, and nearby resorts have sub clubs that can get you down, although boat and equipment hire is often quite expensive. Many resorts, such as San Remo, hire out **deltaplanes** if you want to soar high over the sea.

For further information, contact the **Italian State Tourist Office** or write to the following organizations:

Federazione Italiana Vela (Italian Sailing Federation), Via Brigata Bisagno 2/17, Genoa, ℘ 010 565 723.

Federazione Italiana Motonautica (Italian Motorboat Federation), **Federazione Italiana Sci Nautico**: both these organizations are at Via Piranesi 44b, Milan, ℘ 02 761 050.

Telephones

Public telephones for international calls may be found in the offices of **Telecom Italia**, Italy's telephone company. They are the only places where you can make reverse-charge calls (*a erre*, collect calls) but be prepared for a wait, as all these calls go through the operator in Rome. Rates for long-distance calls are among the highest in Europe. Calls within Italy are cheapest after 10pm; international calls after 11pm. Most phone booths now take either coins (L100, 200, 500 or 1000) or phone cards (*schede telefoniche*), available in L5000, L10,000 and sometimes L15,000 amounts at tobacconists and news-stands—you will have to snap off the small perforated corner in order to use them. In smaller villages, you can usually find a *telefoni a scatti*, with a meter on it, in at least one bar (a small commission is generally charged). Try to avoid telephoning from hotels, as this can often add 25% to the bill.

Direct calls may be made by dialling the international prefix (for the UK ℘ 0044, Ireland ℘ 00353, USA and Canada ℘ 001, Australia ℘ 0061, New Zealand ℘ 0064). If you're calling Italy from abroad, dial ℘ 0039 and then the whole number, including the first zero. Many places have public fax machines, but the speed of transmission may make costs very high.

Time

Italy is on Central European Time, one hour ahead of Greenwich Mean Time and six hours ahead of Eastern Standard Time. From the last weekend of March to the end of September, Italian Summer Time (daylight saving time) is in effect.

Tourist Offices

Known under various initials (EPT, APT, IAT or AAST), Italian tourist offices usually stay open 8am–12.30 or 1pm, and 3–7pm, possibly longer in summer. Few open on Saturday afternoons or Sundays. Information booths can also be found at major railway stations and can provide hotel lists, town plans and terse information on local sights and transport. Queues can be maddeningly long. If you're stuck, you may get more sense out of a friendly travel agency than an official tourist office. Nearly every city and province now has a web page, and you can often book your hotel direct through the Internet.

Liguria: Via Fieschi 15, 16121 Genoa, ✆ 010 54851, *www.regione.liguria.it.*

UK: 1 Princes St, London W1R 8AY, ✆ (020) 7408 1254, ✉ (020) 7493 6695. For brochures, ring ✆ (0891) 600 280 (50p a minute).

USA: 630 Fifth Ave, Suite 1565, New York, NY 10111, ✆ (212) 245 4822.

12400 Wilshire Blvd, Suite 550, Los Angeles, CA 90025, ✆ (310) 820 0098.

500 N. Michigan Ave, Suite 1046, Chicago, IL 60611, ✆ (312) 644 0990.

Australia: c/o Italian Embassy, 61–9 Macquerie St, Sydney 2000, NSW, ✆ (02) 9247 8442.

Canada: 1 Place Ville Marie, Suite 1914, Montréal, Quebec H3B 3M9, ✆ (514) 866 7667.

New Zealand: c/o Italian Embassy, 36 Grant Road, Thorndon, Wellington, ✆ (04) 736 065.

Tourist and travel information may also be available from **Alitalia** (Italy's national airline) or **CIT** (Italy's state-run travel agency) offices in some countries. In the UK, contact the **Italian Travel Centre** at Thomas Cook, 45 Berkeley Street, London W1A 1EB, ✆ (020) 7499 4000.

Where to Stay

All accommodation in Italy is classified by the Provincial Tourist Boards. Price control, however, has been deregulated since 1992. Hotels now set their own tariffs, which means that in some places prices have rocketed. After a period of rapid and erratic fluctuation, tariffs are at last settling down again to more predictable levels under the influence of market forces. Good-value, interesting accommodation in cities can be very difficult to find and you will need to book well in advance for some of the most desirable places.

The quality of furnishings and facilities has generally improved in all categories in recent years. Many hotels have installed smart bathrooms and electronic gadgetry. At the top end of the market, the Riviera is endowed with a number of exceptionally sybaritic hotels, furnished and decorated with real panache. But you can still find plenty of older-style hotels and *pensioni*, whose eccentricities of character and architecture (in some cases undeniably charming) may be at odds with modern standards of comfort.

Hotels and Guesthouses

Italian *alberghi* come in all shapes and sizes. They are rated from one to five stars, depending what facilities they offer (not their character, style or charm). The star ratings are some indication of price levels, but for tax reasons not all hotels choose to advertise themselves at the rating to which they are entitled, so you may find a modestly rated hotel just as comfortable (or more so) than a higher rated one. Conversely, you may find a hotel offers few stars in hopes of attracting budget-conscious travellers, but charges just as much as a higher-rated neighbour. *Pensioni* are generally more modest establishments, though nowadays the distinction between these and ordinary hotels is becoming blurred. *Locande* are traditionally an even more basic form of hostelry, but these days the term may denote somewhere fairly chic. Other inexpensive accommodation is sometimes known as *alloggi* or *affittacamere*. There are usually plenty of cheap dives around railway stations; for somewhere more salubrious, head for the historic quarters. Whatever the shortcomings of the décor, furnishings and fittings, you can usually rely at least on having clean sheets.

Price lists, by law, must be posted on the door of every room, along with meal prices and any extra charges (such as air-conditioning, or even a shower in cheap places). Many hotels display two or three different rates, depending on the season. Low-season rates may be about a third lower than peak-season tariffs. Some resort hotels close down altogether for several months of the year. During high season you should always book ahead to be sure of a room (a fax reservation may be less frustrating to organize than one by post). If you have paid a deposit, your booking is

valid under Italian law, but don't expect it to be refunded if you have to cancel. Tourist offices publish annual regional lists of hotels and pensions giving current rates, but do not generally make reservations for visitors. Major city business hotels may offer significant discounts at weekends.

Main railway stations generally have accommodation booking desks; inevitably, a fee is charged. Chain hotels or motels are generally the easiest hotels to book, though not always the most interesting to stay in. Top of the list is CIGA (*Compagnia Grandi Alberghi*) with some of the most luxurious establishments in Italy, many of them grand, turn-of-the-century places that have been exquisitely restored. The French consortium *Relais et Châteaux* specializes in tastefully indulgent accommodation, often in historic buildings. At a more affordable level, one of the biggest chains in Italy is *Jolly Hotels*, always reliable if not all up to the same standard; these can generally be found near the centres of larger towns. Many motels are operated by the ACI (Italian Automobile Club) or by AGIP (the oil company) and usually located along major exit routes.

If you arrive without a reservation, begin looking or phoning round for accommodation early in the day. If possible, inspect the room (and bathroom facilities) before you book, and check the tariff carefully. Italian hoteliers may legally alter their rates twice during the year, so printed tariffs or tourist board lists (and prices quoted in this book!) may be out of date. Hoteliers who wilfully overcharge should be reported to the local tourist office. You will be asked for your passport for registration purposes.

Prices listed in this guide are for double rooms; you can expect to pay about two-thirds the rate for single occupancy, though in high season you may be charged the full double rate in a popular beach resort. Extra beds are usually charged at about an extra third of the room rate. Rooms without private bathrooms generally charge 20–30% less, and most offer discounts for children sharing parent's rooms, or children's meals. A *camera singola* (single room) may cost anything from about L25,000 upwards. Double rooms (*camera doppia*) go from about L60,000 to L250,000 or more. If you want a double bed, specify a *camera matrimoniale*.

Breakfast is normally optional in hotels, though it tends to be obligatory in *pensioni*. You can usually get better value by eating breakfast in a bar or café. In high season you may be expected to take half-board in resorts if the hotel has a restaurant, and one-night stays may be refused.

Prices (for a double with bath)

luxury (*****)	L450–800,000
very expensive (****)	L300–450,000
expensive (***)	L200–300,000
moderate (**)	L120–200,000
cheap (*)	up to L120,000

There are three youth hostels (*alberghi* or *ostelli per la gioventù*) in Liguria, at Genoa, Savona and Finale Ligure. The **Associazione Italiana Alberghi per la Gioventù** (Italian Youth Hostel Association, or AIG) is affiliated to the International Youth Hostel Federation. For a full list of youth hostels, contact AIG at Via Cavour 44, 00184 Roma, ✆ 06 487 1152; 📠 06 488 0492. An international membership card will enable you to stay in any of them. You can obtain these in advance from:

UK: Youth Hostels Association of England and Wales, 14 Southampton St, London, WC2, ✆ (020) 7836 1036.

USA: American Youth Hostels Inc., Box 37613, Washington DC 20013-7613, ✆ (202) 783 6161.

Australia: Australian Youth Hostel Association, 60 Mary Street, Surry Hills, Sydney, NSW 2010, ✆ (02) 9621 1111.

Canada: Canadian Hostelling Association, 1600 James Naismith Drive, Suite 608, Gloucester, Ontario K1B 5N4, ✆ (613) 237 7884.

Cards can usually be purchased on the spot in many hostels if you don't already have one. Hostels usually close for most of the daytime, and many operate a curfew. During the spring, noisy school parties cram hostels for field trips. In the summer it's advisable to book ahead. Contact the hostels directly.

Villas and Flats

If you're travelling in a group or with a family, self-catering can be the ideal way to experience Liguria, although there are relatively few properties here compared to, say, Tuscany. The National Tourist Office has lists of agencies in the UK and USA which rent places on a weekly or fortnightly basis. If you have set your heart on a particular area, write to its tourist office for a list of agencies and owners, who will send brochures or particulars of their accommodation. Maid service is included in the more glamorous villas; ask whether bed linen and towels are provided. A few of the larger operators are listed below:

in the UK and Ireland

Citalia, Marco Polo House, 3–5 Lansdowne Road, Croydon CR9 1LL, ✆ (020) 8686 5533.

Eurovillas, 36 East Street, Coggeshall, Essex CO6 1SH, ✆ (01376) 561 156.

Inghams, 10–18 Putney Hill, London SW15 6AX, ✆ (020) 8780 4450.

Interhome, 383 Richmond Road, Twickenham, Middx TW1 2EF, ✆ (020) 8891 1294.

International Chapters, 47–51 St John's Wood High Street, London NW8 7NJ, ✆ (020) 7722 9560.

Magic of Italy, 227 Shepherds Bush Road, London W6 7AS, ✆ (020) 8748 7575.

CIT, ✆ (800) 248 8687, in New York ✆ (212) 730 2121, who can also arrange fly-drive rental car packages.

At Home Abroad, 405 East 56th Street 6-H, New York, NY 10022-2466,
✆ (212) 421 9165, 🖅 752 1591, e-mail *athomabrod@aol.com*.

CUENDET: Rentals for Italy (and Elsewhere!), ✆ (800) 726 7602,
www.rentvillas.com; they also offer car rental schemes.

Hideaways International, 767 Islington Street, Portsmouth NH 03801,
✆ (617) 486 8955.

Homeowners International, 1133 Broadway, New York, NY 10010,
✆ (212) 691 2361.

RAVE (Rent-a-Vacation Everywhere), 135 Meigs Street, Rochester, New York, NY 14607,
✆ (716) 246 0760.

Rural Self-Catering

For a breath of rural seclusion, the gregarious Italians head for a spell on a **working farm**, in accommodation (usually self-catering) that often approximates to the French *gîte*. Often, however, the real pull of the place is a restaurant in which you can sample some home-grown produce. Outdoor activities may include riding, fishing, and so forth. In Liguria, you'll find most of these up in the mountain villages.

This burgeoning branch of the Italian tourist industry is run by various *Agriturismo* agencies. Prices of farmhouse accommodation are still relatively reasonable. To make the most of your rural hosts, it's as well to have a little Italian under your belt. Local tourist offices will have information on this type of accommodation in their areas; complete listings are available from three regional organizations:

Agriturist, Via Tomaso Invrea 11/10, Genoa, ✆ 010 553 1878.

Turismo Verde, Via Colombo 15/15, Genoa, ✆ 010 570 5633.

Terranostra, Via Gropallo10/5, Genoa, ✆ 010 876262.

Alpine Refuges

The Italian Alpine Club operates refuges (*rifugi*) on the main mountain trails (some accessible only by *funivie*). These may be predictably spartan, or surprisingly comfortable. Many have restaurants. Even Liguria has a few. For an up-to-date list, write to the Club Alpino Italiano, Via Fonseca Pimental 7, Milan (✆ 02 2614 1378). Charges average L18,000–L25,000 per person per night, including breakfast. Most are open only from July to September, but those used by skiers are about 20% more expensive from December to April. Book ahead in August.

Life under canvas is not the fanatical craze it is in France, nor is it necessarily any great bargain. Liguria has only a few camp sites and these are particularly popular in August, when you can expect to find many sites at bursting point. Unofficial camping is generally frowned on and may attract a stern rebuke from the local police. Camper vans (and facilities for them) are increasingly popular. You can obtain a list of local sites from any regional tourist office. Campsite charges generally range from about L6–8000 per adult; tents and vehicles additionally cost about L7000 each. Small extra charges may also be levied for hot showers and electricity. A car-borne couple could therefore spend practically as much for a night at a well-equipped campsite as in a cheap hotel.

To obtain a camping carnet and to book ahead, write to the **Centro Internazionale Prenotazioni Campeggio**, Casella Postale 23, 50041, Calenzano, Firenze, © 055 882 381, ✆ 055 882 3918 (ask for their list of campsites with the booking form). The **Touring Club Italiano** (TCI) publishes a comprehensive annual guide to campsites throughout Italy which is available in bookshops for L29,5000. Contact TCI, Corso Italia 10, Milan, © 02 85261/852 6245.

Women Travellers

Italian men, with the heritage of Casanova, Don Giovanni and Rudolph Valentino as their birthright, are very confident in their role as Great Latin Lovers, but the old horror stories of gangs following the innocent tourist maiden and pinching her bottom are way behind the times. Italian men these days are often exquisitely polite and flirt on a much more sophisticated level, especially in the more 'Europeanised' north.

Still, women travelling alone may frequently receive hisses, wolf-whistles and unsolicited remarks (complimentary or lewd, depending on your attitude) or 'assistance' from local swains—usually of the balding, middle-age-crisis variety. A confident, indifferent poise is usually the best policy. Failing that, a polite 'I am waiting for my *marito*' (thereby avoiding damaged male egos, which can turn nasty), followed by a firm '*no!*' or '*Vai via!*' (Scram!) will generally solve the problem. Flashers and wandering hands on crowded buses may be an unpleasant surprise, but rarely present a serious threat (unless they're after your purse!).

Risks can be greatly reduced if you use common sense and avoid lonely streets or parks and train stations after dark. Choose hotels and restaurants within easy and safe walking distance of public transport. Travelling with a companion of either sex will buffer you considerably from such nuisances (a guardian male, of course, instantly converts you into an inviolable chattel in Italian eyes). Avoid hitchhiking alone in Italy.

The First Ligurians

Some of the first known Europeans had the good taste to settle on the Riviera. Just over the border in France near Menton, in the Grotta del Collonet, are signs of human habitation (animal bones, rough stone tools—but no fires) going back as far as 900,000 years ago. Jump ahead 700,000 years, to a time when the Alps were covered by an ice cap and the low level of the Mediterranean made Italy a much wider peninsula than it is now, and we find the Neanderthals gracing the Italian side of the Riviera with their low-browed presence, notably in the Balzi Rossi caves. The Middle Palaeolithic (80,000 BC) Neanderthals at Balzi Rossi were succeeded in 30,000 BC by their more handsome Cro-Magnon cousins who left Italy its very first works of art—lumpy fertility goddesses known as Venuses.

When Italy first made written history in the 8th century BC, the various powerful, distinct tribes with related languages living on the peninsula were lumped together as 'Italics'. Everything north of the fabled Rubicon (a dinky nondescript stream near Rimini) belonged to the classical Cisalpine Gaul, the stomping ground of Celts and the **Ligurians** or Ligures, who first debuted on the scene some time around 1800 BC and occupied not only present Liguria but northern Tuscany, Piedmont and part of Lombardy.

Just who were the Ligurians? No one is really sure—the Phoenicians and Greeks traded with them, most notably at Genoa, but by the time the first Roman historians posed the question, the Ligurians themselves had forgotten. No one is even sure if they were Indo-European or pre-Indo-European. The first mention of them in writing was in the 8th century BC, when the Greek poet Hesiod said they were a people living on the western edge of the world. A Phoenician legend declared they were the offsping of Albione and Ligure, sons of the sea god Poseidon, who were overcome at the Foce del Rodano by a mighty hail of pebbles. Curiously enough, an ancient Lapp tradition has it that the Lapps were cousins of the Ligurians, who fled north following a cataclysm of some nature, pebble or otherwise.

To add to the confusion, there were several tribes of Ligurians, and even then no one is sure if they were related. Most seemed to have mingled with their Celtic neighbours, while others are believed to have fled into the mountains to avoid them. The archaeological record is uneven: on the Riviera, at least, they built villages surrounded by a ring of stone walls (*castellari*) on hilltops high over the coast, on crags or on other easily defensible sites, which developed into small trading and religious centres (in some atavistic way, they may also be behind the hundreds of sanctuaries dedicated to the Madonna that more recent Ligurians have built in similar locations). The ancients were primarily shepherds, keeping domestic animals for pork and beef and mutton, although they apparently did little hunting and even less fishing, proving that from the first the Ligurians were landlubbers. Mont Bégo (in the upper Val Roja, now part of France) was an important holy site, followed by Monte Béigua west of Genoa, where the Ligurians (or Celto-Ligurians) left rock etchings from *c.* 1800 BC–1000 BC. Mont Bégo has them by the thousands—the usual Neolithic spirals, stick figures, animals and scenes of war. On the opposite end of

Liguria, around the Lunigiana (and on Corsica) they left their distinctive statue steles (*see* p.221–2).

The one thing that's certain is that the Ligurians were among the toughest nuts the Romans had to crack. They were recruited, along with the Celts, Celtiberians and Numidians, to fight with the Carthaginians by Hannibal's brother Hasdrubal in 207 BC; a third brother, Mago, landed in Genua (Genoa) in 203 but was pinned down by the Romans. This support was enough to earmark the Ligurians for later conquest, besides the fact that they stood square in the way of Rome's plans to build an overland road to Spain. In 177 BC the Romans founded the colony of Portus Lunae (Luni) on the far east end of Liguria, and, not long after that, Albintimilium (modern Ventimiglia) on the far west. Sandwiched between the legions, the Ligurians were at last sufficiently subdued under Augustus to build the Via Julia Augusta.

Romans (177 BC–475 AD)

The Romans were clever in managing their conquests, maintaining most of the tribes and cities as nominally independent states, while planting Latin colonies everywhere—Genua, Vada Sabatia (Savona), Albintimilium (Ventimiglia), Albium Ingaunum (Albenga) and Luna were the main ones. Nor was it long before Genua first gained its prominence as the Mediterranean port of Mediolanum (Milan), linked to it by the Via Postumia.

For the most part, this coast was marginal to the Empire, enjoying a few rewards but taking most of the lumps in an Italy where things began to go very wrong even as it was enjoying a hitherto unknown level of prosperity—for a select few, at least. Taxation ceased for Roman citizens, as booty provided the state with all the revenues it needed, and tens of thousands of slaves were imported. Meanwhile, vast amounts of cheap grain brought from Africa and Egypt ruined the Italian farmer, who had the choice of selling his freehold and becoming a sharecropper, joining the army, or moving to Rome as part of the burgeoning lumpenproletariat. The men who profited the most from the wars bought up tremendous amounts of land, turning Italy into a country of huge estates (*latifundia*), and becoming a new aristocracy powerful enough to stifle any attempts at reform. Only Rome (of course) and a few other cities prospered. Rural Italy knew constant famine and plagues, while in Rome the new rich were learning the delights of orgies, gladiatorial combats and being carried about the streets by slaves.

For all the huge sums it cost to maintain them, the legions in the 3rd century AD were no longer the formidable military machine of Augustus' day. They were bureaucratic and a little tired, and their tactics and equipment were also falling behind those of the more clever German barbarians. The Goths were the first to demonstrate this, in 251, when they overran the Balkans, Greece and Asia Minor. Although **Diocletian** (284–305) completely revamped the structure of the state and economy, his fiscal reforms, such as the fixing of prices and a decree that every son had to follow the trade of his father, ossi-fied the state and made the creeping decline of western Europe harder to arrest. Taxes reached new heights as people's ability to pay them declined, and society's waning ener-gies became entirely devoted to supporting a bloated, all-devouring army and bureaucracy.

Medieval feudalism actually had its origins in the 4th century, as the remaining freehold farmers sold their lands and liberty to the local gentry—for protection's sake, but also to get off the tax rolls.

The confused politics of the 4th century are dominated by **Constantine** (306–337), who founded the new eastern capital of Constantinople and moved to increase the empire's political support by favouring Christianity. Though still a small minority in most places, the Christians' strong organization and determination made them a good bet for the future. The religious revolution that followed was remarkable. Constantine's predecessor Diocletian had been the most ferocious of the persecutors of Christianity; by 400, it was the turn of the pagans and Jews to be persecuted, as the Church itself became the most powerful and coherent instrument of the Roman élite.

In 408, when the Visigoths sacked Rome itself, St Augustine, probably echoing the thoughts of most Romans, wrote that it seemed the end of the world must be near. Rome should have been so lucky: after incursions by the Huns and Vandals, things had changed so completely that it was scarcely possible to tell the Romans from the barbarians. By the 470s, the real ruler in Italy was a Gothic general named **Odoacer**, who led a half-Romanized Germanic army and probably thought of himself as the genuine heir of the Caesars. In 476, he decided to dispense with the lingering charade of the Western Empire and had himself crowned King of Italy.

475–1000: The Dark Ages

At the beginning, the new Gothic-Latin state showed some promise. Certainly the average man was no worse off; trade and cities even revived a bit. In 493 Odoacer was replaced (and murdered) by a rival Ostrogoth, **Theodoric**, nominally working on behalf of the Eastern Emperor at Byzantium. Theodoric proved a strong and able ruler, but from the start stability was compromised by religious quarrels between the Arian Christian Goths and the orthodox Catholic populations in the cities.

A disaster as serious as any of those of the 5th century began in 536, with the invasion of Italy by the Eastern Empire, part of the relentlessly expansionist policy of the great Justinian. The historical irony was profound: in the ancient homeland of the Roman Empire, Roman troops now came not as liberators, but foreign, largely Greek-speaking conquerors. The Greeks ultimately prevailed over the Goths in 563, but the damage to an already stricken society and economy was incalculable. The repercussions were felt as far west as Liguria; Roman fortifications along the coast were shored up and controlled by the Byzantines, whose chief legacy consists of numerous place names and Albenga, the powerful bishopric they created on the Riviera di Ponente that would remain a force until the 14th century.

Italy's total exhaustion was exposed in 568, when the **Lombards**, a Germanic tribe who worked hard to earn the title of barbarian, overran northern Italy and parts of the south. A new pattern of power appeared, with semi-independent Byzantine dukes and exarchs defending coastal areas, and Lombard chiefs ruling most of the interior. The Byzantines saw their Riviera holiday come to an end in 641, when the Lombards under their chief, Rotari, chased them out and plunged the coast into a Dark Age as bleak as any. Their legacy was more to the gene pool than to the stream of culture: surnames ending in *aldo* or *aldi* are Lombard, and it may not be too far-fetched to say they contributed a tough chromosome or two to the already fibrous Ligurian stock.

With trade and culture at their lowest ebb, the 7th century marks the rock bottom of Italian history. In the 8th century, the popes, along with other bishops who had taken advantage of the confused times to become temporal powers, intrigued everywhere to increase their influence; they finally cashed in with a Frankish alliance in the 750s. At the time the Lombard kings were doing well, conquering territories claimed by the popes, who invited in **Charlemagne** to protect them. He eliminated the last Lombard king, Desiderius (his father-in-law, incidentally), and tucked all Italy as far south as Rome except Venice into his short-lived patchwork empire, sanctified by a papal coronation as the heir of the Roman Empire.

When Charlemagne's empire disintegrated following his death in 814, Italy reverted to a finely balanced anarchy and endless wars of petty nobles and battling bishops. Unlike the other regions' little Caesars, however, the Ligurian lords and bishops found their quarrels stymied by an outside force. In the 8th century, the **Saracens** established a permanent base in Provence at Fraxinet (above St Tropez), and made their first recorded incursion into Liguria in 901, raiding the Ligurian coast and marching up the Alpine valleys; one of their towers still stands just over the border in Piemonte, between Ormea and Garessio. Besides sacking and raiding, the Saracens also introduced a number of useful things such as pears and *grano saraceno* (buckwheat), watermills and irrigation techniques, and words like *dogana* (customs) and *darsena*, which turned into arsenal. They too contributed to the Ligurian gene pool, apparent in the occasional dark complexion you'll see, especially in the mountain valleys.

Elsewhere, in less precarious parts of Italy, life was slowly beginning to change. Sailing and trading over the sea always lead to better technologies, new ideas and economic growth, and in these respects the maritime cities of Italy were becoming the most advanced in Europe—Pisa and Amalfi were the most precocious and, unlike Venice, were not beholden to Byzantium. Genoa, however, still languished at the starting block. One of the few records pertaining to it from the period was the report of an early 10th-century Imperial envoy, who described it as a primarily farming community. But it obviously differed from other farming communities in one important aspect: it knew how to build ships and sail them.

In 950, the King of Italy, **Berengar II**, divided northeast Italy into three marches to organize its defence. To the west was Arduinica, including Ventimiglia and Turin; the second march, Aleramica, encompassed Albenga, Savona and Monferrato; and the third, Obertenga, included Genoa, Tortona, Luni and lands stretching almost to Milan. The *marchese* in charge of these territories—the Del Carretto, the Clavesana and Bosco in the Riviera del Ponente, and the Malaspina and Da Passono—created the first feudal powerhouses along the Riviera. These would endure for centuries and make a crazy-quilt political map of the region with their various alliances and betrayals.

A big break for Italy came in 961 with the invasion of the German **Otto the Great**, heir to the imperial pretensions of the Carolingians. He deposed Berengar II and was crowned Holy Roman Emperor the following year. Not that any of the Italians were happy to see him, but the strong government of Otto and his successors helped to control the great nobles and allowed the cities to expand their power and influence; one of his legacies was his 'Diploma' of 963 that put down in writing what pertained to the emperor and what belonged to the pope, an important source of information about Liguria at the time. A new pattern was established; Germanic Emperors would be meddling in Italian affairs for centuries, not powerful enough to establish total control, but usually able to keep out important rivals.

1000–1300: Crusades, Guelphs and Ghibellines

On the eve of the new millennium, most Christians were convinced that the turn of the calendar would bring with it the end of the world. On the other hand, if there had been economists and social scientists around, they would have had ample evidence to reassure everyone that things were looking up. Especially in the towns, business was very good, and the political prospects even brighter. The first mention of a truly independent *comune* (a free city state) was in Milan, in 1024.

Throughout this period the papacy had declined miserably, a fall that was finally arrested in 1073 with the election of the Tuscan reformer Hildebrand as **Pope Gregory VII**. The new pope immediately set himself in conflict with the emperors over the issue of investiture—whether the church or secular powers could name church officials. The various Italian (and European) powers took sides on the issue, and 50 years of intermittent war followed. The result was a big revival for the papacy, but more importantly the cities used the opportunity to increase their influence, and in some cases achieve outright independence, defeating the local barons in war, razing their castles and forcing them to move inside the towns.

It was during this period that the Ligurians found the wherewithal to free themselves and their sea of the Saracens, with enough momentum left over to catapult Genoa directly into Mediterranean affairs, just in time for the **First Crusade** (1097–1130). For Italy, and most especially for Genoa and Pisa, the states with boats to help ship Crusaders, the affair meant nothing but pure profit. In 1099, Genoa became a *comune* or, to be precise, a *Compagna comunis*, an association of citizens' groups bound to support the city's maritime adventures. Because these crusading expeditions were led by bold ambitious men, Liguria from the beginning was dominated by ambitious individuals who behaved obnoxiously at home and were hungry and clever enough to seize the main chance abroad when they saw it; more than anyone else the Genoese cashed in on the Crusades, its chameleon nobility adroitly changing their roles from sea captain to merchant at a moment's notice.

But trade was booming everywhere. The accumulation of money helped the Italians to create modern Europe's first banking system; Florence and Venice get credit for inventing modern accounting. By the 12th century, far in advance of most of Europe, Italy had attained a prosperity unknown since Roman times.

Politically, however, trouble was never far off. Emperor Frederick I **Barbarossa** of the Hohenstaufen—or Swabian—dynasty was strong enough in Germany, and he made it the cornerstone of his policy to reassert imperial power in Italy. Beginning in 1154, he crossed the Alps five times, molesting free cities that asked nothing more than the right to fight one another continually. Genoa had grown so quickly that it had to build a new 'Barbarossa' wall to protect itself against him (1155–60), but the emperor's main target was Milan, which he demolished in 1161; as a result, a united front of cities called the Lombard League defeated him in turn in 1176. Frederick's greatest triumph was arranging a marriage that left his grandson Frederick II not only emperor but king of Sicily, giving him a base in Italy itself.

The second Frederick's career dominated Italian politics for 30 years (1220–50); the popes, most notably Innocent IV of the Fieschi family of the Riviera di Levante, excommunicated him at least twice. As the battle between pope and emperor became deadly serious, all Italy divided into factions: the Guelphs under the leadership of the popes supported religious orthodoxy, the liberty of the *comuni* and the interests of their emerging merchant class. The Ghibellines stood for the emperor, statist economic control, the interests of the rural nobles and religious and intellectual tolerance. In an attempt to find a solution to the turmoil in 1261, Pope Urban IV set an ultimately disastrous precedent by inviting in **Charles of Anjou**, a powerful, ambitious leader and brother of the King of France. As protector of the Guelphs, Charles defeated Manfred, Frederick's son (1266), and murdered the last of the Hohenstaufens, Conradin (1268). He held unchallenged sway over Italy until 1282, when the famous revolt of the Sicilian Vespers started the party wars up again.

Some real changes did occur out of all this sound and fury. In 1204 Venice hit its all-time biggest jackpot when it diverted the Fourth Crusade to the sack of Constantinople, winning for itself a small empire of islands in the Adriatic and Aegean. Genoa emerged as Venice's greatest rival in 1284, when its fleet put an end to Pisa's prominence at the Battle of Meloria. Elsewhere around the peninsula, some cities were falling under the rule of military *signori* whose descendants would be styling themselves counts and dukes. Everywhere the freedom of the *comuni* was in jeopardy; after so much useless strife beween Guelphs and Ghibellines, the temptation to submit to a single strong leader often proved overwhelming.

In Liguria, the conflict was particularly ugly. In Genoa, the four most powerful families divided into factions of hatred and envy and pursued vendettas on a scale that left the other Italians in awe, with the Doria and Spinola on the Ghibelline side and the Grimaldi and Fieschi on the Guelph. All had lands elsewhere on the Riviera, and on Corsica and Sardinia; the Grimaldi, of course, even aced a principality, when one of their scions,

Francesco the Spiteful, disguised himself and his followers as monks in 1297, gained entrance into the Ghibelline fortress at Monaco, and knifed the proprietors (they later officially purchased Monaco and much of the surrounding coast from Genoa). Elsewhere, the people were totally dependent on their lords, who belonged to one side or another and busily fought their own little wars, against themselves, against Genoa and against the dukes of Savoy, who constantly made incursions south from Piemonte in an effort to control the essential trading routes, or salt roads, to the coast.

The Italian economy never seemed to mind the trouble. Trade and money flowed as never before; cities built new cathedrals and created themselves incredible skyscraper skylines, with the tall tower-fortresses of the now urbanized nobles—Albenga still has a fine collection. And it was, in spite of everything, a great age for Italian culture; the era of Guelphs and Ghibellines was also the time of Giotto (b. 1266) and Dante (b. 1265).

1300–1494: Renaissance Italy

This paradoxical Italy continued into the 14th century, with a golden age of culture and an opulent economy existing side by side with almost continuous war and turmoil. With no serious threats from the emperors or any other foreign power, the myriad Italian states were able to menace each other joyfully without outside interference. The cities were usually free from grand ambitions; everyone was making too much money to want to go and wreck the system. Without heavy artillery, walled towns and castles were nearly impossible to take, making the incentives to try hard even less. Best of all, the worst schemers and troublemakers on the Italian stage were fortuitously removed from the scene. Shortly after the election of the French Pope Clement V in 1305, the papacy moved to Avignon, becoming a puppet of the French king that temporarily had little influence in Italian affairs.

By far the biggest event of the 14th century was the **Black Death** of 1347–8, in which it is estimated that Italy lost about one-third of its population. The shock brought a rude halt to what had been 400 years of almost continuous economic growth, but the plague's grim joke was that it actually made life better for most of the Italians who survived; working people in the cities, no longer overcrowded, found their rents lower and their labour worth more, while in the country farmers were able to increase their profits by only tilling the best land.

Italian statesmen understood and used the idea of a balance of power long before political theorists invented the term, and, despite all the trauma, clatter, fighting, plague and noise, most of them probably believed Italy was enjoying the best of all possible worlds. Four major states, Venice, Tuscany, Naples and Milan, each a European power in its own right, were the most responsible for the gilded, opulent Italy of the 15th century, all complacently secure in its long-established cultural and economic pre-eminence. A long spell of freedom from outside interference lulled them into believing that its political disunity could continue safely forever, and, except perhaps for the notoriously clear-eyed realistic Florentine Niccolò Machiavelli, no one realized that Italy was in fact a plum waiting to be picked.

In contrast to the other major states, the nasty little money-making oligarchy of the Republic of Genoa contributed nothing to the cultural life of the times. Hard hit by the plague (its population was halved) and defeated by Venice at Chioggia, it found the 15th century the occasion for more intramural warfare in the good old Guelph and Ghibelline style, and clobbering the feudal nobles along the Riviera, a process of bringing them to heel under the Republic that would continue into the mid-16th century. The Genoese would later look upon this time as a period of preparation for their Republic, a time of *reculer pour mieux sauter.*

1494–1600: The Wars of Italy and the Counter-Reformation

The Italians brought the trouble down on themselves, when Duke Ludovico of Milan invited the French King **Charles VIII** to cross the Alps and assert his claim to the throne of Milan's enemy, Naples. Charles did just that, and the failure of the combined Italian states to stop him (at the inconclusive Battle of Fornovo, 1494) showed just how helpless Italy was at the hands of emerging monarchies. When the Spaniards saw how easy it was, they too marched in, and restored Naples to its Spanish king the following year (an Aragonese dynasty, cousins to Ferdinand and Isabella, had ruled Naples since 1442). Before long the German emperor and even the Swiss entered this new market for Italian real estate. The popes did as much as anyone to keep the pot boiling. Alexander VI and his son Cesare Borgia carried the war across central Italy in an attempt to found a new state for the Borgia family, and Julius II's madcap policy led him to egg on the Swiss, French and Spaniards in turn, before finally crying 'Out with the barbarians!' when it was already too late.

By 1516, with the French ruling Milan and Genoa, and the Spanish in control of the south, it seemed as if a settlement would be possible. The worst possible luck for Italy, however, came with the accession of the insatiable megalomaniac Charles V to the throne of Spain in that year; in 1519 he bought himself the crown of the Holy Roman Empire, making him the most powerful ruler in Europe since Charlemagne. Charles felt he needed Milan as a base for communications between his Spanish, German and Flemish possessions, and as soon as he had emptied Spain's treasury, driven her to revolt, and plunged Germany into civil war, he turned his attentions to Italy.

The wars began anew, bloodier than anything Italy had seen for centuries. Genoa was brutally sacked in 1522 by Spanish troops, who went on to defeat the French at Pavia in 1525. After an even worse sack of Rome by the imperial army in 1527, the French invaded once more, in 1529, and were defeated, this time at Naples, by the treachery of their Genoese allies. The final treaties left Spanish viceroys in Milan and Naples, and pliant dukes and counts toeing the Spanish line almost everywhere else. France would soon get back at Genoa by making alliances with the pirates and Turkish corsairs she couldn't control, and setting them to prey on Liguria.

The broader context of these events, of course, was the bitter struggles of the **Reformation and Counter-Reformation**. In Italy, the new religious angle made the Spaniards and the popes natural allies. One side had the difficult job of breaking the spirit of a nation that, though conquered, was still wealthy, culturally sophisticated and ready to resist; the other saw an opportunity to recapture by force the hearts and minds it had lost long before. With the majority of the peninsula still nominally controlled by local rulers, and an economy that continued to be sound, both the Spanish and the popes realized that the only real threat would come not from men, but from ideas.

Under the banner of combating Protestantism, they commenced a reign of terror across Italy. In the 1550s, the revived Inquisition began its manhunt for free-thinkers of every variety; the Index of Prohibited Books followed in 1559, accompanied by public book-burnings in Rome and elsewhere. Italian intellectuals trudged to the stake, while many more buried their convictions or left for exile in Germany or England. The job of re-educating Italy was put in the hands of the new Jesuit order; their schools and propaganda campaigns bore the popes' message deeply into the Italian mind, while their sumptuous new churches, spectacles and dramatic sermons helped redefine Catholicism.

Despite the oppression, the average Italian at first had little to complain about. Spanish domination brought peace and order to a country that had long been a madhouse of conflicting ambitions. Renaissance artists attained a virtuosity never seen before, just in time to embellish the scores of new churches, palaces, and villas of the mid-16th-century building boom. The combined Christian forces had turned back the Turkish threat at that battles of Malta (1566) and Lepanto (1571), and some Italians were benefiting greatly from Spanish imperialism in the New World—above all the Genoese financiers, who rented ships, floated loans, and snatched up a surprising amount of the gold and silver arriving from America.

1600–1796: The Age of Baroque

While Genoa began to wallow in lucre, after 1600 nearly everything started to go wrong for the rest of the Italians. The textiles and banking of the north, long the engines of the economy, both withered in the face of foreign competition, and many port towns began to look half-empty as the English and Dutch muscled them out of the declining Mediterranean trade.

As compensation, the architects invented baroque—the florid, expensive coloratura style that serves as a perfect symbol for the age itself, an age of political repression and thought control where art itself became a political tool. Baroque's heavenly grandeur and symmetry helped to impress everyone with the majesty of Church and State. At the same time, intimidated baroque scholars wrote books that went on for hundreds of pages without saying anything. Baroque impresarios managed the wonderful pageantry of Church holidays, state occasions and carnivals that kept the ragged crowds amused. Spanish fashions became the rage; manners and clothing became decorously berserk, and a race for easily bought noble titles occurred that would have made a medieval Italian laugh out loud. Italy was being rocked to sleep in a baroque cradle.

By the 18th century, there were very few painters, or scholars, or scientists. There were no heroic revolts either. Italy in this period hardly has any history at all; with Spain's increasing decadence, the great powers decided the futures of Italy's major states. In 1713, after the War of the Spanish Succession, the Habsburgs of Austria came into control of Lombardy under the enlightened despotism of Empress Maria Theresa (1740–80) and her son Joseph II (1780–92). Lombardy's old rival Piemonte, which during the War of the Austrian Succession shook loose from the tutelage of France and joined the winning side, earned a royal title in 1720 for Vittorio Amedeo II. The infant kingdom, with its brand-new capital of Turin, was poor and a little backward in many ways, but as the only strong and free state in Italy it would be able to play the leading role in the events of the next century, and in Italian unification.

1796–1830: Napoleon, Restoration and Reaction

Napoleon, that greatest of Italian generals, arrived in the country in 1796 on behalf of the French revolutionary Directorate, sweeping away the Piemontese and Austrians. Italy woke with a start from its baroque slumbers, and local patriots gaily joined the French cause. Perhaps because he only just missed being born a citizen of Genoa (Genoa's Bank of St George had sold Corsica to France the year before he was born) Napoleon had a soft spot for the old Republic; he obliged it to change its name to the Republic of Liguria, looted it as thoroughly as he did every other region of Italy, and imprisoned the recalcitrant pope in Savona (*see* p.139), but otherwise left much of the old Genoese constitution written by Andrea Doria intact, including the office of Doge. The Ligurians, among the most enthusiastic revolutionaries in Italy, also added some highly radical elements on human rights and duties and the right to an education.

Although Napoleonic rule lasted only until 1814, in this busy period important public works were begun (in Liguria, the coastal highway, the Via Aurelia was laid out) and laws, education and everything else reformed after the French model; the state also expropriated immense Church properties. At the same time, the French implemented high war taxes and conscription (some 25,000 Italians died in the invasion of Russia), and brutally repressed a number of local revolts, systematically exploiting Italy for the benefit of the Napoleonic élite and the crowds of speculators who came flocking over the Alps. The Republic of Liguria went into a depression caused by the Continental blockade. When the Austrians and English came to chase all the little Napoleons out, no one was sad to see them go.

The experience, though, had given Italians a taste of the opportunities offered by the modern world, as well as a sense of national feeling that had been suppressed for centuries. The 1815 Congress of Vienna put the clock back to 1796; the Habsburgs and Bourbons thought they could pretend the Napoleonic upheavals never happened. Political reaction in their territories was fierce; Liguria, which unwillingly found itself annexed by the Congress of Vienna to Piemonte Savoy (the Kingdom of Sardinia) and its reactionary absolutist kings, was livid.

Almost immediately, there emerged revolutionary agitators and secret societies like the famous *Carbonari* that would keep Italy convulsed in plots and intrigues. The French July Revolution of 1830 spread to Italy, encouraged by the liberal King Carlo Alberto in

Piemonte-Savoy, but once more the by now universally hated Austrians intervened. In Liguria, the disappointment was made worse by a cholera epidemic that caused the deaths of thousands; discouraged by politics and disease, hundreds of thousands emigrated to South America.

1848–1915: The Risorgimento and United Italy

Conspirators of every colour and shape, including Genoa's legendary **Giuseppe Mazzini**, had to wait another 18 years for their next chance. Mazzini (*see* pp.74–80) agitated frenetically all through the years 1830–70, inspiring all (Garibaldi was one of his first converts) but with little practical effect. In retrospect, his career as a revolutionary can bear a slight comparison to Marx's—though less Karl than Groucho. It was typical of the times, and the disarray and futility among republicans, radicals and those who simply wanted a united Italy set the stage for the stumbling, divisive process of the Risorgimento.

The big change came in the revolutionary year of 1848, when risings in Palermo and Naples anticipated even those in Paris itself. Soon all Italy was in the streets. Carlo Alberto of Piemonte, the hope of most Italians for a war of liberation, marched against the Austrians, but his two badly bungled campaigns allowed the enemy to re-establish control over the peninsula. By June 1849, only Venice, under Austrian blockade, and the recently declared Roman Republic were left. Rome, led by Mazzini and Garibaldi, beat off several attacks from foreign troops invited in by the Pope before succumbing to a large force sent by, of all people, President Louis Napoleon (soon to declare himself Napoleon III) of Republican France.

Despite failure on such a grand scale, at least the Italians knew they would get another chance. The unification of the country was inevitable, but there were two irreconcilable contenders for the honour of accomplishing it. On one side, the democrats and radicals dreamed of a truly reborn, revolutionary Italy, and looked to the popular hero **Garibaldi** (*see* 'Tales of Tenacity', pp.78–9) to deliver it; on the other, moderates wanted the Piemontese to do the job, ensuring a stable future by making **Vittorio Emanuele II** King of Italy. Vittorio Emanuele's minister, the polished, clever Count Camillo Cavour, spent the 1850s getting Piemonte in shape for the struggle, building its economy and army, participating in the Crimean War to earn diplomatic support, and plotting with the French for an alliance against Austria.

War came in 1859, and French armies did most of the work in conquering Lombardy. Tuscany and Emilia revolted, and Piemonte was able to annex all three. In May 1860, Garibaldi and his red-shirted 'Thousand' sailed from Genoa—Cavour almost stopped them at the last minute—and landed in Sicily, electrifying Europe by beating the Bourbon army all the way to Naples by September, where Garibaldi proclaimed himself temporary dictator on Vittorio Emanuele's behalf. The King met Garibaldi on 27 October, near Teano, and after finding out what little regard the Piemontese had for him, the greatest and least self-interested leader modern Italy has known went off to retirement on the Sardinian island of Caprara.

Napoleon III had helped to make Vittorio Emanuele King of Italy, but at a price: a piece of Liguria and Savoy, what is now the French *département* of the Alpes-Maritimes. To make the secret treaty between Napoleon III ('that fox of a Bonaparte' as Garibaldi called him) and Cavour more palatable to any of the inhabitants who might have preferred to remain Italian, a plebiscite was set up in 1860. Vittorio Emanuele openly encouraged his subjects to vote for French union, but even more encouraging was the presence of the French army holding manœuvres in Nice, and French agents bullying the majority Italian-speaking population to achieve the official result: 24,449 pro-France to 160 against.

If not the Ligurians, at least the other Italians had some good news, as more unexpected help from outside allowed the new Italy to add two missing pieces to the nation. When the Prussians defeated Austria in the war of 1866, Italy was able to seize the Veneto. Only Rome was left, defended by a French garrison, and when the Prussians beat France at Sedan in 1870, the Italian army marched into Rome almost without opposition.

The first decades of the Italian Kingdom were just as unimpressive as its wars of independence. A liberal constitutional monarchy was established, but the parliament almost immediately decomposed into cliques and political cartels representing various interests. Finances started in disorder and stayed that way, and corruption became widespread. The outlines of foreign policy often seemed to change monthly, though like the other European powers Italy felt it necessary to snatch up some colonies. The attempt revealed the new state's limited capabilities, with embarrassing military disasters at the hands of the Ethiopians at Dogali in 1887, and again at Adowa in 1896.

The Riviera's First Tourists

Meanwhile, something unexpected was happening along the Riviera: an English invasion, but a peaceful one. It began with a book: Giovanni Ruffini, from Taggia near San Remo, had emigrated to England, and, feeling homesick, he wrote a novel in English called *Doctor Antonio* (1855), the story of Sir John Davenne and his daughter Lucy who come to San Remo and are swept away by the Mediterranean climate and beauty (Lucy also gets swept away by the local doctor). It was very much the *A Year in Provence* of its day: the Brits under Queen Victoria, busily covering up the limbs of their pianos, read Ruffini and flocked down to the Riviera in droves, especially to San Remo and Bordighera, the two warmest towns on the entire coast. They were followed in short order by other cold Europeans with money, and more than a few crowned heads from Germany, Holland, Sweden and Russia.

Elsewhere, after 1900, with the rise of a strong socialist movement, strikes, riots and police repression often occupied centre stage in Italian politics. Even so, important signs of progress showed that at least the northern half of Italy was becoming a fully integral part of the European economy. The 15 years before the war, prosperous and contented ones for many Italians, came to be known by the slightly derogatory term *Italietta*, the 'little Italy' of modest bourgeois happiness, an age of sweet Puccini operas, the first motor cars, blooming Liberty-style architecture, and Sunday afternoons at the beach.

1915–1945: War, Fascism and War

Italy could have stayed out of the First World War, but let the chance to do so go by for the usual reasons—a hope of gaining some new territory, especially Trieste. Also, a certain segment of the intelligentsia found the *Italietta* boring and disgraceful: irredentists of all stripes, some of the artistic futurists, and the perverse, idolized poet Gabriele D'Annunzio. The groups helped Italy leap blindly into the conflict in 1915, with a big promise of boundary adjustments dangled by the beleaguered Allies. Italian armies fought with their accustomed flair, masterminding an utter catastrophe at Caporetto (October 1917) that any other nation but Austria would have parleyed into a total victory. No thanks to their incompetent generals, the poorly armed and equipped Italians somehow held firm for another year, until the total exhaustion of Austria allowed them to prevail (at the battle of *Vittorio Veneto* you see so many streets named after), capturing some 600,000 prisoners in November 1918.

In return for 650,000 dead, a million casualties, severe privation on the home front and a war debt higher than anyone could count, Italy received Trieste, Gorizia, the South Tyrol and a few other scraps. Italians felt they had been cheated, and nationalist sentiment increased. The economy was in shambles, and revolution was in the air; workers in Turin raised the Red Flag over the Fiat plants and organized themselves into soviets. The troubles had encouraged extremists of both right and left, and many Italians became convinced that the liberal state was finished.

Enter **Benito Mussolini**, a professional intriguer in the Mazzini tradition with bad manners and no fixed principles. Before the war he had found his real talent as editor of the Socialist Party paper *Avanti*—the best it ever had, tripling the circulation in a year. When he decided that what Italy really needed was war, he left to found a new paper, and contributed mightily to the jingoist agitation of 1915. In the post-war confusion, he found his opportunity. A little bit at a time, he developed the idea of fascism, at first less a philosophy than an astute use of mass propaganda and a sense for design.

The basic principle, combining left- and right-wing extremism into something the ruling classes could live with, proved attractive to many. After Mussolini took power and had himself declared prime minister in the anarchic month of October 1922, he governed Italy at first with undeniable competence. Order was restored, and the economy and foreign policy were handled intelligently by non-fascist professionals. Compared to the governments that preceded him, Mussolini looked quite impressive. Industry advanced, great public works were undertaken, and the Concordat of 1929 was signed with the pope, founding the Vatican State and ending the Church's isolation from Italian affairs. The regime evolved a new economic philosophy, the 'corporate state', where labour and capital were supposed to live in harmony under syndicalist government control.

But the longer fascism lasted, the more unreal it seemed, a patchwork government of Mussolini and his ageing cronies, magnified and rendered heroic by cinematic technique—stirring rhetoric before oceanic crowds, colourful pageantry, magnificent larger-than-life post offices and railway stations built of travertine and marble. In a way it was the baroque all over again, and Italians tried not to think about the consequences. In the words of one of Mussolini's favourite slogans, painted on walls all over Italy, 'Whoever stops is lost'.

Mussolini couldn't stop, and the only possibility for new diversions lay with the chance of conquest and empire. His invasion of Ethiopia and his meddling in the Spanish Civil War, both in 1936, compromised Italy into a close alliance with Nazi Germany. Mussolini's confidence and rhetoric never faltered as he led an entirely unprepared nation into the biggest war ever. Liguria was bombed badly. For all the defeats and humiliations Italy was to suffer, however, it did find something to be proud of: a determined, resourceful Resistance that established free zones in many areas, and harassed the Germans with sabotage and strikes—one famous member in Liguria was writer **Italo Calvino**, who grew up in San Remo. The *partigiani* caught Mussolini in April 1945, while he was trying to escape to Switzerland; after shooting him and his mistress, they hung him by his feet from the roof of a petrol station in Milan. At the end of the war, Italy's territorial concessions were relatively slight: France was awarded one last piece of Liguria—Monte Bégo and its valley.

1945–the Present

Post-War Italian *cinema verità*—Rossellini's *Rome, Open City*, or de Sica's *Bicycle Thieves*—captures the atmosphere of this time better than words ever could. In a period of serious hardships that older Italians still remember, the nation slowly picked itself up and returned things to normal. A referendum in June 1946 made Italy a Republic, but only by a narrow margin.

The 1950s was Rome's decade, when Italian style and Italian cinema caught the imagination of the world. Gradually, slowly, a little economic miracle was happening; *Signor Rossi*, the average Italian, started buzzing around in his first classic Fiat Cinquecento, northern industries boomed, and life cruised slowly back to normal. Meanwhile, Italy was run by an unprincipled political machine whose members were raking in as much for themselves as they could grab, and everyone knew it, only it couldn't be said openly, for lack of proof. Even more sinister was the extent to which the machine would go to keep on top. The 1970s, Italy's 'years of lead', witnessed the worst of the political sleaze, along with a grim reign of terrorism, culminating in the kidnapping and murder in 1978 of an honourable Christian Democrat prime minister, Aldo Moro. All along, the attacks were attributed to 'leftist groups', though even at the time many suspected the truth, that some of the highest circles in the government and army were controlling or manipulating them, with the possible collusion of the CIA.

The economic miracle that began in the 1950s continues today, propelling the Italians into sixth place among the world's national economies. 'God made the world and Italy made everything in it,' was the slogan of the 1960s. The rotten Christian Democratic corruption behind the glittering mask was revealed in the early 1990s, when a small group of judges and prosecutors in Milan took a minor political kickback scandal and from it unravelled the golden string that held together the whole tangle of Italian political depravity—what the Italians call the *tangentopoli*, or 'bribe city'.

The Christian Democrats and the Socialists, the two leading parties, collapsed like a house of cards, leaving a vacuum filled by a jostling array of new parties and personalities, none of whom so far has been able to put the brakes on the merry-go-round of Italian politics. Noisiest of all was media tycoon Silvio Berlusconi's rightist Forza Italia, which won Mr Television a brief tenure as prime minister in 1994. Plagued by allegations of scandals and bribery, Berlusconi was forced out in early 1995 and, after a year's interim government by banker Lamberto Dino, new elections produced the more enduring, middle-of-the-road Olive party of Romano Prodi, with the support of the former Communists. Prodi's stringent economic measures allowed Italy to squeak into Euroland in January 1999, but led to the Democrazia di Sinistra withdrawing their support for his government in late 1998, and giving it to one of their own, Massimo d'Allema. At the time of writing, d'Allema continues to run Italy with integrity as the country battens down the hatches for the new millennium, and an expected 25 million pilgrims in Rome.

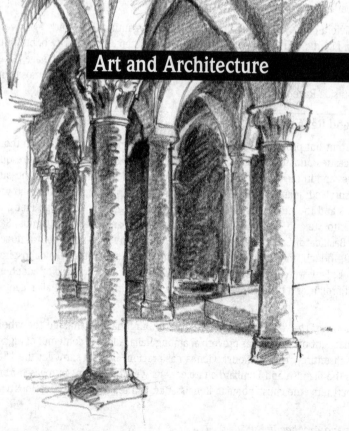

Art and Architecture

Prehistoric, Roman and the Dark Ages

Some of the very first works of art created in Europe were made along the Riviera: the stubby little fertility figures known as Venuses, sculpted by the Upper Palaeolithic Ligurians back in 40,000 BC and now in the museums at Balzi Rossi, Pegli (west Genoa), Toirano and Finale Borgo. Skip ahead 38,000 years or so to the Neolithic era and the first Ligurians, who left two singularly enigmatic kinds of art to recall their passing: 100,000 rock engravings in the upper Val Roja above Ventimiglia (there are casts in the Museo Bricknell in Bordighera), and the statue steles in eastern Liguria, now in the museums in La Spezia and Pontrémoli.

Even the Romans who took their place left little, or little that has survived—the great monument at La Turbie, built to celebrate their victory over the fierce Ligurians, is just over the border in Provence, which the Romans preferred to the Italian Riviera. There are a couple of exceptions, such as the ruins of Luni, the port for Carrara marble, an important Roman garrison town that died on the vine in the early Middle Ages. Ventimiglia, on the other side of Liguria, has a theatre, and remains of the its former incarnation as Albintimilium. Road building was the Romans' main accomplishment along the Riviera, and, perhaps fittingly, their chief legacy in the area is dozens of Roman bridges, some of which are still perfectly intact.

Although the Riviera coast was nominally protected by Byzantium, the Dark Ages were pretty gloomy in Liguria; you'll find a few towers here and there, a crypt or two, but little else. That said, Albegna, seat of a powerful bishopric, is an evocative relic of the age, especially its 5th-century baptistry, containing the only surviving early Byzantine mosaic in northern Italy outside Ravenna.

Middle Ages and Renaissance

Liguria's belligerent but prosperous Middle Ages are most remembered today in a thousand and one castles and tower houses in various states of repair, in its picturesque mountain villages and in the narrow lanes or *carrugi* of the cities. Some fine Romanesque churches have survived, many with black or grey and white stripes (a decoration allowed only to churches and the most illustrious families): San Paragorio at Noli, San Pietro at Portovenere, Santo Stefano, San Matteo and the Cathedral San Lorenzo in Genoa, San Fruttuoso, the Basilica di San Salvatore dei Fieschi above Lavagna and about a dozen others. By 1400, though, there was a school of sculptors working around Genoa inspired by Tuscan models. Few were actually from Liguria, but they became Genoese by adoption: among the most prolific and talented were the **Gagini** family from the Swiss-Italian canton of Ticino.

In *The Civilization of the Renaissance in Italy*, Jacob Burckhardt dismissed the whole region: 'The inhabitant of Liguria was proverbial among Italians for his contempt of higher culture.' It wasn't entirely true: although Genoa has precious little to show for the 15th century besides the Flemish and Lombard altarpieces its wealthy citizens purchased from their trading partners (the most popular Renaissance painter in Genoa was Joos van

Cleve), the Riviera di Ponente, between 1435 and 1515, had many churches frescoed by a school of earnest itinerant painters. Their favourite theme was the *Golden Legend*, by Ligurian Jacopo da Varagine, especially his accounts of the *Last Judgement*, the cycles of *Life and Death* and the *Passion of Christ*—paintings produced in illiterate communities that therefore still had a didactic purpose, and are colourful and dramatic, inspired as much by the Flemish school as the Italian.

Giovanni Canavesio (*c.* 1420–1500) stands head and shoulders above the others, a native of Pinerolo in Piemonte, whose bright palette, exquisite stylized draughtsmanship and ability to put genuine religious feeling in his frescoes make him something of a minor Fra Angelico. His masterpiece, Notre-Dame-des-Fontaines, is in the upper Val Roja (now part of France), near La Brigue; his frescoes in San Bernardo in Pigna are also excellent. There were other vigorous Ligurian painters of the period, led by **Antonio Monregalese**, **Pietro Guido** from Ranzo, **Gabriele della Cella** from Finale Ligure, and **Tomaso and Matteo Biazaci** from Busca.

Nice, then called Nizza, was the birthplace of **Lodovico Brea** (1450–1522), who painted in the elegant if retro International Gothic style, and worked in many places in Liguria, along with his two younger kinsmen Antonio and Francesco. In the later part of his career the Renaissance began to influence Lodovico, and although he was still commissioned to paint hieratic medieval subjects, his precise line and beautiful sense of light and shadow stand out, favouring a shade of wine-red that French artists still call *rouge brea*. There are a few of his works on the Italian side of the border, including a polyptych in Dolceacqua; San Domenico in Taggia has a particularly fine collection of works by all three Breas.

Mannerism

It was the Admiral Andrea Doria, the 'Saviour of Genoa', who also saved his philistine city's reputation in the annals of art when he hired Florentine **Perino del Vaga** (d. 1547), a pupil of Raphael, to help design and fresco his Palazzo del Principe in Genoa in 1527; if the city missed out on the Renaissance quattrocento, it was at least going to get hold of the peculiar tail end of the period, known as Mannerism. The year was a watershed in Italian art and liberty: in 1527 Emperor Charles V's brutal sack of Rome had turned the world upside down; Perino himself was a refugee from the terror. Mannerism, in its own way, turned the most precious classical tenets of the Renaissance upside down. It, too, had begun in Florence with Michelangelo, but the Florentines had the background and intellect to understand it; transplanting it to Liguria, as Perino del Vaga did, was like exporting bowler hats to Bolivia—completely out of context, it became pure decorative fashion.

Perino's work in Genoa was especially stylized, and was the biggest influence on the native founder of the Genoese school, **Luca Cambiaso** from Moneglia (1527–85). Son of the painter Giovanni Cambiaso, Luca was best known for his innovative draughtsmanship and monumental decorative frescoes, which would become the hallmark of the Genoese style (works in Palazzo Bianco, Villa Imperiale di Terralbe and San Matteo). He often painted with **Giovanni Battista Castello**, a Mannerist from Bergamo (1509–69) who spent most of his career in Genoa, decorating interiors and façades. Luca Cambiaso's work increasingly reflected the Counter-Reformation, and earned him an invitation from Philip II to become the court painter at the Escorial.

In the 1550s, **Galeazzo Alessi** of Perugia designed the Villa Cambiaso Giustiniani in the Genoese suburb of Albaro and invented what was to become the stately Genoese palazzo with its interior courtyard atrium or *cortile*. His contemporary, **Rocco Lurago**, took Alessi's basic design and scenographically adjusted it to fit Genoa's exciting terrain, in the long vistas through the courtyard to the staircase in Palazzo Doria Tursi (1568) on Via Garibaldi. Among the sculptors of the day, the Florentine Mannerist **Giovanni Angelo Motorsoli** (d. 1563), a student of Michelangelo, was in demand after his work for Andrea Doria and remained the major influence among a not very exciting pool of local talent until the mid-17th century.

Baroque, Rococo and Beyond

In the 17th century, the obscenely wealthy old and *nouveau riche* families of Genoa required a large number of fluent, virtuoso painters to fill up their new palaces with suitable family allegories and flattering portraits. As a result, the city became a major meeting place of artists from all across Italy, who either came to seek their fortune in person or sent their paintings to the eager patrons there: **Reni, Domenichino, Orazio Gentileschi, Barocci** and other Bolognese masters; various reactionary Tuscans (**Pietro Sorri, Ventura Salimbeni, Aurelio Lomi**); and some Milanese, including the innovative **Giulio Cesare Procaccini**. The Genoese, unlike most 17th-century Italian schools, were very little affected by Caravaggio (who visited Genoa in 1605) and his dramatic use of light and shadow.

Instead, the key formative influence in Genoese baroque was **Peter Paul Rubens**, who arrived in 1606 and painted a number of portraits in the new grand and vibrant style he had evolved during his Italian sojourn, combining his native Flemish realism with vibrant Venetian colours and scintillating brush strokes. He loved Genoa, and, convinced that its stately palaces were the ideal of beauty, made sketches of them and later published a collection of plans and elevations called *The Palaces of Genoa* (1622); he designed his own home in Antwerp with numerous Genoese echoes. A second key influence derived from the works of Rubens' protégé **Antony Van Dyck**, who left the city a number of refined portraits during his stays in 1621–2 and 1626–7 and was the chief inspiration for the popular aristocratic portrait painter **Giovanni Battista Carbone** (1614–83).

Rubens' grand sensuous style and Van Dyck's more sensitive, refined techniques combined in the work of the greatest Genoese painter of the first half of the seicento, **Bernardo Strozzi** (1581–1644); his style, however, was distinctively his own, characterized by bold brushstrokes and light-filled colours. In 1598 Strozzi became a Capuchin monk, but was released in 1610 to care for his ill mother; in 1630, after his mother died, he was imprisoned by his Order and pressured to return, so, much to Genoa's loss, he moved to more tolerant Venice, where he spent the rest of his life. Besides religious paintings, Strozzi was also adept at intimate genre scenes and portraits of musicians; his most famous work in Genoa is *The Cook*, in the Palazzo Rosso. His contemporary, and the most popular painter among the Genoese nobility, was the dull as toast **Domenico Fiasella** (Il Sarzana, 1589–1669); the best was **Gioacchino Assereto** (1600–49), who could equal Strozzi, although most of his work is still in private collections.

The greatest baroque architect of the period was **Bartolomeo Bianco** (c. 1590–1657), designer of Via Balbi and its great Palazzo della Università (1630), where he used the steep grade of the terrain to create one of the most stunning baroque buildings in northern Italy. Rome and Bernini so dominated Italian sculpture that it sucked in most of the talent in Italy; in Genoa, the best sculpture of the period was commissioned from **Alessandro Algardi** (1598–1654), Bernini's chief rival.

The last half of the seicento saw the full flowering of the Genoese school, with its bravura and bold handling inspired by Rubens and influenced by Velazquez, who made two visits to the city, in 1629 and 1649. One of its leading lights, however, **Giovan Battista Gaulli**, left for Rome in 1660, where he painted the revolutionary, dramatic frescoes in the apse of the Gesù church following the theories of Bernini. Another major figure, **Giovanni Benedetto Castiglione** (Il Grecchetto, d. 1665), also spent much of his career in Rome and Mantua; in his unusually versatile career he was always open to change and went through a variety of styles, as Rudoph Wittkower explains it, 'torn between a philosophical scepticism and an ecstatic surrender' that was typical of his generation. Castiglione produced magnificent etchings, inspired by Rembrandt, and prints in monotype, a technique that he invented (Blake would later use an adaptation of the process). In painting, Strozzi, Rubens and Van Dyck were his mentors, and he interpreted them with verve (see the altarpiece in San Luca, Genoa).

Castiglione inspired the two greatest Genoese fresco painters, **Domenico Piola** (1628–1703) and **Gregorio De Ferrari** (1647–1726), both masters of fluid rhythms and superbly decorative frescoes, where life is a grand, hedonistic holiday, overflowing in fantasy settings of Bolognese-style *quadratura* (*trompe-l'œil* architectural settings); the two painters often worked side by side in friendly rivalry, as in the Palazzo Rosso and at Palazzo Balbi-Senarega. De Ferrari, generally considered the superior artist, spent four years in Parma, where he discovered Correggio and adopted his *sfumato* technique; his mature style looks ahead to the rococo. A third important painter of the period was **Valerio Castello** (1624–59), a student of Fiasella, who reacted strongly against baroque classicism and in his brief career left highly dramatic yet highly sophisticated canvases of dissolving forms.

Valerio Castello's spiritual heir was one of the greatest and strangest Italian painters of the day, **Alessandro Magnasco** (Il Lissandrino, 1667–1749). From the start Magnasco was known for his ability to paint *piccole figure*, and his early commissions were to supply his distinctive wraith-like people for the landscapes of Antonio Francesco Peruzzini and scenes of imaginary ruins by Clemente Spera. He worked in Florence for the Grand Duke Ferdinand di Medici, where he saw prints of Jacques Callot's *Misères de la Guerre*, which affected him deeply, leading him to a sombre *chiaroscuro* colouring and phantasmagorical subjects, often demonic or grotesque—beggars and friars, wars and the Inquisition were favoured subjects, painted quickly and nervously as if infected by the distemper of the times, his shadowy figures energized with a few brushstrokes. At the end of his career he returned to Genoa, where he painted two of his greatest works: *The Reception in a Garden* (in the Palazzo Bianco) and the *Supper at Emmaus* (in the Convent of San Francisco in Albaro). He had no followers in Genoa, but his proto-Impressionistic technique influenced 18th-century painters in Venice, especially the Guardi brothers.

It was also in the late 17th century that Genoa's sculptors found their stride. A long residency in the 1660s by **Pierre Puget** (1620–94), a talented sculptor from Marseille who spent a number of years in Rome studying the works of Bernini and Cortona, motivated the locals, especially **Filippo Parodi** (1630–1702), another student of Bernini, who found a kindred spirit in Puget and added a certain French rococo grace to the High Roman style of his master: see the *Ecstasy of St Martha* in Santa Marta, in Genoa. One of his Genoese pupils, **Angelo de'Rossi**, went on to a successful career in Rome; others were his son **Domenico Parodi**, and the brothers **Bernardo** (1678–1725) and **Francesco Schiaffino** (1689–1765). Another important Genoese sculptor of the period, **Anton Maria Maragliano** (1664–1771), was a student of the painter Domenico Piola, and became one of the few baroque masters with the ability to sculpt expressively in wood. Maragliano often used designs supplied by Piola, and managed adroitly to combine the essential ecstastic attitudes required with a rococo charm; many churches along the Riviera contain his work. But, as often as not, the most delightful works of the 18th century are the churches themselves: among the most delightful are at Cervo, Laigueglia and Bogliasco.

The invention of winter tourism on the Riviera led to the creation of a monumental but festive style of holiday architecture, the florid *belle époque* and Liberty-style (Italian Art Nouveau) hotels and villas that have mostly survived intact, although many are now condominiums: the most elegantly dandified are in San Remo and Bordighera, where the architect of the Paris Opéra, Charles Garnier, lived and built. The outer suburbs of Genoa at Pegli and Nervi, popular locations for villas even in the 15th century, were given a whole new set of summer homes. Of special note in Pegli are the remarkable romantic gardens of the Villa Durazzo-Pallavincini, laid out in 1840 by an opera set designer and recently restored to their original state.

Although the once strong regional schools of art in Italy have pretty much lost their special character in the last hundred years, you'll find works by 19th- and 20th-century artists in Genoa, at the Villa Croce museum and the three galleries in Nervi. Genoa is also where much of the Riviera's newest architecture is concentrated, although much of this is in the state of the art restorations of historic buildings, from the Teatro Carlo Felice to the old cotton warehouse. The signal exception to this is Renzo Piano's Biga, or Crane, rising high above the port like a bouquet of giant ships' masts.

Tales of Tenacity

Just Who Was Christopher Columbus?

The Genoese are not Neapolitans, so if you pop the question you won't get a theatrical gesture of despair or an imploring glance up to heaven to please preserve the cosmic order from such ignorant ninnyhammers. This being the new kinder and gentler Genoa, you won't even get knifed. Instead, expect a gentle sigh, and the polite reply that actually, for once, what you learned in school was correct: the great Admiral of the Ocean Sea was from Genoa. Christopher Columbus, who should know, said so himself.

So then why do people, 500 years after his famous voyage, keep trying to prove that he was something else, or from some other place, that he was Jewish and/or from Mallorca, or from Calvi, Corsica (part of the Republic of Genoa at the time) or Cogoleto (between Savona and Genoa), or Pradello, or Cuccaro in Piemonte? The one person responsible for all the enigma, of course, is Christopher Columbus himself. He went out of his way to shroud himself in mystery, and the clues he left behind are so tangled that it's surprising that a pulp sci-fi writer didn't use the 1992 celebrations to try to prove he was a bungling alien from outer space. So much of his private life is unexplained that even the ponderous Italian documentation doesn't convince many. In fact, it contradicts Columbus' own words and his first biographers. A renowned 19th-century criminal psychologist, studying the case, declared that one of history's greatest discoverers was decidedly paranoid.

When was he born, for instance? In his own autobiographical writings, Columbus himself suggests birthdates ranging between 1447 and 1469. Bartolomé de Las Casas and Columbus' son, Fernando, who were his earliest biographers, who knew him intimately and had all his papers, never mention a date. Who were his parents? Columbus never told anyone, not even his own son, the name of his father.

Christopher and his first biographers all claim that he went to sea as a lad—traditionally a Genoese would start off as a deckhand at age 14. But documents in Savona dated 1472 say that he was an apprentice wool-carder at 12 and have him down as a weaver at age 21. To add to the confusion, once he left Genoa (that much, at least, everyone agrees on!) he used a variety of aliases—Colon, Colonus, Colomo—but never his presumed Genoese name, Cristoforo Colombo, or the Latinized Columbus.

The names Cristovam Colón and Christovao Colom are first recorded when he moved to Portugal. According to Las Casas and Christopher himself, he arrived there in 1470, already a well-known navigator, with credentials that impressed the Crown with his vision of sailing west to the Indies. The notarial deeds in Genoa and Savona, however, have it that he didn't even go to sea until 1473, most likely as a trade representative, that his experience at sea was that of a passenger, and that he didn't arrive in Portugal until 1476, and then only by grasping an oar and floating to shore after his ship sank. His Portuguese biographer João de Barros (1496–1571) describes how he was injured, cared for by the locals, then later moved to a Genoese neighbourhood in Lisbon. If true, and it seems to be, Christopher had *chutzpah* on a truly heroic scale, amongst all his other qualities; not every shipwrecked Italian salesman in his mid-20s (presumably) could pass himself off as a great mariner to the Kings of Portugal and the Catholic Kings of Spain.

In Lisbon, Christopher found his young brother, Bartolomé, who was a gifted cartographer and who helped his brother get a job in the field. According to Christopher and his first biographers, he made up a globe in 1474 (note, two years before he apparently arrived in Portugal) and sent it the Florentine astronomer Paolo Dal Pozzo Toscanelli, who sent him an encouraging note and a nautical chart showing the westward approach to Japan (a sketch of this was actually found in the 19th century among Toscanelli's papers in Florence). Christopher took the map along with him in 1492.

No documents survive that begin to explain just when and where the Colombo brothers learned the art of map-making, which has led to the speculation that our man may have been Jewish. The most accurate maps of day were made in Mallorca, by Jewish cartographers, and in the dawn of the Age of Exploration were treated as state secrets. One theory, proposed by Salvador de Madariaga in his *Vida del muy magnifico señor Don Cristobal Colón*, is that Christopher was the son of a Jewish family who had moved to Genoa from Spain, fleeing the growing bigotry, and that he completely recreated himself when he was shipwrecked in Portugal in 1476. De Madariaga's evidence is mostly circumstantial but intriguing: after all, Colombo is among the recorded surnames of Italian Jews, one of whom had served as a rabbi in Livorno in the 19th century.

Whatever his experience at sea or lack thereof, Christopher soon proved to be a bold and able mariner. In 1477, he convinced Prince João to give him a ship to sail to Iceland, where he made observations on tides that were confirmed in 1497 by another Genoese-born explorer, Giovanni Caboto (John Cabot). He voyaged down the west coast of Africa. He also married Doña Filipa de Perestrelo y Moniz, who gave him his first son, Diego, in 1479, but died a few years later.

Most historians agree Christopher the widower and little Diego moved from Portugal to Spain in late 1484 or 1485, after King João II refused to sponsor his vision of sailing west to reach the east. They travelled in secret, perhaps one step ahead of the law; a letter from the king dated March 1488, addressed to Cristovam Colón, says that the King was willing to re-examine his plans and that he could return to Portugal without fear of persecution.

The rest of the famous story falls into place from here: Christopher arrives in Spain, destitute, at Palos de La Frontera, and seeks help at the Franciscan monastery of Santa Maria de La Rabida where he meets Friar Juan Perez, a confessor of Queen Isabella, and Friar Antonio de Marchena, who agreed to work to obtain him an audience with the Catholic Kings of Spain. Christopher left Diego in the care of the friars, met the queen in 1486, and made an impression; a document from 1487 refers to a payment to Cristobal Colomo in regards to some service rendered. In that same year Christopher met Beatriz Enriquez in Córdoba: she became his mistress and in 1488 gave birth to his second son and biographer Fernando.

It was not until 1492, after completing the Reconquista, that Ferdinand and Isabella were ready to give ear seriously to the Genoese. On April 17 1492, at Villa de Sancta Fe de La Vega de Granada, the *Capitulaciones* were spelled out between the Spanish sovereigns and their Admiral Don Cristobal Colón. The *Capitulaciones* stated that if he reached the

Indies by sailing westward, he would be given the titles of Admiral of the Ocean Sea, Viceroy and Governor General of all lands that he discovered, and get a ten per cent cut of all merchandise acquired there; and that these entitlements, upon the death of Don Cristobal Colón, would be passed to his successors in perpetuity. After all his years of waiting, Christopher had learned to become wary and suspicious of kings.

Rightly so. By the time he returned from his second voyage (of 1493–6) the Spanish were already arguing that the *Capitulaciones* were only a draft for an agreement and withdrew the first of his privileges. Occasionally the Crown granted him a few 'mercies' to keep him from claiming the whole things was a fraud. For the rest of his life, Christopher would find himself falling deeper and deeper into debt, scorned by the Spanish court, surrounded by detractors and indifference. His only reliable income turned out to be the 10,000 *maravedis* granted to him by the Crown as a life pension in 1493.

But discouragement that would have driven a lesser man to despair was water off a duck's back to Christopher. After suffering two years of poverty, confinement and abuse in Spain, he set sail again in 1498 and discovered the continent of South America. He left behind his will, a *Mayorazgo*, a strange document in which he made the point repeatedly that his name and that of his heirs is Colón, and that he was a true Colón born in Genoa, and that his successors should return to Genoa, and 'always endeavour for the honor and welfare of the city of Genoa'. He then goes on to command how Diego and his future heirs should sign their papers: they must imitate him, and never use any family name, identifying themselves only by their first name (in Christopher's case, Xpo FERENS, a Latinization of his name) or simply as 'the Admiral' under a cabalistic pyramid of letters:

.S.
.S.A.S.
X M Y
El Almirante

On November 20 1500 Christopher returned from his third voyage—in chains, charged with badly administering the new territories, after he had been unable to put down a rebellion of the first colonists on Hispaniola. Humiliated, all of his privileges revoked and fearing that his two sons would never receive a peso, the Admiral collected copies of all the promises on paper made to him by Spain, and sent them for safekeeping to the most reliable institution in Genoa: the Bank of St George. Which brings up another Columbian mystery: why did he always write in Castilian Spanish (using many Portuguese spellings) even when writing home to Genoa? But he could presumably read his presumably native tongue—at least, all the letters from the bank addressed to 'Our beloved fellow citizen Christopher' were in Italian.

Despite ill health, poverty, dispiriting ingratitude and outright scorn, Christopher managed to get together four tiny decrepit caravels, and set sail with his 14-year-old son Fernando on his fourth and final voyage. He discovered Central America during his two years there, and was shipwrecked on Jamaica where he was left to die, unaided and unsought, even after Governor Ovando of Hispaniola knew he had survived. He came home against all odds, sick with gout, and, having no home to go to, lodged in a boarding house in Valladolid and died in 1506.

Who was that guy? The question arose while he was still warm in the grave. A Genoese Dominican, Agostino Giustiniani, came out with a book claiming that Christopher was of plebeian origin and had been a manual labourer. This was enough to offend the prickly honour of Fernando, who went to Italy in search of some noble Columbus relatives but failed to find a single one. When he replied to Giustiniani by writing his father's biography, he reluctantly conceded the plebeian origins, but denied the manual labour—no man so well read and learned in cartography could have been a humble worker. And as for his father's name, Fernando had to admit, 'with respect to the truth about such a name and last name it did not come about without some mystery.'

His older brother Diego had gone to court to claim his rights, and had won the title of Admiral and governor of Hispaniola. Diego's son Luis had to go to court as well, and reached a settlement with the Crown: in exchange for giving up all claims to the ten per cent in the *Capitulaciones*, he and his heirs would have the honorary title of Admiral of the Ocean Sea, two noble titles, Duke of Veragua and Marquese of Jamaica, and with them an annuity of 1000 gold doubloons, all in perpetuity (which lasted until 1830 when by Royal Order the 1000 gold doubloons were reduced to 23,400 pesos).

In 1578, the identity issue flared up again when there appeared to be no direct male heirs. It was duly confirmed that the names Colón and Colombo were one and the same, and two hundred potential Colombos were located. Curiously, although some of these were Genoese and the reward was great, not a single one of them petitioned the Spanish crown (the rights eventually passed to a great-great-nephew in Spain). Genoa, naturally prudent, remained out of the fray, but by 1618 a Genoese school of scholars emerged to root out the truffle of truth.

One of the most important scholars was Filippo Casoni, who studied the genealogy of Christopher's family in 1708 and whose results were published posthumously in Genoa in 1799 as the *Annali della Repubblica di Genova*. Here we learn at last that the Colombos were a respected family in Liguria, from a place near Nervi and Fontanabuona, where an old tower called the Colombi is still located. Christopher's father, Domenico Colombo, a successful woolweaver, was a citizen of Genoa from the parish of Santo Stefano, and his mother was named Susanna Fontanarossa; she and Domenico had 'lived together for many years' and their 'first fruit' was Cristoforo.

Casoni's work has pretty much stood up to further researches by generations of Columbian scholars in Genoa. Their efforts were published by the Italian state in 15 volumes in three multilingual editions in 1892–6, and were complemented by a prodigious publication of the city of Genoa called *Colombo* (1932) with fascimiles of all pertinent deeds and documents from the church records and other archives (many only discovered in the 19th century). Both establish beyond any reasonable doubt that a Christopher, son of Domenico, was born in Genoa or nearby in 1451. As the Mayor Eugenio Broccardi wrote in the preface:

To reject the documents here assembled in their authentic and legitimate form is to deny the light of the sun; their acceptance signifies the freeing of truth from the infinity of idle words that are increasing every day in vain attempts to find outside Genoa the origin of the discoverer of America.

So there. But the question remains: why did Christopher to go to such extremes to cover up his tracks? In his *The Discovery of North America*, Maurizio Tagliattini comes up with a plausible answer: that Christopher may have been the firstborn of Susanna, but not of Domenico Colombo. Tagliattini bases his theory on two important pieces of evidence. The first is in Fernando's biography of Christopher. Fernando spends an entire chapter inconclusively musing about the names of his father's parents, but further along states that the Admiral's brother and lieutenant Bartolomé was the founder of the city of Santo Domingo, which he named in memory of his father, whose name was Domenico. *His* father, this is, not Christopher's.

The second is a notarized Latin document of 1473 from Savona, in which Susanna, wife of Domenico, agrees to the sale of rights to Domenico's house. With her as witnesses are her two sons, Christopher and Giovanni (who is never mentioned elsewhere) with the surname of Pelligrino. In the document, the notary described them also as the sons of Domenico, but then crossed it out. Tagliattini surmises that, while living in Genoa, Christopher only pretended to be the legitimate son of Domenico Colombo, to hide the disgraceful fact that his true father, Pelligrino, had abandoned him and his mother—hence the change of name once he left Genoa, and his frequent references to Moses, born out of wedlock and abandoned by his father. Of course, Tagliattini has found that Pelligrino is a Jewish surname in Italy... See Tagliattini's website, at *www.millersv.edu/~columbus/ tagliattini.html* for more information.

Typically, no one is quite sure where Christopher is buried (both Seville and Santo Domingo claim his bones) or whether or not his ghost suffers over the ambivalence of his legacy; it seemed as if the general consensus that came out of the review of his career in 1992 was that he should have stayed put in Genoa. The greatest mystery of all is just where he found the heart and courage to carry on; his resilience seems almost superhuman. He wrote: 'And the sea will grant each man new hope, as sleep brings dreams of home.' Which, in his own case, in spite of everything, must have been dreams of the Genoa he knew as a child.

Liguria's Idealists: Mazzini and Garibaldi

Proud, stubborn tenacity must always have been a characteristic of the Ligurians for them to survive on their rocky, vertical homeland. Tenacity kept Columbus going when the chips were down, and it kept the leading families of the Genoese Republic embroiled in feuds and vendettas for generations. Even after Andrea Doria put Genoa under Spanish protection, tenacity kept him from surrendering to Spanish pressure to change the republic into a principality. This enabled Genoa to maintain at least the illusion of a being a free agent, with its own constitution, and unlike Venice it was able, during the Napoleonic years, to keep up appearances as the Republic of Liguria. No region in Italy was more democratically minded in the early 19th century, and when the reactionary kings of Piemonte inherited the Republic by treaty in 1815, they were pleased to have a port but very wary of being burned by the political hot potato that came with it. One of their first acts was to spend buckets of money on fortifications around Genoa, as if they could bottle up the genie.

Fortunately for Italy, Ligurian tenacity and love of independence had already taken root in two young souls, one a dreamer and schemer, the other a man of action, both of whom also possessed a (very non-Genoese) disinterested idealism of staggering proportions. Without the generous and unflagging spirits of Giuseppe Mazzini and Giuseppe Garibaldi, the Risorgimento and Italian unification would have been a different thing altogether, a patched-together political answer to questions about 'a geographical expression' as Metternich disdainfully called Italy in 1847. Mazzini and his impossibly lofty aims and romantic failures contributed mightily to the idea that there was indeed a nation called Italy that could be governed by Italians, inspiring Garibaldi to lead the fight that galvanized the world and give the people of Italy a genuine sense of unity for the first time since the Romans, defying Dante's famous curse:

> *Oh servile Italy, house of suffering*
> *a ship without a pilot in a great tempest*
> *not mistress of provinces, but a brothel!*

Act I: Birth of an Idea

Mazzini was born in Genoa in 1805, the son of a doctor enamoured of the French Revolution and a mother who, even more than the typical Italian mamma, thought her son was the Messiah. Although physically frail, he was a precocious child, and read before he could walk. At age 16, he witnessed a tide of refugees pouring though Genoa, hoping to escape to Spain after their failed revolution against the yoke of Piemonte of 1821. The sight of people suffering for political ideals moved him deeply. He started wearing black, as if in mourning for freedom, and dressed that way for the rest of his life, single-handedly inventing the stereotype of the romantic revolutionary. He devoured the writings of humanist philosopher Johann Gottfried Herder, who believed that empires were monsters and that a people who shared a common language naturally shared a past and organically made up a nation, and that if all states were so composed, a peaceful world would inevitably result.

Mazzini briefly followed his father's career as a doctor but fainted at his first operation, then obeyed his parents' wishes and studied law. His real vocation, as an agitator, began in 1827 when he joined the Carbonari, a hierarchical secret society that planned armed revolution in Italy. Mazzini was not one to take orders blindly, however, and in 1830 he was betrayed to the police by the leader of his cell and sent to prison for three months. Like St Francis, the young Mazzini used his time in the clink to reflect and change his life, developing a philosophy and belief that distilled Herder to the purest essences. He believed in God, not the Christian God, but a God incarnate in the will of the people: Mazzini's religion was pure democracy. His bedrock beliefs were in the equality of humanity (including women and workers, a radical view back then) and in its ability to progress with a proper education. Every individual was born with equal rights, but that alone was not enough, as everyone learned from the French Revolution:

> *The theory of Rights may suffice to arouse men to overthrow the obstacles placed in their path by tyranny, but it is impotent where the object in view is to create a noble and powerful harmony... With the theory of happiness as the primary aim of existence, we shall only produce egoists who will carry the old passions and desires into the new order of things, and introduce corruption into it a few months after. We have, therefore, to seek a Principle of Education superior to any such theory... This principle is DUTY... to struggle against injustice and error (wherever they exist), in the name and for the benefit of their brothers, is not only a right but a Duty; a duty which may not be neglected without sin; the duty of their whole life.*

Essay on the Duties of Man Addressed to Workingmen (1844)

From exile in Switzerland, Mazzini founded his own semi-secret society called *Le Giovine Italia*, 'Young Italy', with the goal of instilling a sense of national identity in the Italian people and educating them to lead a revolution from within, one that would make Italy a democratic republic as a model for Europe. One of his first recruits was a sailor named Garibaldi, who participated in Mazzini's first insurrection in 1834. Unfortunately, the revolt was botched before it began, when Mazzini's commander lost all of Giovine Italia's funds in the gambling dens of Paris. As a result, Garibaldi and Mazzini were both sentenced to death in Genoa, but managed to escape—Garibaldi to Marseille and Mazzini to London.

In London (where the only thing he loved was the fog) Mazzini kept the flame of revolt alive by making contacts and writing endless letters. There are accounts of him giving most of his meagre income from journalism to beggars, who knew that the affable, other-worldly Italian in black could never say no. He lived an austere life in a cramped book-filled room, smoking cigars (his one self-indulgence) while his canaries flew about everywhere because he could not bear to keep them in cages. He founded and taught in a free evening school to teach poor Italian immigrant adults and children to read and write. His personal magnetism charmed all who met him, especially Thomas Carlyle, who thought Mazzini was an impossible dreamer, but adamantly refused ever to hear anyone speak ill of him.

Giuseppe Garibaldi, the impossible doer, was born in Nice in 1807, his father a sailor from Chiavari and his mother from Loano. He loved the sea from an early age, and was hired as a cabin boy at age 15, travelling all over the Mediterranean and Black Sea, having blood-curdling adventures from the start. He later wrote that the influential event in his life was a visit to Rome in 1825 with his father. The ancient monuments thrilled him, and inspired him to imagine that the city could one day again be the capital of a united Italy; it became, as he wrote: 'the dominant thought and inspiration of my whole life'.

Garibaldi got his first commission as a captain in 1832, just before the Mazzinian débâcle, and afterwards carried on his career from Marseille. Discouraged and weary of his life in exile, he joined tens of thousands of other Ligurians who left for South America. Garibaldi had taken to heart Mazzini's notions on one's duty to fight oppression wherever it existed, and at once got involved in Rio Grande's war of independence from Brazil and, later, in Uruguay's war against Argentina. From his very first conflict he showed extraordinary personal courage, disregard for danger, and leadership, using imaginative guerrilla tactics and shockingly brutal (but effective) bayonet charges. Garibaldi's battles in South America were nearly all defeats—most were suicide missions from the start—but they were popular moral victories. Yet from the beginning Garibaldi was to find the rug constantly pulled out from under him by less than idealistic politicians, whom he soon learned to distrust and hate.

When Garibaldi was put in charge of the Italian Legion at Montevideo, he was wounded by disparaging remarks about Italian military prowess. To help make his rag-tag band into a serious fighting force, he absconded with a shipment of red shirts intended for slaughter-house workers and made them into a uniform, creating the first *garibaldini*, who defied all the nay-sayers by acquitting themselves with courage and distinction. But the politicians of Uruguay found the Red Shirts expendable, and in 1847 Garibaldi and some 70 *garibaldini* returned to Genoa, where they received a tumultuous welcome from Mazzini's republicans, who had read accounts of their bold exploits in the papers.

Act II: 1848 and the Roman Republic

By this time, however, Garibaldi regarded Mazzini's dreams for a revolution that would happen without outside help as totally impractical, and although he hated the monarchy, he like many others believed that a unified Italy required the support of Carlo Alberto, the King of Piemonte. With his usual forthrightness, Garibaldi went to the king directly, demanding an army to fight the Austrians in Lombardy. Carlo Alberto, already wary of Garibaldi and his popular support, refused, so Garibaldi gathered together a do-it-yourself band of volunteer *garibaldini* and went about it in the name of Lombardy. When the king's blundering armies went down quickly to defeat at Custoza, Garibaldi and his volunteers fought on, impressing all Europe with their guerrilla tactics. Carlo Alberto ordered Garibaldi's arrest, but the Italian Legion, reduced to 500, only gave up the fight after they were surrounded by 5000 Austrian troops and escaped after a daring bayonet charge. Garibaldi returned to the Riviera, disappointed that so few Italians had rallied to the cause.

But an unexpected second chance fell into his lap: the people of Rome, furious that Pius IX, in spite of his liberal talk, had failed to send troops to help the Piemontese fight the Austrians, rose up against him and sent the Pope fleeing for his life. Garibaldi was made a general of the newly proclaimed Roman Republic, and Mazzini, thanks to his reputation and integrity, was the natural leader of the first governing triumvirate, and true to form gave Rome the most tolerant, enlightened government it ever had—while working for no pay and dining in a workers' canteen. Meanwhile, Garibaldi laboured day and night to organize the Roman defence—needed soon enough when, in the name of the Pope, President Louis Napoleon of France sent an expeditionary force to Rome to restore papal power. An argument erupted in the Assembly: Mazzini hoped to reach a peaceful accommodation, while Garibaldi wanted no appeasement at all, and won the day.

The usually world-weary Romans, aided by not a few foreigners (one was the American political cartoonist Thomas Nast), put up a gallant and heroic defence of the Republic, although they were outgunned and outmanned, as the French force was augmented by Neapolitans and Spaniards. On July 1 1849, the Roman assembly passed the most liberal and advanced constitution Italy ever had. Two days later, after a three-month siege, the French entered Rome. Just before leaving, Garibaldi gave his famous speech in St Peter's Square: 'Whoever wishes to continue the war against the foreigner, let him come with me. I offer neither pay nor quarters nor provisions. I offer hunger, thirst, forced marches, battles and death.'

Act III: Discouragement and Failures

After barely escaping from Rome with his life and watching his beloved wife Anita die in the subsequent hardship, Garibaldi found himself all but abandoned, and all doors fearfully closed against him. Writing bitterly that 'the name of Italian will be a laughing stock for foreigners in every country. I am disgusted to belong to a family of so many cowards', he went off to make candles in a factory on Staten Island for four years and applied for American citizenship.

While he sulked, nostalgic for Italy, Mazzini was back in London, rallying the democrats and scheming away. When Garibaldi couldn't bear to stay away any more and returned to Italy by way of England, Mazzini was anxious to discuss an incursion into Sicily he was planning, but Garibaldi avoided him, blaming him for the failure of the Roman Republic. He took no part in the romantic republican insurrections supported by Mazzini (then secretly living in Genoa) in 1853, 1856 and 1857, all of which went down to tragic defeat; instead, he bought Caprera, an island off the north coast of Sardinia, and bided his time farming. After 1857, however, he was summoned to Turin to discuss the evolving situation with the new, pro-unification King Vittorio Emanuele II and his prime minister Count Cavour.

Act IV: the Unification of Italy

In 1860, Mazzini's idea of a Sicilian expedition, followed by a battle of liberation up the peninsula, persuaded émigré Sicilians to propose it themselves to Garibaldi. Cavour, who was busily cutting deals with Louis Napoleon (now Emperor Napoleon III) and who dreamed of a modern state with an economy based on northern European models, refused to support the idea, so Garibaldi took matters into his own hands and sailed south with a thousand volunteers. Cavour attempted to stop the popular hero, whom he regarded as a loose cannon, but as the Italians say, Garibaldi's *stellone* (the lucky 'big star' that guides Italy through its trials) was on the rise.

What Cavour had hoped would be just another hopeless Mazzini-style insurrection succeeded beyond anyone's dreams. Garibaldi and his Thousand Red Shirts electrified Europe by taking Sicily from the regular Bourbon army, and declaring himself dictator in the name of Vittorio Emanuele (unlike Mazzini, Garibaldi didn't concern himself too closely about the social aspects of revolution). When the *garibaldini* crossed the Straits of Messina, their ranks had swelled to 20,000; when they captured Bourbon Naples, Garibaldi learned that Cavour had outmanoeuvred him in the north and closed off his dream of marching on to French-held Rome. In disgust, Garibaldi refused all honours and rewards and retired to his farm, taking only a sack of seed, coffee, sugar, dried fish and a bag of macaroni, as poor as he was when he started.

Act V: To the Bitter End

Although their dream of Italian unification was accomplished, it was controlled and compromised by their adversaries, and both Giuseppes, the doer on Caprera and the dreamer in exile, could not help but feel disillusioned. Nevertheless, both agitated for the annexation of Rome and Venetia to complete the Italian state. Garibaldi passed his time with his large family, a true Cincinnatus, planting crops and talking to his cows and goats, racked by rheumatism but ready to return to action whenever he thought he could do good, offering on several occasions to capture Rome for Italy and to lead the Union armies in the American Civil War (Lincoln politely refused). Against the will of the French generals, he went to France to lead more *garibaldini* against the Prussians in 1870, only to suffer once more the ingratitude of politicians. Declaring even in his last year that he would rise up to do war with Italy if she ever oppressed any people, the old warrior died in Caprera in 1882.

Mazzini, for his part, declared that the Italy of Vittorio Emanuele II was not the real Italy, not the tolerant democracy of his dreams, and refused to live in it. With his many close contacts with English workers, he helped to organize the First International in London, but his beliefs in private property and insistence on a social as well as a political revolution meant that he was soon eclipsed by Marx and Bakunin, especially after he failed to support the Paris commune in 1871 (because French republicans had destroyed his Republic of Rome, he could not bring himself to trust them). In 1872, sad and lonely and sensing the end was near, Mazzini returned clandestinely to Italy, to Pisa, under the alias of John Brown, the American abolitionist, and died. His chief memorial is the nice big tomb in Genoa's Staglione Cemetery, with its angry epitaph by the greatest Italian poet of the day, Giosuè Carducci:

THE LAST

OF THE GREAT ANCIENT ITALIANS

AND THE FIRST OF THE NEW

THE THINKER

WHO FROM THE ROMANS FOUND HIS STRENGTH

FROM THE COMMUNES HIS FAITH

FROM OUR TIMES HIS IDEAS

THE POLITICAL MAN

WHO THOUGHT, AND WILLED, AND MADE ONE THE NATION

WHILE MANY JEERED AT HIS GREAT PURPOSE

WHO NOW ABUSE HIS ACHIEVEMENT

THE CITIZEN

TOO LATE HEEDED IN 1848

REJECTED AND FORGOTTEN IN 1860

LEFT IN PRISON IN 1870

WHO ALWAYS AND ABOVE ALL LOVED

THE ITALIAN FATHERLAND

THE MAN

WHO SACRIFICED EVERYHING

WHO LOVED MUCH

AND NEVER HATED

GIUSEPPE MAZZINI

AFTER FORTY YEARS OF EXILE

TODAY PASSES FREELY ON ITALIAN SOIL

NOW THAT HE IS DEAD

O ITALY

SUCH GLORY AND SUCH BASENESS

AND SUCH A DEBT FOR THE FUTURE

The Italian Village Model

The Italians, at least until the 19th century, had a near-perfect instinct for creating streets and squares with a maximum of delight. From medieval times, they developed a way of urban design that depended not on paper plans and geometry, but on arranging buildings and monuments to form an artistic composition, as a painter would. The result was asymmetrical, seemingly haphazard townscapes that always seem somehow 'right'; you can learn to explore their subtleties not by standing still, but by walking through a town and seeing how the composition changes. Unexpected perspectives and angles, and carefully planned surprises as you turn a corner, are all part of their art. With the passion for geometry and order that began with the baroque, this old sense of design began to fade. Now, rather belatedly, in a reaction to the dystopia of modern cities and sprawling suburbs, some planners are beginning to look towards the 'Italian village model' for ideas that might recapture some of the visual delight that draws people to be out and about, and create a sense of community, while leaving the surrounding countryside open for agriculture and recreation.

Although the beautiful hill towns of Tuscany hog most of the attention, many of the villages of Liguria, clinging tenaciously to the mountains or jammed into a coastal nook on the rocks, are wonderfully imaginative in the arrangement of their buildings in a tiny space. Much of the best building is not done by architects, as they say, and you will soon notice how urbane a place of 300 souls can be, closely knit together but never dull, with narrow lanes and steps, vaults and archivolts. Bell towers double as defensive towers—in Lingueglietta the church itself, with nice economy, moonlighted as a castle. By the sea, houses are painted intense colours—warm ochres, reds and pinks—so their sailors could spot them from afar, but also to add beauty and dignity to the village. In fact, many of the villas and palaces of the nobility that seem rather austere today originally had *trompe-l'œil* frescoes on their façades imitating architectural features.

There's a whole unique Ligurian vocabulary for streets and lanes, although it may remind an outsider of the Eskimos and their 50 different words for snow. *Carrugio, caréra, chu, ciassa, chibo* (a shadowy side street), *capitoli* (steep vaulted stairs, easy to defend) up to a *crösa* (a boulevard designed for fancy villas). A favourite technique for building on hill tops is in concentric rings crisscrossed by narrow *chibi*; two striking examples are the medieval quarter of San Remo and a hill-town above Bordighera, both called La Pigna (pine cone). One town, Varese Ligure, was planned by its feudal lords in a cosy circle in 1300.

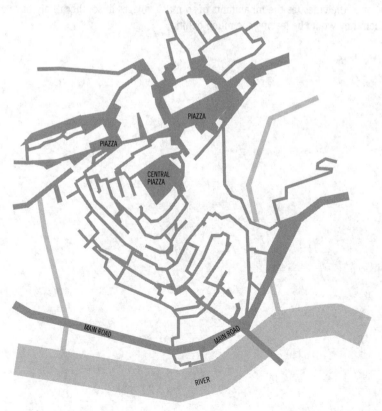

In the early days, separate baptistries and churches offered an opportunity to arrange winsome architectural ensembles in a piazza, the idea that created so many great city centres in Tuscany, reflected in small Ligurian towns like Albenga. The late 16th century introduced a new fad for building oratories near the church, creating a sacred area (*sagrata*), which was set apart with a *risseu*, a figurative black and white pebble mosaic— one of the most spectacular examples of this art form is in Moneglia. Space, however, was often very tight and led to imaginative solutions on various levels—a prime example is Montalto Ligure's complex of church and oratory. Other villages achieve remarkable urban showpieces and theatrical effects in a constricted space. Tiny Buggio has a unique *piazzetta principale*, including a bridge (attractive stone bridges are a distinct Ligurian feature). Àrcola's Piazza della Parrocchiale has the air of an opera set, with its grand stair and balustrade; Apricale's main square is so dramatically perfect that it is used as a natural stage for a summer theatre festival.

Best of all, unlike the *villages perchés* on the French Riviera, Liguria's villages have not been converted into arty trinket shopping malls. Although emigration and the lure of easy money on the coast have led to a decline in population over the past 150 years, and a few villages, inevitably, have become clusters of second homes, the hill towns are still places where people live as they have for centuries. They could have all moved down to the coast, or to the cities (as the inhabitants of so many villages in southern Italy have done), but then they would be leaving too much behind.

The Riviera di Ponente

Stretching between France and Genoa, the Riviera di Ponente is the coast of the setting sun, nightly kissed by that golden orb as it bids Italy sweet dreams. The more fertile and populous of Liguria's two shores, the Ponente is streaked with the silver of olives under emerald Alpine peaks, its coastal towns splashed with colour, its hilltowns as spectacular as any. San Remo, its biggest holiday resort, is larger than the provincial capital, Imperia; Savona, the Ponente's biggest city, was long a bitter rival of Genoa and outdid the bossy Republic in at least one respect by producing a pair of Renaissance popes, including the calamitous Julius II. In between you'll find plenty of surprises: a new independent principality, whose prince will sell you a sticker for your car; the 'Little Dolomites' by Buggio, perfect Roman bridges, a museum dedicated to songs and another to church tower clocks, a shop that sells witch's philtres, and stalactite caves where our stone age ancestors got up to some curious monkeyshines indeed.

PIEMONTE

FRANCE

Calizzano
Garéssio
Bardineto
Castelvécchio di Rca.
Barbena
Balestrino
Toirano
Zuccarello
Campo-chiesa
Ormea
N28
C. di Nava
Ranzo
Pornássio
Pogli
Ortovero
N453
Arróscia
Garlenda
Villanova d'Albenga
Vessálico
Pieve di Teco
Monesi
N.D. des Fontaines
M. Saccarello
Mon. al Redentore
Verdéggia
Téstico
Mérula
Alássio
Mt Bégo
Vallée des Merveilles
Tende (Tenda)
St-Dalmas-de-Tende (S. Dalmazzo di T.)
La Brigue (Briga Marittima)
Realdo
Molini di Triora
Andagna
C. d'Óggia
Borgomaro
Chiusavécchia
Andora
Laiguéglia
Capo Mele
Roia
Roja
Triora
Búggio
Pigna
Lucinasco
Pontedássio
Diano Castello
Marina di Andora
Montalto Lígure
Badalucco
Molfedo
Montegrázie
Cervo
S. Bartolomeo al Mare
Diano Marina
Castèl Vittório
Baiardo
Bestagno
Dólcedo
Rocchetta Nervina
Fanghetto
Ciyezza
C. Berta
Oliveta
S. Michele
Airole
Isolabona
Apricale
M. Bignone
Ceriana
Pietrabruna
Linguéglietta
Onéglia
Porto Maurizio
Impéria
Torri
Dolceacqua
Perinaldo
S. Romolo
Arma di Tággia
Cipressa
Tággia
Bussana
S. Stefano al Mare
S. Lorenzo al Mare
Seborga
Camporosso
Nervia
Bévera
Móntola
Ventimiglia
Vallecrosia
Bordighera
Ospedaletti
Argentina
San Remo

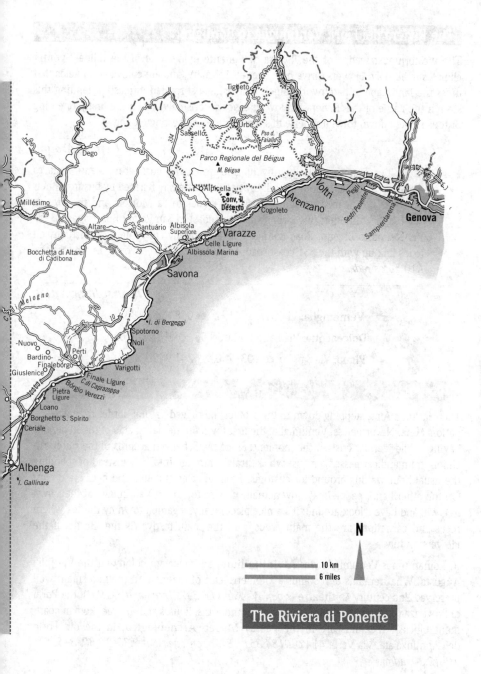

The Riviera di Ponente

The Riviera dei Fiori: Ventimiglia to Bordighera

The westernmost wedge of the Riviera di Ponente enjoys one of the mildest winter climates in all Italy. Flowers thrive here even in February, and are cultivated in fields that dress the landscape in patchwork (albeit increasingly shrouded in plastic), lending this stretch the name of the 'Riviera of Flowers'. Not surprisingly, when the first pioneering Britons flocked down to winter here, this was their prime nesting ground.

Getting Around

Trains run frequently up and down the coast from Ventimiglia to Genoa. Inland, the hill towns are most easily reached by bus from their nearest coastal towns: Bus 1 goes to La Mortola and the French frontier; Bus 2 runs along the coast to San Remo; Bus 7 goes up the Val Nervia to Buggio. Road connections are equally convenient, as virtually all roads link up with the SS1 coast road, the Via Aurelia, or, if you're in a hurry, the A10 *autostrada*.

Tourist Information

Ventimiglia: Via Cavour 61, ✆/🖷 0184 351 183.

Dolceacqua: Via Patrioti Martiri 58, ✆ 0184 206 666.

Pigna: Via San Rocco 103, ✆ 0184 241 040.

Ventimiglia

The Maritime Alps, stepping down to the sea, form a rugged natural border to match the national one. Nevertheless, Ventimiglia, the first town on the Italian side of the Riviera, is having a mild identity crisis at the moment. Since the Schengen accords of the European Union, train and car passengers just whisk straight through into Italy instead of spending the usual hour waiting around for customs. Frontier sales of coffee and beer are down. On the other hand, people may now actually choose to stop in Ventimiglia of their own free will and have a look around: it's a nice place, really, a garden town by the sea where roses and carnations are the main crops, and the main festival is the 'Battle of the Flowers' in July.

In Roman times Ventimiglia was **Albintimilium**, an important colony on the Via Julia Augusta. What remains of it stands a kilometre east of the modern town: a small, well preserved 2nd-century AD **theatre** (*open Wed and Fri 3–7, Thurs and Sat 9–1*), the Porta di Provenza (the Provence gate), and traces of the baths, houses and *insulae* (Roman apartment blocks); the finds are in the nearby **Museo Archeologico**, in the old Forte dell'Annunziata, Via Verdi 41 (*✆ 0184 351 181, open Tues–Sat 9.30–12.30, 3–5, Sun 10–12.30; adm*).

Post-Roman Ventimiglia grew up by the 20th milestone on the Via Julia, and is divided into old and new by the River Roja. In the modern town, built around the winter flower market and lined with typical Riviera seaside promenades, the big event is the Friday market, a cornucopia that brings the French pouring over the border to form a weekly bi-national congress of fanatical bargain-hunters.

Medieval Ventimiglia, with its plan of twisting cobbled lanes, hangs over the edge of Roja, a favourite year-round resort for swans. The main street, **Via Garibaldi**, is lined with handsome palazzi, especially the **Palazzo Pubblico** with its 15th-century Gothic Loggia dei Mercanti. Inside, in the atrium of the old Teatro Civico, the **Civica Biblioteca Aprosiana** is Liguria's oldest public library, founded in 1648; it contains Italy's best collection of 17th-century books outside the Biblioteca Marciana in Venice and is open every morning in the summer if you want to look at its display of rare books.

Further along Via Garibaldi, the attractive 11th–12th-century **Cattedrale dell'Assunta** was built by the Counts of Ventimiglia, the lords of much of this coast at the time of the first millennium, over the ruins of an 8th-century original. It has a Romanesque façade and a Gothic porch added around 1222, and, despite constant tinkering over the centuries, manages a certain harmony on both the outside and interior, although there's little in the way of art, except for a Byzantine font and a two-ton 17th-century painted wooden tabernacle; the cathedral's octagonal **Baptistry** has a magnificent 12th-century total immersion font. Isolated near the Renaissance walls, **San Michele** (*open Sun only, 10.30–12*) with its warm-coloured stones is another fine Romanesque church, founded before the 10th century by the Counts of Ventimiglia; its crypt has an altar made of Roman columns from a temple of Castor and Pollux and a milestone from the time of Caracalla.

From the *centro storico*'s Porta Nizza, a road climbs up to three fortifications west of Ventimiglia that tell of the many battles fought over this choice piece of real estate (claimed, at various times, by the Byzantines, Provençals, the Angevins, the Grimaldi, and the Republic of Genoa): the **Forte San Paolo**, the **Tower-gate Canarda** (bearing the arms of Genoa's Bank of St George) and, uppermost, the ruins of the 12th-century **Castel D'Appio**, named after Consul Appio Claudio, who defeated the Ligurians here in 185 BC. The site was a Ligurian *castelliere*, and later a Roman *castrum*; the castle was the headquarters of the often piratical Counts of Ventimiglia.

Balzi Rossi

Ventimiglia is also a garden of history, with some of the most ancient roots in Liguria, thanks to the relics left by Neanderthal man in the **Balzi Rossi** ('Red Cliffs') caves, just a few feet from France on the beach below the village of Grimaldi. Here, some 200,000 years ago, thrived one of the most sophisticated societies of *Homo erectus* discovered in Europe. In the caves themselves are the traces of several elaborate burials by the caves' later Cro-Magnon tenants, who adorned their dead with seashell finery; and in one cave, the *Grotto del Caviglione*, is an etching of a Prewaleski horse, of a breed now common only on the Russian steppes. At the caves' entrance, the **Museo Preistorico** (*© 0184 381 113, museum and caves open 9am–7pm, closed Mon*), founded by Sir Thomas Hanbury in the 1890s, displays the most important finds from within—ornaments, tools, weapons and the bones of elephants, hippopotamuses and rhinoceroses as well as reindeer (evidence of the extreme climate changes the Riviera has undergone; recently, an Upper Palaeolithic drawing of a penguin was discovered in the Grotte Henri Cosquer near Marseille). Here, too, are some of the earliest works of art ever discovered: lumpy fertility figures called Venuses.

Hanbury Gardens

Nearby, at Mortola Inferiore (and reached by the same municipal bus from Ventimiglia), you can take in the **Hanbury Gardens** (© *0184 229 507, open April–Sept 9–6, Oct–Mar 10–4, closed Wed; adm*), an enchanted botanical paradise founded in 1867 by Londoner Sir Thomas Hanbury and his brother Daniel. Sir Thomas was a wealthy dealer in silks and spices from China, who fell in love with the spot during a holiday on the Côte d'Azur in 1867. He bought the villa there and the surrounding 30 acres, and during the period of his travels brought back rare and exotic plants from Africa, Australia, the Americas and Asia, which he acclimatized to co-exist with native Mediterranean flora. Queen Victoria stopped by to visit in 1882; by 1912 the garden had some 6000 species and a permanent staff of 45 gardeners.

After Sir Thomas died, his daughter-in-law beautifully landscaped the gardens, never suspecting that they would have two rather unwelcome guests in the 1930s: Mussolini (who had a soft spot for the English and their gardens) chose it as the perfect spot to host General Franco, who let his soldiers march all over the flowers and plants in their jack-boots. During the war, the gardens fell even further into decay and in 1960 they were sold to the Italian state. Now managed by the green thumbs of the University of Genoa, the gardens are back in shape—highlights include the Australian forest, the Garden of Scents and the Japanese garden.

Within the gardens there's a section of the ancient Via Julia Augusta, with a plaque along-side listing the famous who have passed this way, from St Catherine of Siena to Napoleon. The main road leads to the former customs post at Ponte San Ludovico, with its landmark **Castle**, where Russian surgeon Count Serge Voronoff (d. 1951) performed his experiments, seeking the Fountain of Youth in monkey glands. He chose Ventimiglia because the sea here has the highest concentration of iodine in the whole Mediterranean; one of his famous patients was Eva Peron.

The Val Roja: the Valley of Marvels and Notre-Dame-des-Fontaines

Inland from Ventimiglia, the N20 and the railway run to Cuneo up the Val Roja on the French-Italian frontier, following a hoary trail through a wild landscape of white cliffs and crags to Monte Bégo, which was either an ancient Ligurian holy site or their favourite outdoor art gallery. The more recent inhabitants of the upper valley voted in the plebiscite of 1860 to become French along with Nice—although 73 per cent of the electorate abstained—but their votes were ignored when King Vittorio Emanuele II personally inter-vened; he may have been utterly useless as a king (his nickname in the courts of Europe was 'the Royal Buffoon') but as a hunter few crowned heads could match him, and he asked Napoleon III to let him keep the upper Val Roja as a hunting reserve. Another plebiscite in 1947 made it France's last territorial acquisition. You can make the journey by train, on a railway that is something of an engineering marvel, threading through 81 tunnels and over 400 bridges, although you'll need a taxi to get to the sights.

The Dutch have restored many of the old houses along the lower, still Italian part of the valley, especially around **Airole** and **Olivetta-San Michele**, two steep grey stone villages that resemble Tibetan monasteries, and were favourite bases for smuggling people and goods over the unguarded border in days of yore. A third village, **Torri Superiore**, at the top of the Val Bevera (a fork in the Val Roja), has been restored by an environmentalist group based in Turin, who take in stressed-out urbanites and give them useful things to do like building walls. North, **Fanghetto** is now the last village in Italy, and has a striking stone bridge for its landmark.

The French part of the valley has two star attractions: the Valley of Marvels and the best Renaissance frescoes on this coast at Notre-Dame-des-Fontaines. The entrance to the **Vallée des Merveilles**, now part of the Parc National du Mercantour, is by way of **St-Dalmas-de-Tende** (25km from Fanghetto), where the train station has a park information office, © 0493 046 700, an essential stop if you want actually to locate the 'marvels'. The ancient Ligurians started scratching their designs in this valley under Mont Bégo not long after they arrived on the Riviera, *c.* 1800 BC, and kept at it for about 800 years, leaving over 100,000 engravings in the rock: human figures, religious symbols (plenty of bulls, horns and serpents), weapons and tools. Most of them defy a conclusive interpretation—the circles, spirals and ladders or chequerboard patterns are of the kind found all over the Neolithic Mediterranean. Why they were made is an open question. One appealing hypothesis is that is this valley, beneath uncanny **Mont Bégo**, the highest of the mountains along the Roja, was a pilgrimage site, and the carvings can be taken as *ex votos* made by the pilgrims, very much in the vein of all the hilltop sanctuaries dedicated to the Madonna, filled with quaint votive paintings. If you can't make it to the park, there are casts in the museums at Tende, a dullsville just up the valley, and at Bordighera, east of Ventimiglia.

Other marvels are north of Tende, in a country chapel 4km from La Brigue: the magnificent frescoes by Giovanni Canavesio and his assistant Giovanni Baleison (completed, according to the records, on 12 October 1492) covering every square inch of wall in **Notre-Dame-des-Fontaines**, 'the Sistine Chapel of the Maritime Alps': subjects include the *Passion of Christ* and a tremendous *Last Judgement* that vividly reminds parishioners that God wasn't joking.

The Val Nervia

The next valley east of the Val Roja, the Val Nervia, is linked by buses hourly from Ventimiglia. The lower part of the valley, where some 140 species of waterfowl and other birds have been sighted, has recently been made a wildlife oasis under the World Wildlife Federation. Fertile farmland surrounds **Camporosso** near the bottom of the valley, an old town that has preserved little of its original character, although it does have three 16th-century polyptychs in the church of **San Marco**, including one by Lodovico Brea.

Dolceacqua

In contrast to Camporosso, the main town of the valley is as picturesque as you could wish. Dolceacqua occupies both banks of the Nervia, spanned here by a singular, poetic, airy 110ft span of a 15th-century **bridge**, painted by Monet in 1884. The town's name means 'Sweet water' but most people seek out something with a little more punch: the hillsides are terraced with vineyards producing Liguria's best red wine, DOC Rossese, of which Napoleon was so fond that he gave Dolceacqua the right to rename the wine after his imperial self. The rarer white Rossese has made recently made a comeback; look for both colours at the Non Solo Vino wine shop, at Via Patrioti Martiri 26.

Dolceacqua was the ancient fief of some other bigwigs, the Doria family. The founder of the dynasty, Oberto, picked it up in 1270 and they held on to it through thick and thin. Their 16th-century and reputedly haunted **Doria Castle**, where the lords are said to have taken full advantage of their *droit de seigneur* with local brides, now stares down lugubriously from its rock, with vacant window eyes. The Dorias' nasty habits (it's safe now; they died out in 1902) and the resistance of a certain bride named Lucrezia to their claims are still remembered today, in a wacky fashion, in the *Sagra della Michetta* on the night of 15 August. A *michetta* is a kind of long brioche, and the young bloods of the town fill up their donkey panniers with them, and, accompanied by musicians, stop under the balconies of unmarried girls and offer their *michetta*; nowadays the girls can just say no.

Of the town's churches, **Sant'Antonio Abate** has fine stucco work and a beautiful polyptych of *Santa Devota* by Lodovico Brea, and the **Oratorio di San Sebastiano** has a figwood statue of the eponymous saint, attributed to Maragliano, who goes for a tour of the town on his feast day (20 January). This Dolceacqua celebrates in another quaint way—a religious procession led by the 'tree man', who bears a huge branch hung with large, coloured communion hosts. After the procession the hosts are distributed to the inhabitants, who keep them all year for luck. The story is said to celebrate Sebastian's martyrdom; his gaolers refused to give him communion, so an angel came down and delivered a host when they weren't looking.

Dolceacqua stays abreast of modern technology, too: one of its newest attractions is the **Visionarium**, Via Doria 12bis, a unique 3D virtual reality tour of the Val Nervia through the four seasons, with special effects (*www.sportour.masterweb.it, open Apr–Sept, Sat and Sun 4–7, Oct–Mar Sun only 3–6, or by booking a day ahead, © 0184 206 638; adm*).

Beyond Dolceacqua

A road runs northwest up to the Y-shaped village of **Rocchetta Nervina** (6km), the attractions of which include little lakes good for summer swimming, two hog-backed bridges, a watermill and a dense fir forest. The main valley road, for its part, continues to **Isolabona**, which sits at the confluence of the Nervia and Merdanzo rivers and has a pretty octagonal fountain of 1486 in the centre; its square Doria castle has been restored and hosts an international harp festival in July. Along the main road, the **Santuario della Madonna delle Grazie** has a classical pronaos and is covered with 16th-century frescoes attributed to Luca Cambiaso.

From here you can make another detour, northeast, to the remarkable medieval village of **Apricale**, 'open to the sun', cascading gracefully from its hilltop perch. Apricale preserves another Doria castle, known as the 'lizard castle', the **Castello della Lucertola**, with Art Nouveau décor and a little museum, including a copy of the town's communal statutes, the oldest in Liguria, and a collection of landscapes by Eugenio Corradi inspired by the writings of Italo Calvino (© *0184 208 126, open Mon–Sat 3–7, Sun 10–12.30 and 3–7*). It preserves three gates in its walls, and a perfectly charming **Piazza Principale**, which looks like a stage set—and is used as one on summer nights, when actors from the innovative Teatro della Tosse in Genoa put on shows in the narrow lanes.

Pigna and the Upper Val Nervia

Pigna, beautifully set in the lushly forested foothills of the Maritime Alps, was founded by the Counts of Ventimiglia. In looks it is rather like its name, which means 'Pine cone', with its concentric medieval lanes rising up the hill. Pigna's thermal sulphurous waters, down in the valley, were quite popular in the 19th century, and may soon be again, thanks to the newly renovated Centro Termale by Lake Pino.

Pigna has some exceptional art and churches: down below, before the town, are the impressive ruins of **San Tommaso**. Just off the main square, **San Michele** (1450) has a lovely rose window in white marble by Giovanni Gaggini, where the spokes of divine salvation radiate from the central Agnus Dei to a ring of pretty Renaissance floral motifs; the stained glass showing the Twelve Apostles is original as well. Inside, the polyptych of *St Michael and other Saints* (1500) by Giovanni Canavesio is one of the last and greatest works of the 'Fra Angelico of the Maritime Alps' (*ring ahead to make sure it's open, © 0184 229 700 or © 0184 229 507*). The cemetery church of **San Bernardo** has more by Canavesio: earlier and excellent frescoes of the *Passion* and *Last Judgement* (1483) that have recently been beautifully restored. From Pigna, a road heads north up the **Gola di Gouta**, a lush, green and thoroughly enchanting drive.

In the crazy quilt of territorial claims in this part of Liguria, Pigna belonged to the kingdom of Savoy for centuries. The village you see hanging among the trees 3km further up the valley, **Castel Vittorio**, belonged to Savoy's frequent rival, the Republic of Genoa, and has changed little since the 13th century, when its thick walls defended it from predatory raids by its arch-enemy Pigna. Some bravos from Pigna once managed to get in anyway and steal Castel Vittorio's bell from under its pretty tiled campanile; in revenge Castel Vittorio boldly made off with the paving stones from Pigna's main square.

From here, drivers can circle back, by way of Baiardo (*see* below), to the coast at San Remo, or you can continue up to **Buggio**, at the foot of Mount Taggio, a perfect example of an intact rural village, with a unique piazzetta with the parish church and oratory and a little bridge. Buggio is also the base for visiting the **Parco Naturale Regionale Alpi Liguri**, where oak and fir and rhododendron take over and the mountains are known as the 'Little Dolomites' for their beauty. In the winter you can ski here; the Rifugio Allavena, (© *0184 241 155, open Dec–Oct*) has rooms and can set you on the path up to the top of Monte Toraggio. A remarkably beautiful spot to aim for (especially if you have a jeep, or at least good walking shoes) is the **Colla di Langàn**, just above the Lago di Tenarda.

Ventimiglia, with its abundant black and red coral, grottoes and marine life, has perhaps the best diving on the Riviera: contact the **Pianeta Blu Diving Center**, ✆ 0184 239 273, who can arrange weekend excursions as far west as Marseille, or **Divemaster**, ✆ 0184 357 265.

Where to Stay and Eating Out

Ventimiglia ✉ 18039

Although Ventimiglia is midway between Monte Carlo and San Remo, prices here are reasonable, at least for hotels. The top hotel choice is **★★★La Riserva**, ✆ 0184 229 533, ✆ 0184 229 712 (*moderate*), up in the olive groves at Castel d'Appio, 5km west of the town, a fine family-run inn with magnificent views, a pool and very comfortable rooms. *Open April–Sept and Christmas holidays only.* The **★★★Sea Gull**, Via Marconi 24, ✆ 0184 351 726, ✆ 0184 231 217 (*cheap*) is a comfortable establishment on the waterfront, with a bit of garden and its own private beach.

Balzi Rossi, Piazzale De Gasperi, ✆ 0184 38132 (*very expensive*), long the premier restaurant in the Ventimiglia area, is right on the frontier at San Lodovico, with a dining room full of flowers overlooking the Mediterranean. The cuisine magnificently blends the best of France and Liguria, and includes a legendary *terrina di coniglio*, pasta dishes with fresh tomatoes and basil, scallops of sea bass, divine desserts and excellent wines. Definitely reserve. *Closed Mon, Tues lunch; also Sun lunch in July and Aug; also half of March and half of Nov.*

Its rival and near neighbour at Grimaldi Inferiore, **Baia Beniamin**, Corso Europa 63, ✆/✆ 0184 38002 (*very expensive*) is set in a lush subtropical garden, where you can dine in season. The food is as beautiful as the setting, featuring both sea and land dishes on the order of cannelloni filled with shellfish and courgette in lobster sauce, or saddle of rabbit baked with olives and pine nuts, followed by sublime desserts. It also has very lovely (and *expensive*) rooms, open in summer and winter. *Closed Sun eve, Mon, three weeks in Nov and a week at Easter.*

For something more modest, try the **Usteria d'a Porta Marina**, Via Trossarelli 22, ✆ 0184 351 650 (*moderate*), which specializes in fish, particularly sea bass in Rossese wine.

Camporosso ✉ 18030

If you need an excuse to stop at Camporosso, there's always **Gino**, Via Braie 10, ✆ 0184 291 493 (*expensive*), one of the Riviera's most all-round pleasant restaurants, where everything is prepared just so; this is a good place to try Pigna's famous beans in a salad with tuna, dressed with fragrant olive oil. *Open only for lunch and Sat dinner, closed Tues.*

Dolceacqua ✉ 18035

Gastone, Piazza Garibaldi 2, ✆ 0184 206 577 (*moderate*) is a relaxed and friendly place, where you can try *capron magro* or imaginative dishes such as gnocchetti with courgette flowers and shrimp, followed by a traditional baked rabbit in casserole. *Closed Mon eve and Tues.* There's an exceptional *agriturismo* lodging, **Locanda del Bricco Arcagna**, just out of the village at Arcagna, ✆ 0184 31426, 🖃 0184 31230, *terrebianche@terrebianche.com* (*moderate*), with simple rooms on a working farm, a pool, mountain bikes and horses for guests to ride. The restaurant serves up good, homegrown food.

Pigna ✉ 18037

The most memorable place to dine here is **La Castellana**, in the castle walls, ✆ 0184 241 014 (*moderate*), if not for the food, certainly for the singing proprietor. Try the beans, the *fagioli di Pigna*, which Alain Ducasse orders specially for his celebrated restaurant Louis XV in Monte Carlo. *Closed Mon.*

Bordighera

Once a favourite winter residence of Europe's pampered set, especially those of the British persuasion, blessed with a good beach and regal promenades, Bordighera is one of the most jovial resorts on the Riviera, perhaps due to the lingering effects of its Festival of Humour. The British get all the credit for instilling Bordighera with the proper attitude for this annual September funfest, which does everything possible to make you laugh, with films, plays, comedy acts and more. As in Ventimiglia, the environs contain vast fields of cultivated flowers, but here the speciality is palms, especially date palms; ever since Sant'Ampelio brought the first seeds from Egypt in 411, Bordighera has supplied the Vatican with fronds during Easter week. But there's even a better story.

The Sailor of Bordighera

The year was 1586, and Pope Sixtus V was busy transforming Rome, wanting to outdo the monuments of the pagans, whose ancient monuments, even in ruins, still threatened to outshine those of the Church. Now the Pope had in his possession a most fantastical obelisk from the ancient Egyptian city of Heliopolis, founded by Akhenaton, the religious reforming pharaoh, who according to Sigmund Freud founded the first true monotheistic religion, influencing Moses and all who came after. This obelisk had arrived in Rome by sheer coincidence and had been erected as the spina in Nero's Circus Vaticanus, where it had overlooked the martyrdom of St Peter. Ever since then it had stood just to the left of the present Basilica of St Peter, until Sixtus decided he wanted it moved down into the centre of St Peter's Square, just to show how puny this heathen ornament was compared to the Biggest Church in the World.

Vatican architect Domenico Fontana was put in charge of the project, but faced a major problem. No one since antiquity had moved an obelisk, and Fontana wasn't quite sure how it was done. He made careful, elaborate plans (the Pope had hinted that failure meant the chopping block) and, on 18 September, gathered 900 men, 150 horses and 47 cranes to re-erect the mighty piece of Egyptian granite. A vast crowd had gathered to watch the procedure, but the Pope insisted on perfect silence so the workmen could hear Fontana's orders, and erected a gallows to underline the point. Slowly the obelisk was hauled upright by the cranes, then hesitated, the ropes too taut with the strain to finish the task. Suddenly the silence was broken by the cry of a sailor from Bordighera: 'Water on the ropes!', saving both the obelisk and Fontana's neck. Sixtus showed his gratitude by henceforth giving the sailor's home town the monopoly of supplying St Peter's with fronds for Palm Sunday.

Tourist Information

Bordighera: Palazzo del Parco, Via Roberto 1, ✆ 0184 262 322, 📠 0184 264 455.

Ospedaletti: Corso Regina Margherita 1, ✆ 0184 59085.

Around the Town of Palms and Mimosa

Compared to Ventimiglia, Bordighera is a baby. Its original nucleus, shoe-horned behind its gates above the Spianata del Capo, is only about 500 years old; from here you can continue up the flower-bedecked **Via dei Colli** for excellent views of the shimmering coast. Down by the sea, the Romanesque Chapel of **Saint'Ampelio** stands on its little cape, above the grotto where the saint lived and perhaps swam, as people do today, in clear turquoise waters. What looks like a rotunda is actually all that survives of a casino bombed during the war. From here you can walk west to the spa along the pleasant Lungomare Argentina (named after Evita came to visit in 1947) or east along the seaside Via Arziglia, past the port, with views of Charles Garnier's white asymmetrical villa, and further on to Bordighera's palm and mimosa plantations at the **Winter Garden** and the **Giardino Madonna della Ruota**, a 45-minute walk all told.

Back in the 19th century, the British outnumbered the native Bordigotti, at least in the winter, and a large part of their elegant ghetto of villas and hotels remains intact, especially around Via Romana and Via Vittorio Veneto. On the latter was **Casa Coraggio**, the home of George Macdonald, author of *At the Back of the North Wind* and a major influence on C.S. Lewis, who was well loved in Bordighera for his generosity. His villa has now been altered and contains new apartments. In Via Shakespeare, the Tennis & Bridge Club was the first of its kind in Italy, founded in 1878, but has fallen in the world to become a *carabinieri* barracks; the Anglican church in Via Regina Vittoria is now a cultural centre. The grandest of the grand hotels were along Via Romana, a lovely street lined with old trees and bougainvillaea. Most have since been converted into condominiums, with the notable exception of the astonishing Hotel Angst. The Angst (the name of the owner!) was one of the showpieces of the Riviera until the Nazis occupied it and left it a wreck. And a haunted wreck the Angst remains.

The most beautiful building, by contrast, is the **Villa Etalinda** (No. 36), designed by Charles Garnier and purchased by the saintly Queen Margherita of Savoy, who died here in 1926; it now serves as a rest home. An enormous magnolia almost hides the entrance to the **Museo Bicknell**, founded by Rev Clarence Bicknell, on Via Romana 39bis (© *0184 263 601, open Mon–Fri 10–12, 3–5, closed first two weeks of Aug*) which keeps plaster casts of the ancient Ligurian rock engravings from the Valle delle Meraviglie (Vallée des Merveilles), discovered by Bicknell (*see* p.89); it also has his butterfly collection, and copies of original coins minted in the principality of Seborga (*see* below). The adjacent **Istituto Internazionale di Studi Liguri** has a permanent exhibit on the elusive Ligurians, and further down you'll find a bust of **Claude Monet**.

After a tour of the Riviera with Renoir, Monet returned by himself to capture it on canvas. He based himself in Bordighera for three months in early 1884, but initially he was unimpressed. The town was, he claimed, 'a confusion of forms, terribly difficult to render'. After a few weeks, however, he found some subjects worthy of being committed to canvas (including Villa Etalinda) and started to enthuse about 'this brilliance, this magical light'. During the summer, the tourist office organizes free guided tours around Bordighera and its environs, pointing out the places, such as the Giardino Moreno and Valle di Sasso, that caught Monet's eye during his stay.

Around Bordighera

Vallecrosia

Just west of Bordighera, a new development merges with the seaside village of **Vallecrosia**. This has an older inland section: its original name, 'Vallechiusa' or Closed Valley, refers to the days when it was a Byzantine border town, 'closing' the valley against Lombard and other invaders, until its inhabitants were drawn to the coast by the presence of the railroad. Today the old steam engine and carriages in the depot have been converted to hold the Ristorante Erio's collection of all things musical, officially inaugurated in 1988, in the commanding presence of Pavarotti, as the **Museo della Canzone** (*visits by appointment,* © *0184 291 000*), full of records, old gramophones, sheet music, and just about anything else associated with Italian song.

The Principality of Seborga

The mountain valley rising behind Bordighera has a surprise as well. **Seborga** may look like any Ligurian hill village, but it's not: in September 1995, it became a pint-sized democratic principality, having elected a flower gardener as Prince George I (304 votes for, 4 against). Seborga is only picking up where it left off in the 19th century. Its history is even longer and perhaps even more dignified than that of the Riviera's more famous principality: in 959, the Benedictine monastery on the Iles de Lérins near Cannes purchased Seborga from the Count of Ventimiglia and gave its abbot the title of prince. From 1660–86 the now secular principality even minted its own coins. It was sold in 1729 to the Dukes of Savoy, but the act was drawn up so wrongly as to invalidate it. Seborga the anomaly was so small that it was overlooked in 1815 at the Congress of Vienna, which defined the territories that made up Savoy-Piemonte, whose king became the king of united Italy—but legally not the king of Seborga. Prince George will sell you a passport for a few thousand lire, some stamps or a sticker for your car, or some of the coin of the realm (the 'Luigino'). At the time of writing the principality has ambassadors at Alassio just up the coast, and one in Scotland.

Perinaldo

Perinaldo, further up the valley, is high on a ridge, way above all light and air pollution. Even before such things existed, however, it was the birthplace of Italy's great astronomer Gian Domenico Cassini (1625–1712), who was the first to discover many things—the first asteroid, Ceres; the first moons of Saturn (he picked out four of the 17); the space between Saturn's rings; and the speed at which Mars, Venus and Jupiter rotate on their axes. He spent much of his career in Paris, working for Louis XIV who, as the Sun King, had a keen interest in the planets. You can have a look at them for yourself on the astronomical evenings at the **Osservatorio Cassini** (*for information © 0184 672 001; L8000 adults, L4000 children*). Another Cassini legacy is the sundial on the parish house (formerly a Doria hunting lodge), made according to the specifications of Gian Domenico's astronomer grandson.

Ospedaletti and Coldirodi

Driving east of Bordighera on the Via Aurelia, right after a tunnel, you'll find a surprising little patch of desert—the **Giardino Esotico Pallanca** (*© 0184 266 347, open Tues–Sun 9–5, Mon 12–5; adm*). Here, on one of the most sheltered and hottest spots on the Riviera, cacti grow like crazy—one stands 21ft high. There are some 3500 different kinds, and nearly all burst into bloom in March: not to be missed if you're in the area.

Just beyond is **Ospedaletti**, a quiet seaside oasis set between the two worldly resorts of Bordighera and San Remo, shaded by a luxuriant ensemble of pines, palms and eucalyptus and guarded by two medieval 'Saracen towers'. The name of the town derives from the Knights Hospitallers of Rhodes (who later became the Knights of Malta), a band of knights shipwrecked here *c*. 1300, who built a pilgrims' hospice that has long since vanished and the surviving church of **Sant'Erasmo**, patron of sailors. The biggest and grandest building in Ospedaletti, **Villa Sultana** on Corso Regina Margherita, was the very first casino in Italy (1886), and in its day offered some keen competition to the Grimaldi enterprise over in Monte Carlo. Katherine Mansfield stayed in Ospedaletti in the early 1900s, before moving on to Menton; her villa has since been replaced by the Hotel Madison.

The Knights of Rhodes also bestowed their name on the nearby hill town of **Coldirodi** (reached by bus from San Remo), to where the good folk of Ospedaletti could hotfoot it if the Saracens showed up. Its church of **San Sebastiano** has some good baroque paintings and frescoes by Maurizio Carrega, and some even better works in its **Rambaldi Art Gallery** (*© 0184 670 131, open 10–12, Fri and Sat also 3.30–6, closed Mon and Wed; adm*), a crammed and disorderly collection but with some gems among the dross: a fine *Madonna col Bambino* by Tuscan Lorenzo di Credi, paintings by Salvator Rosa, and some very credible forgeries of Rembrandt, Veronese and Guido Reni.

The **Kursaal**, on the beach in Bordighera, rents windsurfers, waterskis, boats and mountain bikes, ✆ 0184 264 487. One of the legacies of the Brits is Bordighera's excellent public library, the **Biblioteca Internazionale**, Via Romana 52 (✆ 0184 266 332) with 50,000 volumes, many in English.

Where to Stay and Eating Out

Bordighera ✉ 18012

For real elegance check in at the modern ★★★★**Del Mare**, Via Portico della Punta 34, ✆ 0184 262 201, ✆ 0184 262 394, *g.h.mare@rosenet.it* (*very expensive*), in a beautiful panoramic position over the sea, with private beach, sea-water pool, gardens and tennis courts. *Closed Nov–Christmas.* Another luxurious hotel is the ★★★★**Cap Ampelio**, Via Virgilio 5, ✆ 0184 264 333, ✆ 0184 264 244 (*expensive*), which overlooks both the town and the sea, and can offer designer furnishings, a heated pool and a garden.

★★★**Bordighera & Terminus**, Corso Italia 21, ✆ 0184 269 561, ✆ 0184 266 200, *terminus@rosenet.it* (*moderate*) is a luminous, stylish hotel, in the centre but surrounded by a garden; rooms are very pretty and well-equipped. Excellent breakfast buffet. ★★★**Britannique & Jolie**, Via Regina Margherita 35, ✆ 0184 261 464, ✆ 0184 260 375 (*moderate*) is a traditional favourite, with a garden near the sea. *Closed Oct–Nov.*

★★★**Villa Elisa**, Via Romana 70, ✆ 0184 261 313, ✆ 0184 261 942, *villaelisa@masterweb.it* (*moderate*) is an inviting villa above the town, standing in pretty gardens, with very attractive rooms. Sweet, family-run ★★★**Enrica**, Via Noaro 1, ✆/✆ 0184 263 436 (*cheap*) has bright rooms and a roof garden, a short walk from the station. Down in the town, in front of the station, ★**Palme**, Via Roma 5, ✆ 0184 261 273 (*cheap*) offers basic rooms.

For a sumptuous, superb meal with all the frills, book a table at the **Via Romana**, Via Romana 57, ✆ 0184 266 682 (*very expensive*) in the elegant dining room of the former Grand Hotel. Refined, aromatic combinations of seafood and fresh produce are the speciality (*zuppa* of cuttlefish and artichokes, prawns au gratin with Mediterranean herbs). The desserts, dessert wines and petits fours are equally lovely. *Closed Wed, Thurs lunch.*

The most spectacular place to eat in Bordighera, inserted in the cliffs, is **La Reserve Tastevin**, at Capo Sant'Ampelio, Via Aurelia 20, ✆ 0184 261 322 (*expensive*). The views are fantastic, and so is the food, a delightful combination of ingredients from the sea and the Valle Argentina. The very elegant and tiny **Le Chaudron**, Piazza Bengasi 2, ✆ 0184 263 592 (*expensive*) will win your heart with delicious dishes like spaghetti with artichokes, and the Ligurian speciality, *pesce al sale* (fish baked in a bed of salt, skinned, then dressed with olive oil). Be sure to reserve.

Antica Maddalena, Via Arziglia 83 (the Via Aurelia in disguise), ✆ 0184 266 006 (*expensive–moderate*) is a popular place, with some meat dishes mixed in with the seafood, and all of them good. *Closed Tues.*

Vallecrosia ✉ 18019

Hidden away in a back street off the Via Aurelia, **Giappun 1918**, Via Maonaira 7, ✆ 0184 250 560 (*very expensive*) is an institution on the Riviera for its gourmet versions of everything Ligurian, from *focaccia* nibbles to a remarkable *zuppa di pesce* that is only available on request; book it when you reserve your table. *Closed Wed, two weeks in June and July and two weeks in Nov.*

Ospedaletti ✉ 18014

★★★**Le Rocce del Capo**, Lungomare C. Colombo 102, ✆ 0184 689 733, ✆ 0184 689 024 (*moderate*) offers good value, with a covered pool, private beach and well-equipped rooms that come in three sorts: carnation, lily or rose. ★★★**Delle Rose**, Via dei Medici 17, ✆ 0184 689 016 (*cheap*), set back from the sea, has only 14 rooms but a pretty garden, a good restaurant, and plenty of peace and quiet.

San Remo

San Remo is the opulent, ageing queen of the Italian Riviera, her grand hotels and aristo-cratic villas as beautiful and out-of-date as antimacassars on an armchair. Yet even if the old girl isn't as young and as fashionable as she once was, she's still a game corker with a Mae West twinkle in her eye. Other resorts may be more glamorous, but few have more character. San Remo also has considerable bargains, both in hotels and in the shops—the French pour over from the Côte d'Azur to buy designer clothes and furnishings that cost 20 to 30 per cent more in Paris or Nice.

Set on a huge, sheltered bay, San Remo was long a favourite watering hole for a variety of drifting aristocrats. First the English toffs (among them the duke of nonsense, Edward Lear, who ended his lifelong travels through the Mediterranean here in 1888), followed by the Russians, led by Empress Maria Alexandrovna, wife of Czar Alexander II. The Empress arrived in state in 1874 on the newly built railroad, and was followed by a sizeable Russian colony, including Tchaikovsky, who found the place inspiring enough to compose *Eugene Onegin* and the Fourth Symphony during his stay here in 1878. In 1887 Kaiser Frederick Wilhelm had a pleasant stay at Villa Zirio.

In this century, San Remo was the hometown of Italo Calvino (1923–85), who was born in Cuba but brought here as a small child by his parents, both avid botanists, who planted a beautiful garden by their villa in Via Meridiana. Calvino fought in the Resistance at Baiardo, but after the war he moved to Turin and never returned, because the changes in San Remo made him too sad; only a tiny fraction remains of his parents' garden, now subdivided into second homes for the Torinese and Milanese. But, as he once said in an interview, he never forget this city of his childhood: 'San Remo continues to jump out in my books, in the most varied views and prospects, especially when viewed from on high, but most of all in many of the invisible cities.' In his masterpiece, *Invisible Cities*, in the dialogues between Marco Polo and Kublai Khan, Polo at one point says all the stories he tells Kublai about cities are really about Venice—it's interesting to learn that for Calvino, they were really about San Remo.

San Remo, the fourth largest city in Liguria, is made up of three quite distinct parts: the shopping district around Corso Matteotti, the steep old town called La Pigna (another 'pine cone' town) and the smart west end, where most of the grandest hotels are situated, and which still maintains much of its old glamour. In no part, however, will you find a church or legend for Remo, the non-existent saint; the closest anyone has found is a 7th-century hermit named Romolo, who lived nearby and had his name chewed up by the local dialect. In fact, the locals prefer to see their city written Sanremo, just so people stop asking embarrassing questions.

Getting Around

The **train** station is on the west end of town near the casino; **buses** depart from the big station in Piazza Colombo; *Riviera Transporti* will take you to Nice and Cannes to the west, to Taggia (Bus 13) or as far as Androa (Bus 12) to the east, © 0184 502 030. Piazza Colombo is also a good area to find a parking space. For a taxi, © 0184 541 454.

Tourist Information

San Remo: Via Nuvoloni 1, © 0184 571 571, ✆ 0184 507 649.

Arma di Taggia: in the Villa Boselli, © 0184 43733.

Triora: Corso Italia 7 (in the witchcraft museum), © 0184 94477.

Modern San Remo

To get the full flavour of San Remo take the famous *passeggiata* down the palm-lined **Corso dell'Imperatrice**, named in honour of Maria Alexandrovna; here, overlooking the sea and Lido and springing out of luxuriant, almost tropical foliage, are San Remo's most prestigious hotels and the utterly charming onion domes of the dainty **Russian Orthodox Church** (*open April–Sept Tues, Thurs, Sat 9.30–12.30 and 4–7; Oct–Mar Tues, Thurs, Sat 9.30–12.30 and 3–6.30*), built in the 1920s by the exiled nobility, who lavished a considerable sum on this bright little jewel box. It contains the tombs of some other deposed blue-bloods, the royal house of Montenegro.

This west end of town reaches its zenith at the white, brightly lit, Liberty-style **Municipal Casino**, built in 1904, a legacy from those golden days of fashion and still the lively heart of San Remo's social life, with its gaming rooms, roof garden cabaret, and celebrated restaurant complete with a live orchestra (*open 10am–3am; roulette wheels rolling from*

2pm–3am; there is a dress code in the French gaming rooms but not the American; adm Mon–Thur L5000, Fri–Sun L15,000). This is the only active casino on the Italian Riviera, and it also has something that flamboyant Las Vegas has never dreamed of: 'Literary Tuesdays' in its intimate Teatro dell'Opera, an institution founded in the 1930s by a local poet to amuse the wives of the gamblers and keep them from trying to stop their husbands from going broke. It attracts some of Italy's top scribes and journalists; musical evenings are held on the roof garden.

East of the Casino begins **Corso Matteotti**, San Remo's main shopping street, lined with boutiques selling all the big name Italian and international designers. It also has a relic of the past, the handsome Renaissance-baroque Palazzo Borca d'Olmo, now site of the **Civico Museo Archeologico** at No. 143 (© *0184 531 842, open Tues–Sat 9–12.30 and 3.30–6; adm*), which contains finds from the palaeolithic caves in the region, especially the Grotta dell'Arma; one room is dedicated to Garibaldi, who moved to San Remo for a few years after his political nemesis Count Cavour sold his home town Nice down the river to Napoleon III.

In February, the **Teatro Ariston** on the Corso hosts the biggest event in the wonderland of Italian pop, the *Festival della Canzone*, an extravagant, five-day-long lip-synch ritual of glitter and hype, where this once gloriously musical nation parades its contemporary talents with all the self-confidence of the Emperor in his new clothes. The Festival also serves as the prelims for the lollipop Olympics of the Eurovision Song Contest. In 1967 one hopeful contestant named Luigi Tenco committed suicide when he didn't make the cut; in memory of the man who died for the sake of a song, the Rassegna Tenco takes place in October, drawing singing songwriters from around the world.

La Pigna

Medieval **La Pigna** is San Remo's 'casbah', a tangled, mystery-laden mesh of steep lanes and stairs weaving under archways and narrow tunnels, fortified around the year 1000 as a refuge against the Saracens, back when San Remo belonged to the bishops of Genoa. Get there by way of Piazza San Siro (back from Corso Matteotti) and its 12th-century but much altered **Cathedral of San Siro** (*open 7–11.15 and 3–6*) with two side doors decorated with bas reliefs, one with a 15th-century Madonna and two saints, the other from the 12th century, with motifs so unusual for the area that no one has a clue who might have carved them. Inside there's an unusual black crucifix, formerly believed to be miraculous, and a tabernacle carved by the Gaggini family. The baroque **Oratorio dell' Immacolata Concezione** (1563) stands opposite, and nearby the large, covered **market** in Piazza Eroi Sanremesi draws hundreds of Italian and French gourmets every Tuesday and Saturday.

Inside La Pigna's tangled skein are a number of tiny piazzas, one hosting the 17th-century church of **San Giuseppe**, with a 12th-century door and a fountain topped with the quarter's pine cone symbol. From here you can wend your way up through the casbah to the **Giardini Regina Elena**, which is rather dull as gardens go but has fantastic views of the town and harbour. Standing majestically at the top of La Pigna, at the head of a long lane and the largest pebble mosaic *sagrato* in all Liguria, is the **Santuario Madonna della Costa**, rebuilt in 1630 (*open April–Sept daily 9–12 and 3–6.30; Oct–Mar daily 9–12 and 3–5.30; buses run regularly from San Remo*). The Sanremesi pulled out all the stops in the lavish interior; the Madonna on the high altar (1401) saved a local sailor, who donated the first gold coin to establish the shrine, from shipwreck. On *Ferragosto*, 15 August, this event is celebrated with fireworks and a feast, in one of the Riviera's most attractive traditional festivals.

Lastly, on the east edge of town, above the pleasure port, are the gardens of the Villa Comunale and the **Villa Nobel** (© *0184 507 380, closed for repairs at the time of writing*), a Moorish-style confection on Corso Cavallotti. Built in 1874, it was the favourite residence of the Swedish father of dynamite and plywood and founder of the famous prizes, Alfred Nobel, who died in 1896. You can stop in to look at his laboratory and library, and at the exhibit dedicated to his life. Flowers from San Remo decorate the prize-giving ceremonies in Stockholm. The nearby gardens of **Villa Ormonde** are packed with palms.

A bit further east in the Valle Armea, a few minutes' walk from the Via Aurelia, early risers can take in the intoxicating colour and scent of the **San Remo Flower Market** (© *0184 514 101, open Monday to Friday 4am–8am*)—this is very much a working, wholesale market, but fascinating nonetheless. Nowadays, however, it's not so apparent where this bevy of blooms comes from; most of the greenhouses on the hillsides have been replaced by condominiums.

Above San Remo

If you're driving, the road to take is the panoramic **Corso degli Inglesi** from the Casino; at No.374 is a **Via Crucis** with life-sized bronze figures by Milanese sculptor Enrico Manfrini (1990) set in a beautiful shady grove, with a big car park nearby. Not so long ago a funicular went up from Corso degli Inglesi to **Monte Bignone** (4281ft), the highest peak in the amphitheatre of hills wrapped around San Remo. A committee has formed to restore it, but until then you can drive on Via Galileo halfway up to **San Romolo**, where you'll find a golf course and great views of the Riviera, and also one of the biggest chestnut trees in Europe, 18ft in diameter, a tree that was a mere nut back in the year 1200 or so.

Further inland, **Bajardo** (or Baiardo) was spread out over a conical hill once sacred to the Celto-Ligurians with an enchanting backdrop of mountains and forests. Devastated by the great Ash Wednesday earthquake (*see* below), it was rebuilt further down; its reputation for healthy air has made it a modest summer resort. One intriguing relic of old Bajardo is the ruined church of **San Nicolò** at the top of the town, with its ancient capitals carved roughly with the heads of Mongols, perhaps representing some who accompanied the Saracens to Liguria. Two hundred people were killed when the roof of San Nicolò crashed down on their heads. The views are especially lovely from the **Terrazza sulle Alpi**.

In the Middle Ages, the surrounding forests were used to build ships. In the year 1200, a Pisan employed by Ventimiglia (Pisa's ally back then) came to search for wood and fell in love with the daughter of the Count of Bajardo. Her father, an ally of Genoa, was so adamantly opposed to their marriage that he cut off his daughter's head. Bajardo solemnly remembers this horrible demonstration of paternal wrath in the *Festival della Barca* (of the boat) on Pentecost Sunday, when a large tree trunk topped by a smaller pine tree is erected in the middle of the piazza, around which the people dance slowly while singing the 44 verses of the Ballad of the Count's Daughter in dialect. The ritual is so important to the villagers that they have performed it even during times of war and occupation. A week after Pentecost the tree is auctioned off: it, at least, brings good luck.

If you don't mind the narrow, spaghetti-like mountain roads that prevail here, you can circle back to the coast from here by way of **Ceriana**, another pretty hill-town surrounded by terraces, its narrow lanes built in concentric rings, all crowned by a campanile. Pretty baroque churches dot the lanes; **SS. Pietro e Paolo**, with its two bell towers, has some good 16th-century painting and a beautiful altar in the sacristy, carved of linden wood.

San Remo ✉ *18038*   **Where to Stay**

In San Remo, if you arrive without a booking, there's a hotel-finding service in the station, ℰ 0184 80172 (*closed Sun*). On the whole, though, you shouldn't have too much trouble finding a room outside of July and August. Note that many hotels in this area still prefer guests to take full- or half-pension, particularly in the high season.

The top hotel in San Remo, the ★★★★★**Royal**, Corso Imperatrice 80, ℰ 0184 5391, ✆ 0184 661 445, *royal@sistel.it* (*luxury*), near the Casino, is more of a palace than accommodation for rent. Surrounded by lush gardens, with palms, flowers, tennis court and an enormous heated sea-water pool, this turn-of-the-century *grande dame* has rooms that vary from imperial suites to more modest, refurbished doubles. And, true to tradition, the hotel orchestra serenades guests in the afternoon and gets them dancing in the evening.

One of the region's oldest hotels, the ★★★★**Astoria West End**, Corso Matuzia 8, ✆ 0184 667 701, ⊠ 0184 663 318, *astoria@tourism.it* (*very expensive*) sounds as if it belongs in New York, but instead sits in all its confectionery elegance—grand chandeliers, elaborate stucco ceilings and carved lifts—opposite the sea in San Remo. It also has luxuriant gardens with a pool and a pretty outdoor terrace.

Away from the hustle and bustle, ★★★★**Nyala**, Strada Solero 134, ✆ 0184 667 668, ⊠ 0184 666 059, *www.nyalahotel.com* (*very expensive*) is a wonderfully welcoming hotel in the hills on the west edge of town. It has large bedrooms with sun terraces for sitting and gazing at the splendid hillside views, a restaurant and bar, and a heated outdoor pool with poolside bar. The only smirch on its escutcheon is the bedroom décor—blue satin bedspreads with embroidered fluffy bits and flowery embossed wallpaper.

If you prefer something with a Liberty-style touch, ★★★★**Grand Hotel Londra**, Corso Matuzia 2, ✆ 0184 668 000, ⊠ 0184 668 073, *londra@tourism.it* (*expensive*) can oblige. Built around the turn of the century, it has a lovely garden and pool, and fine original interior details. *Closed Oct–Nov.* Another alternative is the recently refurbished ★★★★**Nazionale**, Corso Matteotti 3, ✆ 0184 577 577, ⊠ 0184 541 535 (*expensive*) which enjoys a privileged position beside the casino. It has 87 modern, air-conditioned and soundproofed rooms, most with fine views.

If you seek peace and quiet, try the ★★★**Paradiso**, Via Roccasterone 12, ✆ 0184 571 211, ⊠ 0184 578 176 (*moderate*), set just back from the seafront, above most of the hurly-burly, and enveloped with flowers on the terrace and balconies. It has a distinguished, glass-enclosed restaurant and a lovely sunny breakfast room. *Closed Nov–first half of Dec.* The ★★★**Lolli Palace**, Corso dell'Imperatrice 70, ✆ 0184 531 496, ⊠ 0184 541 574, *lolli@tourism.it* (*moderate*) is a lovely little seafront hotel with a decent restaurant. The sea-facing rooms are superb: large, bright and airy with great big bay windows and cute little balconies—all tastefully decorated in white and wood.

Further along the front, at Corso dell'Imperatrice 27, ★★★★**Europa**, ✆ 0184 578 170, ⊠ 0184 508 661 (*moderate*) is one of the few hotels not to have been fully refurbished, and so retains a rather *fin de siècle* character in its main rooms. In the same area, ★★★**Bel Soggiorno**, Corso Matuzia 41, ✆ 0184 667 631, ⊠ 0184 667471 (*moderate*) is a friendly Liberty-style hotel with its original stained glass and some original furnishings; the dining room has a gorgeous view over the gardens.

In the centre, ★★★**Eletto**, Corso Matteotti 44, ✆ 0184 531 548, ⊠ 0184 531 506 (*moderate–cheap*) is a very pretty 19th-century hotel, furnished with antiques, and also blessed with a welcoming little garden. Tiny, eight-room ★★**Sole Mare**, Via Carli 23, ✆ 0184 577 105, ⊠ 0184 532 778 (*cheap*) is a comfortable choice, especially popular with Italians.

On the east end of town, near the Villa Comunale, ★★**Corso**, Corso Cavallotti 194, ✆ 0184 509 911, ⊠ 0184 5090 231 (*cheap*) is quiet and simple, and a short walk from the beach by Porto Sole. Cheaper hotels like the old-fashioned **★Terminus E Metropoli**, Via Roma 8, ✆ 0184 577 110 (*cheap*) abound on Corso Matteotti, Via Roma, Corso Mombello and Corso Massini, where rooms can be found for around L20,000 per person.

San Remo ✉ *18038*   **Eating Out**

You can easily drop lire by the hundred thousands in San Remo's restaurants. **Da Giannino**, Corso Trento e Trieste 23, ✆ 0184 504 014 (*very expensive*) offers exquisitely prepared dishes based on fresh, natural ingredients, including a speciality of the region, *tagliolini al sugo di triglia* (wholewheat pasta with red mullet sauce), polenta with cheese and vegetable sauce, and pigeon with ginger, accompanied by an excellent wine list. *Closed Sun evening and Mon.*

Another highly acclaimed restaurant, **Paolo e Barbara**, Via Roma 47 (conveniently near the Casino, if you've hit the jackpot) ✆/✍ 0184 531 653 (*very expensive*) is generally rated one of the tops in all Liguria, run by a couple dedicated to perfect food and all the trimmings. Paolo Masieri in the kitchen is a wizard of invention, which he deftly combines with Riviera traditions—homemade *focaccia* and breads, the famous *gamberoni San Remo* flambéed in whisky, and much more; the average bill with a good wine comes to L160,000. Reserve. *Closed Wed, Thurs lunch, two weeks in June and July, some of Dec and Jan.*

Bagatto, Via Matteotti 145, ✆ 0184 531 925 (*expensive*) is one of the brightest and most relaxed restaurants in San Remo, with tempting *antipasti*, risotti and other dishes using sun-ripened vegetables, as well as delicious seafood and lamb dishes. *Closed Sun and July.* More fish can be found at **Mare Blu**, Via Carli 5, ✆ 0184 531 634 (*moderate*), a happy restaurant near the harbour. **Vittorio**, Piazza Bresca 16, ✆ 0184 501 924 (*moderate*) is another good bet, with a good choice of seafood *antipasti*, *trenette al pesto*, and good fresh seafood and fish. *Closed Wed.*

There is a wide selection of other *medium–cheap* pizzerias and restaurants, concentrated around Piazza Eroi Sanremesi and Via Palazzo, between the sea and the old town. Or head outside San Remo, to Verezzo Cava and **Silvestro**, ✆ 0184 559 066 (*cheap*), who offers an alternative to the constant barrage of seafood in the shape of delicious homecooked meat, chicken and rabbit dishes. *Closed Tues.*

East of San Remo: Bussana New and Old

A few kilometres down the coast from San Remo, **Bussana** is relatively new by Riviera standards, built in the late 19th century. The chief monument is the massive **Santuario del Sacro Cuore**, lavishly decorated inside; the sacristy contains an excellent *Birth of Christ* by Caravaggioist Mattia Preti.

The original Bussana, 2km inland, is now **Bussana Vecchia**, Italy's trendiest 'ghost town'. On 23 February 1887, an earthquake killed thousands and turned the town into the picturesque ruin you see today. The earthquake knocked in the roof of the baroque church (packed at the time for the Ash Wednesday service), but nearly all the parishioners managed to escape death in the side chapels; one survivor, Giovanni Torre detto Merlo, went on to invent the ice cream cone in 1902. The church is open to the sky behind its façade, the stucco decorations now sprout weeds, trees grow in the nave and apse, and cherubs smile down like broken dolls on a shelf.

It is a rather typical Italian contradiction that although Bussana Vecchia officially no longer exists, it has a number of arty inhabitants who are equally officially non-existent, but who have restored the interiors (though not the exteriors) of the ruined houses, and been hooked up with water, lights and telephones. They support two mild-mannered llamas from Peru, and make a living selling paintings and all sorts of artsy-fartsy dust magnets and New Age gizmos—disdainful Italian purists compare it to the 'French method' of managing their Riviera hill-towns by turning them into quaint shopping malls.

Up the Valle Argentina

Taggia

Just east of Bussana, at the mouth of the Valle Argentina, **Arma di Taggia** has one of the finest sandy beaches in the area, and is devoted to the pleasures of the sea. The culture is kept three kilometres inland, in the lovely medieval village of **Taggia**, carefully preserved and wrapped in its 16th-century walls. The biggest dose of art, however, is just outside the walls, in the convent of **San Domenico**, which has recently been made a national monument (*open 9.30–12 and 3–5; closed Thurs*). Built between 1460 and 1490, San Domenico was the wealthiest art patron in these parts for three centuries, making the church a veritable gallery of 15th-century Ligurian painting: there are two polyptychs featuring the Madonna by the elegant Lodovico Brea, along with works by his sons Francesco and Antonio, paintings and frescoes by Giovanni Canavesio, and a beautiful *Epiphany* attributed to the great Mannerist Parmigianino. Other works are in the refectory, in the cloister with its black stone columns, and in the Sala Capitolare, which has Canavesio's superb fresco of the *Crucifixion*. As well as supporting the arts, the Domenicans also introduced the quality olive trees that made Taggia's fortune, to this day known as *taggiasca*.

The walled town is one of the finest on the whole Riviera, a striking sight next to its remarkable, dog-leg 16-arched **medieval bridge** over the Argentina. Within the walls, the lanes are lined with handsome palaces, fountains, gateways and a beautiful baroque parish church, **SS. Giacomo e Filippo**, said to have been built to a design by Bernini. The main streets **Via Soleri** and **Via San Dalmazzo** are lined with porticoes, sculpted architraves and noble houses with their coats of arms. Another church outside of the walls, the **Madonna del Canneto**, has a charming campanile and frescoes by Giovanni and Luca Cambiaso. Next to it, note the handsome Villa Ruffini; Taggia was the hometown of Giovanni Ruffini, the author of *Doctor Antonio* (1855) and the man most responsible for the 19th-century tourist boom on the Riviera (*see* 'History', p.59).

Come on the third Sunday of July for the ancient Festival of Mary Magdalen, a personage who, according to tradition, once paid Taggia a call. She is remembered by members of her red-capped confraternity with an eerie Dance of Death, performed by two men, one playing the role of 'the man', and the other that of Mary Magdalen, who dies and is brought back to life with a sprig of lavender.

Badalucco and Montalto Ligure

A number of attractive old villages dot the Valle Argentina. **Badalucco**, with another pretty bridge of two asymmetrical arches, has murals and ceramic works hidden in every alley—a project funded by the *comune*. The powers that be in Badalucco weren't always so nice: the nearby village, **Montalto Ligure**, was founded by newlyweds fleeing the Count of Badalucco's insistence on his first night *droit de seigneur* (the Ligurian nobles seem to have been real creeps in that regard). Half of Badalucco followed them in protest. Not long after, the Count regretted his ungentlemanly behaviour and invited his ex-subjects to a reconciliatory banquet, but their desertion had left him so poor he only had dried chestnuts to offer them. The good people of Montalto had a word with one another, went home, and returned with all the fixings of a sumptuous feast. And so they were reconciled. But the protestors never went back to Badalucco.

The village they built stands out as one of the most impressive of Liguria's 'mini-cities', condensed into a tiny hilltop space. This reaches an astonishing level of sophistication in the arrangement of Montalto's centrepiece, the 18th-century church of **San Giovanni Battista** and the older **Oratorio di San Vicenzo Ferreri**: the church is built over a vaulted passageway, its façade half hidden behind the bell tower, in turn half hidden beyond the oratory, also built over a portico, with stairs ascending and descending, all in a 'piazza' measuring only a few square yards. San Giovanni's polyptych by Lodovico Brea (1516) spent time in the Louvre after Napoleon pinched it, but the French had a change of heart (and better polyptychs) so they sent it back. The sacristan can give you the key to visit the cemetery church, **San Giorgio**, with some good trecento frescoes.

Further up, the villages take on a more mountainous character and have slate roofs over their bare stone walls. **Andagna** is a steep 3km off the main Argentina road, enjoying a fine panoramic view over the valley below. Another reason to visit is its little **Cappella di San Bernardo** with a fine fresco cycle of 1436, showing scenes from the Passion, along with the Seven Virtues and Seven Vices. **Molini di Triora** down in the valley was named for the 23 watermills that made it the local industrial centre back in the Middle Ages; it was destroyed by the Piemontese in the 17th century. But they missed the attractive 15th-century **Santuario della Madonna della Montata** on the top of Molini.

Triora and its 'Witches'

Hill towns were relatively safe in those centuries of endless war, at least from passing armies. Fortified **Triora** (from the Latin *tria ora*, or 'three mouths', after the streams that join the Argentina here) was from 1216 on an outpost of the Republic of Genoa. In the 17th century it defied two major sieges by the Piedmontese; worse happened in 1944 when it became the victim of Nazi reprisals. Still, Triora looks much the same as it always did, defences and houses intact with a backdrop of Ligurian Alps, a picture postcard of a village of just over 400 souls, its fountains trickling with water brought in in the original 15th-century pipes.

All this belies the fact that Triora is the Salem of the Riviera. The story goes that in the late 16th century, witches, or *bàgiue*, would gather at the now ruined **Cabotina** just outside the village to communicate with the devil. They were also expert herbalists and healers, but in 1588 famine struck, and the *bàguie* (13 women, four girls and a boy) were accused by some of their fellow citizens of having brought the hunger down on their heads. In the collective neurosis of the Counter-Reformation they were hauled before the Inquisition. Five perished, but for the eight survivors their story had a rare happy ending—their condemnation was revoked and their accusers were excommunicated. The curious **Museo Etnografico e della Stregoneria** in Corso Italia is dedicated to the trial (*open 3–6*).

Besides a modest amount of tourist footfaraws spawned by the poor witches, Triora has some serious art, especially in the Romanesque-Gothic **Collegiata dell'Assunta**, with a beautiful *Baptism of Jesus* (1397) by Sienese master Taddeo di Bartolo and works by Luca Cambiaso. The nearby baroque **Oratorio di San Giovanni** has a fine marble portal. Just outside Triora, the pretty little church of **San Bernardino** has an interior completely coated with quattrocento frescoes in the style of Canavesio, complete with a *Last Judgement*. Nearby, a stepped path leads up to the 12th-century towers of the castle on top of the village. You may have seen loaves of *pane di Triora* sold elsewhere on the Riviera di Ponente; it's good mountain bread, famous for staying fresh for a week.

Beyond Triora, in the upper Valle Argentina, beautiful mountain scenery awaits near the highest peaks of Liguria, including the stunning hamlet of **Realdo**, balanced on a sheer crag 3500ft above sea level. **Verdeggia** is even higher up, if not quite as picturesque, having been rebuilt after an avalanche in 1805. Quarrying slate is a big part of the local economy, and the houses have balconies of slate and wood, with wrought iron rails. From Verdeggia a not very difficult path leads up in three hours to the **Passo della Guardia** (2166m) crowned by a statue of the Redeemer; from here you can climb up Saccarello (2200m) and descend into France. The tourist office in Triora has details and maps.

Sports and Activities

There's certainly no lack of things to do in San Remo. You can take a day trip by sea to Montecarlo or go **whale watching** (*avvistamento cetacei*) on summer Sunday afternoons with the Riviera Line, Molo di Levante 35, ℗ 0184 505 055; the whales are attracted to the good seasonal feeding grounds off the coast here. You can **hire a boat** up to 24 metres at Solmar, ℗ 0184 256 486, or go **diving** with Polo Sub, ℗ 0184 535 335, or play **tennis** at the Tennis Club Solaro, ℗ 0184 665 155, or go **riding** nearby at the Campo Ippico del Solaro, ℗ 0184 660 580 or in Arma di Taggia at San Martino, ℗ 0184 477 083. To get above it all in a **deltaplane**, try Ponente Flight San Remo, ℗ 0184 700 087. Midway between San Remo and Monte Bignone, you can shoot bogeys at the 18-hole **Ulivi**

golf course, ✆ 0184 557 093. If your adrenalin is congested, you can **bungee jump** 393ft off an old bridge above Triora over the Argentina river at the No Limits Bungee Center, ✆ 0229 403 136 or ✆ 0229 524 852, or go **rock climbing** up the sheer cliffs, Pukli Centri Arrampicata Sportiva, ✆ 0184 688 900.

Where to Stay and Eating Out

Arma di Taggia ✉ 18011

One advantage of staying at ★★★★**Vittoria Grattacielo**, Via Lungomare 1, ✆ 0184 43495, ✆ 0184 448 578 (*expensive*) is that you won't have to look at it; however, its height does guarantee a sea view from every room. There's a sea-water pool, private beach with cabins, private seaside garden, and well equipped rooms.

Arma also has one of the most highly regarded restaurants on the Riviera, **La Conchiglia**, Via Lungomare 33, ✆ 0184 43169 (*expensive*), which serves Ligurian delights based on seafood, local cheese and delicate olive oil—the prawn and white bean salad is delicious. There's a very good set lunch. Reserve. *Closed Wed, exc in July and Aug, also closed 15 days in June and Jan.* Lost in the olive groves along the road from Arma to Castellaro, **Uliveto**, ✆ 0184 479 040 (*expensive*) is a romantic place to dine, offering a single but refined fixed price L60,000 menu. *Closed Mon.*

Badalucco ✉ 18010

For good homecooking, get a table at **Il Ponte**, Via Ortai 3, ✆ 0184 408 000 (*moderate*), with vegetables fresh from the garden and exquisite pesto. *Closed Wed, Sun eve.*

Molini di Triora/Triora ✉ 18019

Santo Spirito, Piazza Roma 27, ✆ 0183 94019 (*cheap*) is the oldest restaurant in Molini, and a good place to tuck into a steaming dish of homemade pasta. Another good reason to stop is a shop run by 'good witch' **Angela Maria**, Piazza Roma 26, where she sells her delicious homemade cheese, including Alpine *tome* and *brusso* (fermented ricotta) and a 'witch's philtre' made of alpine herbs, a recipe handed down from Angela Maria's ancestor, Francesca Ciocheto, one of the women dragged before the Inquistion in 1588.

Up in Triora, a convent has been converted into the village's only hotel, ★★**Colomba d'Oro**, Corso Italia 66, ✆ 0184 94051, ✆ 0184 94089 (*cheap*), a rather sombre but atmospheric place to sleep.

Entertainment and Nightlife

In all the resorts, most of the clubs, night bars and discos are very expensive. At night, in San Remo, all roads lead to the casino (for details *see* p.99); otherwise, to the right of it, the **Disco Loco** also doubles as a cabaret-revue venue. **Caffé Columbo** is another night-time hangout, or there's the perennially popular **Odeon Music Hall**. The old port along Corso Nazario Suaro, Piazza Bresca and Via Nino Bixio are favourite places just to hang out after dark, with lots of tables outside to watch the passing crowd; medieval La Pigna with its little bars is also popular.

The Riviera dei Olivi

Imperia divides the 'Riviera of Flowers' from the more rugged 'Riviera of Olives'. Olive oil connoisseurs rate Liguria's the tops in Italy, although of course there are plenty of other regions ready to dispute this most slippery of crowns. This stretch of coast, especially the area around Imperia, also gets a lot fewer tourists.

Getting Around

Road and **rail** connections are as easy as in the sections of the Riviera further west. If you plan to rely on the bus, Riviera Bus offer a seven-day Travel Card, good for all coastal destinations from Ventimiglia to San Bartolomeo al Mare, for L20,000. Among the more spectacular drives in the area are the SS582, from Albenga to Garessio, and the SS490, inland from Finale Ligure.

Tourist Information

Imperia: Corso G. Matteotti 37, Porto Maurizio, ✆ 0183 660 140, ✉ 0183 666 510.

From Santo Stefano to Imperia

After San Remo, you can already see the olive groves taking over from the greenhouses. The first villages on the coast, **Santo Stefano** and **Riva Ligure**, have merged together, with fishermen's houses right on the sea; out of season they hibernate in a serious way. Just off the coast, **Cipressa** was named after Cyprus by its founders—three shepherds who escaped here. Devastated by Turkish pirates in the 16th century, the inhabitants survived by taking refuge in the mighty Torre Gallinara. Up the road, set in the olives, **Lingueglietta** has kept its medieval appearance and one of the most peculiar looking churches in Liguria: the 12th-century **San Pietro**, transformed into a fortress against these same pirates in the 1500s. Its little rose window is topped by machicolations (from where the defenders could drop boiling oil on invading corsairs; in one corner is a watch tower, in the other a bell tower). Behind the church are the ruins of the castle of the Della Lengueglia lords, while off the road you can visit the picturesque ruins of the church of **San Sebastiano**.

San Lorenzo al Mare, back on the sea, is another small-time resort dominated by the railway, but with two tiny pedestrian-only centres and pebbly beaches that, for once, are free, if *stabilimenti balneari* drive you crazy. The town's pride and joy is its covered *bocciodromo* for all-weather *bocci*-balling. Inland, **Civezza**, lost in olive groves, was founded by exiles from Venice, who left five towers (now all private houses) and dedicated the parish church to their patron **San Marco**; in 1783 it was rebuilt by Tommaso Carrega. **Pietrabruna**, further up the San Lorenzo valley, is another picturesque village, one that used to cultivate lavender in a big way but in the last decade has turned to greenhouse anemones as an easier way to make a buck. Remains of the old distilleries and lavender fields lie along the pretty ring trail, a walk of three and a half hours along the slopes of Monte Faudo, starting from the parking lot under the town.

Imperia

In 1923, two towns, Porto Maurizio and Oneglia, were married by Mussolini to form a new provincial capital with a name that warmed the cockles of his little fascist heart: Imperia. The towns had the longest possible engagement; by the year 1000 they were already distinct towns under different lords—Porto Maurizio belonged to Genoa, while Oneglia was an insignificant port of Albenga, only to become, after 1567, the only seaport of the Dukes of Savoy, although they didn't do much with it. The two towns were first 'introduced' in 1815 when both entered the kingdom of Sardinia together; in 1848 they were 'betrothed' by a bridge over the river Impero. When Nice was ceded to France in 1860, Porto Maurizio became the provincial capital. This began a luxury building boom, interrupted in 1887 by a mighty earthquake. Relations with Oneglia, its bride, remain cool.

Imperia is one of the rare cities in Italy that fits Gertrude Stein's famous description of Oakland, California: 'there's no there there.' While bits are very pleasant, Imperia remains estranged from itself, and no matter how often you go, you leave with a warm, fuzzy but ultimately anonymous feeling.

Porto Maurizio

Porto Maurizio itself has three distinct parts. Rather dull seaside **Borgo Foce** to the west, the aristocratic **Paraxio** quarter on the acropolis in the centre and, to the east, another maritime quarter, **Borgo Marino**, with a sandy beach. The latter was a port of call protected by the Byzantines after the fall of Rome, and later became important as the Vicarate of Liguria di Ponente, when the town's first fancy palaces were built. The Knights of St John used Borgo Marino as one of their ports to Jerusalem, Rhodes and then Malta; the little deconsecrated church of **San Giovanni** is all that remains of their passing. A pretty seaside footpath links Borgo Foce and Borgo Marino.

Halfway up the hill above Borgo Marino you can't miss the enormous and opulent neoclassical **Duomo di San Maurizio**, built between 1781 and 1838 and full of nondescript 18th-century painting. More of the same fills the nearby **Pinacoteca**, while ships' models and nautical instruments fill the small **Museo Navale del Ponente Ligure**, Piazza Duomo 11 (*© 0183 65541/65572, open July–Aug Wed–Sat 9pm–11pm*) which should give you a good idea of life on board a caravel of old.

From Piazza Duomo, Via Acquarone will take you up to the Paraxio (Ligurian dialect for Palatium, like the Palatine Hill in Rome), its steep lanes and steps and medieval vaults lined with palaces and baroque churches that make such a grand sight from sea level. One is dedicated to Imperia's official patron, **San Leonardo**, and linked to his birthplace; another place to aim for is the **Convento di Santa Chiara**, to see the impressive grand arches behind the convent. In the summer many of these make pretty settings for classical music concerts.

In the neighbourhood of Cascine, you can visit one of the most unusual villas along this coast: the **Villa Grock**, set in a pretty park, once the home of the famous Swiss clown Grock (Adrien Wettach) and now run by a private foundation; ring them to make an appointment, ✆ 0183 293 377.

Oneglia

East of Porto Maurizio, the oil port (olive oil, that is) of **Oneglia** was sold by the bishop of Albenga to the Doria in 1298. It saw the birth of two famous men: Andrea Doria in 1466, and composer Luciano Berio in 1925. Its citizens tend to regard their town's marriage to Porto Maurizio as a shotgun affair: when the Church recently declared that the two halves of Imperia should unite behind one patron saint, St Leonardo, who was born in Porto Maurizio, Oneglia refused to go along and still sticks stalwartly to St John, to his harmonious late baroque parish church of **San Giovanni Battista** (1762) and especially to his big traditional festival in July.

The centre of Oneglia is the theatrical **Piazza Dante**, but the centre of life is in the porticoes along the port. Fishing remains important; at four o'clock in the afternoon all the excitement is around the portside fish auction. The **Museo dell'Olivo**, Via Garessio 13 (*✆ 0183 720 000, open 9–12 and 3–6; closed Tues*) was opened by local oil barons, the Carli brothers, and dedicated to the history of olive-growing from Roman times to the present. Another nice things is that cars have been banned from the incomplete coastal road to Diano Marino, to allow foot access to the wild beaches along **Galeazza Bay**; near Capo Berta you'll find one of the few places in Liguria where you can skinny dip.

Liguria's Liquid Gold

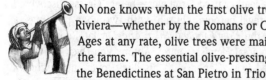 No one knows when the first olive trees were planted along the Riviera—whether by the Romans or Crusaders. In the early Middle Ages at any rate, olive trees were mainly used to define the borders of the farms. The essential olive-pressing know-how was in the hands of the Benedictines at San Pietro in Triora, who over the decades showed farmers how to build the dry stone terraces you see everywhere, how to plant and irrigate the young trees, and how to press the olives in the *frantoio*. The friars at San Domenico in Taggia are given credit for elevating Ligurian olive oil to the top of the class, thanks to the small black *taggiasca* olives they planted, which are also famous for the work they require—they are harder to pick and yield less oil per bushel, but from the 16th to the 19th century their golden-green nectar was in great demand across Italy. For many people in the *entroterra* olive oil was their major, and often only, source of income. But raising olives on these steep slopes is

hard, hard work and when tourists first began to appear on the coast, not a few people abandoned their groves with few regrets and found new jobs along the coast.

Recently, of course, with the much vaunted virtues of olive oil as a basis for a healthy diet, the Ligurians are finding it worthwhile to return to their terraces, to squeeze out their famous *extra vergines* and *spremuta d'oliva*, fresh olive juice. Although olives grow all along the coast, the Riviera di Ponente produces the finest and best; inland from Imperia, Taggia or Albenga you'll find *frantoios* to visit that sell their product. You won't find a better (or healthier) souvenir.

Inland from Imperia

Imperia's *entroterra* is a vast forest of olive groves, swathed around old villages. Above Porto Maurizio, **Dolcedo** has the most renowned olive groves in the region, and several medieval bridges, one of which was built by the Knights of St John in 1292 and still bears their cross. The parish church contains a fine *Martyrdom of St Peter of Verona* by Gregorio De Ferrari—the Inquisitor Peter getting an axe in his head from the medieval heretics he tormented was a favourite Counter-Reformation subject. Further up the valley, above Prelà and Pantsina, there are the expected lovely views from the **Santuario della Madonna della Guardia**. Further up, you can cross east into the Valle Argentina (*see* above) by way of **Colle d'Oggia**, through a wild rocky landscape.

Closer to Imperia, **Montegrazie** (9km) sits high on its hill, a typical medieval village with two rather exceptional churches: a regal late baroque **parish church** designed by Domenico Belmonte, with the only known work signed by Milanese painter Carlo Braccesco, a lovely polyptych painted in 1478; and the nearby **Santuario di Nostra Signora delle Grazie**, dedicated in 1450 and containing the best frescoes in the region, by Ligurian painters Pietro Guido and Gabriele della Cella, and a *Last Judgement* and *Punishment of the Damned* by Tomaso and Matteo Biazaci; the views from the church stretch for miles. Another fork in the road leads to **Moltedo**, a town scented by myrtle. During the Renaissance, these fragrant leaves were exported to Grasse in Provence, where myrtle was used to scent fine leather used for gloves—before Grasse discovered perfume. Moltedo, too, has a very regal baroque church, with two good paintings, a *St Isidore* by Gregorio De Ferrari and the *Holy Family with an Angel* by Jan Roos. This for a long time was attributed to an even great Flemish painter, Antony Van Dyck, who took refuge in Moltedo when he escaped from Genoa with his illicit lover, noblewoman Paolina Adorno.

In the Valle Impero above Oneglia, the main SS28 road leads to pretty **Pontedassio**, hometown of the Agnesi pasta-making dynasty, whose first flour mill still stands intact in Via Garibaldi. Sadly, however, they've closed their spaghetti museum, which was devoted to showing that the world's favourite noodle is a Genoese invention, and not Chinese or Neapolitan (the first known mention of spaghetti is in the Genoese annals, in a document dated 1244). You can, however, visit Pontedassio's **Frantoio Calvi**, ✆ 0183 292 851, home to Liguria's biggest olive-squashing millstones.

From Pontedassio you can make a loop to the east, through **Bestagno**, under the impressive ruins of a powerful medieval castle, or continue up the valley to **Chiusavecchia**, with its mighty stone bridge; a road from here twists up **Lucinasco**, in a panoramic spot overlooking thousands of ancient olives in the valley below. Lusinasco has a small **Museo di Arte Sacra** (*© 0183 52534 to visit*), with seven painted wooden statues from the 15th century, mourning the Dead Christ. The pretty parish church, 13th-century **Santo Stefano**, is just outside the village, reflected in a little lake. Another 3km up the road is the isolated 15th-century **Santuario della Maddalena**, a simple white church made from cut stone blocks, a national monument in a beautiful setting.

Continuing up the main Valle Impero from Chiusavecchia, **San Lazzaro Reale** has yet another medieval bridge, and is worth a stop if the parish church is open, to see the 16th-century anonymous triptych of the *Madonna*. **Borgomaro**, the most important village in these parts, has its work of art as well, a good polyptych of *SS Nazarino e Celso* from the 16th century; outside Borgomaro, the picturesque church dedicated to the same saints is in part from the 11th century. Further up at the valley, the most impressive sight of all is the **oak tree** in Ville San Sebastiano, believed to be the biggest if not the oldest in Europe (follow the sign for *ruve de mégu*).

Where to Stay and Eating Out

Santo Stefano al Mare ✉ 18010

Santo Stefano is known for its restaurants. **La Riserva**, Via Roma 51, © 0184 484 134 (*expensive*) is prettily set in the old bishopric, and serves good fresh seafood and other dishes, including some French ones, using the owner's own olive oil. *Closed Mon*. For a change of pace, **San Giacomo**, Lungomare Colombo 19, © 0184 486 808 (*expensive*) serves pasta and meat with truffles, as well as Ligurian seafood and vegetable dishes (*closed Mon and Tues lunch*).

Imperia ✉ 18100

Seaside ★★★**Croce di Malta**, Via Scarincio 148, Porto Maurizio, © 0183 667 020, ◉ 0183 63687, *cmalta@tourism.it* (*moderate*) is a good comfortable hotel with a pretty breakfast terrace and, most importantly, phones in the bathrooms, just in case. Nearby, ★★★**Corallo**, Corso Garibaldi 29, © 0183 666 164, ◉ 0183 64691, *corallo1@tourism.it* (*moderate*) has functional rooms, but a pretty garden and private beach, and special weekend rates. ★★★**Robinia**, Via Pirinoli 14, © 0183 62720, ◉ 0183 60635 (*moderate*) is a pleasant albeit unexceptional choice, with its own beach, a lovely terrace, a restaurant and 55 rooms, most with sea view. There are any number of one- and two-star hotels, mainly around Viale Matteotti in Oneglia.

The excellent **Lanterna Blù**, Via Scarincio 32, Borgo Marina, in Porto Maurizio, © 0183 63859 (*very expensive*) prepares fine dishes using ingredients from two local farms; be sure to try the hot seafood *antipasti*. *Closed Wed*. Book ahead if you want a chance at a table at **Vecchio Forno**, Piazza della Chiesa, ✆ 0183 780 269 (*expensive*) where you can feast on seafood crêpes or ravioli filled with fresh herbs, as well as classically prepared seafood. *Closed Wed, two weeks in June.* Locals are proud of their prize-winning pizzeria, **Hobo's**, at Via Rambaldo in Porto Maurizio (*cheap*), where an exquisite *Quattro Stagioni* with a beer is L9500.

The Gulf of Diano: Beaches East of Imperia

East of Imperia, the coastal road skirts the abrupt rocky lump of Capo Berta, covered with Mediterranean *macchia* and Aleppo pines and the inevitable watchtower dating from the centuries when living on this coast was hardly a carefree holiday. Beyond lies a string of popular resorts, which, like about a million others, claim to enjoy the most mild climate on the Italian peninsula, although no one really wants to have a thermometer war to prove it once and for all.

Tourist Information

Diano Marina: Piazza Martiri della Libertà 1, ✆ 0183 496 956, ✆ 0183 494 365.

San Bartolomeo al Mare: Piazza XXV Aprile 1, ✆ 0183 400 200, ✆ 0183 403 550.

Cervo: Piazza Castello 1, ✆ 0183 408 197, ✆ 0183 403 133.

Andora: Villa Laura, Via Aurelia 122/a, ✆ 0182 681 004, ✆ 0182 681 807, *iatandora@infocomm.it.*

Laigueglia: Via Roma 150, ✆ 0182 690 059, ✆ 0182 699 191, *iatlaigueglia@infocomm.it.*

Diano Marina

The first resort east of Capo Berta, Diano Marina has a long sandy beach, and palm trees, with a fertile coastal plain stretching behind, all sheltered from the cold and wind—but not, unfortunately, from earthquakes. Shattered by the big one of 1887, Diano had to be completely rebuilt, which gave the inhabitants a chance to forget their old job as an olive oil centre and port, and make their town into a purpose-built resort. They salvaged all the marble altars and paintings they could find and stuck them in the big new church, **Sant'Antonio Abate**.

In ancient times Diano's immediate hinterland was covered with an oak forest, the sacred *Lucas Bormani*, where the Ligurians worshipped their gods Borman and Bormana. It was the Roman custom to be extremely circumspect towards the deities of the people they conquered; during a war the Romans would promise the enemy gods temples and offerings if they changed sides, and after the war they would take their cult images to Rome, and give the deity the name of a Roman equivalent, in this case the virgin goddess of the hunt, masculinized to suit Borman. The late 19th-century Palazzo del Parco on Via Matteotti contains the **Museo Civico** (*✆ 0183 496 112, open April–Sept only*), with finds from an Iron Age necropolis discovered in the centre of Diano, amphorae from the *Felix Pacata*, a Roman shipwreck from the 1st century BC, and a room of Garibaldi memorabilia. Since 1993, Diano has hosted one of the funniest events on the Riviera in August—Vascup, a regatta of bathtubs.

Diano's *entroterra* villages were spared by the quake and, like those to the west, all are surrounded by slopes divided laboriously by stone terraces planted with olives. When pirate sails were spotted on the horizon, the coastal population would flee 2km inland to **Diano Castello** (Roman *Castrum Diani*) which still bristles with towers. The Municipio, opposite the lavish baroque church of **San Nicola di Bari**, has a 17th-century fresco that recalls Diano's participation in the historic Genoese victory over Pisa at Meloria in 1284. This is also a good place to bring the kids when it rains; there's a ten-pin-bowling alley, Via San Pietro 71, ✆ 0183 494 131. Another 2km up the valley, **Diano Borello** has a good 14th-century church, **San Michele**, with a Renaissance fresco in the lunette and a polyptych by Antonio Brea inside. Besides olives, this is the land of Liguria's finest white wine, Vermentino, made from malvasia vines brought over long ago from Spain; try it at the Cantina Maria Donata Bianchi, Via delle Torri 16, in Diano Castello.

Next along the coast, modern development at **San Bartolomeo al Mare** has completely choked the two medieval hamlets of San Bartolomeo and Rovere that once made up the town. In Rovere, the medieval **Santuario della Madonna della Ròvere** has a neoclassical façade and a wooden statue of the Virgin which she handed in person to some local shepherds; in the summer the sacristy is used in classical music competitions. San Bartolomeo's parish church, also much altered over the centuries, contains a polyptych by Cristoforo Pancalino, the Betty Crocker of the art, at least in the respect that he never existed; the name was invented to attribute 16th-century works by Ligurian painters under the influence of the Tuscans. Another polyptych by 'Pancalino' is in the church in lovely **Villa Faraldi**, a medieval village lost in the olive groves some 8km above San Bartolomeo. This holds an important arts and music festival in July and

August, and usually has an exhibition of some kind or another going on, thanks to the initiative of a Norwegian sculptor named Fritz Roed.

The east end of the Golfo di Diano is occupied by **Cervo**, a curl of white, cream and pale yellow houses sweeping up from the sea on to a small promontory, forming one of the most beautiful townscapes on the whole Riviera. At the top of the curl stands the pretty cream-pastry San Giovanni Battista, better known as the **Chiesa degli Corallini** (of the coral fishermen), designed by Giovanni Battista Marvaldi in 1686, with a distinctive concave façade emblazoned with stuccos and a stag, or *cervo* in Italian. It was built, unusually, with money raised by the fishermen themselves, who used to dive for coral around the Ligurian coast, Corsica and Sardinia, a life recorded in the chapel dedicated to their patron Saint Erasmus. In 1964, Hungarian violinist and conductor Sandor Vegh began Cervo's chamber music festival in July and August, featuring internationally known pianists and violinists.

The old town has a delightful, sunny, vaguely Moorish atmosphere. Until the 12th century Cervo was the fief of the Clavesana family, whose castle, above the church, combines the medieval structure with a baroque manor house, now seat of the **Museo Etnografico del Ponente Ligure** (© *0183 408 197, open 9–1 and 3–6.30*) with exhibits on costumes and customs. For all that, Cervo has just five small hotels near its shingle beach.

East of Cervo, modern **Andora** is a small resort on the banks of the torrent Mèrula, encompassing medieval **Andora Marina** and its Genoese watchtower. The ten-arched bridge over the Mèrula is called the **Ponte Romano**; it was used on the Roman road, but in its current incarnation is medieval. The Roman road (pedestrians only, or you can drive up the back way on Via al Castello) continues up to isolated **Andora Castello**, one of the most impressive medieval monuments on the Ponente: an egg-shaped fortified medieval hamlet built by the Clavesana around the year 1000 and sold to Genoa in 1252, and all but abandoned after a flood of the Mèrula caused the inhabitants to relocate to Laigueglia. It makes an impressive sight: a tower gate with Ghibelline crenellations leads into the lovely 13th-century Romanesque-Gothic church of **SS. Giacomo e Filippo**, built of stone from Capo Mele in 1100. The church itself was part of the defences; today it is used as one of the venues for a series of classical concerts, Musica nei Castelli di Liguria.

You can continue up the 'Strada Romana' on foot (or drive from Laigueglia) to **Colla Micheri**, a pretty little rural hamlet, restored by Thor Heyerdahl, the Norwegian ethnologist who sailed the *Kon Tiki*. 'I have spent my life exploring the world,' he wrote. 'But when I arrived in this place, I did not hesitate: my own house would be here in this little paradise.' Beyond this little paradise, Andora's *entroterra* is very sparsely populated, with approximately one inhabitant per thousand olive trees; if you want to go exploring one place to aim for is **Testico**, once a possession of the Doria, but taken over by the Dukes of Savoy. The road above Testico has lovely views over the Maritime Alps.

On the other side of Capo Mele ('Cape Apples') lies the attractive old town of **Laigueglia**. Like Cervo, Laigueglia made a living from coral fishing, and has taken on the postwar demands of tourism more graciously than some. Also like Cervo, it has a majestic baroque church for a centrepiece: **San Matteo** (1745) with two bell towers at angles, crowned with cupolas covered in majolica tiles, their crosses oriented to the prevailing sea winds, the *maestrale* and the *libeccio*; inside there's an *Assumption* by Bernardo Strozzi. The coral fishermen paid for the nearby **Oratorio di Santa Maria Maddelena**. In the summer Laigueglia is a lively place at night, taking in some of the overflow from nearby Alassio.

Where to Stay and Eating Out

Diano Marina ✉ 18013

****Bellevue & Méditerranée**, Via Gen. Ardoino 2–4, ✆ 0183 402 693 (*moderate*) is one of the nicest hotels on the beach, with a pool and garden in addition to its beach facilities. A good bet for families, ***Sasso**, Via Biancheri 7, ✆ 0183 494 319, ✉ 0183 494 310 (*moderate–cheap*) is a well-run hotel 200 yards from the sea (guests have free use of the hotel's beach cabins); rooms are modern and functional, and nine come equipped with kitchenettes. Excellent breakfast buffet. Big off-season discounts. Family-run ***Caprice**, Corso Roma Est 19, ✆ 0183 495 061 (*cheap*) is quite a classy place for this price, with a garden and beach, and a fine moderately priced restaurant, with fresh pasta dishes and wonderful home-made desserts (*open to non-guests, but get there early*).

San Bartolomeo al Mare ✉ 18016

In a 16th-century oil press in a handsome old mansion, **Il Frantoio**, Via Pairola 65, ✆ 0183 401 098 (*very expensive*) offers a vast assortment of *antipasti* and delicious daily specials, not exclusively seafood, according to the season and the day's catch. *Closed Thurs, exc in summer.* For excellent Neapolitan-style pizza, **Partenopea**, Via Martiri della Libertà 5, ✆ 0183 400 748 (*cheap*) is hard to beat.

Cervo ✉ 18010

The nicest of Cervo's few hotels, family-run ***Nuovo Hotel Columbia**, Via Aurelia 17, ✆/✉ 0183 400 079 (*moderate*) has 22 functional rooms by the beach. **San Giorgio**, in the old town, on Via Volta 19, ✆ 0183 400 175 (*expensive*) serves well-prepared Ligurian specialities like *trenette al pesto* or *verdure ripiene* (stuffed vegetables) in an intimate, art-filled setting. Reserve. *Closed Tues lunch, Jan, Nov.*

Andora ✉ 17020

A comfortable hotel on the seaside, ***Moresco**, Via Aurelia 96, ✆ 0182 89141, ✉ 0182 85414 (*cheap*) has nice extras like satellite TV, a restaurant with a special children's menu, and bike hire. An old stone manor house on Via al Castello has been converted into a romantic restaurant: **Casa del Priore**, ✆ 0182 87330 (*expensive*). The dishes have a decidedly French touch, and there is often live music in the bar downstairs. *Closed Mon, Jan–mid-Feb.*

Laigueglia ✉ 17020

For something special on this stretch of coast, book a room at ★★★★**Splendid**, Piazza Badarò 3, ✆ 0182 690 325, 🖷 0192 690 894, *splendid@dg.sv.it* (*expensive*), an 18th-century monastery that has been completely and elegantly refurbished with antiques. The rooms are light and airy, some have sea views, and there's a small pool too. *Open April–Sept.* Another good choice, ★★★**Mediterraneo**, Via A. Doria 18, ✆ 0182 690 240, 🖷 0182 499 739 (*moderate*) is peacefully set back among the olives, although the beach is only a short walk away. *Closed mid-Oct–Christmas.* Dine at **Baia del Sole**, Piazza Cavour 8, ✆ 0182 690 019 (*moderate*), a pretty place with brick vaults and imaginative cuisine; seafood reigns supreme, with *taglioni* tossed with fresh scampi and lovely baked fish with artichokes. Children's menu available. *Closed Mon exc in summer, and Jan–Easter.* The town is also known for its chocolates, *baci di Laigueglia*, made at **Pasticceria Guido**, Via Dante 105.

The Riviera delle Palme

After the Riviera dei Fiori and the Rivieri dei Olivi comes the Baia del Sole and the Riviera delle Palme, where the big-time seaside resort action picks up again at Alassio.

Tourist Information

Alassio: Viale Gibb 26, ✆ 0182 647 027, 🖷 0182 647 874, *iatalassio@infocomm.it.*

Alassio

A suntrap with 3km of beaches made of sugar-fine sand, **Alassio**, according to some scholars, is named after Aldelasia, the daughter of the 10th-century Holy Roman Emperor Otto the Great, who eloped here with her lover Arelamo. Back then it was a fishing village belonging to the Benedictines; in 1541 the Republic of Genoa took over. In the 19th century, the Hanburys (of the garden fame, in Ventimiglia) were the pioneers who first saw in Alassio its potential as a winter resort, and to this day the hills above Alassio are dotted with English-built villas and gardens. Alassio's destiny underwent its most recent twist when summer tans became the rage, thanks to Coco Chanel, who dared to go brown on the French Riviera in 1923. Of pre-resort Alassio, little remains to be seen other than a defence tower, some old *palazzi* and the pretty church of **Sant'Ambrogio** (1597), with a Romanesque campanile, a Renaissance portal and a statue of St Michael stabbing the devil.

Back in the 1930s, when Alassio's **Caffè Roma** was *the* celebrity rendezvous, owner Mario Berrino looked across at the little wall of the garden opposite and said to Ernest Hemingway, 'Caro Ernesto, wouldn't it be something if all the famous people who ever sat in the café left their autographs there?' Papa agreed and contributed his John Hancock, which Berrino made into a ceramic plaque, starting a custom that endures to this day, making the **Muretto** (off Via Cavour, near the train station) Alassio's equivalent of Hollywood Boulevard; in August there's even a 'Miss Muretto' beauty contest. Alassio's main Via XX Settembre (better known as the **Budello**) crosses here and runs parallel to the beach, or at least next to the houses that give directly on to the sands.

You can, by arrangement, take an excursion boat to the tiny privately owned islet, **Isola Gallinaria**, a mile off the coast between Alassio and Albenga. Named after the wild hens that used to populate it, the island provided sanctuary for St Martin of Tours when he was fleeing Arian persecution in the 4th century. For over a thousand years the island was also home to a wealthy Benedictine abbey, with properties all over the Riviera and into Provence; its ruins stand next a villa. Today Isola Gallinaria is a nature reserve, the last place on the entire Riviera to preserve its original vegetation of *macchia*; it is also a popular destination for skin-divers. Another pleasant outing from Alassio is up to the 13th-century Benedictine church of **Santa Croce**, once a dependant of Gallinara and one of the best viewpoints in the area. From here you can follow the Roman Via Julia down to Albenga.

Alassio ✉ *17021*   ***Where to Stay***

The biggest resort in the area, Alassio's finest hotel is probably the ★★★★**Grand Hotel Diana**, Via Garibaldi 110, ✆ 0182 642 701, ✇ 0182 640 304 (*very expensive*), with its own beach, beach bar, beach restaurant, free bike hire and heated indoor swimming pool. The seafront rooms are nice and large with balconies and there is a small restaurant serving decent fare (*7.30–9pm*). Rooms without a sea view are much cheaper.

★★★★★**Spiaggia**, Via Roma 78, ✆ 0182 643 403, ✇ 0182 640 279 (*very expensive*) which, despite its name, is not actually on the beach, does have a private one. The rooms are modern, air-conditioned and well-equipped, if small. There is a pool and a restaurant, but it's not really five-star material.

Out of a very extensive choice, the ★★★★**Ambassador**, Corso Europa 64, ✆ 0182 643 957, ✇ 0182 645 472 (*expensive*) is one of the more popular hotels, with comfortable rooms. Directly on the beach, ★★★**Beau Sejour**, Via Garibaldi 102, ✆ 0182 640 303, ✇ 0182 646 391 (*expensive*) has well-furnished rooms, a terrace and garden, and is good for a longer stay. *Open April–Sept.*

The excellent ★★★**Milano**, Piazza Airaldi e Durante 11, ✆ 0182 640 597, ✇ 0182 640 598 (*moderate*) is right on the beach; its rooms are well-equipped, with balconies and fine sea views. There is also a very nice restaurant serving various Ligurian specialities. ★★★**Ligure**, Passeggiata Italia 25, ✆ 0182 640 653, ✇ 0182 660 641 (*moderate*) is another good hotel, in the heart of the old town but still with sea views, with modern, airy rooms and a very good restaurant.

The ★★**Bel Air**, Via Roma 40, ✆ 0182 642 578, ✇ 0182 640 238 (*cheap*) is wonderful value: its rooms are modern and it has its own beach. The similar ★★**Kon Tiki**, Via delle Palme 11, ✆ 0182 660 110 (*cheap*) is a short walk from the beach, with its own bar and restaurant.

What Alassio may lack in grand hotels it makes up for with a gourmet palace, **La Palma**, Via Cavour 5, ✆ 0182 640 314 (*expensive*), where you can choose between two *menus degustazione*, one highlighting basil, the totem herb of Liguria, and the other Provençal-Ligurian specialities, with an emphasis on seafood. La Palma is not large, so be sure to reserve. For a seafood orgy, head out to the local yacht club's **Al Mare**, Porticciolo Ferrari, ✆ 0182 44186 (*expensive*) where each course (except the delicious ice cream), is delightfully fishy. In the heart of the old town, **La Cave**, Passeggiata Italia 7, ✆ 0182 640 693 (*expensive*) is an atmospheric old restaurant, serving typical Ligurian cuisine like *troffie al pesto* and fish soups. *Closed Wed*. For pizza in a traditional atmosphere, try **Della Quintana**, Via Gastaldi 5, ✆ 0182 643 301 (*cheap*), housed in a medieval building.

Entertainment and Nightlife

During the summer season this area is one of the liveliest on the coast, with several festivals and events as well as lots of clubs, bars and discos. Throughout summer, the **Musica nei Castelli di Liguria** music festival takes place, in which a series of classical concerts by Italian and international ensembles are presented in the many castles of the region. Full details are available from local tourist offices.

As regards **nightlife**, Alassio attracts a fairly young, hip crowd who meet up from about 10pm in the bars lining the seafront such as **Zanzibar**, Via Vittorio Veneto 143, with lots of loud music and 1950s memorabilia, and **La Tavernetta**, Via Gramsci 30, a good place to meet before or after clubbing. All ages can bend an elbow at **Sandon**, Passegiata Cadorna 134, with a maritime theme and lots of photos of Hemingway, who came here for his *centenario*, a concoction of rums.

Clubs and discos generally get going about midnight and close at 4 or 5am. The trendiest places in Alassio are **Rapsodia**, Vico Berna 6, which plays an excellent selection of 70s disco to latest chart music, and **U Brecche**, Via Dante 204. A slightly older clientele patronizes the more mainstream **Boccaccio Club**, in Via Privata Londra. In summer, roofs and inhibitions come down in Alassio at **La Vela**, Via Giancardi 46, and in nearby Laigueglia at **La Suerte**, just by the sea, which gets very crowded very early. **Live music** can also be found in Alassio, at **Fred Music Bar**, on Via XX Settembre, and **Tropicana**, Passeggiata Italia 3, where you can sit outside and listen to the bands.

Albenga

Swinging Alassio's neighbour, Albenga is the most historic and interesting town on the Riviera del Ponente, owing its centuries of good fortune and prestige to the river Cento and its affluents, which formed the largest and most fertile alluvial plain in all Liguria. The settlement dates back at least to the 6th century BC, when it was the *Albium Inguanum*, port of a Ligurian tribe called the Inguani. Once in Roman hands, the name was elided into Albinguanum and the town was rebuilt in the typical colonial *castrum* grid.

Partially destroyed by the Goths and Vandals, Albenga was rebuilt in the 5th century by General Constantius, the husband of Gallia Placida and future emperor of the West at Ravenna. During the dark years of Lombard invasions from the mountains and Saracen invasions from the sea, Albenga endured it all as the capital of the Byzantine Marca Arduinica. It was a free *comune* by the 11th century, and joined in the First Crusade on the same footing as Genoa, thereby obtaining a number of mercantile privileges for itself in the Middle East.

After the 12th century, however, Albenga fell prey to typical Ligurian intramural quarrels. As elsewhere, powerful families took control (here the Clavesana, followed by the Del Carretto) and by the 15th century, weakened and strife-torn, Albenga lost its freedom altogether to the Republic of Genoa. At this point, however, it didn't really matter. Albenga's harbour shifted away with the course of the Cento river, and the port became a malarial marshland. Nowadays the town stands a kilometre from the sea, and Albenga grows asparagus and other vegetables in the fertile soil of its old river bed.

Tourist Information

Albenga: Via B. Ricci, ✆ 0182 558 444, ✉ 0182 558 740, *iatalbenga@infocomm.it.*

Villanova d'Albenga: Via Albenga 46, ✆/✉ 0182 582 241.

Garlenda: Via Roma 4. ✆/✉ 0182 582 114, *iatgarlenda@infocomm.it.*

The Medieval Centre

Albenga's evocative and urbane centre retains its *castrum* layout from Roman times. Via Enrico d'Aste was the Roman *decumanus* and Via Medaglio d'Oro the *cardus*; and the beautiful main square, **Piazza San Michele**, was for centuries the seat of civil and spiritual authority, all in the shadow of an impressive collection of 13th-century brick towers from the days when Albenga was a free *comune*. All Italian cities used to have these proto-skyscrapers, but few have preserved so many (a dozen, of which seven are perfectly intact) in such a small area, most of them leaning, due to the marshy soil. Three stand like slightly tipsy bridesmaids around the elegant campanile (1391) of the 11th-century Romanesque **Cattedrale di San Michele**, rebuilt on the palaeochristian original; inside you can see the Carolingian crypt under the presbytery, and an enormous 19th-century organ.

Steps from the nearby **Loggia Comunale** (1421) lead down to the street level of Albenga 1500 years ago, and to the entrance of its most celebrated monument, the 5th-century **baptistry** (*open Tues–Sun 10–12 and 3–6*). Emperor Constantine set the fashion for geometrical baptistries when he built the very first one, the octagonal baptistry of St John Lateran in Rome. Albenga's is a minor *tour de force* of the genre, its architects combining an unusual 10-sided exterior with an octagonal interior. Some of the niches inside have windows covered with beautiful sandstone transennas, carved with stylized motifs; there are fine granite columns from Corsica, topped with reused Corinthian columns. The original cupola was dismantled by confused 19th-century restorers, who thought it was from the Renaissance. The interior contains early medieval tombs carved with Lombard-style reliefs, and a total immersion font. In one niche the original blue and white mosaics remain, depicting 12 doves, symbols of the Apostles—the only surviving example of Byzantine art in northern Italy outside Ravenna.

Next to the Baptistry and Loggia Comunale stands the tower (*c.* 1300) of the Palazzo Vecchio del Comune, which now houses the **Museo Civico Ingauno** (*✆ 0182 51215, open Tues–Sun 10–12 and 3–6*), containing finds from the Roman and medieval periods; you can also enjoy a lovely view over Albenga from the top floor. The third tower, also from the same era, was joined in the 17th century to form part of the **Palazzo Peloso Cipolla** ('Hairy Onion Palace'), with a Renaissance-era façade. The interior, frescoed in the 1500s, contains the **Museo Navale Romano** (*✆ 0182 51215, open Tues–Sun 10–12 and 3–6*). Here you'll find wine amphorae and other items salvaged from a 1st-century BC Roman shipwreck discovered near the Isola Gallinaria, as well as 16th–18th-century blue and white pharmacy jars from Albisola. A new section on prehistory, containing recent discoveries from the Val Pennavaira, is being arranged on the ground floor.

Just the north of the cathedral's buxom rounded apse, **Piazzetta dei Leoni** is named after the three 17th-century stone lions brought here from Rome by the wealthy Costa family to show off their handsome **Palazzo Costa Del Carretto di Balestrino** (1525). This is now the residence of Albenga's bishop; the Costa also owned the piazza's medieval house and tower with Ghibelline swallowtail crenellations.

From Piazza San Michele, **Via Bernardo Ricci** (the continuation of the *decumanus*) is lined with medieval porticoes and houses (including yet another tower) and the grandiose 17th-century **Palazzo d'Aste**. Opposite, the former Palazzo Vescovile, decorated with black and white stripes and frescoes attributed to Giovanni Canavesio, now houses the **Museo Diocesano** (*open Tues–Sun 10–12 and 3–6*), containing a handsome collection of 17th-century tapestries, paintings, reliquaries and illuminated manuscripts. Where Via Bernardo Ricci meets Via Medaglie d'Oro, the 13th-century **Loggia dei Quattro Canti** marks the centre of the Roman town, where three more tower houses stand, or rather tilt.

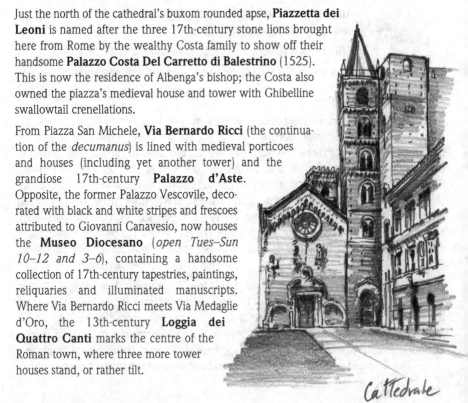

Cattedrale

A short walk from here, east along Viale Pontelungo, will take you to part of the ancient Via Julia and an impressive bridge, the 495ft **Ponte Lungo**, built in the 13th century to span the Cento; apparently it only did the job for a few years before the river changed course. Along the road, note the ruins of the 4th-century basilica of San Vittore, one of the oldest in Liguria.

Around Albenga

Villanova, Garlenda and Campochiesa

Besides asparagus and artichokes and Pigato wine, the plain of Albenga is the site of **Villanova d'Albenga**, laid out in the 13th century as a new town in a polygonal plan by the Clavesana to form an outer defence for Albenga, back when it still dreamed big. Although now minus a large part of its walls and towers, Villanova has kept all of its medieval charm within, a charm augmented by a fondness for potted flowers and plants that cascade in every nook and cranny. Just outside the town stands a round Renaissance church, **Santa Maria della Rotonda**, the kind of geometric ornament more common in Tuscany in the 15th and 16th centuries. Villanova has something else you really don't expect to find on the Riviera: an international airport that has grown from an old air base from the 1920s. Further inland and up into the hills, **Garlenda** is the major resort in these parts, one without a beach but with a fine 18-hole golf course and new hotels and facilities (*see* below).

There's one last sight in the immediate environs of Albenga: **Campochiesa**, on a hill 3km north, where an important series of mid-15th century frescoes decorates the apse of its cemetery church of **San Giorgio**: a *Last Judgement*, based on the description of the *Divine Comedy*, complete with the figures of Dante and Virgil.

Albenga's *Entroterra:* Roads into Piemonte

Two historic mountain roads converge at Albenga: the N453 towards Pieve di Teco and the N582 to Garessio. It's easy to see both by way of a circular route, if you continue up the N28 from Pieve di Teco to Ormea in Piemonte, drive east to Garessio, and from there return to Albenga. The term *via del sale* (salt road) is still used to describe these old routes of exchange between the people of the sea and the people of the Padana, or greater Po valley. One Riviera export in great demand was anchovies, which became an integral part of Piemontese cuisine, especially in its hot vegetable dip, *bagna cauda.*

The N453 follows the *via del sale* to Piemonte, up the river Arroscia up the plain to **Ortovero** and **Pogli**, the latter an important rose-growing centre and scene of a July festival of roses. Further up, **Ranzo** (just before Borghetto d'Arroscia) is the site of the church of **San Pantaleo**, with a pre-Romanesque apse and a 15th-century carved portal with painted frescoes. Those inside were mostly lost when the church was given the old baroque once-over. Continuing up the valley, **Vessálico** is the garlic capital of the Riviera, and honours its fragrant little bulbs in a garlic festival, also in July, making it possible to celebrate both roses and garlic in the same valley on the same holiday.

The key town in these parts is **Pieve di Teco**, its name derived from a Byzantine fort (*teichos*). Its feudal bosses, the Clavesana, rebuilt the castle here, of which a few bits remain, in the 12th century; their much more impressive citadel, which was completely destroyed in the 17th century, was the family's chief stronghold until 1385, when the Republic of Genoa took over and made it the seat of a captain, although his job wasn't easy with the Piemontese coveting the town and control of the salt road. Pieve remains the major market town of the area, and continues to make its bread and cheese the old-fashioned way; workshops still line the main **Corso Ponzoni**. The oldest houses are near the parish church, **Santa Maria della Ripa**, while the 18th-century **Collegiata San Giovanni Battista** has a *Last Supper* by Domenico Piola and a *St Francis de Paul* attributed to Luca Cambiaso.

The road becomes increasingly pretty on the way up to **Pornassio**, which has the *de rigueur* castle and a pretty 15th-century frescoed church, **San Dalmazzo**, in the hamlet of Villa; this area produces good wine, notably a Rossese similar to Dolceacqua's. From here the road winds its way up to the meadows of the **Colle di Nava** (900m) with its fields of lavender and bees that combine to make a famous lavender honey. From here you can turn west, where the narrow but panoramic mountain roads eventually reach Monesi, Liguria's highest ski resort, on the French border. The easier road north leads through the narrow Val Tànaro to **Ormea**, a picturesque medieval town with wrought iron balconies and an old town gate, incorporated into a bell tower. From here it's 12km to Garessio (*see* below).

The second road from Albenga, the N582, follows the river Neva, which is guarded by two impressive medieval castle villages. **Zuccarello** was founded in 1248 by the Clavesana, who lost it to another powerful family, the Del Carretto, who must have been teases, for in the 17th century they ceded their rights, half to Genoa and half to Genoa's rival Savoy. Both, of course, wanted the whole shebang, and their quarrel erupted in the so-called war of Zuccarello, which ended in 1625 with a Genoese victory and total possession of the valley. The amazing thing about Zuccarello is that nothing has happened since: it is so well-preserved that students of the Middle Ages come to examine it, with its perfect main street, lined with lovely porticoes, with gates on either end. Its ruined castle was the birthplace of Ilaria del Carretto, whose beautiful tomb by Jacopo della Quercia is one of the jewels of Lucca.

Further up the valley, the even older **Castelvecchio di Rocca Barbena** sits high on a crag, its castle dating from the 11th century, encircled by the walled village, with magnificent views down the valley. During the war between Genoa and Savoy in 1672, the castle here was the base of the deliciously named Bastion Contrario, the 'Piemontese Robin Hood' (but not so well dressed, the Italians hasten to add), who fought against the wicked Genoese, and eventually lost. From here you can descend by way of Balestrino to Toirano (*see* below), or continue into Piemonte to **Garessio**, a pleasant summer resort back in the days when people wanted to cool off in the summer instead of fry. The main Via Cavour has picturesque houses; the old parish church has a pretty campanile with an octagonal lid.

Garlenda's **Golf Club**, opened in 1965, has 18 holes and is open year-round to the public, ✆ 0182 580 012, ✉ 0182 580 561; the club also has a riding stable, football field, tennis courts, rollerskating rink, gym and *bocci* courts. You'll also find horses to ride at Villanova's **Country Club**, ✆ 0182 580 641. The **airport** at Villanova is the base for a number of air sports—parachuting, gliding and so on; for information ✆ 0182 582 919.

Albenga ✉ 17031

There is not a great choice of accommodation in Albenga, but prices are a good deal cheaper than in the fashionable beach resorts. Family-run ★★★**La Gallinara**, a kilometre south of the historic centre on Via Piave 66, ✆ 0182 53086, ✉ 0182 541 280 (*moderate–cheap*) is another good choice. Near the station you can take a trip back to the 1930s at the **Hotel Italia**, Via Martiri della Libertà, ✆ 0182 50405 (*moderate*), and dine well in the same classy old atmosphere (*open to non-guests*). For beach views, there's the ★★**Sole e Mare**, Lungomare Colombo 15, ✆ 0182 51817, ✉ 0182 52752 (*moderate*), with simple but pleasant rooms.

★**Il Bucaniere**, Lungomare Colombo 8, ✆ 0182 50220 (*cheap*) has basic rooms and a nice garden. If you have a car, ★★★**Ca' di Berta**, 6km east of Albenga at Salea, ✆ 0182 559 930, ✉ 0182 559 888 (*moderate*) is a lovely place to stay, a complex of several stone buildings isolated in the countryside by a swimming pool and solarium. Rooms (all doubles) are well equipped, and there's a good restaurant, **Carlotta**, serving up fresh homemade pasta dishes and Ligurian specialities based on ingredients grown in the owner's garden (*expensive, open to non-guests, closed Wed*).

Little **Cristallo**, a simple family-run restaurant in the centre at Via Cavalieri di Vittorio Veneto 8, ✆ 0182 50603 (*expensive*) is renowned for the freshness of its fish, prepared with a knowing touch in the kitchen. *Closed Mon.* Near the cathedral, the **Antica Osteria dei Leoni**, Via Mariettina Lengueglia 49, ✆ 0182 51937 (*expensive*) offers a change, giving Ligurian seafood a Neapolitan touch—try the lasagne with aubergines and clams. There are also tables ouside. *Closed Mon and two weeks in Oct.* Above Albenga at Monti, you can dine well on Riviera classics at **Punta San Martina**, ✆ 0182 51225 (*moderate*) while enjoying a lovely view from the veranda. For pizza and the best *farinata* in Albenga, join the crowds at the long wooden tables at **Puppo**, Via Torlaro 20, ✆ 0182 51853 (*cheap*).

Garlenda ✉ 17033

★★★★**La Meridiana**, Via ai Castelli 11, ✆ 0182 580 271, ✉ 0182 580 150 (*very expensive*) is a golfer's paradise, next to the course, amid pretty olive groves, ancient oaks and vineyards. A member of the Relais et Châteaux group, it is a contemporary building constructed with traditional stone walls and wooden ceilings, and simple but attractive furnishings. The restaurant is expectedly recherché, serving refined Franco-Italian gourmet dishes, including a delicious breast of duck with caramelized pears. *Open all year.* Golfers with smaller budgets can still be near the links at the ★★★**Golf Club**, at Bra, Via del Golf 7, ✆ 0182 580 013, ✉ 0182 580 561 (*cheap*), which has seven rooms that are simple but nice.

Entertainment and Nightlife

In Albenga, start the evening out in the historic centre, at La Piazzetta degli Artisti, before moving on to dance at **Blackout**, Via Piave 2, small and trendy, with an interesting mixture of rock and funk, or the popular and lively **Moghi**, Regione Moino Pernice 7. In Ceriale, just up the coast there's live **jazz** every night till 3am at the **Blue Monk Pub**, Via Ponetto 2, from local and international performers.

Focaccia al formaggio (*focaccia* with cheese)

250g flour
30ml water
salt
125g butter
four eggs
an egg white
250g groviera cheese, diced

Put the water in a pot with a pinch of salt and the butter and heat it up until the water is just about to boil. Take the pot off the heat, pour in the flour and work energetically with a spoon. Put the pot back on the heat and mix continually until the dough is smooth and begins to stick to the bottom of the pot. Then take the pot from the heat and add the four eggs all at once, stirring constantly. Add the diced cheese (except for three spoonfuls) and mix it all together.

Butter a rectangular cake pan. Pour in the dough and spread evenly. Brush on the egg white and sprinkle on the remaining cheese. Bake at a low temperature and serve hot.

Toirano, Loano and Pietra Ligure

Up the coast from Albenga you'll find the most beautiful and interesting caves along the whole Riviera at Toirano, where our distant ancestors hung out with bears, as well as the popular resorts of Loano and Pietra Ligure.

Tourist Information

Ceriale: Piazza Nuova Italia, ✆ 0182 993 007, ✉ 0182 993 804, *iatceriale@infocomm.it.*

Loano: Corso Europa 19, ✆ 019 676 007, ✉ 019 676 818, *iatloano@infocomm.it.*

Pietra Ligure: Piazza Martiri della Libertà 31, ℗ 019 629 003, ℗ 019 629 790, *iatpietraligure@infocomm.it.*

Borgio Verezzi: Via Matteotti 158, ℗/℗ 019 610 9412, *iatborgioverezzi @infocomm.it.*

Toirano and its Grottoes

Next up the coast from Albenga, **Ceriale** is a small resort with a long beach, palm trees, campsites, and the only **aquapark** in the region, at **Le Caravelle**, Via Sant'Eugenio, ℗ 0182 931 755 (*open April–Sept daily 10–7*), where you'll find loads of slides, chutes and waterfalls for serious wet fun. Just beyond Ceriale, **Borghetto Santo Spirito** is the junction (and bus pick-up point) for Toirano.

Toirano was founded as Varatelia, an outpost of Byzantine Albenga. In the 9th century its fortunes improved when Charlemagne founded a Benedictine abbey on a crag above town, **San Pietro** (the locals like to claim it was founded by St Peter himself); although now only a few ruins remain, this was, until it closed in 1495, one of the major powers in the area, and its monks were pivotal in improving local agriculture, especially the cultivation of the olive. In the 12th century, Toirano came under the bishop of Albenga, and in 1385 the town was annexed by the Republic of Genoa. Some of the walls and defensive towers remain intact—one of the latter was converted into an enormous campanile for the church of **San Martino**, in the charming main piazza. In Toracco, the oldest part of Toriano, tall medieval houses loom over the lanes; a cut stone bridge from the 1100s crosses the river Caratella.

All of this seems spanking new, especially after visiting the caves in the limestone massif, a mile up the valley from Toirano. Some 50 caverns pock these white cliffs, which in the Middle Ages were believed to be entrances to hell, entrances guarded by ocellated lizards, Europe's largest, which can grow to over two feet long if you measure right up to the tip of their tails. The secrets they guard are rather older than hell, however, especially in the **Grotta della Basura** ('of the witch' in Ligurian dialect), where in 80,000 BC Lower and Middle Palaeolithic inhabitants made their abodes; like modern Italians, their Cro-Magnon ancestors had excellent taste, and chose one of the loveliest caves in the region, tarted up by Mother Nature with draperies and designs of pastel-coloured stalactites.

The most intriguing thing about the Grotta della Basura is that the humans apparently had some interesting company: one section is called the **Bear Cemetery**, where masses of bear bones (the extinct *Ursus spaeleus*) were found; another is the **Corridor of the Imprints**, where both bears and humans left foot, hand and knee prints, claw marks, and torch marks, all helter-skelter, as if from some mad prehistoric boogie woogie. Then there's the so-called **Room of Mystery**, where the Homo Sapiens Sapiens (the 'smart smarts', because they had bigger brain pans than we do) hurled balls of clay at the cave wall. Although this is inevitably interpreted as having some religious or ritual significance, it's just as easy to imagine the smart-smarts doing it for the fun of watching them stick. Maybe they bet mastodon steaks on the outcome.

A path from the Grotta della Basura leads to the **Grotta di Santa Lucia**, which more recent residents, especially in the Middle Ages, regarded as a holy place; the spring behind the altar is credited with curing eye diseases, hence the dedication to Lucy, a native of Sicily whose luminous name has made her the patroness of sight—her unpleasant martyrdom, having her eyes gouged out, was a little extra touch added by the martyrologists. Her sanctuary is impressively built into the vertical cliff, next to two needle-like cypresses. A third cave, the **Grotta del Colombo**, is a beautiful natural hypogeum, formed by eons of water melting the limestone (✆ *0182 98062, 1½ hour guided tours of the caves, from 9–12 and 2–5; adm*). The ticket to the caves includes admission to the **Prehistoric Museum of the Val Varatella**, which contains remains found in these and other caverns in the valley, and a reassembled bear skeleton.

Dances with Bears

Have you ever wondered why children respond so viscerally to teddy bears? One possible answer may be sheer atavism: way back in the Middle Palaeolithic or Mousterian culture (120,000–35,000 BC) bears often occupied the same caves as our ancestors, and perhaps not always as dangerous rivals for shelter. The Grotta della Basura is one of the most intriguing examples of possible cohabitation, but it's not the only one. In the 1950s, in the Grotte de Regourdou (next to the famous but much later Cave of Lascaux in southwest France) a bear cemetery from the same era as Basura was found; unlike Basura, where bones were just massed together willy-nilly, some 20 bears were laid out in proper tombs, their bones carefully arranged around their skulls, sprinkled with red ochre dust, and covered with a slab. Around them were the fossilized remains of smaller animals, presumably funerary gifts for the bear to enjoy in the afterlife.

Much later, in the vivid mural art of the Upper Palaeolithic period (20–12,000 BC) in southwest France, bears (like people) are rarely depicted among the bison, horses, mammoths and other favourite animals; there's a fine one engraved in the Grotte du Pech Merle in the Lot, where bears lived for thousands of years; there's another at Lascaux, hidden in the body of a bull, almost as if it were part of a children's find-the-hidden-picture game. Other drawings and etchings in the decorated caves are often accompanied by bear claw marks. People never actually lived in the caves they so beautifully painted, sculpted or etched; they seem to have been holy places, with an important if unknowable religious or ritual meaning. The bears were there, though.

Perhaps the most suggestive of all are carvings found on bone throwing-staffs found at the Upper Palaeolithic shelters at La Madeleine (Dordogne) and Massat (Ariège). Few other works of the period are as explicitly, and mysteriously, sexual; they apparently show the bears licking disembodied human male and female genitalia. Then of course there are the statuettes made by the Old Eskimo, from a culture technologically similar to the Upper Palaeolithic, and demonstrating an intimacy with bears positively shocking, at least by the standards set by Christopher Robin and Winnie the Pooh.

Judging by the various bear cults that survived into historical times, our ancestral relationship with bears was limited to hunting cultures. Two examples come from the Ainu people of northernmost Japan and the indigenous folk of Siberia, where bears were not only an important source of food and clothing, but were also regarded as earthly representatives of the gods. According to their own legends, the Ainu descended from the son of a woman and a bear. Ainu hunters would apologize profusely when they slew one, and set up bear skulls (where the animal's spirit resides) in a place of honour. When a bear cub was captured, it would be suckled by an Ainu woman and raised with her children until its own strength made it a dangerous playmate; then for two or three years it would be put in a cage and pampered with delicacies, in preparation for the Bear Festival. Then the bear would be given a huge last meal in a great show of sorrow, as the Ainu apologized and carefully explained to the bear their reasons for sending it to its ancestors, before it would be ritually strangled and eaten. In his comments on the Ainu in *The Golden Bough*, James Frazer wrote (a hundred years ago, before savage took on its current meaning):

> *the sharp line of demarcation which we draw between mankind and the lower animals does not exist for the savage. To him many of the other animals appear as his equals or even his superiors, not merely in brute force but intelligence; and if choice or necessity leads him to take their lives, he feels bound, out of regard to his own safety, to do it in a way which will be as inoffensive as possible not merely to the living animal, but to its departed spirit and to all the other animals of the same species, which would resent an affront upon one of their kind much as a tribe of savages would revenge an injury or insult offered to a tribesman.*

Another road from Toirano passes the two-hour path up to the ruined monastery of **San Pietro dei Monti** (*see* above) before reaching the medieval village of **Balestrino**, still defended by a picturesque sunbleached **Del Carretto** castle, this one built in the 16th-century residential style.

Above Toirano: A Circular Route through the Forests

This route, through the *entroterra* behind Toirano, to Calizzano and back to the coast at Pietra Ligure, is especially lovely, passing through deep beech and chestnut woods at Colle del Melogno. The road from Toriano rises up the Val Varatella to cheese-making **Bardineto** and the mountain village of **Calizzano**, both medieval Del Carretto properties. Head back to the coast from here, through the enchanting **Colle del Melogno**; lush green and cool in the summer, and golden in the autumn, when the woods echo with the tramp of *porcini* mushroom hunters. On the way back down to the Riviera, don't miss **Bardino Nuova**, site of the **Museum of Tower Clocks** (© 019 637 138), dedicated to a local family who make them, revealing all their inner workings.

Loano and Pietra Ligure

If you've ever spent time in Paris reading the inscription on the Arc de Triomphe you'll recognize **Loano** as the site of Napoleon's first victory in Italy. An attractive, palm-shaded town with a long beach, Loano was one hell of a hot property throughout history. It originally belonged to the bishop of Albenga, who sold it to Oberto Doria in 1263; the Fieschi took it briefly, and then Milan, but in 1547 it was officially bestowed back on the Doria by Emperor Charles V in gratitude for services rendered by its admirals.

The entrance to the old town is through a clock tower gate, built in honour of King Vittorio Amedeo III, who rarely gets honoured with anything, but here gets credit for picking up Loano from the Doria in 1737. Among the town's 16th-century palaces, the biggest is naturally the **Palazzo Doria** (now the Palazzo Comunale); pop in to see the beautiful 3rd-century AD Roman mosaic pavement kept here. Opposite, the 17th-century church of **San Giovanni** has a dodecagonal central plan wearing a peculiar copper cupola cap on its head, added after the earthquake of 1887. The oldest part of town, Borgo Castello, surrounds a castle that the Doria converted into a magnificent villa in the 18th century. The same family also founded, in 1608, the **Monte Carmelo** convent in a panoramic spot in the hills; the church contains numerous Doria tombs.

Another old seaside town and modern beach resort, **Pietra Ligure**, was inhabited back in Neolithic times, when the caves of Monte Trabocchetto were *the* place to stay. In Roman times it was an important stop along the Via Julia Augusta; the Byzantines, feeling rather less secure, built their *Castrum Petrae* high up, where a ruined Genoese castle now stands. Pietra has a mix of medieval buildings and 18th-century palaces; in central Piazza del Mercato, the **Oratorio dei Bianchi** was redone in baroque and has a campanile crowned by a bronze St Nicholas who, according to legend, rang the bell in 1525 to announce the end of a plague. Here too is the late 18th-century church of **San Nicolò di Bari**, dedicated to Pietra's patron (better known as Santa Claus) containing two noteworthy paintings: *St Nicholas Enthroned* by Giovanni Barbegelata, 'Frozen Beard' (1498) and *SS Anthony Abbot and Paul the Hermit* by Domenico Piola (1671).

High above Pietra, the village of **Giustenice** (from *Jus tenens*, 'where one obtains justice') has magnificent views. It once had a proud castle, which, after standing up to a long siege, was razed to the ground by the armies of the Republic of Genoa in 1448 when it made war on Giustenice's lord, Giovanni Del Carretto. In July, Giustenice dresses up in costumes and re-enacts the battles, serves a 15th-century banquet and plays a game of Renaissance football, similar to the famous *calcio storico* in Florence, with no rules whatsoever, much less justice.

Next up the coast, **Borgio Verezzi** is a shade calmer as resorts go. It has two medieval nuclei, most notably Verezzi, set 700ft over the sea. At Borgio you can turn off for

Valdemino and the **Grotta di Valdemino**, a labyrinth of colourful stalactites that goes on and on, but the tour stops after half a mile (*open Tues–Sun 9–11.30 and 2.30–5; adm*).

Where to Stay and Eating Out

Calizzano ✉ 17057

★★★**Hotel Miramonti**, Via Cinque Martiri 6, ✆ 019 79604, ✆ 019 79796 (*cheap*) is a cosy place to stay over, but also an exceptionally good place to eat, which draws in weekend diners around Liguria for its delicious selection of *porcini* mushroom dishes in season; year-round, however, you'll find well prepared *salame*, fresh pasta, game and poultry dishes and homemade comfort desserts on the order of *budino della nonna*, 'Grandma's pudding'. *Closed Mon, except in the summer, Jan, Feb.*

M'se Tutta, Via Garibaldi 8, ✆ 019 79647 (*moderate*) is another good restaurant in a charming old-fashioned setting; the chef adds a touch of class to local ingredients—start with ravioli filled with porcini and finish with a lavender *semifreddo*. *Closed Mon exc in summer, and a month in winter.*

Loano ✉ 17025

★★★★**Garden Lido**, Lungomare N. Sauro 9, ✆ 019 669 666, ✆ 019 668 552 (*expensive–moderate*) overlooks the little port; it has exceptionally well furnished rooms, including VCRs and hydromassage baths, and a wide range of facilities—private beach, pool, gym, bicycles, and a babysitting service.

Peaceful ★★★**Villa Beatrice**, Via S. Erasmo 6, ✆ 019 668 244, ✆ 019 668 245 (*moderate*) offers 30 rooms in an early 19th-century villa, as well as pool, fitness room and private beach. *Closed Oct–mid-Dec.*

Pietra Ligure ✉ 17027

★★★**Grand Hotel Royal**, Via G. Baldo 129, ✆ 019 616 192, ✆ 019 616 195 (*moderate*) might not be quite so grand and royal any more, but it's a fine enough place with a private beach among the palms, where nearly every bedroom and the dining room have sea views; air-conditioning extra. *Closed mid-Oct to mid-Dec.*

Borgio Verezzi ✉ 17022

★★★**Ideal**, near the sea at Via XXV Aprile, at Borgio, ✆ 019 610 438, ✆ 019 612 095 (*moderate*) is a good economical choice with its own beach and recently renovated rooms. *Closed mid-Oct to mid-Dec.*

Borgio also has an exceptional restaurant, **DOC**, Via Vittorio Veneto 1, ✆ 019 611 477 (*expensive*), a romantic place in a refined villa, serving food with the usual emphasis on fresh fish and delicious pasta dishes with garden-fresh vegetables. *Closed Mon, Feb.*

Beyond Borgio and bulky Capo di Caprazoppa ('Lame Goat Cape') begins the territory of Finale Ligure. Way back, 30 million years ago, this was under the sea, where zillions of ancient molluscs turned into reddish limestone.This is now a popular building stone, *pietra di Finale*, in which cliffs and caves eroded over the eons, a magnet not only for prehistoric types looking for a place to hang their hats in old times, but also for modern rock climbers.

Tourist Information

Finale Ligure: Via San Pietro 14, ✆ 019 681 019, 🖷 019 681 804, *iatfinale@infocomm.it*. Also general information office run by the local bus company, Via Mazzini 28, ✆/🖷 019 692 275, near the train station.

Varigotti: Via Aurelia 79, ✆/🖷 019 698 013, *iatvarigotti@infocomm.it*.

Noli: Corso Italia 8, ✆ 019 749 9003, 🖷 019 749 9300, *iatnoli.infocomm.it*.

Spotorno: Piazza Matteotti 3, ✆ 091 741 5008, 🖷 019 741 5811, *iatspotorno@infocomm.it*.

Finale Ligure

Throughout history Finale has been on the edge: its name comes from the long-ago days when it marked the border between two Ligurian tribes, the Ingauni to west of Caprozoppa, and the Sabazi, who lived east of Capo Noli. In Roman times it was the end (*ad fines*) of the municipium of Vada Sabatia. Under the Lombards it separated the western March of Arduinica from the eastern March of Aleramica. The Del Carretto, Marchesses of Arduinica, were the dominant force at Finale and at Noli, and a Ghibelline needle in the side of Genoa.

This lively resort, like so many Riviera towns, has more than one frock in its closet, and actually consists of three Finales, like some very long opera where the fat lady refuses to die. The resort action and nightlife are concentrated in **Finale Marina**, with its wide swathes of fine pebble beaches framed by Caprazoppa. The town of Finale Ligure itself grew up in the mid-15th century, when the coast was clear; its castle changed hands several times between the Del Carretti and the Genoese.

Finale Pia, across the river Sciusa, is older, built around the 12th-century church of **Santa Maria di Pia**, with a Romanesque-Gothic campanile. In the 16th century, the church was joined by a Benedictine abbey, and later given a rococo façade; it has a beautiful 15th-century tabernacle inside. One of the monks' tasks is beekeeping, and a shop sells their honey and sweets, wax and royal jelly.

The medieval village of **Finaleborgo**, two kilometres inland, was founded in 1100 as *Burgus Finarii* by the Del Carretto, destroyed in their ongoing tussle with Genoa and rebuilt in the 15th century by Enrico II Del Carretto. Their impressive if derelict **castle** remains, while the walled town has a splendid ornament, the 13th-century octagonal **campanile** of **San Biagio**, built over one of the defensive towers. The church itself keeps a number of treasures: fine works in marble, including a magnificent pulpit sculpted in 1765 by Pasquale Bocciardo, and a polyptych by 'Cristoforo Pancalino' dated 1540 (*see* p.115). In 1359 the Del Carretto founded the convent of **Santa Caterina**, which had the sad fate of serving as a penitentiary for a century, until 1965; the restoration revealed a good cycle of Tuscan-inspired frescoes from the quattrocento. Its cloisters now contain the **Museo Civico del Finale** (*open June–Sept Tues–Sun 10–12 and 3–6; Oct–May Tues–Sun 9–12 and 2.30–4.30*) housing pottery, an early Christian sarcophagus, palae-olithic Venuses, Neolithic tools, burials, another huge bear skeleton and other items from Finale's caves, most famously the **Grotta delle Arene Candide**, although the most spec-tacular finds are in the regional museum at Pegli.

Just above Finaleborgo, before the *autostrada*, **Perti** is an interesting old place up in the limestone heights. Its 14th-century parish church, **Sant' Eusebio**, has a pretty campanile and Romanesque crypt; a bit further on, isolated in an olive grove, there's **Nostra Signora di Loreto**, a Renaissance gem known as the 'church of five bell towers'. Also near Perti stands all that remains of the **Castel Gavone**, built by Enrico II Del Carretto in the 1180s, destroyed by the Genoese, rebuilt by Giovanni Del Carretto, and destroyed again by the Genoese in 1713, leaving only the picturesque 'Diamond Tower', containing some original frescoes. A pretty path leads up from Finale, beginning at the Spanish castle of San Giovanni.

The lofty patch of *entroterra* between Finale Pia and Noli is now protected as the **Parco della Mànie**, a high-altitude meadow crisscrossed by paths through the pines and Mediterranean flora. One of the most memorable excursions is to make your way along the Roman Via Julia Augusta, which weaves through the Parco della Mànie and the Val Ponci (near Finale Pia), traversing **five Roman bridges** built in 124 AD, when the locals improved the road; one, called the Fairies' Bridge, the **Ponte delle Fate**, is in perfect condition.

The next place up the coast, built on Saracen Bay and tucked under the limestone cape, **Varigotti** is about as picturesque and laid-back as a seaside village can get, its houses painted in rich shades of ochre and pink. The village has a stunning setting, giving directly on to a wide sandy beach and sparkling turquoise sea. This was the Byzantine *Varicottis*, destroyed in 643 by those heavy metal barbarians, Rotari and the Lombards, and only rebuilt in the 14th century by the Del Carretto. Ernest Hemingway was known to have been very fond of it and modern painters seem to find it a very attractive subject. The castle—what remains there are of the Byzantine *castrum* and the Del Carretto fort—can be seen over Punta Crena, while a lone watchtower stands on the summit of the cape. The narrow coastal Via Aurelia, carved out of the bleached cliffs between Varigotti and Capo Noli, is one of the most scenic stretches of road on the Riviera di Ponente; there are rare plants growing on the cliffs, and peregrine falcons can often be spotted soaring over the cape.

Noli: the Fifth Republic

Every Italian schoolchild learns of the four great Maritime Republics of medieval Italy: Genoa, Pisa, Amalfi and Venice. But in Liguria at least they learn that there were really five; at least if you count the not-so-great maritime republic of Noli. Noli's independent spirit goes way back; stories tell how its first inhabitants, unlike the other Ligurians, joined up with the Romans against the Carthaginians. The Byzantines made it their *castrum* Neapolis, which was shortened to Noli by the time the Marchese Del Carretto led its fighting men in the First Crusade in 1097. Like Genoa, Noli fought well enough in the Holy Land to jump-start its career back home. When Savona threatened to take over in the 12th century, Noli allied itself with Genoa and managed to remain an independent republic for 600 years, from 1192 to 1797, when Napoleon wiped it off the map as an anachronism. It's not a bad record, however, and Noli commemorates its centuries of independence with regattas that pit its four quarters, or *rioni*, against one another every September.

Lying under **Monte Ursino** (an impressive white bulk, which some say inspired Dante's description of Purgatory as 'rugged and difficult of access'), Noli even physically resembles a mini Genoa, with its narrow lanes and tall houses. Of its original 72 medieval skyscrapers, eight remain, including the 125ft **Torre del Canto** and the perfectly intact 13th-century **Torre Comunale**, topped with Ghibelline crenellations, next to the Palazzo Comunale. This is on Noli's main street, **Corso Italia**, which once had a portico that sheltered both the people and their boats; a part of this remains, encompassing the **Loggia del Comune**. Note the antique street lamps. Noli's 13th-century **Cattedrale di San Pietro** was covered with a baroque skin, and contains in the apse a polyptych by the school of Lodovico Brea.

Noli's most important monument, however, is the beautiful 11th-century church of **San Paragorio**, one of the finest Romanesque monuments in Liguria. Founded in the 8th century (the date of the sarcophagi that line its left flank) and beautifully restored in the 19th century, the façade is decorated with blind arches in the Lombard style; inside, there's a 13th-century bishop's throne, an ambone, and a 12th-century crucifix called a *Volto Santo* because of the picture on it, said to be a true portrayal of Christ—similar to the more famous one in Lucca. Other medieval buildings to look for in Noli are secular: **Casa Repetto**, the 14th-century tower gate **San Giovanni**, and the **Palazzotto Trecento**. If you have enough puff, there's also a path up to the **castle** on Monte Ursini, built by the Del Carretto in the 12th century. The views are lovely, although you may find Dante's description of Purgatory more than apt on a hot day.

There's a good beach at Noli, and an even better one nearby at **Spotorno**, which has grown into a large resort, but still keeps a 14th-century **castle** tucked in behind all its new development. Off rockbound Capo Maiolo, closing off Spotorno from Savona, is the little islet of **Bergeggi**, now a nature reserve, but used at various times in the past as a monastic retreat and outer defence. To visit, enquire at the Spotorno tourist office. The little seaside village of the same name has one of the most famous restaurants on the Riviera (*see* below).

Sports and Activities

Divers can explore the depths of Finale's coast with Peluffo Sport, Via Molinetti 6, ✆ 019 601 620, while the Lega Navale, in the little port at Capo San Donato, ✆ 019 600 440, can fix you up with a **sailboat**. The *entroterra* of Finale, especially around Pia Finale with its sheer limestone cliffs, is the **rock climbing** capital of the Riviera: the fantastical Rocca di Corno in the Parco Naturale delle Mànie is a special favourite. For information, contact La Pietra del Finale, CAI Guida alla Palestre Finalesi, Via Brunenghi 178, ✆ 019 694 381; if you, too, long to be a human fly, you can take a course at the Rockstore, Piazza Garibaldi 18, ✆ 019 690 208.

Where to Stay and Eating Out

Finale Ligure ✉ 17024

Hotels in Finale Ligure mainly cater to families, and if you arrive without a reservation, there's a hotel finding service, ✆ 019 694 252. *Open June–Sept.* The ★★★**Park Hotel Castello**, Via Caviglia 26, ✆ 019 691 320, ✆ 019 692 775 (*moderate*), near the top of the town, has more character than most and a pretty garden; it's also one of the few that remain open all year. ★★★★**Moroni**, Via San Pietro 38, ✆ 019 692 222, ✆ 019 680 330 (*moderate*) has big, air-conditioned rooms without sea views, or smaller ones with. Seaside ★★★**Medusa**, Lungomare di Via Concezione, ✆ 019 692 545, ✆ 019 695 679 (*moderate, but full pension required*) makes for a good carefree family base for a seaside holiday, with remodelled rooms, satellite TV and breakfast buffet, and discounts at the bathing concession in season.

For a change from the fairly anonymous modern establishments try the ★★★**Conte**, Via Genova 16, ✆ 019 600 670 (*moderate*), in its own secluded garden in a lovely setting. Inside, it's like stepping back in time fifty years—old prints line the walls and period furniture sits in reception. All the rooms are different and large, and some have modern fittings. In the old town, 30 yards from the sea, ★★★**Colibri**, Via Colombo 57, ✆ 019 692 681, ✆ 019 694 206 (*moderate*) is a very efficiently run, modern place, whose rooms have views of the hills. There is also a sun-roof and a good restaurant.

★**San Marco**, Via Concezione 22, ✆ 019 692 533 (*cheap*) is a fairly basic cheap hotel, with a good restaurant, that has the advantage of being right on the seafront. Finale also has a youth hostel, **Wuillermin**, Via Caviglia 46, ✆ 019 690 515.

Raffa, Via Concezione 64, ✆ 019 692 495 (*expensive*) is run by Raffaele Ciuffo, who prides himself on choosing only the freshest of local fish, which is served in an intimate atmosphere. Don't leave without trying the speciality, *pescespada alla Raffa. Closed Wed.* **Torchi**, Via dell'Annunziata in Finaleborgo, ✆ 019 690 531 (*expensive*) has warm *antipasti*, herb-filled ravioli and a couple of meat dishes as well as good fish dishes. *Closed Tues, out of season also on Mon.*

One of the best reasonably priced places to eat is **Al Cantuccio**, Via Torino 54, ✆ 019 691 394 (*cheap*), which offers two fixed-price menus of local delicacies, one around L12,000 and the other at L30,000. There is also a good wine list. For a sweet pick-me-up, stop by **Pasticceria Ferro**, Via Garibaldi 5, ✆ 019 692 753 for its renowned almond *chifferi.*

Above Finale at Perti Alto (follow the signs for Calice Ligure), the **Osteria del Castel Gavone**, ✆ 019 692 277 (*moderate*) offers an exceptionally varied menu that includes plenty of dishes rarely seen in Liguria, including wild boar.

Varigotti ✉ 17029

Appropriately enough on the Baia dei Saraceni, you can stay in arabesque luxury at ★★★★**Nik Mehari**, Via Aurelia 104, ✆ 019 698 096, ✆ 019 698 292 (*expensive*) a modern and comfortable place with a beach and good service. Little Varigotti also has a lovely restaurant, **Muraglia-Conchiglia d'Oro**, Via Aurelia 133, ✆ 019 698 015 (*expensive*), where the menu changes daily and the food is authentic and true—pure flavours and fragrances, and seafood fresh from the sea a few feet away; try *fazzoletti* (traditional Ligurian homemade pasta with scampi) and mouth-watering *grigliata*, or red mullet with citrus. The wine list includes Liguria's finest. Reserve. *Closed Tues, Wed (in summer Wed only), two weeks in Jan and Feb.*

Noli ✉ 17026

An old seaside fort has found a new life as hotel ★★★**Miramare**, Corso Italia 2, ✆ 019 748 926, ✆ 019 748 927 (*moderate*); all rooms have sea views and a touch of class; there's also a garden and a nice breakfast buffet. *Closed Oct–mid-Dec.* ★★★**El Sito**, Via La Malfa 2, ✆ 019 748 107, ✆ 019 748 5871, *elsitop@tin.it* (*moderate–cheap*) is set back in a garden, a peaceful and pleasant family-run place with modern rooms and a delicious sun terrace. *Closed Nov.* In the very centre of Noli, **Pino**, Via Cavalieri di Malta 37, ✆ 019 749 0065 (*expensive*) is an elegant place to dine, and serves up very generous portions of pasta and fresh seafood. *Closed Mon except in summer.*

Friendly **Da Ines**, Via Vignolo 1, ✆ 019 748 086 (*moderate*), in the old town, has Ligurian favourites. For a memorable meal, it's worth seeking out (it's not small, but out of the way) **Lilliput**, 4km up in Frazione Voze, regione Zuglieno 49, ✆ 019 748 009 (*expensive*), for well-executed dishes—even simple ones like *minestrone alla genovese* take on a new quality. There's landfood as well as seafood, and a garden for summer dining. *Closed Mon, closed for lunch Tues–Fri.*

Bergeggi ✉ 17042

The little award-winning ★★★**Hotel Claudio**, Via XXV Aprile 37, ✆ 019 859 750 (*expensive*) combines a lush garden setting and luminous rooms, all with terraces overlooking the sea; there's a pretty pool and beach, and a gorgeous homemade breakfast. *Closed Jan.* Claudio's restaurant is one of the biggest wallet busters in Italy: you won't find dreamier seafood, prepared with a light, expert hand, accompanied by perfect wines and desserts in magical surroundings; but be prepared for a bill at around L170,000 a head. *Closed Mon, Tues lunch, Jan.*

Entertainment and Nightlife

Finale is a hot-spot for nightlife: plenty of bars line the seafront, including **Clipper**, with an old-style atmosphere. **Caffè Caviglia** is a favourite rendezvous just back from the sea in Piazza Vittorio Emanuele. Of the discos, **Caligola**, on Via Colombo, plays mainly dance, and **El Patio**, Lungomare Italia, provides less frantic music for a slightly older crowd. In summer the outdoor **Covo**, Capo San Donato, is a popular club with floors on two levels, while on the other end of town, above the little pleasure port at Finale, **Covo Nord Est** is even more trendy.

Savona

Liguria's second city, Savona offers a pleasant change of pace, and more than one surprise. This is a working town rather than a resort, and one of Italy's busiest ports; if you have nothing else to do, it's fun to hang around the docks and watch the aerial cable cars unload coal for the ironworks at San Giuseppe di Cairo. Savona was always a rival of Genoa; if Genoa is on the main *transmontane* route from Milan, Savona plays a similar role with Turin and the upper Po. In Roman times, there were two towns here: Savo on the rock Priamàr, founded over a Ligurian *castellari* and mentioned by Livy, and Vada Sabatia down by the sea. The Byzantines fortified Savo, and this grew up to become an independent city that Genoa only put under its thumb in 1528.

Wandering about Savona, you'll find that many of the churches store impressive processional floats displaying scenes of the Passion, which go out for a solemn airing on Good Friday.

Tourist Information

Savona: Via Guidobono 125r, ✆ 019 840 2321, ✉ 019 840 3672, *iatsavona@infocomm.it*.

Around the Port

Savona's old port, now filled with pleasure craft, is the most picturesque corner of the city, with its collection of medieval towers. One, the **Torre di Leon Pancaldo**, dates from the 13th century, but was renamed to honour Magellan's pilot who was born in a nearby palace but, like Magellan, never made it home. A niche near the top holds a statue of the

Madonna della Misericordia, the patroness of local sailors. Another tower, the 12th-century **Torre del Brandale**, has some medieval frescoes inside and a great big bell called A Campanassa, which summoned the Savonesi in times of emergency. Merchants built their houses in the portside Piazza Salinera and nearby streets, where they only had to glance out the window to see if their ship had come in. The most important of these, a 16th-century palace, is now the **Camera di Commercio**; if they let you in, have a look at the frescoes along the grand stair, inspired by the work of Perino del Vaga in Genoa. The Palazzo Pozzombello, nearby at Via Monte Grappa 5, was a Jesuit school and contains the **Museo di Scienze Naturali** (*call ✆ 019 829 860 to arrange a visit*) with fossils, including those of a one-of-a-kind beast called an Athracotherium.

Behind the Torre di Leon Pancaldo, portico-lined **Via Paleocapa** is Savona's main shopping street; it has a pretty Liberty-style address, the **Palazzo dei Pavoni** at No.3/5, designed by Alessandro Martinengo, and the 18th-century church of **Sant'Andrea** which contains in the sacristy an icon of St Nicolas from the Hagia Sofia. The nearby **Oratorio del Cristo Risorto** (*open afternoons only*) was rebuilt in 1604 and covered with frescoes, including a mighty *Triumph of God* around the altar. It has fine choir stalls from the late 1400s, made by German sculptors, as well as two small German Gothic paintings. A third church, **San Giovanni Battista**, was built by the Dominicans after the Genoese destroyed their original one on Priamàr, and is well topped up with baroque frescoes and paintings. It stands at the crossroads of **Via Pia**, Savona's medieval high street, lined with elegant palaces. Just up in Piazza Diaz is the monumental **Teatro Chiabrera** (1850), dedicated to Savona's 17th-century poet Gabriello Chiabrera, who composed a fawning epic called the *Amedeide* in honour of the dismal Savoy dukes; the theatre's tympanum depicts the poet presenting his opus to a grateful Duke Carlo Emanuele I in all its provincial glory.

Savona of the Popes

Savona gave the world two della Rovere popes: Sixtus IV, who built the Sistine Chapel in the Vatican, and his nephew, Julius II, who hired Michelangelo to paint its ceiling. Sixtus and Julius left their mark on Savona, too, but more discreetly; their **Della Rovere Palace** (No.28, now the law courts) on Via Pia was designed for Julius while he was still a cardinal by one of the architects of St Peter's, Giuliano da Sangallo. This was lavishly decorated inside, until it became a convent and the prudish nuns plastered over the walls; only the part of the palace now housing the post office retains some of its original frescoes.

In the street behind the Della Rovere palace rises the 16th-century **Cattedrale di Santa Maria Assunta**, hiding behind an 18th-century facade. This contains a number of fine works in marble: a baptismal font made from a Byzantine capital, a *Crucifix*, and a pulpit with symbols of the Evangelists (1522). In the apse, note the magnificent carved choir stalls (1515); in the chapel to the right, the *Madonna enthroned between Saints* is considered the masterpiece of Alberto Piazza, a Lombard painter. There are more goodies tucked away in the **Cathedral Treasury** (*open on request if the sacristan is there, or ✆ 019 825 960*), with a fine *Assumption and Saints* by Lodovico Brea, an *Adoration of the Magi* by the Hoogstaeten master, 14th-century English alabaster statues, and religious items donated by the popes. Through the cloister, inhabited by marble statues of the saints, Savona's own **Sistine Chapel** was built by Sixtus as a shrine to his parents, and later frosted with rococo decorations; it contains a marble tomb of his mum and dad.

The Savonese Captivity

A third pope spent, or rather did, time in Savona, in an affair that marks the nadir of the papacy's international prestige. Petrarch labelled King Philip le Bel's corralling of the 14th-century papacy in Avignon as the 'Babylonian Captivity' but it took an even more brazen French agent named Napoleon physically to arrest a pope to try to bend him to his will. Napoleon, declaring himself the new Charlemagne, had forced his Code Napoléon on the papal states in 1801, along with a Concordat that made the Gallican Church practically autonomous. Pius VII had no choice but to go along or risk losing the papal states altogether, but he balked when Napoleon-Charlemagne ordered him in 1808 to expel all British ministers from Rome and not to allow British ships into his ports. Napoleon responded by invading the papal states and revoking the pope's rights to a temporal state; Pius, a mild-mannered liberal, replied by excommunicating Napoleon; Napoleon ordered his police to keep this a secret (they failed), and had Pius arrested and imprisoned in Savona's bishop's palace.

Napoleon did all he could to browbeat Pius, even taking away the Pope's pen and ink when he discovered that he had secretly sent out letters ordering the Church not to accept the Napoleon-appointed bishops. When the chips were down and Napoleon wanted to negotiate with the Pope to appease the allies, he had his prisoner brought to Fontainebleau in a journey that nearly killed him. After being treated extremely rudely by Napoleon for a week, the Pope signed a new Concordat that gave him everything he wanted, except the papal states; in 1813, when the Allies were invading France, Napoleon offered to give these back to the Pope as well. Pius replied that no treaty was necessary for the return of stolen property—a remark that earned him a return to Savona to cool his heels. He was only released and allow to return to Rome in March 1814, when the Allies had reached the outskirts of Paris, and the papal states, 'so awful that even the earth refuses to swallow them up' as Goethe put it, limped on until 1870.

In the street behind the cathedral, the **Oratorio Nostra Signora di Castello** (*open Sundays only*) contains the finest painting in Savona: a polyptych of the *Madonna and Saints* from the late 1400s, begun by Vincenzo Foppa and completed by Lodovico Brea.

Fortezza di Priamàr and its Museums

Savona once had a medieval core called Savo on a hill, with most of its houses, a Romanesque cathedral and churches, but in 1542 the Genoese, who really knew how to bear a grudge, razed the lot to build their fortress, **Priamàr**—not to protect Savona, but to keep it in its place after clobbering it in 1528. These days Savona uses the massive pile for four museums. The **Pinacoteca** (*open Mon–Sat 8.30–12.30*) houses two excellent 15th-century *Crucifixions*, one by Donato De Bardi (from Pavia) and the other by Giovanni Mazone, who also painted the beautiful polyptych of the *Annunciation, Calvary and Saints*. Most of the other works are from the 17th and 18th centuries, offering a chance to become acquainted with the dubious baroque talents of Robatto, Ratti, Fiasella, Brusco and others. Another room is dedicated to ceramics, made in Savona since the 1500s. Modern Italian art given to politician Sandro Pertini over his long career now forms the **Museo Sandro Pertini** (*same hours*), including works by De Pisis, Guttuso and Manzù; from here a walk through the underground passages of the citadel will take you to the **Museo Renata Cuneo** (*same hours*), dedicated to sculptures by Savona native Renata Cuneo, who among other works sculpted several Good Friday floats. The **Museo Archeologico** (*© 019 822 708, open 10–12.30, 3–7, summer 4–6 , closed Sun morning and Mon*) contains artefacts, including ancient Greek and Etruscan ceramics, found on this very hill.

There's an art encore 6km above Savona (take the road from Piazza Aurelio Saffi) in a hamlet called Santuario, where a theatrical piazza holds the **Santuario di Nostra Signora della Misericordia**. This was begun in the 1550s and completed in 1610 by Taddio Carlone, who finished the striking façade. Inside, there's a dramatic *Nativity of the Virgin* by one of Caravaggio's best followers, Orazio Borgianni (second chapel on the right) and, in the third chapel on the left, a superb marble relief of the *Visitation*, believed to be by Bernini.

Savona's *Entroterra*

Thick forests mark Savona's hinterland, which also has the traditional boundary between the Alps and the Apennines at **Bocchetta di Altare di Cadibona**. The trees were used to build ships and fuel the furnaces of **Altare** (on the SS29), a town famous for glassmaking since the 12th century at least. Altare has a museum devoted to the subject, as well as a handful of Liberty-style villas.

Beyond this, **Millesimo** (connected by bus to Savona) is a charming, fortified hill town with a ruined Del Carretto castle of 1206, where even the 15th-century bridge, the **Gaietta**, has a watch tower. Millesimo has a fine 11th-century Romanesque church, **Santa Maria Extra Muros**, restored to its original appearance, and a neoclassical **Santuario della Madonna del Deserto** (1725), frescoed and full of *ex votos*. The town, with a clutch of artisans' workshops, is a popular excursion destination, not least because of its pastry shops selling scrumptious rum chocolates called *millesimini*. Above, on the Colle di Millesimo, there's a rare menhir and a few incisions, similar to the Vallée des Merveilles.

The best scenery is north of Dego (backtrack a bit and turn north at Cárcare) in the little **Parco Regionale di Piana Crixia**, where the rocky landscape is eroded into peculiar forms, including a giant mushroom near the hamlet of Borgo.

Savona ✉ 17100

By the sea, ★★★★**Mare**, Via Nizza 89r, ✆ 019 264 065, ✉ 019 263 277 (*expensive–moderate*) is the nicest hotel in town, with every comfort and an exquisite seafood restaurant with a funny name, **Spurcacciun-A** (*open to non-guests*) where you can dine outside by the sea or in the luminous dining room. The special seven-course menu is a seafood-lovers' heaven, each course served with its own wine (around L130,000); other simpler menus are also available. Leave room for the bitter chocolate soufflé at the end. *Closed Wed, and a month in winter.*

Also near the sea, ★★★**San Marco**, Via Leoncavallo 4, ✆ 019 813 660, ✉ 019 813 688 (*moderate*) makes a good tranquil base. Savona also has two youth hostels, **Ostello Priamàr**, Corso Mazzini, ✆ 019 812 653 (*open all year*) and the **Villa De Franscheschini**, Via alla Strà 29, ✆ 019 263 222 (*open mid-March–mid-Oct*). Besides the Spurcacciun–A, Savona isn't a big restaurant town, but **Oreste**, Vico Gallico 11/13r, ✆ 019 821 166 (*moderate*) has a good name for traditional cuisine. *Closed Sun.*

On to Genoa

There are some good beaches along this coast, before you strike greater Genoa, that long, long tapeworm of a city that has swallowed up many old fishing towns and villa suburbs in its wake. Because of their proximity to both Savona and Genoa, these resorts are favourites for a lazy day by the sea.

Tourist Information

Albissola Marina: Via dell'Oratorio 2, ✆ 019 400 2008, ✉ 019 400 3084.

Celle Ligure: Via Boagno, in the Municipio, ✆ 019 990 021, ✉ 019 999 9798.

Varazze: Viale Nazioni Unite 1, ✆ 019 935 043, ✉ 019 035 016.

Arenzano: Lungomare Kennedy, ✆/✉ 010 912 7581.

Albisola, for Ceramics

Like many Riviera towns, **Albisola** (from the Latin *Alba Docilia*) has a split personality, but in this case the two sides have been separate *comuni* since the 16th century: the seaside **Albissola Marina** and the upper **Albisola Superiore**. Together they form Liguria's most important ceramics centre, making plates and pots and decorative tiles since the mid-15th century, using the rich red clay from the plain behind the city. Although production plummeted in the 19th century, it began to revive in 1891, when Nicolò Poggi began to create Liberty art pieces. A bit later, Tullio di Albisola made the town a centre of the Futurist ceramics, and Albisola hasn't looked back since. There are several permanent exhibits: the 18th-century **Villa Durazzo Faraggiana**, set in a lovely garden in Albissola Marina, has its original furnishings, including a gallery paved in blue and white majolica tiles, as well as a museum on the history of ceramics (*open summer 3–6.30*); the Futurist **Fabbrica Casa-Museo Giuseppe Mazzotti** (1903), Viale Matteotti 29 (✆ 019 489 872), with works by contempory Italian and foreign artists; and the **Museo della Ceramica Trucco** on Corso Ferrari 195, in Albisola Superiore (*open Mon–Sat 10–12*), where you'll also find the **Scuola di Ceramica**, ✆ 019 482 295, which holds summer courses if you're inspired.

There's more, including proof that self-indulgence is nothing new. A vast Roman Imperial **villa** was recently excavated in the middle of Albisola's plain, an enormous agricultural estate from the time when small landowners were being increasingly taxed into selling themselves into serfdom just to survive. There's a beautiful pebble mosaic in front of the church of **Nostra Signora della Concordia** in Albissola Marina, and, up in Albisola Superiore, the **Palazzo Gavotti**, a 15th-century villa that the last Doge of Genoa, Francesco Maria della Rovere, converted into a sumptuous residence (1739–1753).

The *Entroterra*: Sassello and Monte Béigua

Up in the Ligurian Apennines on the SS334 from Albisola, **Sassello** is a popular summer resort that always remains fresh and cool; in winter people come here from the coast to play in the snow. Its name comes from the Statielli Ligurians, and it eventually fell into the hands of the Doria, who built the walls around the lower town, the Bastia Sottana. Sassello still looks pretty much as it did in the 18th century, although only the memory remains of its old iron manufacturers, who combined ore shipped up from Elba with their abundant water power and forests that kept the furnaces ablaze. Paths lead into the woods, which are filled with mushroom hunters in the autumn. Stop in a *pasticceria* to try the local *baci* (kisses)—unlike the famous ones from Perugino, these are *amaretti*, and among the best you'll find in Italy.

From Sassello you can follow a scenic circular route further into the Apennines by way of **Urbe**. This area was long owned by the Cistercian abbey at **Tiglieto**, founded in 1120—perhaps the first one in Italy, although it was later converted into a private residence. There's a pretty stone bridge, and a favourite swimming hole just below. From Tiglieto or Urbe you can head back south through the densely wooded **Parco Naturale del Monte Béigua** (1287m), encompassing the striking rocky outcrop of Béigua which, like that mountain of similar name, Bégo in the Val Roja (*see* pp.88–9), provided a canvas for shepherds to scratch their thoughts from prehistoric times up to the Middle Ages—hence the many crosses. These mountains are rich in titanium, a mineral needed for the manufacture of computer components, although so far the ecologists have won the battle to keep Béigua unscarred by the gaping pits that would be required to extract the stuff. Another road from Urbe crosses over the **Passo di Faiallo**, with a fantastic view over Genoa and as far as Corsica, views that continue east along the road to the Passo del Turchino; from here the SS456 will take you back to the coast at Voltri, in the suburbs of Genoa.

Celle Ligure and Varazze

In spite of its long, popular sandy beach, **Celle Ligure** has maintained its integrity, a colourful old seaside town, one backed by hills that keep it snug. In the centre, a theatrical stair leads up to the parish church **San Michele**, which has kept its 12th-century campanile and, inside, a polyptych of *SS Michele, Pietro and Giovanni* by Perino del Vaga (1535), as well as a peculiar *Crucifixion* in the shape of a tree. The *comune* has an extremely pretty and panoramic pine grove to the west, the **Pineta Bottini**, the perfect place for a picnic, perhaps with a bottle of Celle's own dry white wine, Lumassina, and a plate of *lumasse* (snails), the food that goes so well with it that it gave the wine its name.

Varazze, the major beach resort in these parts, has always had shipyards; its name in Roman times was *Ad Navalia*, which over the centuries became Varagine, and then Varazze. In the 13th century, when it was still Varagine, it produced one of the best-selling authors of the Middle Ages, Jacopo da Varagine. He was a Dominican friar who became an archbishop and wrote the *Golden Legend*, which, among its lives of the saints, included the story of the *Invention of the Cross* which quickly became a favourite subject for painters, especially Piero della Francesca's unforgettable cycle in Arezzo. Varazze was also the birthplace of the Lanzarotto Maloncello, a discoverer of the Canary Islands, one of which takes his name. The shipyards of Varazze built many of the ships for the Third Crusade in 1246, and are famous these days for their Cantieri Baglietto, manufacturers of some of Italy's most prestigious yachts.

Varazze's centre, or *borgo*, is still partly surrounded by city walls, which incorporate the façade (but, strikingly, nothing else) of the 10th-century church of **Sant'Ambrogio**. The rebuilt 1535 Sant'Ambrogio, with a lovely Romanesque-Gothic campanile, contains a rare work by an excellent Genoese painter, Giovanni Barbagelata (1500), a polyptych of *St Ambrose with saints and angel musicians*, and a statue of *St Catherine of Siena* by

Anton Maria Maragliano; in 1300 her prayers to rid Varazze of the plague succeeded, an event commemorated every 30 April with a historic procession. On the west end of Varazze, **SS. Nazario e Celso** is another Romanesque church hiding behind a baroque façade, with a rather grand pebble mosaic of 1902. A third church, **San Domenico**, has the tomb of the locally canonized 'saint' Jacopo as well as a cannonball embedded in its façade, fired by a French ship in 1746.

Inland, a favourite trip is up to the Franciscan convent, the **Eremo del Deserto**; although the region is fairly deserted it's hardly a desert, but lush and well watered, with walking and riding paths radiating into the southern confines of the Parco Naturale del Béigua (*see* above). There's a small archaeology museum in **Alpicella**, with finds from the various prehistoric sites in the area; it also has a picturesque little bridge, built by the Saracens.

Last Stops before Genoa: Cogoleto and Arenzano

A pretty seaside path, the 5km **Lungomare Europa**, replaces the old railway line from Varazze to **Cogoleto**. According to one tradition, Cogoleto was the birthplace of Columbus. At least everyone in the village thinks so, and they've erected a statue and plaque to him in the main piazza.Their conviction is based on a Latin document dated Cogoleto, August 23 1449, that states: 'Maria, wife of Domenico daughter of Jacobi Justi de Lerdra in Cogoleto resides in Cogoleto, with three sons, Christophor, Bartholomé et Jacopo recently born.' Of course, this is only another spanner in the Columbian mystery works; if true, it would make Christopher about ten years older than his accepted birth-date of 1450 does. One explanation is that the names are a sheer coincidence. Nevertheless, a house in town has a venerable history as Columbus' birthplace, and in 1650 a priest named Antonio Colombo living in the house wrote three inscriptions on the façade. One says: *Unus erat mundus; duo sunt ait iste, fuere.* ('There was but one world; let there be two said he, and it was so'.)

Arenzano is another resort dotted with villas and a famous Grand Hotel (*see* below), its *lungomare* planted with palms dating from the late 19th century. It has a little port and, in the pine woods west of town, the **Golf Tennis Club della Pineta** (℘ 010 911 1854); the old part of town is full of boutiques, and there's a pretty park to laze about in, around the 16th-century hilltop **Villa Pallavicini-Negrotto-Cambiaso**, now the town hall. For all that, the main draw in Arenzano is the modern Sanctuary of the Christ Child of Prague.

Where to Stay and Eating Out

Albissola Marina ✉ 17012

> ★★★★**Garden**, Viale Faraggiana 6, ℘ 019 485 253, ✆ 019 485 255 (*moderate*) offers very good value, tranquillity, air-conditioning, bright modern rooms and a pool. All rooms have terraces, and most have sea views. The same owners run the slightly less luxurious ★★★**Villa Chiara**, Viale Faraggiana 5, ℘ 019 480 590, ✆ 019 485 255 (*moderate*), a Liberty-style villa with plenty of character and a garden and sun

terrace. *Closed Nov–Easter.* Get a table at elegant **Gianni ai Pescatori**, Corso Bigliati 82, ✆ 019 481 621 (*expensive*) for generous portions of the classics lovingly prepared (including *bistecca alla fiorentina*, if you can't bear to look at another fish). *Closed Tues.*

Familiare, Piazza del Popolo 8, ✆ 019 489 480 (*moderate*) is a first-rate trattoria, with fish but also plenty of fresh vegetable dishes. *Closed Mon.*

Celle Ligure ✉ 17015

★★★**Villa Costa**, Via Monte Tabor 10, ✆ 019 990 020, ⌨ 019 993 608 (*moderate–cheap*) is just back from the beach, a pleasant place with big ceiling fans and a large terrace for lounging around; nearly all rooms have sea views.

★★**San Marco**, Via Cassisi 4, ✆ 019 990 269 (*cheap*) is simple and near the pines and sea; no restaurant. *Open April–Sept.*

You'll dine well in a pretty, light-filled setting at **Bolero**, Lungomare Crocetta 7, ✆ 019 993 448 (*moderate*), where top quality land- and seafood is prepared with a refined touch; good homemade desserts, too, especially the crème brûlée. *Closed Mon, Nov.*

Varazze ✉ 17019

★★★★**Torretti**, Viale Nazioni Uniti 6, ✆ 019 934 623, ⌨ 019 932 854 (*moderate*) is one of the oldest hotels in Varazze, close to the sea and recently refurbished without sacrificing its charm.

Up above Varazze in Piani d'Invrea, ★★★★**El Chico,** Strada Romana 63, ✆ 019 931 388, ⌨ 019 932 423 (*expensive*) is a modern Mediterranean-style building in a much older park; tranquil and relaxing, with a pool and gym, as well as a reading room, game room and billiards room.

★★★★**Cristallo**, Via F. Cilea 4, ✆ 019 97264, ⌨ 019 96392 (*moderate*) offers exceptionally well-equipped rooms with air-conditioning, as well as a playground, gym and a private beach.

★★★**Cocodrillo**, Via N. Sardi 16, ✆ 019 932 015, ⌨ 019 932 588 (*cheap*) has a pool and a good restaurant, and a pleasant garden atmosphere. For some succulent variations on Ligurian seafood **Antico Genovese**, Corso Colombo 70, ✆ 019 96482 (*expensive*) will not disappoint: the *cuscus di gamberi* is a delicious starter, and there are so many wines on the list it's genuinely hard to choose; elegant service, too. *Closed Sun.*

The extremely popular **Cavetto**, Piazza Santa Caterina 7, ✆ 019 97311 (*moderate*) offers a good mix of land- and seafood, including great homemade pasta with homemade pesto. *Closed Thurs.* Up in Alpicella, wild boar, either stewed with polenta or in ham or salami, holds pride of place at the **Piccolo Ranch**, Via Monte Beigua 7, ✆ 019 918 058 (*moderate*); in the autumn, you'll also find an inspiring *fettuccine al tartufo.*

Arenzano ✉ 16011

The majestic neo-Renaissance ★★★★**Grand Hotel,** Lungomare Stati Uniti, ✆ 010 91091, 📠 010 910 9444 (*very expensive–expensive*), built in the 1920s, has 110 rooms with everything you need, from satellite TV to your own fax machine in the stylish, sound-proof rooms; private parking, pool and beach, and a fitness salon to work or sauna away any excess calories you may have acquired in the hotel's excellent restaurant, La Veranda. Another good choice, near the train station and sea, ★★★**Poggio**, Via di Francia 24, ✆ 010 913 5321, 📠 010 913 5320 (*moderate*) also has a pool and comfortable rooms, with optional air-conditioning.

Cima alla Genovese

1 breast of veal weighing two kilos

For the stuffing:
300g lean veal (mixed with brains and sweetbreads, if you prefer)
25g shelled pistachios
25 pine nuts
2 artichoke hearts, chopped
75g peas
a handful of dried mushrooms
chopped marjoram
chopped garlic
6 eggs, beaten
50g parmesan
50g breadcrumbs
salt and pepper

Boil the meat for the stuffing in salted water until half cooked. Reserve the broth and chop the meat finely. Mix it with the pistachios, pine nuts, artichoke hearts, peas, mushrooms, marjoram, garlic, eggs, parmesan, breadcrumbs moistened in the broth, and add salt and pepper to taste. Stuff it in the opening of the veal breast and sew the opening together. Pierce the breast with a needle. Cook in the broth for three hours.

Piazza de' Ferrari

Genoa (Genova)

For various days I lived in real ecstasy...Paris and London, in the face of this divine city, look insignificant, as simple agglomerations of houses and streets without any form.

Richard Wagner, 1825

There's always a tingling air of danger, excitement, unexpected fortune or sudden disaster in real port cities. The streets are enlivened with sailors, merchants, travellers and vagrants of all nationalities, and you're always aware of the volatility of the sea itself, ready to make or break a fortune. Of the country's four ancient maritime republics (Venice, Amalfi and Pisa are the others), only Genoa has retained its salty tang and thrill. It is Italy's largest port, and any possible scenic effect it could have, enhanced by its beautiful location of steep hills piling into the sea, has been snuffed out by the more important affairs of the port: a godawful elevated highway, huge docks, warehouses, stacks of containers and unloading facilities hog the shoreline for miles, so that from many points you can't even see the sea. And behind the docks wind the dishevelled alleys lined with typical piquant portside establishments that cater to weasely men of indeterminate nationality, old pirates and discreetly tattooed ladies.

Counterbalancing this fragrant zone of stevedores is the other Genoa, the one that Wagner, Rubens, Dickens and countless other travellers have marvelled at, the one that Petrarch nicknamed *La Superba*, the Superb City (or 'Proud', as in one of the Seven Deadly Sins) of palaces, gardens and art; the city whose merchant fleet once reigned supreme from Spain to the southern Russian ports on the Black Sea, the city that gave the Spaniards Columbus but which in return controlled the contents of Spain's silver fleets until it became the New York City of the late 16th and 17th centuries, flowing with money, ruled by factions of bankers and oligarchs, populated by rugged individualists and entrepreneurs, all while the rest of Italy languished. Genoa even left a mark in the fashion industry with its silks and a sturdy blue cotton cloth the French called *de Gênes*, which came to be made into jeans.

Modern Genoa (pop. 680,000) is like a double dose of java after too many lazy days on a Riviera beach. Even its impossible topography is exciting: squeezed between mountains and sea, the city stretches for 30 kilometres—there are people who commute to work by lift or funicular. Tunnels bore under green parks in the very centre of the city, and apartment houses hang over the hills so that the penthouse is at street level. The old quarter is a vast vertical warren of alleys, or *carrugi*—miniature canyons under eight-storey palaces and tenements, often streaming with banners of laundry. Elsewhere, you'll notice the famous aloofness of 'multi-marbled Genoa' as Thomas Hardy called it, in the quiet stately marble streets lined with late Renaissance and baroque palaces, in its collections of Grand Masters, and in one of the most amazing cemeteries on earth.

And now there's more. The Columbus exhibition in 1992 inspired a new razzmatazz spirit in Genoa: its bomb-damaged buildings, in particular the Teatro Carlo Felice and Palazzo Ducale, have been restored to bring big league culture back into the heart of La Superba. It was also the year when the Genoese followed in the footsteps of Baltimore and Barcelona and reclaimed some of their seafront for themselves, taking over the former liner port for the Americas, the Porto Antico, and building and restoring there to create a stunning range of attractions for all ages.

History

Genoa's destiny was shaped by its geography, not only as the northernmost port on the Tyrrhenian Sea, but as a port protected and isolated by a ring of mountains. It was already a trading post in the 6th century BC, when the Phoenicians and Greeks bartered with the native Ligurians. Later the city was a stalwart outpost of the Roman Empire, and as such suffered the wrath of Hannibal's brother Mago Barca in 205 BC; rebuilt after his sacking, it remained relatively happy and whole until the Lombards took and occupied it in 641, initiating a dark, troubled period. While Amalfi, Pisa and Venice were busy creating their maritime republics in the 10th and 11th centuries, Genoa was still an agricultural backwater, far from the main mercantile and pilgrimage routes of the day, its traffic dominated by Pisa, its coasts prey to Saracen corsairs.

Adversity, more than anything, formed the Genoese character. Once it rallied to defeat the Saracens, the city began a dizzily rapid rise to prominence in the 12th century. It captured Corsica, and joined forces in the First Crusade with the Norman Prince Bohemond of Taranto, helping him to conquer Antioch and asking as its reward the right to establish trading counters in the Near East. The Genoese took to trade like ducks to water, and by the next century they had established similar counters and colonies stretching from Syria to Algeria, including the whole district of Pera in Constantinople. The city walls had to be enlarged in 1155, and as the city quickly expanded so did the bravado of the Genoese. At the siege of Acre Richard the Lionheart was so impressed by their courage that he placed England under the protection of Genoa's patron St George, took the red cross from the banner of Genoa and made it the national flag of England.

It wasn't long before business competition with Pisa grew into a battle of blows. Genoa lost the first round at Meloria in 1241, but the turning point came in 1284, at the same location. Both cities were willing to risk all, and according to the chroniclers of the day every able-bodied man on their respective coasts was on board to do battle on nearly equal fleets; but luck (in the form of a strong wind) was with Genoa, and she pummelled Pisa into naval obscurity. Five thousand Pisans perished, and another 11,000 were taken captive and held in ransom for the island of Sardinia, which Genoa coveted; the Pisans preferred to die in prison.

After Pisa, Genoa's only rival in the east was Venice. In 1293, an accidental encounter between the Genoese and Venetian galleys off Cyprus started a vicious war. This time Genoa won the first round, when Admiral Lamba Doria crushed the Venetians at the Curzonali Islands in 1298, burning 66 galleys and bringing 7000 prisoners (including Marco Polo) in triumph to Genoa; the next year the Venetians sued for peace. The Genoese were acclaimed as the bravest and best of mariners; its merchant colonies spread even further afield, from the Black Sea to Spain, and its captains were the first to sail to the Canaries and the Azores.

Medieval Genoa, in spite of its lack of any agricultural hinterland, was one of the most densely populated cities in Europe. Its patricians constructed those characteristic towering houses that seemed so 'superb' to visitors; its fame was so widespread that Genoa appears even in the *Arabian Nights*, the only Western city to be so honoured. At the same time, one of of the most popular fairytales told in Genoa was called 'Money Can Do Everything' and goes about proving just that: who needs goodness or magic, when you have money and cleverness?

Punch and Judy, and Simone Boccanegra

> *Party conflicts here assumed so fierce a character, and disturbed so violently the whole course of life, that we can hardly understand how, after so many revolutions and invasions, the Genoese ever contrived to return to an endurable condition.*
>
> Jacob Burckhardt, *The Civilization of the Renaissance in Italy*

What Genoa singularly failed to do, unlike Venice or Pisa, was govern itself. Genoa's first golden age was marred, as all subsequent ones were to be, by civic strife and turmoil that were disgraceful even by Italian standards. The individualistic, stubborn Genoese never developed any sense of community; every enterprise was privately funded, including most of the city's military expeditions. Like Pisa and Venice, Genoa's merchant-captains brought great treasures and holy relics back from the east, including the relics of St John the Baptist, but they failed to translate their achievement on to any higher plane. Genoa has no Field of Miracles to match Pisa, no Basilica of San Marco to rival Venice; nearly all the medieval art it does have was made by other hands. It was a Republic not by virtue of its institutions but by default. Even Dante found Genoa notably lacking: 'Sea without fish, hills without wood, men without honour, women without shame.' The Genoese achievement, in fact its miracle, is how such a weak and fragmented state not only survived, but actually prospered.

The Republic itself was divided into factions based on hereditary enmity: prominent Guelphs (the Grimaldi and Fieschi) against prominent Ghibellines (the Doria and Spinola); nobles against the mercantile classes; the merchants against the artisans or *popolano*. Each faction dominated its own quarter of the city, forming brotherhoods, or *alberghi*, of their partisans, running their own prisons and armies, and constantly fighting for political control of the city. For two centuries Genoese civic history is an ignoble chronicle of one faction after another gaining the upper hand, while all the others did everything to undermine it. In times of danger, however, these same irksome noble families, especially the Doria, consistently produced brilliant admirals that the Genoese relied on in a pinch. In admiration for their heroes, the *popolano* would join in their blood feuds until they became sick of them again.

The arrival in 1311 of Emperor Henry VII made things worse. At first he was greeted as a saviour by all the factions, and the Genoese declared him absolute sovereign of their republic for 20 years in the hopes that he would enforce the peace that they were always breaking. The emperor, however, soon alienated the Genoese by demanding a 'gift' of 60,000 florins for his services. Life quickly became precarious for the imperial party, and the emperor was glad when a Pisan fleet arrived in 1312 to take him away, while Genoa's Guelphs and Ghibellines overheated to the point of meltdown.

In 1339 the common people won a victory by excluding all the nobles from the government. Admiring the government of Venice, they elected Genoa's first doge, Simone Boccanegra (1301–63), who five hundred years later would become the hero of Verdi's opera. Boccanegra was a lover of liberty and didn't use his position to take more power, but like most Italian politicians he used it to take more money and raised taxes so high that the nobles exiled him to Pisa and invited in the Visconti of Milan. The Visconti behaved as badly as ever, driving Genoa to revolt a few years later; Boccanegra returned and was re-elected doge in 1356, but died suddenly seven years afterwards. Although the original idea had been to elect doges 'in perpetuity' on the Venetian model, Boccanegra was one of only four to die while in office. It was far more common for a doge to be forced to resign on the day of his election.

Meanwhile, rivalry with Venice was heating up again into a fourth hot war for Eastern Mediterranean trade. In 1378 the Venetians sided with the Cypriots in their quarrel with the Genoese and defeated them in a battle fought in a raging tempest. The Genoese sent Admiral Lucian Doria to exact revenge, and when the two fleets met again at Pola, Doria was slain, which infuriated the Genoese sailors: the Venetian fleet was nearly annihilated. Scenting blood, the Republic appointed Pietro Doria to finish off the kill. He started by besieging Chioggia, the southernmost port of the Venetian lagoon, aided by the lord of Padua and the king of Hungary. All refused to accept any terms; Pietro Doria declared he would not leave until he had 'bridled the horses of St Mark with his own hand'.

This time luck was on Venice's side. Her fleet from the east arrived in the nick of time, and blockaded the Genoese at Chioggia; Genoa sent a new fleet into the Adriatic to succour them, but the trapped and starving Genoese were unable to escape, and surrendered with honour. Venice was just as exhausted and glad to put an end to the war. It did mark the end of Genoa's leading role in the east, a blow followed by the loss of most of its colonies to the rising power of the Ottomans.

In the aftermath, in 1382, new Genoese families—the Adorni for the Guelphs, the Fregosi for the Ghibellines—arose from the merchant class to contest the authority of the established power brokers. As soon as they took control, they and their *alberghi* behaved no better than the Doria or Spinola, who remained excluded from power. The Fregosi alone contributed 13 doges; when one, Domenico Fregoso, deposed Gabriel Adorno in 1370, the republic was plunged into its usual state of civil war. Life hit such a nadir that both families threw up their hands in despair and on several occasions gave the lordship of the Republic to foreigners, in the slim hope that they could calm the city's heartburn—Savoy for periods in 1382 and 1390, France in 1396, Monferrat in 1409, Milan in 1463, and France again in 1499.

Bankers to the Rescue

The real power turned out to be a bank. During Genoa's wars with Venice, the city's creditors—Genoa's oligarchs—formed a syndicate, the Casa di San Giorgio, to guarantee their increasingly precarious loans. This the bank did by gradually assuming control of the city's overseas territories, castles, towns, and even its treasury. By the 15th century Genoa, for all practical purposes, was run as a business proposition—once, in 1421, when the bank had a cash flow problem, it sold Livorno to Florence for a tidy sum. One writer in the last century aptly described the Bank of St George as the Bank of England combined with the East India Company, with the added responsibility of collecting the Republic's taxes. The Genoese never had the slightest reason to identify with their government like the Venetians, but, as Machiavelli noted, they were very loyal to their bank.

By forcing the Genoese to transform their economy from the mercantile sphere to the financial, the defeat at Chioggia was actually a blessing in disguise. By the 16th century, the city's population was around 85,000, and the opening up of new sea routes around the Horn of Africa and discoveries in the New World by two native Genoese, Christopher Columbus and Giovanni Caboto, were quickly making its old Mediterranean sphere of influence obsolete. But with the Bank of St George and its exquisite accounting methods (necessary to avoid charges of the sin of usury), no place in Europe was better poised to deal with the great influx of wealth brought over the Atlantic in Spain's treasure fleet.

Andrea Doria, the 'Saviour of Genoa'

After the exclusion of the old nobility from power, the Doria, the proudest and one of the wealthiest clans of Genoa, had chafed in their compound in Piazza San Matteo. Their various attempts at taking over the city were notable failures, until the advent of Andrea Doria (1468–1560). Doria began his career as a member of the guard of Pope Innocent VIII and later served several Italian states as a mercenary. When the Wars of Italy between the Habsburg emperor Charles V and Francis I of France broke out, Doria was employed by France, one of Genoa's traditional allies.

Unfortunately for Genoa, the war broke out during one of its periodic lapses in self-govern-ment, when its doges had placed the Republic under the rule of France. This was sufficient reason for Imperial troops to sack it brutally in 1522, as a practice round for their later Sack of Rome. Under Cesare Fregoso, the Genoese recaptured the city for the French (1527). In the meantime, however, the French made a fatal miscalculation: they granted commercial privileges to Savona at Genoa's expense. Getting funny with the money was the one act a Genoese could never forgive, and Andrea Doria at once offered Charles V his services, in return for assurances that the Republic of Genoa would have its 'liberty', under Spanish-Austrian protection. Charles agreed, and Doria and his men drove the French from Genoa and Savona in 1528. Doria used the occasion to write a new Republican constitution institutionalizing the shared rule of the 28 *alberghi*, and in effect created an oligarchy of plutocrats of both the old and new nobility, even though he made sure that the plums of office, including the dogeship, were hogged by the old. The constitution provided for the annual election of five senators, and punters would wager on the five names in what they called the *lotto*—the origin of our modern lottery.

Charles V rewarded Doria for screwing the French with the titles of Prince of Melfi and Admiral of his Mediterranean fleet, nor was it long before other Genoese took prominent posts throughout the Empire. At home, Doria's aloof neutrality in city politics and near-dictatorial powers did much to cool the feuding, although many Genoese were deeply humiliated by Doria's *realpolitik* terms that bound them to the Habsburgs. One was Gian Luigi de' Fieschi, who in 1547 formed a conspiracy with his partisans and vassals from the mountains in the name of Genoese liberty. Andrea Doria fled, and the revolutionaries succeeded in taking the city—only they couldn't find de' Fieschi, who, when no one was looking, had fallen overboard in his armour and drowned. Without their leader, the conspirators haplessly surrendered, reassured by the promises of an amnesty that Doria gave just before he executed them all. Spain, sensing that its protégé was floundering, made a bold attempt to intimidate Doria into surrending the title of Republic for Genoa, but the old man stalwartly refused, and the motto *Libertas* remained proudly on the city's escutcheon.

Andrea Doria, at the age of 91, gained the Republic's last territorial acquisition when he led an expedition to reconquer Corsica. He was also Genoa's first great patron of the arts, introducing the High Renaissance to a city that had formerly managed without it. The wealthy abandoned their medieval palaces to build new, much grander ones further up on new marble streets and squares, each more sumptuous than the next.

At the same time, a number of prominent families went bankrupt, especially those traders who found their fleets attacked by the Ottomans and their sometime allies, the French, who were keen to get back at the treacherous republic. Counter-Reformation policies in line with the Spaniards and papacy saw the expulsion of the Jews—another set-back for the economy. Spanish taxes were so onerous that the Genoese tried to reopen negotiations with both the Ottomans and the kings of France, to no avail. Under Andrea Doria's nephew and heir, Gian Andrea Doria (d. 1606), the old disputes between the ever prickly old and new nobility flared up yet again. Doria asked the Spaniards to intervene for the old nobility, and a combined Spanish-papal force arrived on the scene. Its leaders at last did the one thing the Genoese were thoroughly incapable of doing themselves: they made peace. They eliminated the *alberghi* and all distinctions between the old and new nobility, and inscribed 170 families from both sides into the Golden Book (the list of those eligible to serve on the Republic's council). Now at relative peace, with a constitution that would survive until 1797, Genoa was ready to get its money back from Spain, with interest.

The 'Genoese Century'

Isabella and Ferdinand and their heirs may have bilked Columbus and his heirs out of a tenth of all the profits from the New World (*see* p.72), but the Genoese got it instead. The late 16th century to late 17th century was Genoa's time; while Italy wilted under Spanish rule, the Banco di San Giorgio and its directors (especially the Pallavicini, Sauli and Spinola) became increasingly fat through worldwide banking manipulations, financing the wars in the Low Countries for Charles V and Philip II, processing Spain's silver and making a fortune on its high resale value, and stealing the international money markets away from Besançon and Antwerp: millions of *scudi* passed through Genoa every year.

Chivalrous, warlike, religion-crazed Spain would have been even more lost without the acumen of Genoa's bankers, whom the great French historian Ferdinand Braudel described as 'discreetly dominating the rest of Europe' as the treasure fleet from the America found its way into Genoese bricks and mortar, stucco and gilt, frescoes and paintings. The nobility grew ever more exclusive and aped the Spanish grandees, going about with large bands of bravos, bodyguards and assassins. They had their reasons. In 1628, Julius Caesar Vachero, member of a great family excluded from the Golden Book, plotted a *coup d'état* with an army of bravos. They planned to capture the Palazzo Pubblico, massacre all the old nobles and take over Genoa, under the support of the Duke of Savoy. The plot was revealed the night before, and Vachero and his co-conspirators were executed.

In 1644, the famous English traveller John Evelyn visited Genoa and wrote that 'this beautiful city is more stained with horrid revenges and murders than any one place in Europe, or haply the world.' A devastating cholera plague struck Genoa in 1657, but it barely caused a blip in the city's financial statements; far more damaging, in 1684, was a bombardment by the fleet of Louis XIV, who took it amiss that Genoa had refused to allow the French to establish a military depot at Savona. After taking 14,000 bombs in three days, the doge agreed to go to Paris and apologize to the king to keep the French from destroying the city altogether.

Decline and Unification, and the New Genoa

> *The sovereign nobility, prodigal and voracious, created by their pomp wants beyond their resources; accordingly, they stooped to the most disgraceful depredations to obtain money. The state could make no contract without being robbed...every place was an object of sale, and justice was venal in the tribunals...*
>
> Sismondi, *A History of the Italian Republics*

As Sismondi describes it, Genoa in the 18th century sounds a bit like our own times. But its days were numbered. Spain's bankruptcies came too frequently; Atlantic commerce overtook the Mediterranean trade, leading to the decline of the city's bread and butter port. In 1734 Genoa chose the wrong side in the war of the Austrian succession, and in 1746, when an Austrian army appeared at the gate, the city could only open it and let them in. The Austrians behaved like cads, demanding that the Republic pay them nine million imperial florins as they began to cart away everything that could be moved, forcing the Genoese to haul their own cannons down to their waiting ships and brutally beating them. This led to a spontaneous revolt and a pitched battle in the narrow medieval streets, pitting armed Austrians against unarmed, rock-throwing Genoese, who trapped and destroyed them. It was the last victory of an Italian republic over a foreign tyrant. At the same time Corsica, Genoa's last colony, was in revolt against the city's heavy-handed ways and the Banco di San Giorgio could do nothing but sell it to France in 1768. Napoleon was born the very next year.

The Genoese tried to stay neutral in his wars, but failed, and under French rule found themselves compelled to change the name of their republic to the Republic of Liguria, meaning that everyone had a share in the government, much to the distaste of the old aristocrats. Although the city underwent the usual thorough Napoleonic looting, many of the *popolani* found much to admire in their new constitution, which helped to make them among the most radicalized and revolutionary in Italy. Genoa, however, suffered grievously. In 1800, a French army was blockaded there by the Austrians and British, causing the estimated deaths of 30,000 citizens from famine and disease. After the French succeeded in retaking it, the Continental blockade strangled Genoa. The Doge threw the desperate city at Napoleon's feet, and after the war the once proud Republic was snuffed out and annexed to the kingdom of Piemonte, an act the Genoese regarded as wholly unfair and unjustified.

For Piemonte, gaining Genoa and its port turned its attention from the Alps to the Mediterranean, and led to Turin's greater involvement in the peninsula. But for Genoa, the reactionary, absolutist policies of the Savoy kings only exacerbated its revolutionary tendencies. The former self-centered city of plutocrats rose superbly to the occasion by giving Italy its philosopher of the Risorgimento, Giuseppe Mazzini, who became a beacon to other patriot luminaries from Liguria: Nino Bixio, Goffredo Mameli, the Ruffini brothers and, of course, Garibaldi himself (*see* **Tales of Tenacity**, pp.74–80).

Unification with Italy brought Genoa its first speculative building, its all-important railroad line and a return of its status as Italy's chief port. This also brought the bombs on its head in the Second World War—the Teatro Carlo Felice and the ducal palace were among the casualties. For decades they languished in ruins, until Columbus came to the city's rescue, or at least the celebrations of the 500th anniversary of his discovery. The impetus behind 1992 continues apace in the redevelopment of the Porto Antico ('the city of fun'—a brand new field for the dour old Genoese) with the opening in 1999 of a state-of-the-art museum on the Antarctic, aptly fitting Genoa's new, spot-on slogan: *La città che non ti aspetti*— 'the city that you didn't expect'.

Getting There and Around

by air

Genoa's international airport, **Cristoforo Colombo**, ✆ 010 601 5410, 6km from the city in Sestri Ponente, has direct flights to Britain and many European destinations as well as to Italian cities. **Buses** to the airport depart an hour before each flight from Brignole Station and Piazza de Ferrari.

by sea

From Genoa you can sail away to exotic lands on a ferry from the **Stazione Marittima**, ✆ 010 246 3686, just below the Stazione Principe. Nearly any travel agency in Genoa can sell you a ticket, or you can make reservations by phone. **Grandi Traghetti** sails several times a week to Palermo, and Porto Torres in Sardinia; **Tirrenia** has ferries to the Sardinian ports of Porto Torres, Cagliari and Olbia, as well as to Palermo and Tunis; **Sardinia Ferries** has services to several points on that island from Genoa; and **Corsica Ferries** sails to Bastia.

by rail

Genoa has two main train stations: **Principe**, in Piazza Acquaverde, just northwest of the centre, and **Brignole**, to the southeast. For information, call ✆ 010 246 2633. Principe in general handles trains from the north and France, while Brignole takes trains from the south, though most long-distance trains do call at both. Bus no.37 links the two.

by long-distance bus

Intercity services and buses to the rest of the province and the Riviera depart from the Piazza della Vittoria, south of Brignole station, or from Piazza Acquaverde, in front of Stazione Principe. For information, call ✆ 010 599 7414.

by road

Three major *autostrade* meet just north of the city centre—the A10 from France and the Riviera di Ponente, the A12 along the Riviera di Levante and the A7 to Milan, which also connects with the A21 for Turin. The elevated branch of the A10, the *Sopraelevata*, runs right along the old port before ending near the Fiera di Genova; use it to get in or out of the city, and to connect up with all three of the main highways.

by public transport

Genoa is 30km long and fairly narrow, and trains run frequently from one end to the other, stopping at many of the smaller stations. Chances are you won't need to make much use of the city's buses (ATM, for information, ✆ 010 558 2414) as most of Genoa's points of interest are in the centre, between the two train stations. However, public transport is relatively cheap; an urban ticket, valid for ninety minutes' travel on **bus, urban FS train, metro, lift** or **funicular**, is L1500. A day ticket is L5000. **Tickets** must be purchased before embarking, from tobacco shops or the transport authority information kiosks at the rail stations.

The **funiculars** run from Piazza Portello and Largo della Zecca and ascend to the city's upper residential quarters; the one served by the latter, **Righi**, has a splendid outlook over the city and harbour. A single ticket costs L600. An Art Nouveau **lift** from Piazza Portello will also take you up to the nearer belvedere at Castelletto. Piazza Manin is the base for visiting the hills above Genoa, and the terminus for the very narrow-gauge **Trenino di Casella**, pulled by the oldest electric locomotive still operational in Italy (1924); the scenery and trattorias along the way are reason enough to make the trip (20 times a day, ✆ 010 839 3285 for information).

Genoa can seem a bit forbidding at first. One way to get a handle on it is a guided tour on the **Artbus**, equipped with an audio-visual system, departing every 20 minutes from Piazza Caricamento by the port, from 9am to 7.50pm. Another bus, the **Girogirotour**, offers live guided city tours from Piazza Caricamento with a daily departure at 3.30pm, returning at 5.10pm.

by car and taxi

Driving in Genoa is not much fun. The old quarter is closed to traffic, and the street plan is chaotic, though one consolation is that the *Sopraelevata*, the ugly elevated motorway that runs along the harbour, is never hard to find for a quick getaway. Car parks convenient for the Old City are by the Porta Soprana/Casa di Colombo and the Piazza Caricamento, down by the Porto Antico. **Taxis**, on the other hand, are plentiful. For a radio taxi, call ✆ 010 5966.

Tourist Information

Porto Antico–Palazzina Santa Maria B5, ✆ 010 24871, ✆ 010 246 7658, *aptgenova@aptgenova.it*. There are branch offices at Stazione Principe, ✆ 010 2462 633, and at the airport, ✆ 010 601 5247.

For information about entertainments, special events and what's on in general in Genoa at any one time, a good source is the city's daily paper, *Il Secolo XIX*.

Fire: ✆ 115.
Carabinieri: ✆ 112.
Police: Via Diaz, ✆ 53661 or ✆ 113.
Ambulance: ✆ 010 570 5951.

Hospital: Ospedale San Martino, Via Benedetto XV 10, ✆ 010 5551.
24-hour pharmacy: Pescetto, Via Balbi 185r, ✆ 010 246 2697.

24-hour automatic change machine at **Bancomat**, Piazza de Ferrari 10.

Main post office: Via Boccardo 2, off Via Dante and near the Piazza de Ferrari (*open Mon–Sat 8.15–7.40*). There are also offices at the two main train stations.

24-hour telephone centre: at the SIP office, Via XX Settembre 139.

Genoa is one of several cities with an unnecessarily complicated street-numbering system: any commercial establishment receives a red (r) number, but any residence a black or blue number.

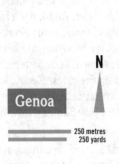

Genoa

250 metres
250 yards

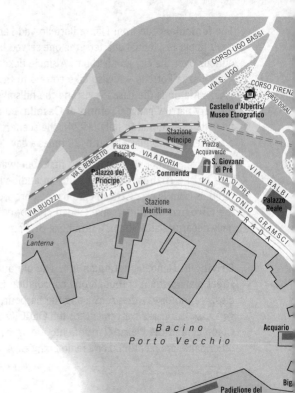

N

CORSO UGO BASSI

VIA S. UGO

CORSO FIRENZ

CORSO DOGALI

Castello d'Albertis/
Museo Etnografico

Stazione
Principe

Piazza
Acquaverde

S. Giovanni
di Prè

VIA S. BENEDETTO

Piazza d.
Principe

VIA A DORIA

VIA DI PRÈ

VIA BALBI

Palazzo del
Principe

Commenda

VIA ADUA

VIA ANTONIO GRAMSCI

Palazzo
Reale

VIA BUOZZI

Stazione
Marittima

STRADA

To
Lanterna

*Bacino
Porto Vecchio*

Acquario

Big

Padiglione del
Mare e della Navigazione

Porta Siberia

San
Ma

Molo Vecchio

Città dei
Bambini

VIA DI CIRCA

MURA MALAPAGA

Stazione Principe, Palazzo del Principe and the Lanterna

Both of Genoa's main train stations are palatial—**Stazione Principe** at the west end of the centre could easily host a fancy-dress ball. In its Piazza Acquaverde visitors are greeted by a **Statue of Columbus** and a view of the port. If you're catching a ferry, Via Andrea Doria will take you down to the Stazione Marittima, passing on the way the **Palazzo del Principe Doria Pamphili**, the only 'Royal' palace built during the secular history of the Genovese Republic (*open Sat 3–6, Sun 10–3; adm L10,000; guided tours outside opening hours, © 010 255 509*). The royal in this instance was Andrea Doria, Prince of Melfi, who in 1528 commissioned Perino del Vaga, Raphael's pupil, to decorate the interior of his new palace and introduce the joys of art to his fellow Genoese oligarchs. Perino designed the grand portal, and on the walls frescoed stories of the kings of

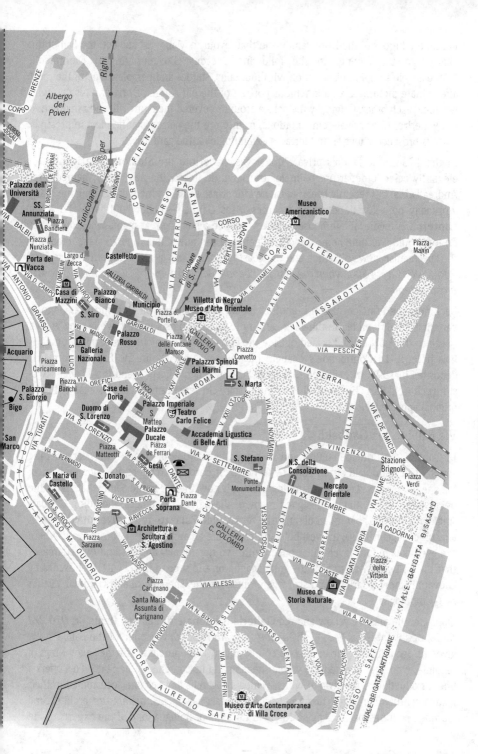

Rome, the heroes of the Doria family and that favourite Mannerist subject, the Fall of the Giants, in the Salone. In the following decade, Giovanni Angelo Montorsoli, Michelangelo's pupil, finished it off with fountains, statues and pergolas. One of the most affectionate pictures is an anonymous portrait of the old Andrea Doria and his cat, who resemble each other. Originally the palace grounds covered the entire hill and ran down to the waterfront, for private embarkations; from there the palace is at its most impressive, with its prospect of loggias and terraces extending over the gardens.

In the 1930s, the Doria's private quay was made into the **Stazione Marittima**, an elegantly eclectic departure point for transatlantic liners; the next quay, named after Andrea Doria, has recently been redesigned for cruise ships. To the west, among the many workaday port installations and facilities, rises Genoa's slender landmark, the 386ft **Lanterna**, a medieval lighthouse, which was once a bold sight at night, when open fires on top would welcome home the city's fleet. You can now climb the 375 stairs to admire the spectacular views of Genoa and the coast (*guided tours by appointment only, ✆ 010 246 5396; except Sun, when the first 100 people who turn up at 2.30pm at the Bigo will be admitted*).

Back near the Principe station is another medieval institution: **La Commenda**, Genoa's very first hotel, founded in the 11th century to give pilgrims a lodging while they waited to sail to the Holy Land. Located outside the city walls to keep out pilgrimaging riffraff, it was here, in La Commenda's chapel, that the relics of St John the Baptist were first deposited in 1098. In 1180 the Knights of St John added a hospital and the adjacent two-storey church, **San Giovanni di Pré**, with a spire-clustered campanile, now restored to its original appearance.

Via Balbi to Via Garibaldi

In front of the Principe station and its piazza begins one of Genoa's most aristocratic streets, **Via Balbi**, laid out in 1606 by Genoa's top baroque architect, Bartolomeo Bianco, for one of Genoa's wealthiest families, although now the car traffic somewhat spoils the once stately effect. Bianco designed many of Via Balbi's residences, including Genoa's single most famous baroque building, the remarkable **Palazzo dell'Università**, begun as a Jesuit college in 1630; the vestibule and *cortile* are an architectural *tour de force*, where the eye takes in four levels all at once, with two tiers of airy arcades and two staircases that divide twice. Ask to visit the Aula Magna on the second floor, with its frescoes by Giovanni Andrea Carlone and six large bronzes on the Theological and Cardinal Virtues by Giambologna.

Opposite, the massive yellow and red **Galleria Nazionale di Palazzo Reale** (✆ *010 271 0236, open Sun–Tues 9–1.45, Wed–Sun 9–7; adm L8000*) was built for the Balbi family, given its decorative façade in the late 1600s, and in 1824 purchased by the Savoy Kings of Sardinia, who later donated the whole shebang and its contents to the State. This offers a fine introduction to the style to which Genoa's oligarchs had become accustomed in their golden century: hanging gardens and superb mosaic pavements; *quadratura* (architectural *trompe-l'œil*) frescoes by Angelo Michele Colonna of Bologna, one of the experts of the genre, and others by Valerio Castello; a hyper-decorated 18th-century ballroom; a Gallery of Mirrors (with a marble *Metamorphosis* group by Filippo Parodi); and rooms hung with Gobelin tapestries and sprinkled with paintings by Veronese, Guercino and Van Dyck, and sculpture, including an 18th-century *Pluto and Proserpina* by Francesco Schiaffino.

Other palaces designed by Bartolomeo Bianco on Via Balbi are the **Palazzo Durazzo-Pallavicini** (No.1), and **Palazzo Balbi-Senarega** (No.4), both of which have been altered over time, their very austere façades offering no hint of the *trompe-l'œil* frescoes that originally covered them. The former palace is the last one on the street still in private hands and is filled with a famous art collection, while the latter now holds the university's department of humanities. It also has one of Genoa's finest fresco cycles, in which all Genoa's baroque masters had a hand, especially Valerio Castello, Gregorio De Ferrari, Domenico Piola and Andrea Sighizzi, another master of *quadratura*. The street's church, **SS Vittore e Carlo** (1632), has sculptures in the right transept by Alessandro Algardi, who introduced Roman baroque to Genoa, and in the left by Bernini's pupil Filippo Parodi (*Virgin and Child*).

Via Balbi gives on to Piazza della Nunziata, one of the city's traffic infernos, under the brooding presence of the 16th-century **Basilica della SS. Annunziata del Vastato**, with a somewhat grubby façade hiding an insanely voluptuous interior. This was redone, beginning in 1591, by the Lomellini, a family as fervently Counter-Reformation Catholic as they were wealthy, who insisted that every square inch of the basilica be covered over with new frescoes and paintings; other surfaces were given new marbles, statues, and more precious materials. Even the stuccoes were covered with gold. Only the façade was neglected, later to be given an outsize neoclassical pronaos in the 1700s that has become an urban landmark.

An even more staggering landmark built by the Lomellini is around the back of the church, at the top of Via Brignole De Ferrari: the enormous 17th-century **Albergo dei Poveri**, theatrically rising over twin stairs, rivalling the one in Naples as one of the most pompous poorhouses in Italy. Built when the demands of the wealthy were increasingly forcing Genoa's poor into the streets and crime, this monster of a building has four inner courtyards with a church in the centre, housing a sculpture by Pierre Puget, who later designed as a similar project the Charité in his native Marseille.

From Via P. Bensa, the wide street just east of Piazza della Nunziata, a little detour to the south leads to one of the shrines of modern Italian history, the Casa di Mazzini, on Via Lomellini 11, where the prophet of Italian unification was born in 1805 and is remembered in the **Museo del Risorgimento** (*© 010 246 5843, open Tues, Thurs, Fri, Sat 9–1*). While on Via Lomellini, note the church of **San Filippo** with a Roman-baroque concave façade, a style later reflected in some of the prettiest Riviera churches, such as Cervo; the oratory, added in the 18th century, now occasionally serves as a charming rococo concert hall.

From the next crossroads, the **Largo della Zecca**, you have several options, including a quick fix of upward mobility: a thrilling ride up to **Righi** on a recently restored funicular built over a century ago that rises some 900ft in under a mile, where you can have a coffee and a view of the walls and forts of Genoa's hinterlands, linked by a panoramic foot path (*see* below, pp.173–4).

The high road of art and culture (and antique shops), however, continues round on Via Cairoli. Just off this, on Via San Siro, is one of Genoa's most prominent churches, the Mannerist **San Siro**, rebuilt in the late 16th century by the Theatines. Although the main façade was redone in 1821, the south face still preserves their grand 17th-century portal over the stair. A double row of columns helps to create an illusion of space in the basilican interior, richly decorated with coloured marbles, frescoes by Giovanni Battista Carlone, and splendid altars with paintings by Orazio Gentileschi, Il Pomarancio and Aurelio Lomi, all culminating in the high altar, a confection in black marble and gilded bronze by Pierre Puget.

After Via S. Siro, Via Cairoli continues around to Piazza della Meridiana (named after the meridian line, which was painted when the square was laid out); its 16th-century palace of the same name was built for Grimaldi and contains Mannerist mythological frescoes by Luca Cambiaso and Giovanni Battista Castello. Beyond lies Genoa's most famous street, Via Garibaldi.

Via Garibaldi

This, the former *Strada Nuova* or Via Aurea, 'Golden Way', was laid out in 1558 and at once became Genoa's Millionaires' Row, with uninterrupted lines of late 16th-century palazzi. Rubens, for one, was besotted by its elegant dignity and understated wealth; from the exterior the mansions put on a solid front of stern respectability, differing from one another only in detail. Originally all were crowned by exotic gardens and aviaries of rare birds. Many have since been converted into banks and city offices, but the street's unique and elegant character has been carefully maintained.

Two of the palaces hold important collections of Grand Masters: the **Galleria di Palazzo Bianco** (© 010 557 33499, *open Tues, Thurs, Fri 9–1, Wed and Sat 9–7, Sun 10–6; closed Mon; adm L6000*), at No.11, another residence of the Grimaldis, is no longer very white, but has the best paintings in the city, especially by 17th-century artists. Key works include Filippino Lippi's *Madonna with Saints*, Pontormo's *Florentine Gentleman*, Veronese's *Crucifixion*, and works by the great Lombards, Caravaggio and Giulio Cesare Procaccini. There's an even more impressive collection of Flemish art, much collected in Genoa: Hans Memling's *Christ Blessing* and Gerhard David's sweetly domestic *Madonna della Pappa*, a very 17th-century and overripe *Venus and Mars* by Rubens, with Mars in the guise of a Counter-Reformation captain, and a *Portrait of Andrea Doria* with remarkable hands by Jan Matsys; other paintings are by Cranach, Van der Goes, Van Dyck, the Dutch artists Steen and Cypt, Simone Vouet from France, and a handful of Spanish masters, especially Murillo, and a fine *San Bonaventura* by the Zurbarán. Another section features some of the best canvases by the Genoese: Luca Cambiaso, Strozzi, Giovanni Andrea De Ferrari, Gregorio De Ferrari, Gioacchino Asserto and Alessandro Magnasco; the latter's solemn *Reception in a Garden* is an elegant, rather twilit work that seems to sum up the end of baroque. The museum also keeps one of Genoa's more exotic treasures, an embroidered purple silk pallium, given to the city in 1261 by Byzantine Emperor Michael VIII in thanks for Genoa's aid in his regaining of Constantinople.

Across the street at No.18, the **Galleria di Palazzo Rosso** (*© 010 557 4741, currently undergoing renovation, but still open Tues, Thurs and Fri 9–1, Wed and Sat 9–7, Sun 10–6; adm L6000*) is in a palace built in 1671 by the Brignole Sale family and donated to the city in 1874 by their last descendant, the Duchessa di Galliera. Named for the reddish tint of its stone, it was bombed badly in the war, but after a major restoration it has regained its position as the apotheosis of Genoese domestic baroque, with its gilt stucco and woodwork, a hall of mirrors designed by Filippo Parodi, and rooms frescoed with allegories of the Four Seasons by Domenico Piola (*Autumn* and *Winter*) and Gregorio De Ferrari (*Spring* and *Summer*), who wielded their brushes here in a friendly competition. The Brignole family produced more than one Doge, and are remembered in their excellent family portraits by Van Dyck. There are other portraits by Pisanello and Dürer, a *Christ Bearing the Cross* by Rubens, works by Caravaggio's followers and a *Judith* by Veronese; here, too, is *La Cuoca*, a favourite work by Genoa's own Bernardo Strozzi, and a sultry *Cleopatra* by Guercino. The gallery also includes an excellent collection of drawings, and some good examples of ceramics made in the city and from Savona and Albisola.

Next to the Palazzo Rosso at No.9 stands the **Palazzo Doria Tursi,** built by Rocco Lurago in 1568 for a Grimaldi banker to Philip II, but soon after purchased by Giovanni Andrea Doria. Now Genoa's City Hall, it has one of most beautiful *cortile* and stairs in the city, and such municipal treasures as native son Paganini's violin (an instrument once believed to be of infernal origin) in the Sala della Giunta, and three letters from Columbus in the Sala del Sindaco. If you get married in Genoa, however, the civil ceremony will be held in a splendid baroque room of antiques and tapestries over in the **Palazzo Doria** (No.6). At No.7, the **Palazzo Podestà** has its elegant façade by Mannerist Giovanni Battista Castello; the door is often open so you can peek into the theatrical baroque *cortile.* You can step inside the **Palazzo Carrega Cataldi** (No.4, now the Chamber of Commerce), built in 1558 with a golden rococo gallery added on the upper floor in the 1700s. The façade of No.3, the 16th-century **Palazzo Parodi-Lercari**, was built by the descendants of Megollo Lercari, who recalled the 'Insult to the Genoese' at Trebizond with earless and noseless caryatids.

The Famous Insult to the Genoese

In 1316 occurred one of the most beloved anecdotes of Genoese history, a story the Genoese like to tell for its perfect evocation of their proud, stubborn character: a Genoese merchant, by name Megollo Lercari, was the guest of the Byzantine emperor at Trebizond, when he disagreed with one of the emperor's pages, who slapped him across the face. The emperor refused to let the Genoese strike back, though he apologized for the youth's arrogant behaviour. It was not enough. Seething, Megollo returned to Genoa, got up a private fleet, sailed back to Trebizond, and demanded the page.

When the emperor refused, the Genoese besieged the city, capturing whoever they could and sending them back, minus their ears or noses. Finally his subjects' despair made the emperor give in. He handed over the youth, and watched, first in trepidation and then amazement, as Megollo made the page stoop over, then gave him a smart kick in the seat of the pants. Honour thus regained, the merchant returned the page to the emperor, lifted the siege and sailed back to Genoa.

Via Garibaldi ends at romantic **Piazza delle Fontana Marose**, a pedestrian island encased in more palaces, including the 15th-century **Palazzo Spinola dei Marmi**, embellished with black and white bands and statues of the Spinola family. Just up Via Interiano, Piazza del Portello has another chance to get above the city, thanks to its venerable Liberty-style lift up to **Castelletto** and its Belvedere Montaldo.

19th-Century Genoa

In the 19th century, after Genoa was joined to Piemonte, an architect named Carlo Barabino was appointed to give the old city some breathing space. He started above Piazza del Portello with the **Villetta di Negro**, a once private oasis built over the bastions of the 16th-century wall, which takes full advantage of Genoa's crazy topography, with streams, cascades, grottoes and walkways. At the top of Villetta di Negro, the **Museo d'Arte Orientale** (© *010 542 285, open Tues, Thurs, Fri and Sat 9–1; adm L6000*) is Italy's finest hoard of Oriental art, donated by Edoardo Chiossone (1833–98), who served the Imperial government in Tokyo as one of its *oyatoi gaikokujin* (hired foreigners) in charge of setting up the new finance ministry. Chiossone sent home a choice collection of statues, paintings and theatre masks, and an extraordinary set of Samurai helmets and armour, all displayed in a sun-filled modern building designed by Mario Labò in 1971.

Below the museum is the circular **Piazza Corvetto**, a busy roundabout with huge trees and parks on either end. One side of Piazza Corvetto is anchored by yet another **Palazzo Spinola**, on the corner of Via Roma; this, built in 1543 by Antonio Doria, admiral of the papal fleet, is now the Prefecture and still bears the exterior frescoes once common in Genoa. Within, there's a lovely *cortile*, frescoes in the public rooms by Luca Cambiaso and his father Giovanni, and fine views over the city from the upper loggia. Here too is the church of **Santa Marta**, embellished by Genoa's choice interior decorators, Domenico Pialo and Valerio Castello, with a highly emotional marble *St Martha in Ecstasy* in the choir by Filippo Parodi. On the corner of Via Roma is your chance to stop off for a history-imbued coffee break at the early 19th-century **Caffè Mangani**.

In Via Roma is the entrance to Genoa's most elegant arcade, the **Galleria Mazzini**, designed as an after-theatre promenade, rather like the Galleria Vittorio Emanuele by La Scala in Milan. It ends up at tumultuous **Piazza de Ferrari**. Under Carlo Barabino, this became an important address in Genoese cultural life, beginning with the construction of the neoclassical **Teatro Carlo Felice** in 1829. After the bombs of 1944, only the façade remained, crumbling away until 1992, when it was restored using the most avant-garde acoustic techniques; it has flourished ever since and now holds a year-round programme of opera, dance and theatre. In spite of the lyrical associations of his name, Carlo Felice was an unpopular and reactionary king, and the Genoese placed a grand equestrian statue of Garibaldi in front of the theatre to neutralize the sour aftertaste of his name. Adjacent, the **Museo della Accademia Ligustica di Belle Arti** (entrance Largo Pertini 4, *© 010 587 810, open Mon–Sat 9–1, closed Sun and hols; adm*), is a good place to learn about the evolution of the Genoese school, with paintings from the 14th–19th centuries: Perino del Vaga's *Polyptych of St Erasmus*, Luca Cambiaso's night scenes of *Christ before Caiaphas* and *Madonna and Child*, Bernardo Strozzi's *St Augustine washing Christ's Feet*.

Across the piazza, and separating it from Piazza Matteotti below, is the giant black and white mass of the 16th-century **Palazzo Ducale**, once the seat of Genoa's doges, which since 1992 has been converted into a culture, shopping and exhibition centre (*see* below). The way down from the Piazza de Ferrari to the Piazza Matteotti is by a huge monumental staircase, once used for the Republic's most theatrical processions.

Into the Old City

> *...if you bring peace, you are permitted to stop within this gate; if*
> *you ask for war, you will fall back deluded and defeated.*
>
> from the inscription on the Porta Soprana

From Piazza de Ferrari you can descend into the skein of medieval Genoa. The proper, imposing introduction is to head down Via Dante to **Piazza Dante** (with its skyscraper by Marcello Piacentini, Mussolini's favourite architect) and through the tall twin-towered **Porta Soprana**, a gate built in 1155 as part of the **Barbarossa walls** designed to keep out the emperor of that name. By the gate you'll find the **House of Columbus**, owned by Domenico Colombo, giving rise to the dubious notion that this was Christopher's 'boyhood home'. Although the Genoese at first were ambivalent about their great admiral (in a mid 16th-century list of the city's great men he doesn't make the grade) they thought enough of him by 1684 to reconstruct this house after it was shattered by a French bomb (*guided tours by appointment only, © 010 247 6575*). Here, too, stands the ruined, 12th-century Romanesque **Cloister of Sant'Andrea**, set out on the lawn amid the olive trees.

Genoa's medieval centre is one of the most extensive in Europe. In some ways it's like Venice, only built on a slope; tall houses here are sliced by corridor-like alleys or *carrugi* rather than canals, and some are so narrow that they live in perpetual shade. One advantage is that you can never get too lost, with the seafront always waiting at the bottom. Partly bombed in the war and now mostly restored, leaning ever so gently towards the harbour below, it has houses with striped white marble and black slate portals, a special honour permitted only to families who performed a good deed for the city. Corners and wall niches are decorated with hundreds of little shrines or *aedicolae* known as *madonnette*, the little madonnas, erected by various corporations, merchants and individuals for grace granted.

The old town is for exploring. To see the highlights, take Via di Ravecca down from Porta Soprana to the 13th-century Gothic monastic church of **Sant'Agostino**, with its bell tower coated with colourful majolica tiles. The church and monastery are now used as an auditorium and headquarters of the innovative Teatro della Tosse, while the unusual triangular cloisters have been converted into the well-designed **Museo di Sant'Agostino** (© *010 251 1263, open Tues–Sat 9–7, Sun 9–12.30*), containing sculptures and architectural fragments salvaged from Genoa's demolished churches. One of the finest works is the 1312 fragment of the tomb of Margherita of Brabant, wife of Emperor Henry VII, sculpted by the great master Giovanni Pisano. Margherita died suddenly in Genoa while accompanying her husband to Rome for his coronation, and Henry, whom Dante and many others had hoped would be able to end the feud between Italy's Guelphs and Ghibellines, died in Siena two years later, many believe of sorrow; his last request was that his heart be taken to Genoa to be interred with his wife. There are also Roman works, Romanesque sculpture, frescoes and the 14th-century wooden *Christ of the Caravana*. Later sculptures are by the Gagini, Parodi, Pierre Puget and Antonio Canova.

Sant'Agostino gives on to elongated **Piazza Sarzano**, both the highest and the largest square inside the medieval walls, and a favourite venue for tournaments and jousts and Genoa's intramural donnybrooks; at other times it served as a market and a place for ropemakers to stretch out their wares. The city stored its water beneath the square, in enormous subterranean cisterns located under a little temple built in the 1600s. In the 1990s, many of the religious buildings that frame the square were converted into a new home for Genoa university's school of architecture.

From Piazza Sarzano, Stradone di Sant'Agostino leads to another good church, the 12th-century Romanesque **San Donato**, with an exceptionally lovely octagonal campanile (echoed in the new octagonal striped skyscraper near the *Genova Ovest autostrada* exit), and portal and interior, combining a pleasant mix of Roman and medieval columns. If it's time for a drink, take a short walk up Via S. Donato to Piazze delle Erbe, site of the picturesque **Bar Berto**, founded in 1906 and covered throughout with tiles from Albisola.

If you walk in the opposite direction down Via S. Donato, you'll reach **Via San Bernardo**, one of the few straight streets in the old city, laid out by the Romans and used by mule caravans to bring goods from the port through the Porta Soprana. The Romans' castle (reached by way of the striking 12th-century tower house, the 135ft **Torre degli Embriaci**) provided the foundations for Genoa's most venerable church and the first of about a zillion dedicated to the Madonna in Liguria, **Santa Maria di Castello**. Founded in the palaeochristian era, it incorporates numerous Roman columns and stones in its Romanesque structure. The crusaders used Santa Maria's complex as a hostel, and when the Dominicans took over in the 15th century they added a friary and three cloisters, all paid for by the Grimaldi, who are glorified for their generosity on the Sacristry portal. Fairest of its artworks is the 15th-century fresco of the *Annunciation* by Giusto d'Alemagna in the cloister, while the strangest is the *Crocifisso Miracoloso* in a chapel near the high altar—miraculous in that the Christ's beard is said to grow whenever Genoa is threatened with calamity.

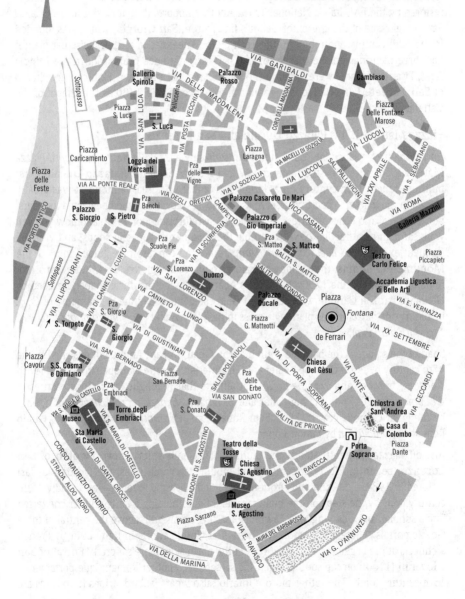

The seafront here has kept its 16th-century walls and a rare survivor, a Roman house, the so-called **Casa di Agrippa** (on the south tip of Piazza Cavour) from the 1st century AD. If you follow Piazza Cavour up two streets, you'll regain Via San Bernardo. Just here, in Vico San Cosima, the church of **SS. Cosma e Damiano** is dedicated to the patron saints of doctors, barbers and surgeons; close by, at Vico Caprettari 7, you can get a haircut at Italy's most beautiful **Barber Shop**, all done up in the purest Art Deco and recently restored by the FAI, Italy's National Trust. Another important node in this area is Piazza San Giorgio, site of the church of Genoa's first patron, **San Giorgio**, which was founded in the 10th century and rebuilt in the 16th by the Theatines in a central circular plan; it has three paintings on the martyrdom of St George by Luca Cambiaso. In the Middle Ages, Pisan merchants were based in the square, and had their own 12th-century church of **San Torpete** (alias St Tropez), rebuilt in a rococo oval in 1730 as the chapel of the Cattaneo family.

Piazza Matteotti: the Palazzo Ducale and San Lorenzo

An alternative entrance into the historic centre from Piazza de Ferrari is by way of Piazza Matteotti, dominated by the main yellow and red façade of the **Palazzo Ducale**. First built in the late 16th century on a design by Lombard Andrea Vannone, it was greatly altered in the following century to serve as the city law courts. It stood neglected for years, but, like the Carlo Felice theatre, it was beautifully refurbished for 1992, and now you can walk through its attractive *cortiles*, sample the restaurants, bars and shops, and visit the frequent exhibitions (*Tues–Sun 9am–9pm; adm*). You can also take guided tours of the **Monumental Rooms**: the Salone and Salonetto of the Maggiore e del Minore Consiglio, rebuilt after a fire in the 1700s, the Doge's Apartments, and the ducal chapel, frescoed by Giovanni Battista Carlone with scenes of Genoese conquests done in the name of God, including one of Columbus planting a cross in the New World (*ring ahead to book, © 010 562 440; adm exp*).

Sharing the square is the baroque church of the **Gesù** (or Sant'Ambrogio) designed in the 17th century by Jesuit Giuseppe Valeriani. The interior is a pure baroque fantasia, all lavish stuccoes, frescoes and *trompe-l'œil* stage effects that highlight its frothy treasures: a *Circumcision* (1607) on the high altar and *St Ignatius Exorcising the Devil* (1622), both by the great Catholic covert, Peter Paul Rubens, an *Assumption* by the 'Divino' Guido Reni and a *Crucifixion* by Simon Vouet.

Just off Piazza Matteotti stands the jauntily black and white striped **Duomo** of **San Lorenzo**, begun in the 12th century and modified several times; the façade was last restored in 1934. Odds and ends from the ages embellish the exterior—two kindly 19th-century lions by the steps on the main façade, a figure holding a knife-grinder converted into a sundial, and a carving of St Lawrence toasting on his grill, above the central of three Gothic portals. These were among the very first Gothic efforts in Italy, built by French architects at the beginning of the 1200s. On the north side, there's a pretty **Portal of San Giovanni** (1160); on the south, Hellenistic sarcophagi, another Romanesque portal and a 15th-century tomb. The rather morose interior also wears jailbird stripes (two sides are currently undergoing renovation). The first chapel on the right contains a marble *Crucifixion* of 1443, and a British shell fired from the sea 500 years later that hit the chapel but miraculously failed to explode, while the last has an altarpiece by Federico Barocci (1597), of the Bologna school. On the left, note the sumptuous Renaissance **Cappella di San Giovanni Battista**, with fine sculptures and marble decorations by Domenico and Elia Gagini (1451), and a 13th-century sarcophagus that once held the Baptist's relics.

In the vaults off the nave to the left, the subterranean **Museo del Tesoro della Cattedrale** (✆ 010 311 269, *open Mon–Sat 9–12 and 3–6; guided tours only, every half hour; adm*), is an Ali Baba-like cavern of genuine treasures, acquired during the heyday of the Republic's adventures in the Holy Land: a basin that was part of the dinner service of the Last Supper, the blue chalcedony dish on which John the Baptist's head was served to Salome, an 11th-century arm reliquary of St Anne, the golden, jewel-studded 12th-century Byzantine *Zaccaria Cross*, and an elaborate 15th-century silver casket holding John the Baptist's ashes, which goes on an outing through the city in a procession on 24 June.

Piazza San Matteo

The Salita del Fondaco follows the back of the Palazzo Ducale from Piazza de Ferrari, then veers right for the Piazza San Matteo, a beautiful little square completely clothed in the honourable black and white bands of illustrious benefactors—and it's no wonder, for this was the public foyer of the Doria family, encompassed by their proud palazzi and their 12th-century church of San Matteo, inscribed with their great deeds. One of the most important of these happened in this very square: in 1528, Andrea Doria gathered the nobles of Genoa here and convinced them to rise up against the French in the name of the Republic's autonomy under the blessing of Spain. One palace was donated by Genoa in 1298 to Lamba Doria, victor over the Venetians at Curzola; another, No.17, with a florid Gothic loggia, was donated by the Republic to Andrea, while No.14, with a beautiful portal and early Renaissance St George and the Dragon, belonged to the nefarious Branca Doria (d. 1325) who invited his father-in-law to dinner and murdered him, and whose soul, at least according to Dante (*Inferno XXXIII*), went straight to hell while his body lived on, inhabited by a devil, occasioning the famous remark of a Tuscan still sore over the defeat of Pisa in 1284:

> *O all you Genovese, you men estranged*
> *from every good, at home with every vice,*
> *why can't the world be wiped clean of your race?*

trans. Mark Musa

The Piazza also has the Doria's private **cloister** (early 1300s), designed by one Maestro Marco Veneto, with charming capitals on twinned columns. Zebra-striped **San Matteo**, the family church, was founded in 1125 but rebuilt in the early 14th century along with the rest of the square. The interior was given a complete Renaissance facelift with marbles, stuccoes and frescoes commissioned by Andrea Doria, whose tomb is within.

The Northern Historic Centre

The northern section of the historic centre, built up mostly in the Renaissance, has survived in somewhat better nick than the area around Porta Soprana, and has, amid its monuments, fine shops, pubs, restaurants and cafés. Get there from Piazza Fontane Marose by descending Via Luccoli, a major shopping thoroughfare, or from the aforementioned Piazza San Matteo and the **Campetto**, a lovely square adorned with the ornate 16th-century **Palazzo di Gio Imperiale**, its Mannerist façade decorated by Giovanni Battista Castello with stuccoes and frescoes—the rest of the palace was shattered in the war. Adjacent, the even larger **Palazzo Casareto De Mari** from the same period is better known as 'pomegranate palace' for the tree by the entrance; the *cortile* has a statue of Hercules and a nymphaeum (fountain) by Filippo Parodi. In the nearby Piazza Soziglia you can take a break at one of the oldest coffee-houses in Genoa, **Kainguti**, at No.98r, or **Romanegro**, at No.74r, both founded by Swiss entrepreneurs at the beginning of the 19th century.

From Piazza Soziglia and the Campetto, pretty Via degli Orefici ('of the goldsmiths') meanders down past the most elaborate and beautiful of all the *centro storico*'s edicolas (little shrines built in nooks in walls), a slate one, commissioned by the goldsmiths from the Gagini family with a sculpture of the Magi and a *Madonna and saints* (original in the Accademia Ligustica) by a young painter, Pellegro Piola, who took his fee on the day it was hung, invited his friends on a spree and was murdered out of jealousy that evening. Via degli Orefici continues down to what was the very core of Genoa from the Middle Ages until the mid-1800s, the **Piazza Banchi**, where the bankers and merchants met in the late 16th-century Renaissance **Loggia dei Mercanti**, supported by a single, daring vault. As the heart of Genoa, this square witnessed a good amount of murder, fire and mayhem in its time, and the bankers' stalls and their church, **San Pietro della Porta** (founded in the 9th century), were often victims. In the 1500s, after the Madonna rescued Genoa from a plague, the Senate found the will to rebuild the church and at the same time give the bankers a new home; the church was built directly over their stalls and the rentals financed its upkeep.

From here Via al Ponti Reale descends to harbourside Piazza Caricamento, lined with the ancient, evocative arcades of **Via Sottoripa**—a perfect medieval shopping street. The big news here is the gaudily frescoed **Palazzo di San Giorgio**, a massive palace built in 1260 for the Capitani del Popolo, namely for Guglielmo Boccanegra, the popular great-uncle of the first doge, using masonry hijacked from the Venetians. In 1298, at the battle of Curzola, the Genoese also snatched a certain Marco Polo and imprisoned him here, where he met a romance writer named Rustichello of Pisa. Marco whiled away the time telling of his adventures, and when they were released Rustichello became the ghost-writer of his famous book, *Il Milione* ('The Million' tales, or tall tales; in English it's simply *The Travels*) of which Columbus possessed a well-thumbed copy. The palace was taken over in 1408 by the Banco di San Giorgio, the shrewd Genoese bankers requiring a headquarters from where they could scrutinize the comings and goings of the port. When

Columbus, about to embark on his third voyage, wanted to safeguard the copies of his privileges granted by Ferdinand and Isabella, the first place he thought to send it was the Banco di San Giorgio. The palace is now occupied by the Harbour Board, but you can ask the guard to show you some of the rooms that have been refurbished in their original 13th-century style.

Galleria Nazionale di Palazzo Spinola

Behind the Palazzo di San Giorgio, off the aforementioned Piazza Banchi, runs **Via San Luca**, the former 'Caruggio Dritto' or straight street, the principal thoroughfare of medieval Genoa, wide enough for doubly-laden mules. This was the turf of another prominent Genoese family, the Spinola, who shared it in an uneasy arrangement with their Guelph enemies, the Grimaldi. The Spinola's little church of **San Luca** is one of the best family chapels in Genoa, rebuilt in 1626 with a palatial interior, entirely frescoed in the ballroom style by Domenico Piola, and endowed with Castiglione's magnificent altarpiece of the *Nativity* (1645) and sculptures by Filippo Parodi.

One of the grandest Spinola palaces, just off Via San Luca in little Piazza di Pellicceria, now houses the **Galleria Nazionale di Palazzo Spinola** (*© 010 270 5300, open Tues–Sat 9–7, Sun 2–7*). The Marquese Spinola donated most of the paintings along with the old homestead, complete with its lavish 16th–18th-century décor and hall of mirrors. The paintings are still arranged as in a private residence, and include Antonello da Messina's sad, beautiful *Ecce Homo*, Joos Van Cleve's magnificent *Adoration of the Magi*, works by Van Dyck (*Portrait of a Child* and the *Four Evangelists*), and a statue of Justice, another fragment of Giovanni Pisano's tomb of Margherita di Brabante. There are excellent works by Genoa's masters (Cambiaso, Strozzi, Valerio Castello, Domenico Piola and Gregorio De Ferrari) and a recent acquisition: the dramatic equestrian *Portrait of Giovanni Carlo Doria* by Rubens. Don't miss the terrace, with its orange and lemon trees and views over Genoa's slate roofs.

The Porto Antico

Seawards from Piazza Caricamento, Genoa's long-neglected old port was dusted off and redeveloped as the showcase for the 1992 celebrations, and it proved so overwhelmingly popular that the Porto Antico has been expanding ever since. Its landmark and tallest attraction is the **Bigo**, or Crane, designed by Renzo Piano (co-architect of the Pompidou Centre in Paris) which towers over the port from the end of one of the quays; a panoramic, revolving lift goes up the tower for the superb views from the top (*tickets L6000*). Other attractions include a marina, an ice skating rink, a giant swimming pool, the largest cinema complex in Italy, and the **Città dei Bambini**, the largest children's educational play area in Italy, designed for ages 3–14 and full of climbing frames and giant plastic insects, as well as a building site where children can dress up in hard hats and push around plastic wheelbarrows full of sand (© *010 247 5702, open 10–6, closed Mon and Sept; adm L8000*).

The former Cotton Warehouses have been converted into an exhibition centre and the **Padiglione del Mare e della Navigazione**, a branch of the Pegli Naval museum, containing artefacts from 16th- and 17th-century ships and an early steam ship, as well as a reconstruction of a medieval shipyard (© *010 246 3678, open Mon–Fri 10.30–6, Sat and Sun 10.30–7; adm L9,000*). Behind the Cotton Warehouse, the grand military gateway, the **Porta del Molo-Siberia**, was designed by Galeazzo Alessi in 1553 and hints at the opulence of the Molo Vecchio, the main quay of old Genoa, considered the greatest of its many wonders in the 17th century. The small walled, thumb-shaped neighbourhood that grew up by the port, the **Quartiere del Molo**, has, curiously enough, a church of **San Marco**, founded in 1173 (perhaps in the hopes of luring Mark's patronage away from Venice); it also has the 13th-century **Palazzo del Boia**, where criminals were hanged over the quay up until 1852.

Then there's Europe's largest **Aquarium**, further up the quayside, a converted ship filled with seals, dolphins, sharks and penguins, and reconstructions of coral reefs. The aquarium is visited by around a million and a half people each year, making it Italy's third most visited 'museum' (© *010 248 8011, www.acquario.ge.it; open Tues–Fri 9.30–6.30, ticket office closes at 5; Sat and Sun 9.30–8pm, ticket office closes at 6.30; adm L19,000, children aged 3–12 L12,000, children under 3 free*). Behind it, the brand new **Museo Nazionale dell'Antartide** (© *010 254 3690, open Oct–May Tues–Sat 9.45–6.15, Sun 10–7; June–Sept 2pm–10pm; adm exp*) is devoted to the Antarctic, in particular an Italian research expedition of 1985 that tested the endurance of the scientists living in tents over a period of several months.

19th-Century Genoa: Via XX Settembre and Around

East of Piazza de Ferrari awaits yet another side of La Superba. Arcaded **Via XX Settembre**, the main thoroughfare of 19th-century Genoa, is still the city's chief shopping street, adorned here and there with Liberty-style flourishes and plenty of good old-fashioned neon. Overhead, the 20th-century **Ponte Monumentale** carries the Corso A. Podesta, near the platform supporting another striped church, the grey and white **Santo Stefano**, consecrated in 1217, with a beautiful apse decorated with blind arcading and an octagonal tribune. Not much in Genoa recalls the Lombards' tenure, but the base of Santa Stefano was a Lombard defensive tower and the crypt, discovered during post-war restoration, may be theirs as well. It contains an excellent *Martyrdom of St Stephen* (1524) by a less flamboyant than usual Giulio Romano.

Genoa's main market, the **Mercato Orientale** (1889), occupies the cloister of the 18th-century church **Nostra Signora della Consolazione**; its name comes not from Chinese vegetables but its location east of the centre. Under the Ponte Monumentale, the avenue

continues to the large **Piazza della Vittoria**, a Fascist-era square presided over by a 1931 War Memorial Arch. Nearby is the **Giacomo Doria Museum of Natural History**, Via Brigata Liguria 9 (*© 010 564 567, open 9–12 and 3–5.30; closed Mon and Fri*), a recently refurbished collection garnered by 19th-century Genoese noblemen in their travels.

Carignano, the 19th-century residential area south of here, has two attractions to seek out: at the highest point, the four-square church of **Santa Maria Assunta in Carignano**, one of the landmarks of Genoa, built between 1552 and 1602 and topped by a cupola; it has fine statues by Pierre Puget in the alcoves and a *Pietà* by Luca Cambiaso. Then there's the new **Museo d'Arte Contemporanea di Villa Croce**, Via J. Ruffini 3 (*© 010 580 069, open Tues–Sat 9–6.30, Sun 9–12; adm L7000*), a beautiful neoclassical villa housing 20th-century works by both Italian and foreign artists.

Behind Genoa: Hills and Walls, and a Glorious Boneyard

Thanks to centuries of shipbuilding, the hills around Genoa are the least forested in all Liguria. Not only are they naked, but vulnerable, and here the seagoing Republic built its first outer walls and forts back in the early 14th century. When the rouble was rolling in the 17th century, Genoa decided, more for show than in response to any military threat, to construct a new wall over the ridge. This system of fortifications, designed by the Republic's architect Bartolomeo Bianco, stretches for 13km, forming a defensive boundary wall surpassed in length only by the Great Wall of China. It also adds a nice dramatic touch to Genoa's upper rim. The easiest way to visit it is a drive along the panoramic **Strada della Mura**, departing from **Piazza Manin**, north of the Brignole station. Piazza Manin itself is the site of one of the stranger fortifications, the early 20th-century **Mackenzie Castle**, a folly with more teeth than a school of sharks. Nearby (just off Via Arecco and the Passo dello Zerbino), the more conventional **Villa Balbi-Groppallo** was built in the 1560s and decorated with magnficent frescoes by baroque's dynamic duo, Gregorio De Ferrari and Domenico Piola. The gardens were laid out in the 1700s by one of Genoa's first naturalists, Ippolito Durazzo.

Piazza Manin is also the point of departure for an inner ring road through the hills, the equally panoramic **Circonvallazione a Monte** that skirts the villa-laden slopes, a route followed by city bus no.33, from Stazione Brignole or Piazza Manin. If you're driving, the Circonvallazione takes Corso Armellini and Corso Solferino from Piazza Manin; at Corso Solferino 39, the privately run **Museo Americanistico F. Lunardi** (*open Tues–Sat 9.30–12 and 3–5.30, Sun 3–5.30*) is installed in the 17th-century Villa Grüber, and has a beautiful and important collection of pre-Columbian art, especially strong in Mayan work. The hillside route continues along Corsos Magenta, Paganini, Firenze and U. Bassi, passing on the way the imposing **Castello d'Albertis**, which is medieval, though it was rebuilt in the 19th century. This, too, houses a **Museo Etnografico**, with a pre-Columbian collection (*closed for years, although it may re-open soon; © 010 557 4738 for information*).

A third excursion from Piazza Manin is to **Casella** up in Genoa's *entroterra*, by way of the pokey old narrow-gauge **Trenino di Casella**, built in the 1920s and much used during the war to bring provisions into the city and to escape the bombs. Although under threat in the 1960s, it managed to avoid extinction and still makes its 25km journey in about an hour. It's a favourite weekend jaunt, when the trattorias along the way do a brisk trade (highly recommended and moderately priced: Caterina, at Cortino, © 010 967 7146).

Staglieno Cemetery

Below Piazza Manin, and up along the Torrente Bisagno, is the extraordinary last port for the Genoese, **Staglieno Cemetery** (*open daily 8–5; bus no.34 from Piazza Acquaverde or Piazza Corvetto*). Founded in 1844, this necropolis covers 160 hectares, and even has its own internal bus system. The Genoese have a reputation for being canny and tight-fisted, but when it comes to post-mortem self-indulgence they have few peers. Staglieno is a veritable Babylon of the dead, a fantastic, surreal city of miniature cathedrals, Romanesque chapels, Egyptian temples and Art Nouveau palaces and statuary. In the centre, Giuseppe Mazzini lies buried in a simple tomb behind two massive Doric columns, surrounded by inscriptions by Tolstoy, Lloyd George, D'Annunzio, Carducci (*see* p.79) and others. Mrs Oscar Wilde is buried in the Protestant section.

On the east bank of the Torrente Bisagno, you'll find Genoa's football stadium L. Ferraris in **Marassi**; in **San Fruttuoso**, completely engulfed by modern buildings, is the **Villa Imperiale di Terralba** (now a public library) and its centuries-old park (now a public garden). The Villa was built in 1502, and used by Lorenzo Cattaneo to host Louis XII in courtly style (note the *fleur de lys* in the vaults of the atrium); within, the villa was given a Mannerist remodelling, and has frescoes by Luca Cambiaso.

West of Genoa: to Pegli and Voltri

Genoa has no suburbs, as it will tell you; instead its surrounding towns are more like lots of satellites hooked into the metropolis. As a general rule, the business end of Genoa is to the west of the city and the residential areas to the east, although there are plenty of exceptions to prove the rule. Just west of the Lanterna, for instance, is **Sampierdarena**, actually a city within the city, but one that has always played an important role in Genoa. The Republic's galleys were originally beached on its long sandy strand. The Doria were big shots here, too, and rebuilt the oldest church in Sampierdarena, **Santa Maria della Cella** (1206) around a cell where St Augustine's remains were kept in the 8th century, en route to their final destination in Pavia. Santa Maria's Gothic interior has baroque stuccoes, Doria tombs and an altarpiece by Castiglione. Although they are now lost among the manifestations of industry, noble villas from the 16th century still haunt Via Dottesio and Via D'Aste: the three most famous ones are nicknamed **Bellezza, Fortezza e Semplicità** (Beauty, Strength and Simplicity), each packed full of important frescoes. A few bits remain of their once splendid gardens, along with a charming rustic grotto (Via D'Aste 9) that once belonged to a Doria villa. Another grand residence, the **Villa Centurione-Carpaneto** in Piazza Montano 4, has the only surviving frescoes by Bernardo Strozzi in Genoa.

Further west, you'll find other woebegone villas in industrial zones; one is the grand rococo summer residence of the Princes of Savoy in **Cornigliano**. Others, including a magnificent Spinola spread, are in **Sestri Ponente**, site of the Cantiere Cadenaccio, the most important ship-building yard in Italy for a century (1868–1960) and now home to Genoa's airport. Beyond is **Multedo**, where the once lovely landscapes have been transformed and wasted in this century; here the 16th-century **Villa Lomellini Rostan**, with its loggias and watch tower, frescoes and bits of the gardens that were once celebrated for elegant parties, is a wistful reminder that it wasn't always so.

Pegli and its Parks and Museums

West of the Villa Lomellini lies **Pegli,** and although there's been plenty of new building here, too, the character of this longtime retreat of the Genoese has not been totally lost, especially as the grounds of the two princely villas are now used as public parks. One belongs to the 16th-century **Villa Centurione Doria**, built by Prince Giovanni Andrea Doria and his heir, the fabulously wealthy banker Adamo Centurione. Decorated with Mannerist mythological frescoes by Nicolosio Granello and Lazzaro Tavarone, the villa is now used as the **Museo Navale** (*Piazza C. Bonavino, ☎ 010 696 9885, open*

Tues–Thurs 9–1, Fri, Sat 9–7, 1st and 3rd Sun 9–12.30), with a fascinating collection of artefacts relating to Genoa's maritime traditions, including ships' models, paintings (among them a portrait of Columbus, attributed to Ghirlandaio, and the famous late 15th-century *View of Genoa*, a copy of the original by Cristoforo de Grazzi), compasses, astrolabes, weapons, armour, logbooks and maps. The park still contains the lake and 'fairy island' laid out by the architect Galeazzo Alessi.

The second park, the magnificent **Villa Durazzo-Pallavicini**, is even more full of fancy. In the 1840s Michele Canzia, an eclectic set designer at the Teatro Carlo Felice, was put in charge of the landscaping and used his stage experience to make it into 'a drama in three acts' that begins at the 'City' and ends at 'Heaven Reconquered', passing by way of 24 acres of romantic gardens, filled with exotic plants and an eclectic programme of statuary, ruins, triumphal arches, rotundas, Turkish temples, coffeehouses and ponds. The palace itself, built for the Marchese Ignazio Pallavicini, now contains the **Museo di Archaeologia Ligure** (*© 010 698 1048, open Tues–Thurs 9–7; Fri, Sat 9–1; 2nd and 4th Sun 9–12.30)*, with a collection of pre-Roman and Roman finds from Genoa and its ancient cemeteries, from the Roman towns of Luni and Libarna, and especially from the prehistoric caves of the Riviera di Ponente. The star exhibit is the 'Young Prince,' discovered in the Grotta delle Arene Candide at Finale Ligure, a youth of about 15, buried with a seashell headdress and a dagger in his hand approximately 20,000 years ago. Recently the bronze *Tabula Polcevera* (117 BC), a unique account of Roman judgements on various rights, privileges and jurisdictions in Liguria that was discovered in the Val Polcevera in 1527, has been restored and put back on display.

Voltri, the westernmost part of the metropolis, is famous for supplying the best *focaccia* in Liguria. Après eating, head up to the **Villa della Duchessa di Galliera** and its English garden, with pines, elms and holm oaks, and a deer and goat park. The 18th-century palace, charmingly decorated with seashells, where the Duchess hosted popes and kings, is one of the most sumptuous in the metropolitan area. At the top of the park, the late 19th-century **Santuario di Nostra Signora delle Grazie** has lovely views and a good collection of *ex votos*.

Eastern Genoa to Nervi

The best way to visit the more genteel eastern districts and beaches of the metropolis is along the scenic coast-hugging Corso Italia, which begins at the **Fiera Internazionale**, the setting for Genoa's biggest annual event, the Boat Show. **Albaro**, the first town to the east, was already a favourite resort of the Genoese in the 14th century and has remained a residential area ever since, although now its fancy villas are engulfed in speculative developments. It was the last home of Alessandro Magnasco, who painted one of his masterpieces, the *Supper at Emmaus*, for the church and convent of **San Francesco**, in Albaro's historic centre. The public park at the crossroads of Via Albaro and Via Montallegro is the address of the **Villa Cambiaso Giustiniani** (1548), masterpiece of Galeazzo Alessi and the prototype for all subsequent Genoese palaces, with its tripartate façade and airy loggia within. Just up Via Albaro, the 16th-century **Villa Saluzzo**

Bombrini, nicknamed simply 'Paradise', is still private and still intact, down to its superb Renaissance gardens, which were the setting for another Magnasco masterpiece, the *Reception in a Garden*.

Other stately villas line the sea, one of which, the **Villa Bagnarello**, hosted Dickens while he wrote *Pictures from Italy* (1843). Genoa, incidentally, met Boz's approval, much to his surprise ('I would never have believed that the time would come when I would be attracted even by the stones of Genoa's streets...'). Next to the east is **Boccadasse**, a bijou little fishing port much beloved by the Genoese. **Quarto dei Mille**, from where Garibaldi and his Thousand set sail to Sicily and glory before Cavour could stop them, has a monument to the Risorgimento heroes and a **Garibaldi Museum**, in Villa Garibaldi (✆ *010 385 493, open 9–1; closed Thurs*), which houses some of the original red shirts of Garibaldi's Thousand, their guns and a variety of documents.

Beyond lies **Nervi**, at the east end of Genoa (bus no.15 from the Piazza Caricamento). This is one of the oldest resorts on the Riviera, where handsome grand hotels line Via dei Palme, although many are now converted to apartments. A lovely path, the **Passeggiata Anita Garibaldi**, follows Nervi's lush, wild and rocky shore.

In Nervi three villas have been converted to museums: the **Galleria d'Arte Moderna**, at Via Capolungo 9, contains an excellent collection of 19th- and 20th-century Italian art by Rubaldo Merello, Arturo Martini, Plinio Nomellini and others (*open Tues–Sat 9–7, Sun 9–1, for information call* ✆ *010 322 396*). The villa's 18th-century English park now belongs to the city and hosts Nervi's prestigious international ballet festival; the adjacent Villa Grimaldi has a beautiful rose garden which doubles as an outdoor cinema in the summer. A second house, the Villa Grimaldi Fassio, is now the home of the **Raccolte Frugone** (✆ *010 322 396, open Tues–Sat 9–7, Sun 9–1; adm*), featuring figurative paintings by Italian and other artists from the 18th and 19th centuries. Further east, at Viale Mafalda di Savoia 3, the **Museo Giannettino Luxoro** (*open Tues–Sat 9–1*) is in another lovely park. It, too, has a small modern art collection, but is especially noteworthy for its decorative arts: clocks (some of the first luminous timepieces), Christmas crib figures, ceramics, furniture, fabrics and lace.

Shopping

'Genoa has the face of business,' wrote Tobias Smollett in 1766, and you won't find any lack of shops. Antiques are a speciality in the streets around Garibaldi. Genoa's huge food market, the **Mercato Orientale** on Via XX Settembre, is a great place to experience the cornucopia of seafood and vegetables that help make Liguria Liguria. For more exotic produce, try the bazaar-like Sottoripa near the port, where you can buy shark's fins and ouzo. The **Palazzo Ducale** is the site of frequent antique shows and has some of the city's better bookshops and fashion showrooms. English books are available at **Bozzi**, on Via Cairoli 6. **Drogheria Torielli** in Via San Bernardo is the last old-fashioned grocer's in Genoa, selling exotic spices and nuts from around the Mediterranean, just as shops did in the Middle Ages.

Genoa's premier cultural event is its annual **Boat Show**, a vast celebration of all things nautical held over ten days in early October. Each year around half a million people come to look at over 2000 boats of all shapes and sizes displayed in and around the port's International Fair (*open daily 9.30–6.30; adm L18,000*).

If you want to get a closer look at the installations of Italy's busiest quays, take the **tour of Genoa's port**. Excursions (most dramatic at night, when everything is illuminated) are run by the Cooperativa Battellieri, ✆ 010 265 712, and by Alimar, ✆ 010 256 775; both companies depart from the Calata Zingari, near the Stazione Marittima, and the trip costs L10,000 return.

Genoa has two professional **football** teams: Sampdoria, one of Italy's top half-dozen teams who last won the Scudetto (the Italian first division championship) in 1991 and have in their time paid the wages of Ruud Gullit, Graeme Souness and Gianluca Vialli; and Genoa, an older but less successful side currently languishing in the second division. Both play at the Stadio Luigi Ferraris, on the north side of the city.

Genoa ✉ *16100* **Where to Stay**

Genoa's hotels range from the fabulous to the scabrous. Most are near one or other of the main train stations—around Brignole is the better area if you're looking for something cheap. Only crusty sailors and bodyguards would feel comfortable in the very cheapest establishments near the port. It can be very difficult finding a room, at any price, during the Boat Show (*see* above).

very expensive

★★★★ **Starhotel President**, Via Corte Lambruschini 4, ✆ 010 5727, ✉ 010 553 1820, is the top hotel in the city (while the Colombia is closed), a six-year-old part of a complex in front of Brignole Station built specifically for the 1992 celebrations, and something like the ultimate in nineties luxury and design. Ultra-modern and super-sleek, it has 192 double rooms, including some vast suites, a palatial reception area and gourmet restaurant.

★★★★ **Bristol Palace**, Via XX Settembre 35, ✆ 010 592 541, ✉ 010 561 756, located near Brignole Station and the Teatro Carlo Felice, is an elegant choice with sumptuous antique furnishings, beautiful air-conditioned rooms and a pleasant English bar.

★★★★ **Brittania**, Via Balbi 38, ✆ 010 26991, ✉ 010 246 9242, is perhaps the best upper-range hotel near Principe Station. It is very smart and slick, if maybe rather garishly designed in black and red, and modern and comfortable. The top floor rooms enjoy fantastic views, and though there's no restaurant, it does have a café, gym and billiard room and garage. There are self-catering flats for longer stays.

★★★★　**Jolly Hotel Plaza**, Via Martin Piaggio 11, ✆ 010 839 3641, 🖷 010 839 1850, *jollyha@primopiano.it*, in the centre, near Piazza Corvetto and the pretty Villa di Negro park, offers the standard Jolly combination of luxuriousness and efficiency for the business traveller, while not being particularly jolly. The bedrooms are superbly comfortable and the décor is a surpringly jaunty Art Deco concoction of greens and blacks. The restaurant has a good reputation and stays open till 10pm, although you are unlikely to be seated after 9.

★★★★　**Villa Pagoda**, Via Capolungo 15, Nervi ✉ 16167, ✆ 010 372 6161, 🖷 010 321 218, *pagoda@pn.itnet*. Beautifully set in its own park near the sea, it has 17 spacious and tastefully decorated bedrooms, housed in an 18th-century villa. There's a big buffet breakfast to wake up to, and a new pool planned for 1999.

expensive

★★★★　**Astor**, Viale delle Palme 16, Nervi ✉ 16167, ✆ 010 329 011, 🖷 010 372 8486, is a fashionable and elegant hotel in an enchanting garden near the sea, far from the hurly-burly of the city centre.

★★★★　**Savoja Majestic**, Via Arsenale di Terra 5, 010 261 641, 🖷 010 261 883, near Stazione Principe, is in an elegant 19th-century building, with a charming hall and American-style bar; rooms are spacious and soundproof; helpful staff and big breakfast buffet; pay garage nearby.

★★★　**Metropoli**, Piazza Fontane Marose, ✆ 010 246 8888, 🖷 010 246 8686, a comfortable Best Western Hotel in a charming, quiet location at the end of Via Garibaldi, with excellent service (including laundry) and a pay garage nearby.

moderate

★★★　**Agnello d'Oro**, Via Monachette 6, ✆ 010 246 2084, 🖷 010 246 2327, is housed in a 17th-century property of the Doria family, near Via Balbi. Although most of the old-fashioned charm is concentrated in the lobby, the rooms are very comfortable.

★★★　**Bellevue**, Salita Providenza 1, ✆ 010 246 2400, 🖷 010 265 932, has a wonderful view of the port. It has smart, modern, air-conditioned rooms, but no restaurant.

★★★　**La Capannina**, Via T. Speri 7, ✆ 010 317131, 🖷 010 362 2692. Out in the eastern residential zone, near the charming fishing port of Boccadasse, with a lovely terrace where breakfast is served, and simple but tranquil rooms. In summer, the hotel's boat goes out on diving expeditions.

★★　**Bel Soggiorno**, Via XX Settembre 19/2, ✆ 010 542 880, 🖷 010 581 418, near the centre, is the friendliest hotel in this category, and in an excellent position, though it can be slightly noisy.

cheap

★★　**Cairoli**, Via Cairoli 14/4, ✆ 010 246 1454, 🖷 010 246 1524, *cairoli@rdn.it*. Among the more respectable and hygienic of the city's inexpensive choices, and very centrally located, it's more like a three-star hotel, with sparkling, modern rooms and a relaxed, friendly and personal atmosphere. Excellent value.

* ★★★ **Vittoria & Orlandini**, Via Balbi 33, ☎ 010 261 923, ✆ 010 246 2656, *vittorin@mbox.vol.it.* A charming, slightly eccentric hotel with rooms around an inner garden; comfortable bedrooms and a pretty breakfast room with views over the historic centre.

* ★★ **Della Posta Nuova**, Via Balbi 24, ☎/✆ 010 246 2005 (*moderate–cheap*), also near Brignole, is the best of a few *pensioni* in the same building.

* ★ **Major**, Vico Spada 4, ☎ 010 247 4174, ✆ 010 246 9898 is a cheaper alternative, in a great position just inside the *centro storico*, and close by Piazza de Ferrari and Via Garibaldi. The rooms are clean and modern, and a real bargain.

* ★ **Carletto**, Via Colombo 16 (signposted off Via XX Settembre), ☎ 010 588 412, ✆ 010 561 229, in the station area, not far from Brignole, has good rooms, with lots of *focaccia* stands nearby.

* ★★ **Villa Bonera**, Via Sarfatti 8, Nervi, ☎ 010 372 6164, ✆ 010 372 8565, is a very attractive option with 26 charming rooms in a 17th-century villa surrounded by a pretty garden.

Genoa ✉ *16100*

Eating Out
expensive

One of Genoa's most famous restaurants, **Toe Drue**, Via Corsi 441, ☎ 010 650 0100, is in the working-class district of Sestri Ponente, west of the centre. Toe Drue means 'hard table', and this very fashionable restaurant has kept the furnishings of the rustic inn that preceded it. On these hard tables are served an array of delightful and unusual Ligurian specialities, many featuring seafood. Reservations are definitely necessary.

First opened in 1939, **Gran Gotto**, Viale Brigata Bisagno (near Piazza della Vittoria), ☎ 010 583 644, is another of the city's classic eateries, and one that seems to be getting better all the time, featuring imaginative and delicately prepared seafood like turbot in radicchio sauce, warm seafood *antipasti*, famous *rognone* (kidney) dishes and delectable desserts. *Closed Sat lunch and Sun.*

Near the centre, **Saint Cyr di Corti Elia**, Piazza Marsala 8, ☎ 010 886 897, serves expensive but tasty fare. The menu is by no means extensive but what they do they do well. The food is always beautifully presented and the staff are charming. Try their Genovese *minestrone* with pesto. *Closed Sat lunch and Sun.*

In the old centre, near Piazza Banchi, **Trattoria del Mario**, Via Conservatori del Mare 35/r, ☎ 010 246 2269, is an old Genoese favourite that offers the freshest of fish prepared in authentic Genoese style, and pasta with pesto as well as *cima*; the delicious seafood salad is a popular starter. *Closed Sat and Aug.*

One of the best traditional choices in the old city, **Pancetti Antica Osteria**, Borgo Incrociati 22/r, ☎ 010 839 2848, offers *pansotti* and some other Ligurian classics that are rarely prepared elsewhere, accompanied by the region's best vintages. *Closed Mon.* Something of a Genoese institution, **Zefferino**, Via XX Settembre 20, ✆ 010 591 990, has been run by the same family since 1939 and offers a taste of 1960s glamour with its mix of delicious Ligurian dishes and 'transatlantic cuisine' and a huge array of desserts. Non-stop service daily from noon to midnight. *Closed Wed.*

moderate

In the maze of the southern old city, **Archivolto Mongiardino**, No.2 in the street of the same name, ✆ 010 247 7610, is the place to go for excellent seafood dishes. *Closed Sun and Mon.* **Genio**, Salita San Leonardo 61, ✆ 010 588 463, off Via Fieschi, near Piazza Dante, is another popular restaurant serving great traditional Ligurian food, and offering a wider choice for non-seafood fans. *Closed Sun.*

Mannori, Via Galata 70/r, ✆ 010 588 461, has excellent home cooking, where the pots simmer all morning to create hearty soups and other fills that a good Ligurian mamma might make. *Closed Sun and Aug.*

cheap

Good inexpensive restaurants abound in Genoa, especially in the *centro storico*. Try the fresh fish in the **Trattoria da Pino**, in Piazza Caricamento, ✆ 010 372 6395, one of Genoa's top portside greasy-spoon districts. **Ostaja Do Castello**, Salita Santa Margherita del Castello, ✆ 010 246 8980, has some of the best cheap food in town, with good Genoese specialities. *Closed Sun.*

Just off Via XXV Aprile, near the Piazza de Ferrari, the wonderfully authentic **Trattoria da Maria**, Vico Testadora 14/r, ✆ 010 581 080, serves up filling three-course meals for under L20,000. *Closed Sat.*

Up by Columbus' house, **Da Bedin**, Via Dante 56/r, ✆ 010 580 996, is famous for its pizza and *farinata*; way up by the Casteletto belvedere, **Baraccia**, Spianata Castelletto 6, ✆ 010 246 5165, is a great place for a light lunch, with the option of ordering two courses for L20,000. *Closed Sun and Aug.*

Genoese snacks

Focaccia, topped with olive oil and salt in its simplest form, is sold throughout the city, in bakeries and pizzerias; follow your nose to find it fresh from the oven, when it's at its best. *Farinata* (made of chick-pea meal, olive oil and water, and baked) and *panissa* (similar, only fried) are a bit more specialized. **Guglie**, Via S. Vincenzo 64/r, serves good versions of each, as well as *torta pasqualina.* Near the Porto Antico, **Antica Sciamadda**, Via S. Giorgio 14/r, is a classic place for Genoese snacks: *farinata*, savoury pies and *frisceu di baccalà* (stockfish croquettes). **Tugnin**, Piazza Tommaseo 42/r, is also good for *farinata*, pies and various croquettes, filled with onions or other vegetables. **Vexima**, Via Cerusa 1/b, is famous for its *farinata*, which comes with various optional extras, from whitebait to artichokes.

Tripe is something of a litmus test of urban authenticity: a real city has a hard core coterie of denizens who like to sink their teeth into an aromatic mess of the stuff, prepared to an age-old recipe; in Genoa the place to go is the **Cucina Trippa**, an institution founded in the late 18th century and still spooning out tripe *alla genovese* in Vico Casana.

cafés/pasticcerie/gelaterie

Genoa has had a long love affair with sweets. The technique for making the candied fruit that plays such a prominent role in the glass counters of the city's *confetterie* was brought back from Syria (the beautiful **Caffè Romanengo**, Via Soziglia 74/r, is famous for them) while the orange flower water, which goes into the city's classic cake, *pandolce*, was learned in Sidon in the Lebanon. The best pandolce is made at **Profumo**, in Via del Portello. The **Pasticceria Traverso**, Via Pastorino 116–188/r, ✆ 010 745 0065, was founded back in 1893 and is the official supplier of sweets to the Italian Senate; try their homemade *Nicolò Paganini* chocolates. **Viganotti**, in Vico Castagna, is another celebrated 'chocolate laboratory'. An all-round delicious assortment of pastries and sweets also awaits at **Klainguti**, Piazza di Soziglia 98/r, an elegant *caffè/pasticceria* founded in 1828, where the speciality is their unique *klaingutino*. **Caffè Gelateria Balilla**, Via Macaggi 84, is a traditional favourite for luscious ice creams.

Entertainment and Nightlife

In Paganini's home town there is bound to be plenty of music. The **Genoa Opera**, now back in the Teatro Carlo Felice in Piazza de Ferrari after years of being without a proper home, presents its main season from January to June, and in the summer sponsors the prestigious **Ballet Festival** in the park in Nervi. The Carolo Felice has two smaller theatres, the Teatro della Corte and the Teatro Duse, used for a mix of classic and avant-garde theatre. For information, contact the box office at Galleria Cardinal Siri 6, ✆ 010 589 329, ✉ 010 53 81 335 (*open Tues–Fri 2–6, Sat 10–12 and 2–6, and 1½hrs before each performance; no phone bookings*). The **Teatro della Tosse** is dedicated to alternative and underground performances. Summer sees a number of travelling companies at **Fort Sperone**, while the villas and parks around Genoa are used for outdoor film showings. In the summer there's also a full schedule of music and theatre in the city itself: there's **jazz** at **Il Millo, the Cotton Club**, Via al Porto Antico; **The Patio**, Via Oberdan 22, in Nervi, has live bluegrass on Mondays and jazz on Wednesdays. Every year Genoa competes with Venice, Pisa and Amalfi in the **Regatta of the Ancient Maritime Republics** (Genoa is to host next in 2000). There are frequent flower shows in the Fiera district, and a lively flea market in Piazzetta Lavagna.

The main centre of **café and bar** life is around the Via XX Settembre, though a noisier and seamier choice of places can be found around the port. Anyone feeling a need for a more English drinking ambience can find it at the **Britannia Pub** on

Vico della Casana just off Piazza de Ferrari, which is very popular with both foreigners and Italians. **Capitan Baliano** is a nice friendly bar in Piazza Matteotti, next to the Palazzo Ducale.

Minestrone con Pesto alla Genovese

For the pesto:

3 bunches of basil
1 clove of garlic
coarse sea salt
a handful of pine nuts
a handful of grated parmesan
handful of grated Sardinian pecorino (or any tangy hard ewe's milk cheese)
5 tablespoons of olive oil

For the minestrone:

150g fresh or tinned beans
a small cabbage, sliced
6 small aubergines (eggplants), cubed
4–5 tomatoes, cubed
a slice of pumpkin, cubed
75g mushrooms preserved in olive oil
100g small pasta
6 spoonfuls of pesto
parmesan

To make the pesto, wash the basil leaves, wring them out well, and crush them with a mortar and pestle, with the garlic, a bit of salt, the pine nuts and the cheese. When you have a uniform paste, slowly drizzle in the olive oil and a bit of hot water.

In a pot of salted water (enough for four large bowls of soup) boil the beans, aubergine, cabbage, tomatoes, pumpkin, mushrooms and a few spoonfuls of olive oil. Cook, and then add the pasta. When the pasta is done, add the pesto, and boil a little longer, until it thickens. Serve in bowls, covered with parmesan.

Genoa's *Entroterra*

For the most part, Genoa has sucked the juices out of its hinterland, leaving few compelling reasons to delve inland. Since the building of the Via Postumia (148 BC) the main roads to Milan and the Po valley go up the busy Val Polcevera; just off this to the west is the queen of all Liguria's numerous hilltop sanctuaries, the **Madonna della Guardia**. In the old days folks would walk up to deposit their *ex votos*; today people drive up to say a prayer, enjoy the stupendous view, and have lunch. The upper Polcevera, especially **Sant'Olcese**, is famous for its slightly smoky-flavoured Genoese salami. Further north, **Ronco Scrivia** has an impressive three-arch medieval bridge, apparently going nowhere in particular; even further north at **Vobbia** you'll find an even more peculiar 11th-century castle sandwiched in the rocks: the **Castello della Pietra**, once the property of the Spinola (© *010 939 394, open Sun 1–6*).

To the east of the Val Polcevera you can make the excursion to **Casella** by electric train (*see* above, p.157). In the Valle Scrivia even further east, **Torriglia** (reached by bus, or by car on the SS45) was a Roman town and today is Genoa's 'Little Switzerland', a small resort with an impressive if utterly derelict medieval castle. Nine kilometres to the east, **Montebruno** was owned at various times by most of Genoa's big families; it has a small museum of country culture and, in the church across the bridge, pieces of hawsers from Andrea Doria's galleys, donated as an *ex voto* for his victories.

Returning to Genoa from Torriglia, near the village of Doria, the Abbey of **San Siro di Struppa** was built some time around the year 1000 to honour Genoa's bishop saint, a famous 4th-century persecutor of the Arians. The church has been restored to its original form and boasts a polyptych of 1516, showing Siro confronting a rather benign-looking and very smartly decked-out basilisk, a symbol of heresy.

Riomaggiore

The Riviera di Levante

East of Genoa, the coast becomes a creature of high drama and romance. The beaches of this Coast of the Rising Sun, the Riviera di Levante, aren't as prominent, nor the climate quite as mild, but there are compensations. From Nervi and the Golfo di Paradiso, past Monte di Portofino to the once nearly inaccessible fishing villages of the Cinque Terre and in and

N

10 km
6 miles

The Riviera di Levante

Map labels:

S. Stéfano d'Aveto, Rezzoáglio, Magnasca, Cabanne, L. d. Lame, Parco dell'Aveto, Neirone, Favale di Málvaro, M. Cavallo, Borzonasca, M. Chiappozzo, M. Porcile, M. Alpe, Libiola, Tassani, Genova, Quarto dei Mille, M. Fasce, Nervi, Bogliasco, Sori, Terrile, Uscio, Cicagna, Avegno, V. Fontanabuona, Recco, Ruta, Rapallo, Camogli, S. Rocco, Zoagli, Margherita Ligure, Gravéglia, Entella, Portofino Vetta, M. de Portofino, Paraggi, Chiávari, S. Fruttuoso, Portofino, Golfo del Tigullio, Lavagna, Sestri Levante, Riva Trigoso, Moneglia, Déiva Marina, Framura, Parco Regionale out of the nooks and crannies of the Gulf of Poets, the mountains and sea tussle and tumble in a voluptuous chaos of azure, turquoise and piney green. Against these deeply coloured coves and cliffs rise villages of weathered pastels and ochres, silvery groves of olives, the striped terraces, gazing out over bobbing fleets of fishing craft, sailing boats and sleek white yachts. Everyone has heard of Portofino, but there are other lovely if less glittering places to anchor yourself—Camogli, Portovenere, Santa Margherita. The Apennines of the *entroterra* offer another world altogether, a world of luxuriant chestnut forests and modest hamlets, where sheep-rearing and farming and quarrying slate for Liguria's roofs and the world's billiard tables are the main occupations.

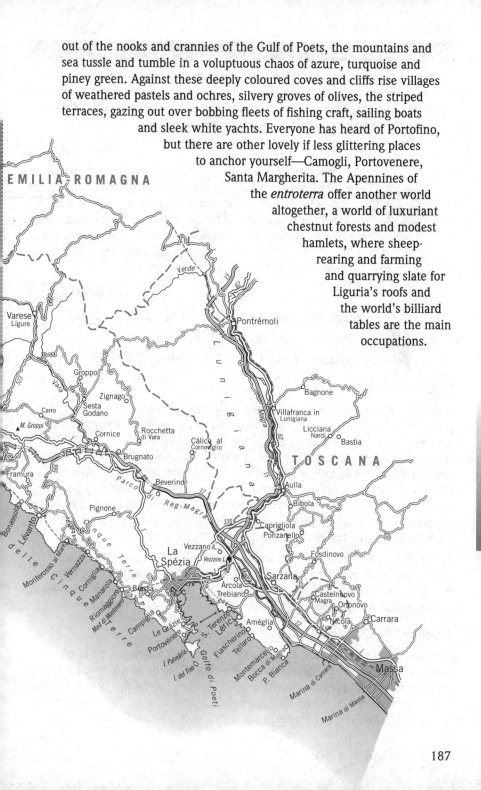

Of all the nubs and notches in the Italian coastline, one of the best beloved is the squarish promontory of Monte di Portofino. It comes into view as you leave Genoa's easternmost toehold at Nervi, and forms on its western side Genoa's own Riviera, the Golfo Paradiso—and if its name may be an exaggeration, well, we've heard worse.

Getting Around

The Genoa–Pisa **railway** hugs the coast, but in many places you can only get glimpses of the scenery between the tunnels. The most scenic of all is the old coastal road, the Via Aurelia (SS1), which is also the route used by most of the **buses**. From Camogli there's a regular boat service, run by the **Battellieri del Golfo Paradiso**, Via Scalo 2, ✆ 0185 772 091, ✆ 0185 771 263, to Recco, Sori, Bogliasco and Nervi one way, and San Fruttuoso, Portofino and Santa Margherita Ligure the other.

Tourist Information

Recco: Piazza Nicoloso di Recco, ✆ 0185 722 440, ✆ 0185 721 958.

Uscio: Via Caduti della Libertà 4, ✆/✆ 0185 91101.

Camogli: Via XX Settembre 33, ✆/✆ 0185 771 066 (very helpful).

Bogliasco to Recco

Beyond Nervi, handsome fishing hamlets dot the coast: **Bogliasco** is a well-nigh perfect one, with its thousand-year-old fortress converted into pastel-washed apartments by the sea, with laundry flapping in the breeze and the delightful oval rococo church of the **Natività** (1731). Next comes little **Pieve Ligure**, hemmed in by Monte Santa Caterina and its olive terraces. Pieve is proudest of another tree, however: as the mimosa capital of the Riviera, it fills up with little yellow pompom blooms in January and early February. It doesn't have a beach, but people swim off the rocks. **Sori**, next, does have a fine sandy beach tucked in a pretty inlet. It also has a few too many holiday homes, and a curvaceous confectionery church, the pink Santa Margherita (1711).

Recco, at the crossroads to Camogli, was bombed into dust during the war. Completely rebuilt, it holds its head high as the gastronomic capital of the Riviera di Levante. One thing the bombs couldn't damage, however, is the perfect little pebble beach at **Mulinetti**, set among villas and gardens.

A Detour into Columbus Country

A twisting road from Recco leads up steeply through the trees to **Avegno**, the village of bell-makers, where that foundry has been in business since 1594; the nearby church at **Tesana** has a remarkable 16th-century Flemish wooden high relief of the *Crucifixion*. A by-road leads to **Terrile**, an even smaller hamlet, where craftsmen make everything else a fashionable campanile needs—the bell supports and clocks. **Uscio**, the main village in these parts, was once a Lombard stronghold, and has a 12th-century Romanesque church, recently restored to its original appearance. Mostly, however, Uscio is renowned for its refreshing climate and was one of the first health resorts in Italy (*see* below). The surrounding chestnut forests do double duty, supplying the flour to make the local pasta, *trofie*, and the scenery for lovely walks and drives—the high road back to Genoa, by way of **Monte Fasce** (834m), the big bald mountain that looms over the east end of the city, is especially grand at sunset, taking in views as far as Corsica, Elba and the marbly Apuan Alps above Carrara.

Another road above Uscio writhes to **Gattorna**, a toy-making and flower-growing town in the **Val Fontanabuona** that runs parallel to the coast all the way to Chiávari; the valley's river, the little Lavagna, was one of the very few things in Liguria that met Dante's approval (he called it a *fiumana bella*). This quiet vale of slate quarries was the cradle of the Columbus family; Christopher's grandfather Giovanni, a woolworker, hailed from tiny **Terrarossa Colombo**, 2km away, and, with his son Domenico, was one of many who migrated to Genoa to seek a better living. You can follow their presumed path from here to Nervi, the **Itinerario Storico Colombiano**, beginning at the sculpture by Antonio Leveroni erected in 1982. **Neirone**, up a narrow valley north of Gattorna, holds a festival in August honouring one of the greatest gifts the New World was to bestow on the Old: not gold, but spuds. The local lord, Michele Dondero, introduced potatoes in the 18th century, in the face of charges of witchcraft by the locals, who suspected the newfangled crop of being as poisonous as its cousin, deadly nightshade; they quickly changed their minds when famine struck in 1795 and there was nothing else to eat, and have fêted the potato ever since.

The biggest settlement of the Fontanabuona valley is **Cicagna**, famous for good bread, a bridge built by the Fieschi, and the reactionary *Viva Maria* revolt that its priests and peasants led against the Napoleonic Republic of Liguria in 1797. Afterwards, many residents followed the Columbian itinerary all the way to the Americas, so many, in fact, that there's a rather sweet *Monument to the Italian Emigrant* (a bronze fellow with his grip, ready to depart) in **Favale di Málvaro**, a village up the road from Cicagna. In exchange for the potato, Favale gave the New World the parents of Amedeo Pietro Giannini, the founder of what was for a long time the biggest bank in the world, the Bank of America. The Giannini homestead has documents on his career and immigration in general.

Camogli

Returning to the coast, Camogli, only a mile from Recco on the promontory, was luckily spared the bombs that flattened its neighbour. Unabashedly picturesque on its pine-wooded slope, the town has a proud maritime tradition: this was the home port of a renowned republican fleet that fought with Napoleon, and its fishing and merchant vessels were everywhere along the Riviera in the 19th century. Its name derives from *Casa Mogli* (home of wives), since the menfolk were almost always at sea. Many of them still are.

The old harbour, piled high with tall, faded houses with dark green shutters, is the scene of Camogli's famous *Sagra del Pesce* on each second Sunday in May, where Italy's largest frying pan (14ft across) is used to cook up thousands of sardines, which are distributed free to all comers—a display of generosity and abundance carrying with it the hope that the sea will be equally generous and abundant in the coming year. A small promontory, the Isola, separates Camogli's little pebble beach from its fishing port, and wears like a hat the bijou medieval **Dragonara Castle**. Fish now flit where soldiers spent many a bored or harrowing hour—the castle contains the **Acquario di Camogli** (© *0185 773 375, open April–Sept 10–11.45 and 3–6.45; til 5.45 in winter; adm L6000*), with 22 tanks of Mediterranean creatures. Nearby, the **Basilica di Santa Maria Assunta**, last redone in the 19th century with a neoclassical façade, is richly decorated with gilded stuccoes and frescoes.

Camogli recalls its thrilling days as a rough-and-tumble sea power with models, paintings, votive offerings and other salty memorabilia in the **Museo Marinaro**, Via Gio Bono Ferrari 41 (© *0185 729 049, open April–Sept Wed–Mon 9–12 and 4–7; Oct–Mar Wed, Sat and Sun 9–11.45 and 3–5.40, Mon, Thurs and Fri 9–12*). The archaeological section (*open Wed–Mon 9–12*) contains artefacts from, and a reconstruction of, an Iron Age settlement discovered nearby, as well as 2nd-century BC silver coins from the ancient Ligurian settlement at Castellaro.

Pansotti con salsa di noci

If you've mastered the art of homemade pasta, you may want to try this speciality of Recco and Camogli. The pasta should be made with only one egg.

> *One sheet homemade pasta (about 700g)*
> *500g chard, boiled*
> *a handful of fresh borage, boiled*
> *2 eggs*
> *50g ground pine nuts*
> *a handful of grated parmesan*
> *marjoram*
> *500g walnuts, crushed with a clove of garlic*
> *90g butter*
> *a little soft breadcrumb*
> *a bit of cream*
> *olive oil*
> *salt and pepper*

For the salsa di noce (walnut sauce):

> *12 walnuts, ground*
> *250ml cream*

Roll out the pasta in a large sheet. Make the filling with the chard and borage, the eggs, ground pine nuts, parmesan, salt, pepper and marjoram. Mix together well, gradually adding 50g butter, the walnuts, a bit of breadcrumb and cream and more parmesan. Cut the pasta into circles, fill it, fold it in shapes of large caps and cook in boiling salted water. Top with 40g butter and walnut sauce.

For the walnut sauce: reduce the walnuts to a mush, and mix with the warm cream.

The Promontory of Portofino

The coastal road ends at Camogli, although there are two other points on the stunning promontory of Portofino accessible by road by way of **Ruta**, just inland: the hamlet and church of **San Rocco** and **Portofino Vetta** (buses from Camogli), an hour's walk from the summit of **Monte di Portofino** (2001ft), with its priceless views of the Riviera and out to sea as far as Elba.

But to take in the best of this enchanting corner of the Gulf of Paradise, now protected as the **Parco Naturale di Portofino**, you have to go by sea (*see* 'Getting Around', above) or by foot on the paths that crisscross the olive groves and Mediterranean *macchia*. From Camogli it's a strenuous but gorgeous three-hour hike to the main destination, the fishing hamlet of **San Fruttuoso** on the seaward side of the promontory; there are also boats from Portofino, Santa Margherita and Rapallo, so in summer it can be short of elbow-room. Along the way, walkers can visit the pretty little 12th-century Romanesque church of **San Nicolò di Capodimonte**. The path descends to the minuscule fishing hamlet at **Punta Chiappa**, a point famous for the changing colours of the sea, although thanks to the quantity of rubbish floating around nowadays the water is no longer as clear as it once was.

San Fruttuoso is named after its famous **Abbey**, founded in 711 by the bishop of Tarragona, who fled Spain from the Moors with the relics of the third-century martyrs St Fructuosus and his two deacons in his bag. The Benedictines subsequently took over the abbey, and were given a large donation of land by Adelaide, the widow of Emperor Otto I. San Fruttuoso later came under the protection of the Doria family, and in the 16th century Andrea Doria added the **Torre dei Doria** to defend the abbey from Turkish corsairs, who plagued the coast in the name of the king of France. In 1983, the family donated the abbey and its lands to the FAI (the Italian National Trust); you can visit the small museum and the pretty white 11th-century church with its unusual Byzantine-style cupola and tiny cloister, with six 13th-century Doria tombs—the family church of San Matteo was being done up. Another tomb belongs to local heroine Maria Avegno, who drowned trying to save the crew of the English steamship *Croesus* that sank here in 1855 (© *0185 772 703, open Mar–April Tues–Sun 10–1 and 2–4; May–Oct until 6; Nov–Feb public holidays only*). San Fruttuoso is surrounded by a lush growth of palms and olives, and it's a two-hour walk through these groves to Portofino. Another sight, best appreciated by skin-divers (although you can also see it through the bathyscopes on the boats) is the 1954 bronze **Cristo degli Abissi** (Christ of the Depths), eight fathoms under the sea, a memorial to those lost at sea and protector of all who work underwater.

Where to Stay and Eating Out

Bogliasco ✉ 16031

There's one little hotel, ★★**Villa Flora**, Via Aurelia 5, © 010 347 0013, 🖷 010 347 1123 (*cheap*), but an exceptional restaurant, in spite of a name that might imply otherwise: **Tipico**, just out of the centre at San Bernardo, © 010 347 0754 (*expensive–moderate*), serving irresistible *antipasti* and homemade pasta, topped with fresh-picked tomatoes and seafood; in the spring don't miss the *pansotti* with asparagus tips. Follow it with perfectly grilled fish, and homemade desserts. *Closed Mon and mid-Aug.*

Recco ✉ 16063

Though lacking in scenic attractions, Recco is something of a gourmet mecca, famous for its *focaccia* with cheese, and *trofie* with pesto sauce and *pansotti.* The mayor of Recco runs some of the best places to stay and eat: ★★★★**La Villa**, Via Roma 278, ✆ 0185 74128, ✉ 0185 721 095, *manulina@omninet.it* (*expensive*), is a typical Genoese pleasure villa with modern extension, gym and sun terrace, prettily set in a garden with pool; the bigger rooms are in the annexe, but all are very comfortable. The hotel loans out mountain bikes to guests, and has an excellent *enoteca* with theme tastings. Predating the hotel is its restaurant, the celebrated **Manuelina**, ✆ 0185 74128 (*expensive*), just outside the centre, where you can try exquisite *trofie* with pesto, and seafood in a variety of styles for the *secondo*. Next door is **Focacceria** (*expensive*), where you can dine on one of the town's famous *focaccia*, or on other Ligurian dishes such as *cima. Both closed Wed.*

Another renowned restaurant in Recco is the hundred-year-old **Da-o Vittorió**, Via Roma 160, ✆ 0185 74029 (*expensive*), whose specialities include utterly superb *minestrone di verdura alla Genovese* and *trofie al pesto*. Recco has good budget-price restaurants, too, particularly along the seafront and around the Via Roma.

Uscio ✉ 16030

The **Colonia della Salute Carlo Arnaldi**, ✆ 0185 919 400, ✉ 0185 919 418 (*expensive*) was founded in 1906 as one of the first health farms in Italy, guaranteed to make you more healthy and beautiful. Phytotherapy (including a secret herbal potion), beauty and relaxation treatments, tailor-made diet, a pool and tennis are part of the cure.

Camogli ✉ 16032

The lovely ★★★★**Cenobio dei Dogi**, Via Cuneo 34, ✆ 0185 7241, ✉ 0185 772 796 (*luxury*), a former palace of Genoa's doges, is at the water's edge with fantastic views of the gulf—on a clear day you can see the steady winking of Genoa's lighthouse. The bedrooms are light and airy and tastefully decorated in white and wood, and there are two excellent restaurants, one on the hotel's private pebble beach, both open to the public and both with superb views. There are various sun terraces, a flower-filled park, a heated swimming pool and tennis courts.

For something more affordable try the ★★★**Casmona**, Salita Pineto 13, ✆ 0185 770 015, ✉ 0185 275 930 (*moderate*), a quiet, tidy place with a restaurant and a shady little patio. ★★**Pensione La Camogliese**, Via Garibaldi 55, ✆ 0185 771 402, ✉ 0185 774 024 (*cheap*) is very pleasant and also has an attractive restaurant, with a veranda overlooking the port, and good, reasonably priced fish dishes. *Closed Wed.*

Vento Ariel, Calata Porto 1, © 0185 771 080 (*expensive*) is a tiny, charming place on the harbour that bases its existence entirely on the luck of the town's fishing fleet. Only fish and seafood are served, with daily set menus or *à la carte*. Reservations are essential in summer. *Closed Wed.*

There are several restaurants near Camogli at Portofino Vetta, of which the **Rosa**, Via J. Ruffini 11, © 0185 771 088, enjoys some of the finest views, and prepares some of the best seafood from the morning's catch.

San Fruttuoso ✉ 16030

There are a couple of good seafood restaurants: **Da Giovanni**, © 0185 770 047 (*expensive*), a small, charming place, which also doubles as an *inexpensive* hotel, and **La Cantina**, © 0185 772 626 (*expensive*), on the beach, serving fish cooked to order at very reasonable prices.

The Golfo del Tigullio: Santa Margherita, Portofino and Rapallo

The Golfo del Tigullio, on the east of the promontory of Portofino, is just as lovely as its paradisiacal counterpart to the west. After Camogli, the road cuts inland to Santa Margherita Ligure, the crossroads for Liguria's most famous and exclusive resorts, Portofino and Rapallo.

Getting Around

Buses from Santa Margherita station make the journey to Portofino (with constant horn accompaniment) every twenty minutes or so (L1700 one way). From Santa Margherita boat excursions go to San Fruttuoso, Portofino and the Cinque Terre.

Tourist Information

Portofino: Via Roma 35, © 0185 269 024.
Santa Margherita Ligure: Via XXV Aprile 2/b, © 0185 287 485, @ 0185 283 034.
Rapallo: Via A. Diaz 9, © 0185 51282, @ 0185 230 346.
Zoagli: Piazza San Martino 8, © 0185 259 127

Santa Margherita Ligure

Santa Margherita, with its beautiful harbour, is not as spectacular as Portofino, but friendly and lively, a popular winter hideaway for the British since the 19th century, with its share of grand hotels and villas immersed in gardens. The town, formerly two separate villages, was united in the 19th century and named for its church, **Santa Margherita d'Antiochia**, a rococo extravaganza full of Italian and Flemish art. Near here, you can wander through the luxuriant **Parco di Villa Durazzo**, the gardens of a 17th-century villa, complete with allegorical statues (*open 9–12 and 2–4.30*); the nearby Villa Nido is used for concerts. Just below it on the shore, the **Cappuccini** church contains one of Liguria's oldest sculptures: a 12th-century *Virgin*.

The 9km stretch of the SS227 to Portofino, opened in 1878, is one of the most beautiful on the coast, a steeply meandering ribbon of tarmac roughly one and a half cars wide. On the way it passes the **Abbey of La Cervara**, where King Francis I was imprisoned after the Battle of Pavia. **Pariggi**, further along, has a sandy beach on an emerald sea.

Portofino

One of Italy's most romantic little nooks, Portofino was discovered long ago by artists, then by the yachting brotherhood, who fell in love with its delightful little port framed by mellowed, narrow houses, and then by the rich and trendy, who fell in love with its spectacular beauty and seclusion, which made it a favourite setting for illicit trysts and such, far—or so they hoped—from the clicking cameras of the paparazzi. This exclusiveness still exists to a certain extent—linked to the rest of the Riviera only by the narrow coastal road, Portofino is certainly a difficult place to get to. Despite this, and the fact that there are only a handful of hotels, Portofino's hard-fought-for seclusion vanishes every weekend and every day in summer when thousands of trippers pour in for an afternoon's window-shopping in the smart boutiques (some selling the district's famous lace), a drink in the exquisite piazzetta or a portside bar, or perhaps a walk in the cypress-studded hills. In the evening, the yachtsmen and the residents of the hillside villas descend once again to their old haunts and reclaim Portofino as their own.

Portofino's name is derived from the Roman *Portus Delphini*, which had a *mithraeum* (an initiatory sanctuary dedicated to the Persian god Mithras, a favourite of Roman soldiers) on its isthmus. The *mithraeum* is now the site of the church of **San Giorgio,** rebuilt after war damage in 1950 but still housing the supposed relics of the defrocked saint George. It's hardly a formal place—as often as not there's a cat sleeping on or under the altar. Further up, **Castello Brown**, built in the 1500s as a defence against the Turks, converted into a residence in the 1800s, and reconverted into a castle, affords enchanting views of the little port (*open Tues–Sun 10–6; adm L4000*). Another lovely walk, beyond the castle, is to Punta del Capo and the **Faro**, the old lighthouse, taking in magnificent views of the Gulf of Tigullio through the pine forest.

Rapallo and Zoagli

After Portofino, **Rapallo**, in a marvellous setting at the innermost pocket of the Gulf of Tigullio, is probably the most famous resort on the Riviera di Levante. The British in the 19th century were the pioneers, arriving to bask in Rapallo's mild year-round climate and bathe at its fairly good beach, genteel days still recalled along the charming **Lungomare Vittorio Veneto**, with its grand hotels and turn-of-the-century villas. More recent attractions include an 18-hole golf course, busy marina, indoor swimming pool, tennis and riding stables. The **Castle** at the end, surrounded by the harbour's waters, was built after one of the most notorious Turkish pirates, Dragut, destroyed Rapallo in the 16th century; it now holds changing exhibitions. Further along the shore, there's a **Museum of Bobbin Lace** in the Villa Tigullio (*open 3–6, Thurs 10–11.30; closed Mon*), dedicated to Rapallo's proudest age-old craft. Don't miss riding the recently restored **funivia** (*Mar–Oct 8–sunset; Nov–Feb 8.30–5; cars leave every 30 minutes*); the seven-minute trip will take you up 7707ft to the 16th-century **Santuario di Montallegro**, on the site where the Madonna appeared to a local farmer and a Byzantine icon miraculously arrived, having flown from Dalmatia; and from where any sinner can enjoy a heavenly view of the Tigullio Gulf.

Rapallo was the longtime home of Max Beerbohm, who lived in the Villino Chiaro and attracted a literary circle of some note to the resort; it is also a favourite venue for conferences—at the **Villa Spinola**, the Treaty of Rapallo was signed in 1920, setting the border between Italy and Yugoslavia and normalizing relations between Germany and the Soviet Union. The villa lies along the Santa Margherita road, not far from **San Michele di Pagana**, a seaside hamlet with large firework-popping festivals in July and September, and a parish church containing an excellent *Crucifixion* by Van Dyck.

East of Rapallo, **Zoagli** was another casualty of the war, rebuilt after 1945, but it's no fashion victim; Zoagli still produces handmade patterned velvets, just as it did when they were the rage in the Middle Ages, although nowadays people prefer to use them for dressing their furniture. Most of the velvet factories (they also make silks and damasks) are open for visits, among them the Fratelli Cordani, Via S. Pietro 21, © 0185 259 141, and Giuseppe Gaggioli, Via Aurelia 208A, © 0185 259 057. A path cut in the rock follows the shore from the beach with lovely views over the gulf. Along the Via Aurelia towards Chiávari, the 15th-century **Santuario della Madonna delle Grazie** shelters a Flemish Renaissance statue of the Virgin and some fine frescoes, especially a *Last Judgement* by Luca Cambiaso.

Note that many hotels in this area still insist, or at least prefer, that guests take full board, particularly in the high season.

Santa Margherita ✉ 16038

Two hotels have long rivalled one another in the luxury category: **★★★★★Imperiale Palace**, Via Pagana 19, on the edge of town, ✆ 0185 288 991, ✆ 0185 284 223 (*luxury*), formerly a private villa, was converted into a hotel at the turn of the century; in 1922, in one of the palatial marble- and gilt-encrusted public rooms, the Weimar Republic signed an agreement with Russia to re-open diplomatic relations. Antiques litter the hallways, public rooms and more expensive bedrooms, and concerts are held in the music room some afternoons. There's a heated outdoor pool, a lush tropical garden and a seafront terrace. The restaurant is rich and refined and leads on to a wonderful breakfast room overlooking the garden. *Open Mar–Oct.*

The shining white **★★★★Grand Hotel Miramare**, Via Milite Ignoto 30, ✆ 0185 287 013, ✆ 0185 284 651 (*very expensive*) is almost as palatial, though purpose-built as a posh winter hotel in the early 1900s. Surrounded by a lovely garden, with a heated salt-water pool (and a pebbly beach across the road), it has lovely air-conditioned rooms, many with fine views of the gulf from their balconies. The Miramare's water-skiing school is one of the best in Italy.

★★★La Vela, Via N.Cuneo 21, ✆ 0185 284 771 (*moderate*), a former villa located a bit above town, has a friendly, intimate atmosphere and 16 rooms with good sea views. *Closed Nov–Christmas.* **★★★Conte Verde**, Via Zara 1, ✆ 0185 287 139, ✆ 0185 284 211 (*moderate*), also a villa, is in the centre, a short walk from the sea, and is a cheerful place with a small terrace, garden and bar.

Santa Margherita's best value option in this category, though, is the very friendly and welcoming **★★Albergo Fasce**, Via L. Bozzo 3, ✆ 0185 286 435, ✆ 0185 283 580 (*moderate*), part of the 'family hotel' chain. Its rooms are modern and immaculately maintained, and it also offers a laundry service, free bike hire, parking, sun roof and a small garden. There's an excellent restaurant, where you can enjoy a full meal of delicious Ligurian specialities for not much more than L20,000 a head (*high season only*). *Closed Nov–Christmas.* Another good choice is **★★★Terminus**, Piazza Nobili 4, ✆ 0185 286 121, ✆ 0185 282 546 (*moderate*), run by the former owner of two London restaurants, at the top of town just beside the station. Some rooms have wonderful views of the bay and town. **★San Giorgio**, Via N. Cuneo 59, ✆ 0185 286 770, ✆ 0185 280 704 (*cheap*), a bit outside the centre, has nine pleasant rooms and a garden.

If you can escape the board requirements of your hotel, try the finest restaurant in Santa Margherita, **Cesarina**, Via Mameli 2/c, ✆ 0185 286 059 (*very expensive*), located under an arcade in the old part of town. The décor is fresh and modern, and goes well with such specialities as *zuppa di datteri* (razor clam soup) or Liguria's famous spaghetti with red mullet (*triglie*) sauce. Reservations are advisable. *Closed Tues.*

More seafood and tasty fresh fish dominates the menu at **Dei Pescatori**, Via Bottaro 43, ✆ 0185 286 747 (*expensive*). **L'Ancora**, Via Maragliano 7, ✆ 0185 280 599 (*moderate*) offers seafood specialities (an excellent *insalata di pesce*), and a good-value set tourist menu. *Closed Tues.*

Portofino ✉ 16034

The management of the ✭✭✭✭✭**Splendido**, Viale Baratta 16, ✆ 0185 269 551, 🖷 0185 269 614 (*luxury*) believe they run the best hotel in Liguria, if not Italy. It's an arrogant assumption but one with which precious few people would disagree. The views alone, of olive- and-cypress-clad hills gently framing the town, its tiny harbour and the deep blue sea beyond, are well worth the astronomical fees. The bedrooms are sumptuous, the restaurant refined and the breakfast terrace, sheltered beneath a huge sub-tropical canopy, simply delightful. Take a swim in the heated outdoor pool or, for a mere L1,000,000 per day, go for a ride in the hotel's own speedboat. If you are still not impressed, the staff will point you towards their wall of fame where you will find numerous signed photographs of the various film stars, pop stars and members of minor European royal families who have sampled the Splendido and found it to their liking (Winston Churchill, Groucho Marx, Elizabeth Taylor and Richard Burton, Humphrey Bogart and Lauren Bacall, Wallis Simpson and Edward, Duke of Windsor, Liza Minnelli, Barbra Streisand, Madonna and Bill Gates, to name-drop a few). In essence, this is the sort of place where, for just one night, you can be Grace Kelly. Its secluded location high on a hillside preserves its air of exclusivity.

If you want to mingle with mere mortals, check into the Spendido's smaller sibling, the **Splendido Mare**, Via Roma 2, ✆ 0185 267 802, 🖷 0185 267 807 (*luxury*), which recently opened on the Piazza by the harbour. This is a less grand, slightly cheaper version of the original with a delightful *al fresco* restaurant, the Chufley Bar. A shuttle service links the two hotels. *Both open Mar–Jan.*

The ✭✭✭✭**Nazionale**, Via Roma 8, ✆ 0185 269 575, 🖷 0185 269 578 (*luxury*), smack on the port, has a slightly faded charm, furnished with antiques or reproductions. The best rooms, rather more expensive, have Venetian furniture and overlook the harbour. It has no parking, which can be a big problem in Portofino. ✭✭✭**Eden**, Vico Dritto 18, ✆ 0185 269 091, 🖷 0185 269 047 (*very expensive*) is far from cheap, but is the least expensive hotel in town, a charming 12-room establishment in the centre, endowed with a fine garden and good Ligurian restaurant.

Dining out in Portofino can be a rarefied experience. Most of the restaurants are clustered around Portofino's little piazza and port including **Il Pitosforo**, Molo

Umberto I 9, ✆ 0185 269 218 (*very expensive*), where the Ligurian cuisine is among the finest anywhere, whether you order *bouillabaisse*, spaghetti with prawns and mushrooms, the red mullet or sea bream with olives. A tree grows out of the middle of the dining room, and one whole wall is lined with a collection of spirits from around the world that will make any serious drinker's eyes glaze over in delight. Every night at 10pm all the lights are switched off to highlight the magical view of the golden lights in the port. *Closed Tues.*

Da Puny, Piazza Martire Olivetta 7, ✆ 0185 269 037 (*expensive*) serves delicious pasta and seafood dishes for starters, and well-prepared main fish dishes, like sea bass baked in salt.

Taverna del Marinaio, Piazza Martire Olivetta 36, ✆ 0185 269 103 (*moderate*), although by no means cheap, is as reasonable as you'll find. The fish and pasta are excellent. *Closed Tues.*

Rapallo ✉ 16035

Rapallo has more hotels than any other resort on the Riviera di Levante. The bright red ★★★★**Eurotel**, Via Aurelia Ponente 22, ✆ 0185 60981, ✐ 0185 50635 (*very expensive*), located on the outskirts of town, has great views of the hills and harbour, large well-appointed rooms with balconies, smart lounge areas and a heated outdoor pool.

In the centre of Rapallo, the ★★★**Riviera**, Piazza IV Novembre 2, ✆ 0185 50248/9, ✐ 0185 65668 (*expensive*) is a converted villa near the sea.

Remodelled inside, it has a popular glass terrace in the front and a garden at the rear. ★★★**Minerva**, Corso Colombo 7, ✆ 0185 230 388, ✐ 0185 67078 (*moderate*) is good value: an up-to-date hotel near the seashore, with tasteful décor, garden and bar. Close to the seafront and right in the middle of town, the ★**Pensione Bandoni**, Via Marsala 24/3, ✆ 0185 50423, ✐ 0185 57206 (*cheap*) is a comfortable, simple hotel that's good value. There are a good many more *inexpensive* hotels in the same area.

In a garden among the olives **Giancu**, Via S. Massimino 78, ✆ 0185 260 505 (*moderate*) is a delightful family restaurant complete with a small playground. There's no playing around with the food, however—it's all good, traditional stuff. *Closed Wed.* The best cheap eateries are around Piazza Garibaldi and Via Venezia.

Entertainment and Nightlife

In élite Portofino two port-side drinking holes have long competed for the biggest celebrities: **La Gritta American Bar** and **Scafandro American Bar**, both of them elegant and glamorous in the resort's studied, laid-back and very expensive style. There's a good disco, **Covo di Nord Est**, Lungomare Rossetti 1, in Santa Margherita. For later on, **Villa Porticciolo**, Via G. Maggio 4, in Rapallo, plays a varied selection of house and chart music until the early hours.

At Chiávari, the coast flattens out to form a narrow plain for the last time in Liguria. This is the stamping ground of the Fieschi family, which produced a pair of popes and the leader of the famous conspiracy against Andrea Doria, who might have succeeded if he hadn't fallen overboard in his heavy armour and drowned.

Tourist Information

Chiávari: Corso Assarotti 1, ✆ 0185 325 198, ✉ 0185 324 796.

Lavagna: Piazza della Libertà 48a, ✆ 0185 395 070, ✉ 0185 392 442.

Sestri Levante: Via XX Settembre 33, ✆ 0185 457 011, ✉ 0185 459 575.

Chiávari and Lavagna

Chiávari was born on 19 October 1178 as a colony of the Republic of Genoa, and laid out with a nice tidy grid of streets, defended by walls and a castle. Over the centuries it was given various responsibilities and in 1646 it became the first town on the Riviera di Levante to earn the title of city. Made the seat of the governor of the Levante in the 18th century, it felt safe to knock down its walls and fill up its streets with noble residences. Since the last war, tourism jobs have usurped the specialized crafts that Chiávari was known for: ship-building, fine wooden and straw chairs, and macramé, an art brought back by the town's sailors from the Middle East, and still used to adorn towels and tablecloths with intricate fringes and tassels. Orchids are still a local speciality, their blooms best seen at the annual show at the end of February.

The centre of life in Chiávari is **Piazza Mazzini**, with a lively morning market, a tower from the demolished citadel, stern palaces and a monument dedicated to Liguria's favourite revolutionary. A few streets away at Via Costaguta 2, the **Palazzo Rocca** was designed by Bartolomeo Bianco in 1629 and houses two museums: the **Civica Galleria** with works by the Genoese school (*open Sat and Sun 10–12 and 4–7.30*), and the **Civico Museo Archeologico** (*open 9–1.30*), with items discovered in the nearby 8th–7th-century BC necropolis that demonstrate trade links with the Phoenicians, Greeks and Egyptians. The church of **San Giovanni Battista**, rebuilt in the early 1600s by Bartolomeo Bianco and Andrea Vannone, has a modern marble façade and more works by the Genoese school. Chiávari's modern **cathedral** replaces an earlier version, built to house a painting of the Virgin (1493) by Benedetto Borzone that was hung on a garden wall and immediately began working miracles; among the other art inside you'll find two fine wooden sculptural groups by Anton Maria Maragliano (the *Temptation of St Anthony* and *St Francis receiving the stigmata*). Afterwards, treat yourself to an ice cream or pastry at **Caffè Defilla**, founded in 1883 on Via Garibaldi 4. In Chiávari's newer quarters there's a small pleasure port, near the long sandy beach.

Lavagna is separated from Chiávari by the Entella and several bridges, including the splendid **Ponte della Maddalena**, built in 1210 by Ugone Fieschi when the Roman bridge collapsed. It too has a long beach which has brought much new building; it too keeps a few crafts alive, a fact most apparent on Thursdays, when the weekly market sells local handicrafts in wood, iron and slate (*lavagna* means 'blackboard' in Italian).

In the Middle Ages, the Counts of Lavagna were the Fieschi, a litigious family who began to play a leading role in the Republic of Genoa in the 12th century. Their fortunes soared when they produced a pope, Innocent IV (reigned 1243–54), who was the arch-enemy of Emperor Frederick II Stupor Mundi; like most popes, he did all he could for his family, attempting to confirm them as the bosses of the Guelphs in Genoa. A second member of the family was elected pope in 1276 as Adrian V, although like John Paul I he only survived just over a month in office (still, Dante placed him in Purgatory because he was Genoese, and thus naturally guilty of avarice). One member of the clan, Count Opizzo Fieschi, made such a splash in Lavagna when he married the Sienese Countess Bianca dei Bianchi in 1230 that the wedding is annually re-enacted every 14 August, climaxing in the communal eating of the gargantuan *Torta dei Fieschi*.

Innocent IV, on the other hand, is remembered in the beautiful church he founded in 1244 during his first trip home after his election, the **Basilica di San Salvatore dei Fieschi**. Located half an hour's walk from Lavagna, in a setting that by some special papal miracle has changed little since, the church is Romanesque with some inklings of Gothic and has an enormous tower with quadruple mullioned windows, a lovely marble rose window, and a striped façade; the dimly lit interior, bare of decorations, is solemn and spiritual. Next to the church are the overgrown ruins of the Fieschi palace, destroyed by the Turks in the 16th century.

The *Entroterra*: Into the Fief of the Fieschi

As busy as the coast and beaches are, the *entroterra* remains a world apart, of quiet, time-less farming hamlets in the Apennines, lightly sprinkled with 'sights'—on the whole, more a place to be than to see. From Chiávari, a long, winding road follows the Entella up to one of the main centres, **Borzonasca**, from where a road winds up through the olives and chestnut groves to the **Abbazia di Borzone**, founded in this tranquil spot in the 12th century by Benedictines from the monastery of San Colombano in Bobbio, Emilia. The present abbey was built by the Fieschi counts in 1244 over the ruins of a late Roman fortress; the tower, basilica and convent stand intact and lonely by a giant cypress. The altar has a slate tabernacle of 1513.

The SS586 winds up, skirting the Parco dell'Aveto on the Emilian border; the forests here were one of the main sources of lumber for Genoa's shipbuilders, and cutting trees was already strictly regulated in the 1500s. Regulations are still strict (much of the park is off limits to the public), to the extent that, in recent years, even wolves have made a big comeback. **Cabanne** up the road has become a modest summer resort; it belonged to one of Liguria's many minor league feudal families, the Della Cella. Their residence is opposite the little parish church, which proudly houses two paintings purchased from Genoa's Santa Maria di Castello: the *Deposition* and *Resurrection*, attributed to Agostino Carracci and Giovanni Lanfranco. **Rezzoáglio**, another 8km up the road, was another Della Cella property, and has a lovely medieval stone bridge.

At the village of **Magnasco**, you can detour south to the pretty little lake Lame, or continue up to the main town and resort in this neck of the woods, **Santo Stéfano d'Aveto**, where in winter the inhabitants of the Riviera di Levante head for a taste of snow and a bit of skiing at just over 1000m, as well as a scenic 8km cable car excursion. Santo Stefano's landmark is the ruined but still imposing **Castello Malaspina**.

Sestri Levante

Sestri Levante, as *Segesta Tigulliorum*, was an important Roman town that grew up at the junction of the Via Aurelia and the Via Aemilia Scauri. One of the biggest and happiest resorts on the Riviera di Levante, Sestri is endowed with a lovely, curving peninsula, called the Isola, which once upon a time really was an islet. The Isola divides the little 'Bay of Silence' from what Hans Christian Andersen himself named the 'Bay of Fables' with a picturesque sandy beach, and perhaps more than its share of touristic development. The magnificent garden on the peninsula belongs to Albergo dei Castello, where Marconi performed his first experiments with radio waves in 1934; below it stands the fine Romanesque church of **San Nicolò dell'Isola**, with a Renaissance façade. Piazza Matteotti, down on the isthmus, has fine views of the two bays. The **Galleria Rizzi**, Via Cappuccini 8, on the Bay of Silence (*open April–Oct Wed 4–7, Fri and Sat 9pm–11pm, Sun 10–1*), contains works by the Florentine, Emilian and Ligurian schools, ceramics and a small furniture collection. The main shopping street (as it has been for centuries) is Via XXV Aprile, the *carrugio* just back from the seafront. If the main beach is too busy for your tastes, there's another one just east at **Riva-Trigoso**, next to the shipyards.

The *comune* of Sestri encompasses the **Val Gròmolo**, an area rich in minerals from gold and silver to copper and magnesium. **Libiola** was the main centre for copper mining, now abandoned; a charming legacy of its geological wealth is the more colourful than usual *risseu* pavement in front of the church, using black, white, brown and red pebbles. If you want to learn more, in nearby **Tassani** a schoolhouse is now used as a museum of Ligurian minerals.

Where to Stay and Eating Out

Chiávari ✉ 16043

In the historic centre, ★★★**Monte Rosa**, Via Marineti 6, ✆ 0185 300 321, ✉ 0185 312 868 (*moderate*) is a welcoming hotel, with a decent restaurant and satellite TV. Right on the beach, ★★**Zia Piera**, Via Marina Giulia 25, ✆ 0185 307 686, ✉ 0185 314 139 (*cheap*) is modern and recently refurbished to a three-star standard, with a big solarium overlooking the sea. The **Lord Nelson Pub**, Corso Valparaiso 27, ✆ 0185 302 595 (*very expensive*) may have dark woods and bottles, but the resemblance to a pub ends there: this is the most elegant gourmet restaurant in town, with delicate seafood dishes such as ravioli with smoked ricotta and shrimp and *dentice* (similar to sea bream) with pine nuts, olives and potatoes. Save room for the exquisite desserts. *Closed Wed.* **Felice**, Via L. Risso 71, ✆ 0185 308 016 (*moderate*) serves a delicious *zimino* (fish soup) and other Ligurian dishes; it's small, so book. *Closed Mon.* Chiávari offers relief for fish haters at **Dragut**, smack on the marina, ✆ 0185 324 828 (*moderate*) which serves up nothing but meat and chicken dishes, and plenty of both, along with fashion videos. *Closed Wed.*

In Leivi, 6km from Chiávari, **Ca' Peo**, Strada Panoramica, ✆ 0185 319 696 (*very expensive*) is one of the best restaurants on the Riviera. The atmosphere is elegant and charming, and the food imaginatively and delicately prepared, featuring ingredients like radicchio from Treviso, truffles from Alba, porcini mushrooms and very fresh fish, followed by excellent desserts and accompanied by noble wines. Reservations are a must. *Closed Mon, Wed lunch and Nov.*

Sestri Levante ✉ 16039

Sestri Levante competes with Rapallo for the title of most touristy resort in the east, but it is nonetheless home to a number of excellent hotels including ★★★★★**Grand Hotel dei Castelli**, Via Penisola 26, ✆ 0185 487 220, ✆ 0185 44767 (*very expensive*), occupying the tip of the Isola peninsula. Built in the twenties on the site of a Genoese castle, it was constructed from the castle's stone. The views of both bays and the sea crashing against the cliffs all around the hotel's park are magnificent, especially from the dining terrace. There's also a natural sea pool cut into the rock for safe swimming. *Open May–Oct.*

On the seafront is the supremely stately pink palace ★★★★**Villa Balbi**, Viale Rimembranza 1, ✆ 0185 42941, ✆ 0185 482 459 (*very expensive*), built at the beginning of the 17th century for the Brignole family, and full of unexpected treasures: a preserved library and a room decorated entirely with paintings of fish, as well as oak-beamed bedrooms and antique-laden public rooms. Much of the original garden remains, including a large camphor tree growing in the middle (indeed, through the roof) of the restaurant. It also has an outdoor pool and a rather good private beach. *Open April–Oct.* Alternatively, there's the ★★★★**Miramare**, Via Cappellini 9, ✆ 0185 480 855, ✆ 0185 41055 (*very expensive*), in an idyllic location, perched on the Bay of Silence overlooking the gentle sweep of confectionery cottages and bobbing painted sailing boats, with a decent terrace restaurant and its very own strip of beach.

★★★**Helvetia**, Via Cappuccini 43, ✆ 0185 41175, ✆ 0185 57216 (*expensive*) is a welcoming little hotel in the prettiest part of town, right on the Bay of Silence, with a large terraced garden. ★★★**Mira**, Via Rimembranza 15, ✆ 0185 41576, ✆ 0185 41577 (*moderate*) is a family-run hotel with rooms with a view and a restaurant serving excellent fish specialities, including *riso marinara* and *nasello alla mira*, on a covered terrace overlooking the sea. *Closed Mon.* ★**Villa Jolanda**, Via Pozzetto 15, ✆/✆ 0185 41354 (*cheap*) is a good budget hotel, with sea view from some rooms.

For excellent seaside dining, **Angiolina**, Piazza Matteotti 51, ✆ 0185 41198 (*expensive*) is the place to go for an exquisite *zuppa di pesce* and other delicious denizens of the deep. *Closed Tues.* Seafood and traditional Ligurian cuisine comprise the menu at **Fiammenghilla Fieschi**, Via Pestella 6, ✆ 0185 481 041 (*very expensive*), a great place to try marinated swordfish, lobster, *focaccia* or *pansotti*. There's also a very good Ligurian wine list. *Menu degustazione* L100,000. *Open evenings only.*

A few streets back from the 'Bay of Silence', **Polpo Mario**, Via XXV Aprile 163, ✆ 0185 480 203 (*moderate*) is a nice cosy family restaurant. It's very popular with locals, presumably because of the very generous portions. The family also runs an all-day snack bar, **La Cantina del Polpo**, around the corner at Piazza Cavour 2/r. The best budget eateries are around the Via XXV Aprile.

Nightlife

In Sestri, for early drinking, there's an excellent bar, **Il Bistro di Sestri Levante**, Piazza Matteotti 13, ✆ 0185 41613, notable for its vast collection of beer cans and good music. It also serves good, inexpensive food.

The Val di Vara

There are two routes east from Sestri Levante to La Spezia. The first, the Val di Vara, runs inland, parallel to the coast, nearly the entire length of La Spezia province down to the sea. For millennia the main road from points east to Genoa has run here, as does the modern *autostrada*, the coastal progress of both foiled by the tumultuous coast of the Cinque Terre. The ancient Ligurians had several *castellari* along here, and one curiosity of the valley—little rough stone heads (*testine apotropaiche*) with primitive faces you may see outside the houses, used to keep evil away from gates and doors—seems to hark straight back to the faces sculpted in relief on the prehistoric statue steles. On a far more delicate level, the Val di Vara is famous for one of the most beautiful forms of pasta in all Italy: *corzetti* (or *croxetti*), thin discs stamped with arabesques or floral patterns, and served with pesto or another light sauce designed to accent the relief. Once a favourite dish of the Genoese nobility, the end result is almost too pretty to eat.

Tourist Information

Varese Ligure: Via Portici 19, ✆ 0187 842 094.

Cálice al Cornoviglio: ✆ 0187 936 309, 📠 0187 936 451.

Varese Ligure

From Sestri a bus heads inland along the tortuous SS523 to **Varese Ligure**, the chief town of the Val di Vara, an agricultural and market centre and summer resort. The Fieschi constructed the recently restored 15th-century **castle**, a rather striking building with a beautiful slate roof. Varese's strategic location (it's just below two passes over the mountains into Emilia) was behind a late 15th-century special offer by the Fieschi: they would donate the land and protect any merchant who built a house and shop in a ring around the market. With only one entrance, the circular design also had the advantage of instant self-defence, and this unusual core with its ring of porticoes survives intact in the **Borgo**

Rotondo. Just outside town, the church of **SS. Teresa d'Avila e Filippo Neri** has an elegant façade of the 1700s and, on the left of the altar, a painting by Gregorio De Ferrari. The road north of Varese towards the Passo di Cento is especially lovely, lush and rolling.

Downriver, off either side of the main Vara valley road, you'll find quiet, picturesque hamlets lost in the chestnut forests, half-forgotten places such as **Groppo**, **Sesta Godano** and **Carro**. Even places like **Cornice**, a strikingly panoramic medieval hamlet on the main valley, are all but abandoned. **Brugnato** has a historic centre even odder than Varese's Borgo Rotondo, laid out like pincers, gripping the double-naved **parish church**. This has a strawberry parfait bell tower, built over a palaeochristian necropolis, and a Benedictine abbey that flourished under the Lombards, whose abbots warred with the bishops of Luni until 1133 when they themselves were made bishops, an office that left them in a position to take on new opponents: the Malaspina and other noble families of the area. A fresco inside shows San Colombano, the Irish founder of the great abbey in Bobbio, over the mountains in Emilia, but still a strong influence in this part of Liguria. At Brugnato you can pick up the road to **Rocchetta di Vara** and **Zignago**, two other quiet and pretty places with views.

Further down the valley, fortified **Beverino** is a curiosity: like Noli, west of Genoa, it was an 'independent' island in the republic, made a free *comune* in 1247. The bell in its campanile was hung in 1492 and still does the business. North of Beverino, **Cálice al Cornoviglio** is the capital of its own little valley, and has an imposing Malaspina castle with a fat round tower containing a little Pinacoteca (*open summer Sundays, 4–7*). **Pignone** to the south, off the Via Aurelia, has a striking stone bridge and takes pride in producing the best onions in Liguria.

The Coast Route: Sestri Levante to La Spezia

The other way from Sestri to La Spezia is the coastal route. East of Sestri Levante the coastal tunnels begin in earnest again for both trains and cars, while the more sensible Via Aurelia and *autostrada* delve inland. All the coastal villages here have a certain drama, but the Cinque Terre ('The Five Lands'), as they've been known since the Middle Ages, take the cake and frosting too, forming a stunning, unique ensemble of villages audaciously balanced over the sea in a precipitous, vertical landscape: the concentrated essence of Liguria at its most tenacious. Formerly accessible only by sea or by a spectacular series of cliff-skirting footpaths, the five have maintained much of their original charm, even though nowadays they are far from being undiscovered. Now part of a Natural Park that stretches to Portovenere, the Cinque Terre should at least be spared the worst ravages of development made possible by the new road.

Getting Around

The easiest way to reach the coastal villages and Cinque Terre is by **train**. Each of the towns has a station, only a few minutes apart and separated by long tunnels. The second easiest way is by boat; *see* La Spezia, below. The third and most memorable way is by foot, on the strenuous but gorgeous path from Lévanto to Riomaggiore.

The controversial coastal road to the Cinque Terre (*Litoranea delle Cinque Terre*; Italian engineers' bulldozers begin to twitch at the mention of the word 'inaccessible') hardly makes access easier: east of Sestri Levante, the narrow one-way tunnels lead to major traffic jams in the summer. Drivers should be aware, also, that the villages at the end of the winding cliff roads are tiny, and parking is a perennial problem: there is one garage at Riomaggiore, and one car park at Monterosso, and that's it.

Tourist Information

Moneglia: c/o Pro Loco, Corso C. Longhi 32, ✆ 0187 490 576.

Deiva Marina: Lungomare C. Colombo, ✆ 0187 815 858, ✉ 0187 815 800.

Bonassola: Via Beverini 1, ✆ 0187 813 500, ✉ 0187 813 529, *proloco@itline.it.*

Lévanto: Piazza Cavour, ✆ 0187 808 125.

Monterosso al Mare: Via Fegina 38, ✆ 0187 817 506.

Sestri Levante to Monterosso

After Sestri Levante, the Apennines move in and crowd the coast, admitting here and there little glens and sandy strands—one is at sleepy **Moneglia** (from the Latin *monellia*, or jewel) with its quiet stretch of beach framed by two medieval castles, Monleone and Villafranca. Moneglia's 18th-century church, **Santa Croce**, concentrates much of the interest in the village, with one of the most beautiful of all *risseu* pavements in Liguria, made in 1822. It keeps, among other things, a Byzantine cross that washed up on shore here after a shipwreck, an *Immacolata* by Maragliano, and a *Last Supper* by Luca Cambiaso, who was born here, the son of painter Giovanni Cambiaso (another famous local was Felice Romani, who wrote many of the libretti, including some of the awful ones, for Bellini, Donizetti and Rossini). On the side of Santa Croce, note the chain links, a souvenir of the chain that once guarded the port of Pisa, a trophy given to the town by Genoa in honour of its help in the victory of Meloria in 1284. There's more art in **San Giorgio** (rebuilt in 1704) on the west end of town: an *Adoration of the Magi*, a youthful work by Luca Cambiaso, and a *St George* attributed to Rubens.

Deiva Marina is a conglomerate of hamlets: big condos by the shore and more traditional houses on the wooded hillside; towards **Framura** are the romantic, overgrown ruins of a castle of the Da Passano, destroyed by the Genoese in 1180. The road circles inland to another hamlet called Costa, where the striking medieval church of **San Martino de Muris** has stupendous views over the sea. San Martino has three pretty apses and a campanile made from a watchtower and keeps inside a *Madonna and saints* by Bernardo Strozzi; the nearby oratory has a handsome Gothic door. The next seaside village, **Bonassola**, occupies a rare flat spot on this coast, with a long beach. Its parish church is full of *ex votos*, including a striking painting by Antonio Discovolo of the *Pious Women at* the *Foot of the Cross* (1924) and another Strozzi. The favourite thing to do in Bonassola at sunset is to walk out to the tiny chapel of the **Madonna della Punta** on the cliff. On the road to the east, the Renaissance **Convento dell'Annunziata** is decorated with a bas relief and has a sweet cloister; it contains a number of good baroque paintings including the *Miracle of St James* by Strozzi and a *St George* by Pier Francesco Sacchi.

Set in an amphitheatre over the sea, **Lévanto** has the best beach of all in this area, a long and sandy strand in a pretty flower garden setting Originally a possession of the Da Passano *marchese*, it later became a free *comune*. It has several monuments from the 13th century—chunks of its defensive walls, the lovely **Loggia** with a ruined 15th-century fresco, the **Casa Restani**, and the handsome striped church of **Sant'Andrea**, with a rose window added in the 18th century. Two other churches have beautiful 15th-century bas reliefs, **Santa Maria della Costa** and the **Oratorio di San Giacomo**.

The Cinque Terre

Next on the coast comes **Monterosso al Mare**, the westernmost and largest (pop. 1730) of the Cinque Terre. As fantastical as their setting are the stupendous dry stone terraces that corrugate the slopes, the labour of generations upon generations, all for the laudable purpose of producing fine white wines, including the famous potent Sciacchetrà, made from raisins, which can be either dry or sweet. Despite their impossible location, all of the Cinque Terre were doing well enough in the Middle Ages to afford the local status symbol: a rose window for the parish church, sculpted in marble from nearby Carrara. Like all good Ligurian towns, each has the inevitable sanctuary high above, inevitably dedicated to the Madonna and inevitably affording astonishing views of this most astonishing coast.

Monterosso is the most touristy of the five towns, with picturesque beaches (free and 'organized'), hotels, rooms in private houses, and so on, and boats to hire for personal tours of the coast. Most of the facilities are in the new half of town called Fegina, separated from the old by a hill crowned with the **Convento dei Cappuccini** (1622), encompassing the medieval **Torre Aurora** ('Tower of the Dawn') and church of **San Francesco**, home to some surprisingly fine art: Strozzi's *La Veronica*, a *Crucifixion* by Van Dyck and two works by Luca Cambiaso. The parish church, striped **San Giovanni**, has an exquisite marble rose window with lace-like edges. You can walk or drive around to the 18th-century **Sanctuary of Soviore**, built over an older church, which hosts a music festival in the summer. If you have the puff, don't miss the climb up to the breath-taking (literally) **Punta Mesco**.

From Monterosso it's a momentary train ride or an hour-and-a-half walk to the next town, **Vernazza**, founded by the Romans on a rocky spit and guarded by two imposing Saracen towers, a striking vision from the footpath above. It is the only one of the five with a little port. The parish church, **Santa Margherita d'Antiochia**, was built in 1318 on two levels, with the apse overlooking the main piazza.

The hour-and-a-half walk from Vernazza to **Corniglia** is one of the most strenuous, for Corniglia, unlike the other towns, is high up on the cliffs and not on the sea, though it does have the longest (albeit pebbly) beach way down below. It is the centre of the Cinque Terre's winemaking, and has been since Roman times; an amphora bearing its name was found at Pompeii. The parish church of **San Pietro** has a handsome Gothic façade pierced by a lovely rose window. The Cinque Terre wine cooperative is up on the road to Manarola, at **Groppo**.

From Corniglia another hour's walk through splendid scenery leads to the astonishing sight of **Manarola**, a colourful fishing village, piled like a dream on a great black rock by the sea. Founded in the 12th century, the outer walls of the houses follow the lines of the original castle, demolished in 1273. The Gothic parish church has another superb marble rose window, while the interior has been stripped of its baroque foldirols but also, sadly, of its pebble mosaic, which was covered over with cement.

Manarola is linked in 20 minutes or so to **Riomaggiore** by the most popular and singular section of the footpath, the **Via dell'Amore** or Lovers' Lane, carved into the living rock of the cliff over the sea. Riomaggiore is also one of the prettiest towns, and sees plenty of visitors, who crowd its lively cafés and rocky beaches. The parish church also has a good 14th-century rose window, surviving in a neo-Gothic façade; inside there's a lifesize wooden *Crucifixion* by Anton Maria Maragliano. Other pretty walks are up to the ruins of the castle and to the spectacular view point of the **Madonna di Montenero**, 1120ft over the sea (there's also a road).

Where to Stay and Eating Out

Besides hotels, note that the Cinque Terre also have a number of rooms to rent, often connected to the restaurants. The coast here is home to a unique species of silvery anchovy, the *afrore delle acciughe*, caught at night with special lamps, which taste pretty darn good with a glass of chilled white Cinque Terre wine.

Moneglia ✉ 16030

Centrally placed in front of the sea, the welcoming ★★★**Piccolo**, Corso Longhi 19, ✆ 0185 49374, 📠 0185 401 292, *laura@piccolohotel.it* (*moderate*) has 24 air-conditioned rooms and a pool. The bright pink **Villa Edera**, Via Venino 12, ✆ 0187 492 291, 📠 0187 49470 (*moderate*) is a nice, quiet family-run hotel set in the hills a few minutes from the beach, directly next to the medieval Castello Monleone. The rooms are basic but comfortable, with good views of the surrounding countryside. It also has a lovely restaurant featuring homemade regional specialities. The 'Enchanted Citadel', the **Rocca Incatenata**, Punta Rospo, ✆ 0185 49476 (*expensive–moderate*) is a bit hard to reach through the tunnels, but lives up to its name, a lovely spot directly on the wine-dark sea, with a menu based on the day's catch. *Closed Mon except in summer.*

Bonassola ✉ 19011

A minute from the beach, ★★★**Delle Rose**, Via Garibaldi 8, ✆ 0187 813713, 📠 0187 814 268, *lerose@spitline.it* (*moderate–cheap*) is a well run family hotel;

many rooms have sea views, and all have ceiling fans. The even cheaper ★★★**Moderno**, Via G. Daneri 81, ✆/✉ 0187 813 662, *modena@sp.italine.it* (*cheap*) has a certain 1930s charm, a good garden restaurant and terrace, and a play area for the kids.

Lévanto ✉ 19015

One of Lévanto's oldest hotels is still one of the nicest: ★★★**Nazionale**, Via Jacopo da Levanto 29, ✆ 0187 808 102, ✉ 0187 800 901 *hotel@nazionale.it* (*moderate*), located near the sea and set in a garden, with old-fashioned iron beds in comfortable rooms. ★★**Stella Maris**, Via Marconi 4, ✆ 0187 808 258, ✉ 0187 807 351, *renza@hotelstellamaris.it* (*moderate*) offers two kinds of rooms: the more expensive ones with frescoes and antiques in an 18th-century palace, or modern air-conditioned ones closer to the sea. Rooms are well equipped, and there's a garden for children; price includes a generous breakfast buffet. Lévanto is blessed with an innovative restaurant, **Araldo**, Via Jacopo da Levanto 24, ✆ 0187 807 253 (*expensive*), where the chef combines mushrooms, seafood and vegetables with savoir faire. *Closed Tues, exc in summer.*

Monterosso al Mare ✉ 19016

Of the five towns of the Cinque Terre, Monterosso has the best accommodation, with the ★★★★**Porto Roca**, Via Corone 1, ✆ 0187 817 502, ✉ 0187 817 692 (*very expensive*) as the top choice, located on the headland, with lovely views of the sea from all the rooms. ★★★★**Palme**, Via IV Novembre 18, ✆ 0187 829 013, ✉ 0187 829 081 (*expensive*) is a modern hotel with 49 rooms, set in a large garden just five minutes from the sea. The largish, modern ★★★**Cinque Terre**, Via IV Novembre 21, ✆ 0187 817 543, ✉ 0187 818 380 (*expensive*) has a private beach and simple but comfortable rooms.

Next door, the ★★**Villa Adriana**, Via IV Novembre 23, ✆/✉ 0187 818 109 (*moderate*) is large and friendly, with its own beach. Probably the best budget option is ★★★**Degli Amici**, Via Burranco 36, ✆ 0187 817 574, ✉ 0187 817 424 (*moderate*), in the old part of town, and 150m from the beach. The rooms are light and airy, some with balcony, and there's an excellent restaurant. ★★★**Jolie**, Via Gioberti 1, ✆ 0187 817 539, ✉ 0187 817 273 (*expensive*) is much the same, but more expensive.

The best food in Monterosso is served at **Il Gigante**, Via IV Novembre, ✆ 0187 817 401 (*moderate*), with especially good Ligurian specialities—*pansotti, trenette al pesto* and fresh fish.

Vernazza ✉ 19018

The ★**Sorriso**, Via Gavino 4, ✆ 0187 812 224 (*cheap*) is an honest little inn with very inexpensive rooms and a well-known restaurant. ★**Barbara**, Piazza Marcanilo, ✆ 0187 812 201 (*cheap*) has basic rooms, with lovely views overlooking the square.

The **Gambero Rosso** in Piazza Marconi 7, © 0187 812 265 (*moderate*) is a well-known restaurant that's partly carved out of the rock; try the *tegame di acciughe*, a tasty dish made with the Cinque Terre's special anchovies, but there's plenty of less piquant seafood, too. On the square, the **Da Capitano**, © 0187 812 201 (*moderate*) serves fine fish fare—try the *linguine ai granchi*, washed down with a glass of the genial Captain's own wine.

Manarola ✉ 19010

The ★★★**Marina Piccola**, © 0187 920 103, ◙ 0187 920 966 (*cheap*), with 10 simple rooms, is a good place to get away from it all, and it has a very nice restaurant. Rooms are better in the main hotel, rather than the annexe. The new ★★★**Ca' d'Andrean**, Via Discovolo 25, © 0187 920 040 (*cheap*) is a spotlessly clean little family-run place with 10 large rooms (some with terrace), a garden and bar. The choice trattoria is **Aristide**, Via Roma, © 0187 920 000 (*moderate*), serving a delicious *minestra* and fish dishes, also rabbit, game and other meat in season.

Riomaggiore ✉ 19017

Two choices here: the arty ★★**Villa Argentina**, Via A. De Gasperi 39, © 0187 920 143, ◙ 0187 920 213 (*moderate*), with 15 recently renovated rooms in one of the prettiest corners in town, with an optional good buffet breakfast that will give you the oomph to walk the Via dell'Amore; and, 9km from the centre at Campi, ★★★**Due Gemelli**, Via Littoranea 9, ©/◙ 0187 731 320 (*cheap*), a low-key choice in a lovely setting among the pines and olives, overlooking the sea.

La Spezia and Portovenere

Until the 19th century La Spezia, despite its sheltered location, never managed to gather more than 5000 souls to its bosom. Napoleon came up with the idea that it might make a perfect little naval base, an idea that Count Cavour pushed forward in 1860 in the heady early days of the Risorgimento. It quickly grew to become the largest city in the region and provincial capital, although its vocation earned it a heavy bombing in the Second World War. Now all the scars have healed and La Spezia presents a modern but cheerful face to the world, standing at the head of the enchanting 'Gulf of Poets', framed by the rocky peninsula of Portovenere.

Getting Around

Buses for Portovenere (every 15 minutes), Lérici, Sarzana and the rest of La Spezia province are run by the ATC, © 0187 522 522; departure points vary so ask. Several **boat** lines serve the area, and come in handy when coastal roads clog up in the summer. From La Spezia, there's **In-Tur**, Viale Italia, © 0187 24324, and **Battellieri del Golfo**, Via Banchina Revel, © 0187 28066, and **Navigazione Golfo dei Poeti**, © 0187 967 676, ◙ 0187 730 336, *navinfo@navigazionegolfodeipoeti.it*, **Verde Azzurro**, © 0187 967 860, and **Cap Baracco**, Via San Bernardino 1, © 0187 964 412. All have regular sailings between La Spezia, Lérici, Portovenere and the Cinque Terre; **NGP** goes as far as Portofino to the north, and Marina di Carrara in Tuscany. Another company, **Fratelli Rossignoli**, ✆ 0187 817 456, sails between Monterosso and Viareggio during summer. **Corsica Ferries**, ✆ 0187 21282, and **NAVARMA**, ✆ 0187 35484, make the five-hour run between La Spezia and Bastia in Corsica daily in summer, and less frequently at other times.

Tourist Information

La Spezia: Viale Mazzini 45, ✆ 0187 770 900, ✉ 0187 770 908; in the station, ✆ 0187 718 997.

Portovenere: Piazza Bastreri 1, ✆ 0187 790691, ✉ 0187 790 215.

La Spezia

Mostly used by visitors as a base for visiting the Cinque Terre and locations around the Gulf of Poets, La Spezia does have a few attractions in its own right amid its regular businesslike grid of streets and piazzas—among them the **Passeggiata C. Morin**, a seaside promenade of swaying palms and beautifully tended public gardens. At the end of the promenade in Piazza Chiodo, the excellent **Naval Museum** (*✆ 0187 770 750, open Tues–Thurs and Sat 9–12 and 2–6, Mon and Fri 2–6; adm L2000*) contains a fine collection begun in 1560 by Emanuele Filiberto, with relics of the ships sent by the Savoys to the Battle of Lepanto; there are models, a gallery of figureheads, and mementoes from Italy's naval battles. The adjacent Naval Arsenal is off limits to the public, except for one day a year—19 March, the feast day of St Joseph, the carpenter patron of shipbuilders.

Corso Cavour, one of La Spezia's main streets, leads back from the sea to Piazza Beverini and the black and white façade of the church of **Santa Maria Assunta**, last refinished in 1954, but containing a beautiful polychrome terracotta *Incoronation of the Virgin* by Andrea della Robbia and a *Martyrdom of St Bartholomew* by Luca Cambiaso. Further along, on the corner of Corso Cavour at Via Curtatone 9, the **Museo Civico Ubaldo Formentini** (*✆ 0187 739 537, open Tues–Sat 8.30–1.15 and 2.30–7.15, Sun 9–1; adm*) contains an important archaeological section, with prehistoric finds from Palmaria's Grotta dei Colombi, pre-Roman and Roman material from Luni (including a beautiful mosaic pavement with a nereid riding a sea monster) and, best of all, ancient Ligurian statue steles from the Bronze and Iron Ages, male and female figures that look uncannily like prehistoric spacemen, a special treat for all *Chariot of the Gods* fans (for more, *see* below, pp.221–2). The museum also has an ethnographic collection, with traditional costumes and tools from villages in the province.

Thanks to a major donation to La Spezia in 1995, it now has an art gallery of ancient, medieval and modern art, the new **Museo Amedeo Lia**, Via Prione 234, (*✆ 0187 731 100, open 10–6, closed Mon; adm exp*), housed in a former convent, containing, among others, fine works by Giovanni Mazone, Giacomo Recco and Titian. Above on the hill, the medieval **Castello San Giorgio** is currently under restoration.

Just south of La Spezia and off the road to Portovenere, a pair of little roads wind up west to extraordinary viewpoints. The village of **Biassa** offers huge panoramas over La Spezia and the Gulf of Poets with the Apuan Alps for a backdrop, near the ruined 12th-century Genoese Castello di Corderone, the Republic's outermost outpost against Pisa. The tiny **Campiglia**, up the second road, hangs like a balcony high over the stupendously vertical landscapes of the **Tramonti**, a continuation of the precipitous Cinque Terre but much less visited. Paths lead west to Riomaggiore and the Madonna di Montenero, or down to Portovenere, on the west shore of the Gulf of Poets.

Totani ripieni (stuffed squid, from La Spezia)

800g squid, cleaned and washed
1 egg
1 soft roll, soaked in milk and crumbled
100g mortadella, chopped
a bit of marjoram
100g grated parmesan
1 pinch nutmeg
5 tablespoons olive oil
half an onion, chopped
1 clove garlic
a bit of parsley
1 glass of white wine
3 ripe tomatoes, peeled and mashed
salt and pepper

Detach the tentacles from the squid and chop them finely, and mix with the egg, roll, mortadella and marjoram. Season with the parmesan, nutmeg and a bit of salt. Stuff the squid with the mixture and seal them with toothpicks.

In a large pan, heat the olive oil and gently fry the onion, garlic and parsley for 5 minutes. Add the squid and, after a minute, the white wine. Let it evaporate while cooking on a low heat for 7 minutes. Then add the tomatoes and salt and pepper to taste, cover, and cook at a low heat for around 45 minutes.

Portovenere

Like heaven and many other good things, Portovenere isn't easy to reach. The road from La Spezia is very narrow and winding (if you're prone to motion sickness you may prefer to take the equally scenic boat). It passes by way of the pretty cove, tiny beaches and seaside village of **Le Grazie**, named for its 15th-century church of Santa Maria delle Grazie, near the **Convento degli Olivetani**; both have good 16th-century frescoes.

At the end of the road stands ancient, fortified **Portovenere**, one of the most beautiful towns on the Riviera and one that is quickly becoming a rival to Portofino in the Riviera chic sweepstakes. Dignified by a long promontory, three islets, a castle and tall pastel houses right on the sea, Portovenere's name comes from *Portus Veneris*, the port of

Venus. It was on the frontlines in the Middle Ages and was fortified by the Genoese to counter the Pisans, who had made a stronghold of Lérici across the gulf; their gate still reads *Colonia Januensis 1113*, a proud inscription by the proud Republic, which liked to think that 'Genoa' derived from Janus, the two-faced Roman god of ports and doorways, beginnings and the month of January. The mighty tower to the left of the gate was added 50 years later.

One of the tasks of the goddess of love was to protect sailors, and her temple stood at the tip of the promontory, on the site of the present church of **San Pietro**, dedicated to the patron of fishermen. This strange little striped Genoese church, with its loggetta and wall that doubled as part of the city defences, was built in 1277, using a few colourful marble remains of a 6th-century predecessor. There are splendid views from here, of Palmaria and the coast of the Cinque Terre and cliffs of Muzzerone. The pretty cove below once held the Grotta Arpaia (until it collapsed in the 1930s), which provided the inspiration for Byron's *The Corsair*; from here Byron swam across the gulf to Lérici and Shelley's villa.

The best thing to do in Portovenere is wander through its narrow, cat-crowded lanes (Portovenere is Italy's champion kitty city). The tall houses have interesting details on their doorways, and are separated by steep vaulted stairways or *capitoli*. From the port a narrow lane leads up to the lovely church of **San Lorenzo** (1130), built by the Genoese in only three years, with a bas-relief of St Lawrence being toasted on his gridiron over the door. The campanile was rebuilt after the Aragonese hit it with a bomb in 1494. San Lorenzo shelters some unique treasures: Portovenere's most precious relic, the *Madonna Bianca*, said to have floated to the town encased in a cedar log in the 13th century, a 15th-century marble ancona sculpted by the Florentine school, and four ivory coffers from the first millennium, three Syrian and one Byzantine. Further up, a steep but worth-

while walk leads to the 16th-century Genoese **Castello**, with marvellous views (*open April–Oct daily 10–12 and 2–6; Nov–Mar daily 3–5*).

From Portovenere, excursion boats cross the 400m channel to **Isola Palmaria** to visit its famed **Grotta Azzura**—though a much cheaper proposition is to book a passage from La Spezia. Palmaria produces the black, gold-veined marble you may have noticed in Portovenere, and was the site of a Neolithic settlement. A much smaller islet, **Isola del Tino**, has a lighthouse and the evocative ruins of an 8th-century Abbazia di San Venerio, once the address of the hermit saint with the suspiciously venereal name. Even tinier **Tinetto**, further out, had a Benedictine oratory in the 4th century.

La Spezia ✉ 19100

La Spezia's finest accommodation is at the ★★★★**Jolly**, Via XX Settembre 2, ✆ 0187 739 555, 🖷 0187 22129 (*very expensive*), a modern and rather stylish member of the Italian hotel chain, with views stretching to the gulf. Near the station, the ★★★**Firenze & Continental**, Via Paleocapa 7, ✆ 0187 713 210, 🖷 0187 714 930 (*moderate*) is a comfortable hotel convenient for making rail hops into the Cinque Terre. Among the bargains the best are ★**Flavia**, Vicolo dello Stagno 7, ✆ 0187 27465, off Via del Prione (*cheap*), not far from the station, with rooms for under L55,000; and ★**Terminus**, Via Paleocapa 21, ✆ 0187 703 436, 🖷 0187 714 935 (*cheap*), slightly more expensive, with large, clean rooms, albeit a bit noisy.

If you have a car, get directions to **Pettegola**, Via del Popolo 39, ✆ 0187 514 041 (*expensive*), which has some of the city's most expert cuisine, with game, truffles and mushrooms in season and good pasta dishes—try the gnocchi made from pumpkin with seafood—and delicious desserts. *Closed Sun, two weeks in Aug.* Just off the seafront, the elegant **Parodi**, Viale Amendola 210, ✆ 0187 715 777 (*expensive*) has the best gourmet dishes in the city, with a tempting menu of market-fresh ingredients featuring all the best from the land and sea; great choice of wines and spirits too for a memorable night out. *Closed Sun.* There is a good number of low-price restaurants, much patronized by the naval personnel who are everywhere in the town, and mainly concentrated around Via del Prione.

Try **Da Dino**, Via de Passano 17, ✆ 0187 736 157 (*cheap*), a charming, unpretentious place with an excellent-value fixed price menu. *Closed Sun eve and Mon.* Or try the more upscale **Incontro**, Via Sapri 10, ✆ 0187 24689 (*moderate*), with some unexpected dishes such as asparagus wrapped in filo. *Closed Sun.*

Portovenere ✉ 19025

★★★★**Grand Hotel Portovenere**, Via Garibaldi 5, ✆ 0187 792 610, 🖷 0187 790 661, *ghp@village.it* (*expensive*) occupies a 17th-century Franciscan convent, beautifully set by the sea with views across the gulf and Palmaria. The former cells have been converted into stylish, air-conditioned rooms; there's a fitness and beauty centre, parking and a pretty restaurant with a panoramic terrace. The large and modern ★★★★**Hotel Royal Sporting**, Via dell'Ulivo 345, ✆ 0187 790 326, 🖷 0187 777 707 (*expensive*) is built in the Mediterranean style in a fantastic location overlooking sea and town; amenities include a salt-water pool, beach, garden and tennis courts. There is also a place to park, an important consideration in this little town. *Open April–Oct.*

Little family-run ★★★**Paradiso**, Via Garibaldi 34, ✆ 0187 790 612, 🖷 0187 792 582 (*moderate*) also has lovely views from its seaside terrace, and cosy, well-equipped rooms; pay parking available. ★★**Genio**, Piazza Bastreri 8, ✆ 0187 790 611 (*cheap*) has the cheapest rooms in town, and a nice little garden, too.

Fittingly, one of the specialities here is Venus shells or sea truffles, *tartufi di mar* (cockles). Try them at **Al Gavitello da Mario**, ℡ 0187 900 215 (*expensive*) in a former fisherman's house in the picturesque Calata Doria, with a menu devoted to seafood, but prepared in unusual ways—for *primo*, try fish ravioli with prawn sauce, and for *secondo*, scampi with pear brandy. In the same Calata Doria, **Iseo**, ℡ 0187 790 610 (*expensive*) is Portovenere's best known restaurant, featuring accurate renditions of the classics, and an especially delicious spaghetti with seafood. *Closed Wed, Jan, Feb.*

At the beginning of the promontory, **La Taverna del Corsaro**, Lungomare Doria 182, ℡ 0187 900 622 (*expensive*) has one of the most delightful locations in town, where you can savour delicacies like prawn in bell-pepper sauce and *zuppa di datteri* (razor clams). Family-run **La Spiaggia**, on the quay at Piazza Basteri 2, ℡ 0187 901 670 (*cheap*) serves some of the best fried squid rings in Italy, along with a refreshing house wine.

The Gulf of Poets and the Val di Magra

There is a legend that a magical sea monster, pursued by hunters, fled into this gulf, and clawed and scratched out all the numerous little coves and inlets along its shores in its mad efforts to escape. A seductive enchantment lingered in everything it touched, and makes all who see it fall in love with it; poets, like Petrarch, Shelley and Byron, are especially vulnerable to its charm. Today, a bit of poetic imagination may be required to see past La Spezia's military installations and the recent *cementificazione* of the east gulf coast as far south as Lérici. The Val di Magra begins around on the east end of the Lérici peninsula.

Tourist Information

Lérici: Via Biaggini 6, ℡ 0187 967 346.

Montemarcello: Via Delle Mura 7, ℡ 0187 600 324.

Sarzana: in the town hall, Piazza Matteotti, ℡ 0187 6141, ✉ 0187 614 252.

Arcola: Via Valentini 197, ℡ 0187 986 559.

Lérici

Fortunately, the sprawl and industry east of La Spezia ends abruptly at a tunnel: beyond opens the pretty bay of Lérici. The first place you'll come to is **San Terenzo**, the charming fishing village beloved by Percy Bysshe Shelley and his wife Mary Wollstonecraft Shelley, who lived at Casa Magni.

Shelley goes Boating

 After the Napoleonic interlude, Grand Tourists of all stripes began to drift back to Italy, including England's wayward Romantic poets Byron and Shelley, both of whom composed some of their finest verse under the benevolent Italian sun. Shelley wrote the *Ode to the West Wind* and *To a Skylark* while living in Tuscany, and *In the Eugaean Hills* in the Veneto, after the death of his little daughter Clara—who died through neglect, at least according to the wagging tongues of the day.

Not all of Italy agreed with Shelley as much as it suited Byron, who appalled his English acquaintances by slumming with the Venetians, and having one notorious affair after another—a grocer's daughter was as likely a target of his attentions as a countess. Shelley may have been expelled from Oxford for being an atheist, but he was never a traitor to his class. At one point he wrote home:

> There are two *Italies*—one composed of the green earth and trans-
> parent sea, and the mighty ruins of ancient time, and the aereal
> mountains, and the warm and radiant atmosphere which is inter-
> fused through all things. The other consists of the Italians of the
> present day, their works and ways. The one is the most sublime and
> lovely contemplation that can be conceived by the imagination of
> man; the other is the most degraded, disgusting and odious. What
> do you think? Young women of rank actually eat—you will never
> guess what—garlick!

It was from Casa Magni that Shelley sailed, in 1822, to meet Leigh Hunt at Livorno, only to shipwreck and drown on the way back by Viareggio. He was just 30 years old. His friends, including Hunt and Byron, cremated him on the beach, as described in ghastly detail by Edward Trelawney: 'The fire was so fierce as to produce a white heat on the iron, and to reduce its contents to grey ashes. The only portions that were not consumed were some fragments of bones, the jaw and the skull, but what surprised us all was that the heart remained entire.'

Lérici, the Roman *Mons Ilici*, is the chief town of the gulf, and makes a bold sight, circling the skirts of an imposing and rather majestic **Castello** (*open daily 9am–midnight; adm L2000*). This is the best preserved castle on the whole Riviera, towering proudly on its rocky promontory. Genoa acquired the town in 1152 as a bookend to Portovenere, but the Pisans seized it in 1152 and held tight to it for 13 years, thanks to the castle; the Genoese later enlarged it in the 15th century. The highlight of the interior is the Gothic chapel of Sant'Anastasia (1250). Below the castle, the **Baia di Maralunga** with its sandy coves is one of the prettiest places to swim. Near the centre, the **Oratorio di San Rocco** was curiously turned back to front in 1524, when the apse became the façade; it has a pair of Renaissance reliefs on the bell tower, one altarpiece by Domenico Fiasella and another, an anonymous Renaissance painting of saints, on the high altar. The main shopping street, Via Cavour, leads to the 17th-century parish church of **San Francesco** with more good anonymous Renaissance paintings and a fine marble triptych by Domenico Gare (1529). When the charismatic Franciscan preacher (and patron saint of advertising) Bernardin of Siena came to Lérici, he preached from San Francesco's little slate pulpit. There are a number of handsome 19th- and early 20th-century villas above town, and a road leading to the pine-wooded summit of the peninsula for views over the gulf.

The best part of the eastern Gulf of Poets is south of Lérici (in the summer take the bus: there's no place to park) where you'll find the tiny, tranquil cove and beach of **Fiascherino**, a fishing village where novelist and sometime poet D.H. Lawrence lived from 1913 to 1914; beyond is the unspoiled, quintessentially Ligurian fishing hamlet of **Tellaro**, with its tall medieval houses and pink baroque church. If shellfish rules the menus of Portovenere, Lérici and its bay is the land of the *polpo*, or octopus. In a letter, Lawrence recorded a local legend: one night the inhabitants of Tellaro awoke to the sound of the church bell ringing frantically, and ran over to see that the rope in the campanile had been seized by the tentacle of a giant octopus, who dragged it and the entire church besides down into Davy Jones' locker.

Another road from Lérici continues around on a scenic corniche high over the gulf to **Punta Bianca** on the far east tip, where the Magra flows into the sea under the Apuan Alps, streaked white with marble. Along the way is the colourful village of **Montemarcello**, built in a rectangular plan that reflects its origins as a Roman *castrum*. It was named after the Consul Marcellus, victor over the local Ligurian tribes; it has one of those perfect charming piazzas that the later Ligurians seemed to create so effortlessly. From here a road descends to the former fishing village of **Bocca di Magra**, where Italian poet Cesare Pavese spent his summers after the war, now given over wholesale to holiday homes and tourism.

The Val di Magra

From either Montemarcello or Bocca di Magra you can begin the ascent up the Magra, the river that plays a major role in the local geography. The first town is **Ameglia**, a strategic place inhabited since the Iron Age. After the 10th century it became an imperial stronghold, belonging to the Count-Bishops of Luni, who were beholden to the Emperor and did all they could to squash the local nobles, without any notable success; in 1380, the town was annexed to the Republic of Genoa. Concentric streets encircle the 10th-century citadel; note the handsome slate portals of the older houses.

Ancient Luni

At Ameglia a bridge crosses the Magra for **Luni**, ancient *Portus Lunae*, a Roman colony founded in 177 BC as a bulwark against the fierce Ligurians. The settlement, named after the moon—perhaps from the whiteness of the marble of the Apuan Alps—thrived especially in the 2nd century AD as a marble port. Although a bishopric in the early days of Christianity and an important Byzantine port, it eventually succumbed (unlike most Roman cities in Italy) to Lombard and Norman invasions, not to mention the malarial mosquito and the silting up of its port—the sea is now over a mile away. By the time Petrarch visited Luni in the 14th century, it was in such a melancholy state that he used it to evoke the ephemeral nature of human things. Excavations over the years have revealed a sizeable 2nd-century AD amphitheatre capable of seating 5000, the forum, houses (some with frescoes and mosaics), temples, and the palaeochristian basilica; on the site, the **Museo Nazionale di Luni** (*© 0187 66811, open April–Sept Tues–Sun 9–12 and 3–7; Oct–Mar Tues–Sun 2–7; adm L6000*) has a collection of marble statuary, coins, jewellery, portraits and so on, as well as a display of archaeological techniques used in excavating ancient Luni, which can be toured with a guide.

Near Luni, a by-road winds up to **Nicola**, an outpost of the bishop of Luni and a charming little walled village with a spiral plan, in a beautiful bucolic setting. On Easter morning, the men of Nicola still come to the main square to play *manda*, a game with a metal ball played according to ancient rules, which symbolized the end of the hunting season. Also here is medieval **Ortonovo**, a similar village of concentric streets that was sold by Florence to Genoa in 1454. To the north, **Castelnuova Magra** offers a change of pace, a long town stretched out along the crest of a hill with the Malaspina Castle on one end. In 1306 Dante was here, brokering a peace treaty between the Malaspina and the bishop of Luni. The church has a *Calvary* by Brueghel the Younger, and the region's *enoteca*, where you can try the local Vermentino dei Colli di Luni, recently accorded DOC status.

Sarzana

The big town on the lower Magra is **Sarzana**, the easternmost outpost of the Republic of Genoa. After the decline of ancient Luni and the conquest of the Lombards, Sarzana was the most important stronghold on the Riviera di Levante, and the seat of the bishopric of Luni from 1204 until 1929, when it was combined with that of La Spezia. Throughout the Middle Ages, Sarzana's strategic location on the Magra and on the Via Francigena, the main highway that linked Rome to northern Europe, attracted envious suitors: Pisa in 1284, Lucca in the early 14th century, Florence in 1486, and Genoa, which took it in 1562 and held on to it. Although bombed in the war, its fascinating historic centre has survived intact.

The Florentines built quite a bit during their tenure, including the **Palazzo Communale** in Piazza Luni, designed by the excellent Giuliano di Maiano for Lorenzo de' Medici, although regrettably the Genoese obliterated it and rebuilt their own version in the 16th century; it does have an elegant portico, decorated with coats of arms and fragments salvaged from ancient Luni. The main street, Via Mazzini, is lined with palaces and towers, including one tower at No.28 that belonged to the Buonaparte family before they emigrated to Corsica in the early 16th century. Nearby is Sarzana's oldest church, **Sant'Andrea**, founded in the 11th century, with its curious door framed by caryatids.

Further along, Sarzana's **cathedral** was built shortly after the bishopric was transferred here from Luni. It has a fine marble rose window and tower, and an imposing interior containing one of the best works of Master Guglielmo: a *Crucifixion* of 1138, one of the oldest of datable works of its kind in Italy, and two beautiful marble polyptychs made in the 1430s by Leonardo Riccomanni of Lucca. It also has its share of baroque paintings by native son Domenico Fiasello (otherwise known as Il Sarzana) and the *Annunciation with Saints* (1720) by Giuseppe Maria Crespi. From here, Via Castrocani leads north to the church of **San Francesco**, with good sculptures, including the tomb of Guarnerio degli Antelminelli, the infant son of Castruccio Castracani (1328), the rather likeable tyrant of Lucca whose name means 'dog-castrator'. Sarzana has two Tuscan forts. The imposing **Citadella** that still towers over Sarzana was built by Lorenzo de' Medici over an earlier

Pisan fortress. The **Fortezza di Sarzello**, built by Castruccio Castracani, is a mile to the east and in its 14th-century state-of-the-art construction resembles nothing as much as a giant steam iron.

To the east, just over the border in Tuscany, **Fosdinovo**'s Malaspina castle that lodged Dante in 1306 is one of the most beautiful and majestic in the region. Still owned by the family (*open daily exc Mon, 9–12, 3–6; adm*), it contains a collection of arms and ornaments found in local tombs.

Back on the West Bank of the Magra

Returning to the west bank of the Magra, across the bridge from Sarzana, a brief detour to the left takes you to Romito, the base of the road up to **Trebiano**, an intact medieval hill town where the parish church has a 15th-century *Crucifixion* and a holy water stoup made from a Roman altar. North from the bridge, on the other hand, the road leads up to **Árcola**, a perfect example of a compact Ligurian hill town, built around the pentagonal tower (all that remains of a castle); the Piazza della Parrocchiale is one of the most surprising and delightful in Liguria, with its grand stair in an otherwise typically rural setting.

North, **Vezzano Ligure** has two centres, Inferiore and Superiore, both overlooking the Val di Magra. The lower town has a pretty leafy square with lovely views; Vezzano Superiore piled on its knob of a hill has a similar square by the ruined castle, with a top of the line view over the junction of the Magra and Vara valleys. The parish church of **SS. Prospero e Ciro** has a lovely pebble mosaic and more views, stretching for miles on end.

Where to Stay and Eating Out

San Terenzo ⊠ 19036

Palmira, Via Trogo 13, ℰ 0187 971 094 (*expensive*) is a very popular trattoria that serves delightful *zuppa di vongole*, other seafood and meat dishes as well. *Closed Wed, and Sept and Oct.*

Lérici ⊠ 19032

The ★★★**Shelley & Delle Palme**, Lungomare Biaggini 5, ℰ 0187 968 204, ✆ 0187 964 271 (*moderate*) is one of the largest and most comfortable hotels on the 'Gulf of Poets', with fine views of the sea. On the left as you approach the town is the ★★★**Byron**, Via Biaggini 19, ℰ 0187 967 104, ✆ 0187 967 409 (*moderate*), also a good choice, where the slightly small rooms are compensated for by fine views across the bay and, on the third floor, huge balconies. ★★★**Doria Park**, Via Doria 2, ℰ 0187 967 124, ✆ 0187 966 459, *doriahotel@tamnet.it* (*moderate*), just over the headland, is slightly cheaper and also enjoys great views.

Outside town on the cove of Fiascherino ★★★**Il Nido**, Via Fiascherino 75, ℰ 0187 967 286, ✆ 0187 964 225 (*moderate*) enjoys a lovely location, with enchanting views over the sea and beach. The only inexpensive hotel in Lérici is the ★★**Hotel del Golfo**, Via Gerini 37, ℰ 0187 967 400, ✆ 0187 965 733 (*cheap*), just up from the tourist office. It's new and clean, and some rooms have balconies.

Near Lérici, in the more laid-back San Terenzo, ★★★**Elisabetta**, Via Mantegazza 21, ✆ 0187 970 636 (*cheap*) is tiny but comfortable, with a garden. ★★★**Mulino,** Via Garibaldi 30, ✆/✉ 0187 970 801 (*cheap*), on the road into the village, is not as well positioned but has similar prices.

There are even cheaper options along the seafront, including ★**Il Nettuno**, Via Mantegazza 1, ✆ 0187 971 093 (*cheap*), which has clean, big rooms, some with balconies, for under L70,000; or ★★**Giglio**, Via Garibaldi 26, ✆ 0187 970 805 (*cheap*), on the left as you come into the village, which has well-equipped rooms and a restaurant.

The best restaurant in Lérici is **Due Corona**, Via G Mazzini, ✆ 0187 967 417 (*very expensive*), beside the port, the deserving winner of two culinary awards. Seafood is, of course, a speciality; try their *cocktail di antipasti mare* and *grigliata mista*. *Closed Thurs*. **Paolino**, Via S. Francesco 14, ✆ 0187 967 801 (*expensive*) offers three dining choices—light, medium and full, depending on your appetite— with particularly good salads and pasta dishes.

Fiascherino/Tellaro ✉ 19030

★★**Miranda**, Via Fiascherino 92, at Tellaro ✆ 0187 968 130, ✉ 0187 964 032 (*moderate, but half pension only*) is a little seven-room charmer surrounded by lovely views; the restaurant (*expensive*) is open to non-guests and serves mouth-watering seafood dishes like prawn flan in white truffle sauce and fish *gnocchi* with pesto.

Montemarcello ✉ 19031

For a memorable dinner amid sweet old-fashioned décor, try **Pironcelli**, Via delle Mura 45, ✆ 0187 601 252 (*moderate*); look for all the classics of the Levante, including *mesciua*, the soup made of spelt, chick peas and cannellini beans. *Open weekday eves only, weekends for lunch and dinner, closed Wed.*

Ameglia ✉ 19031

Ameglia is the gourmet vortex for this far east end of the Riviera. The pioneer establishment, ★★★★**Paracucchi Locanda dell'Angelo**, at Ca' di Scabello, Viale V Aprile 60, ✆ 0187 64391/2, ✉ 0187 64393 (*moderate*) has a modern, stylish and slick hotel, with a new pool for the summer of '99 and the sea only a couple of minutes away; the restaurant (*very expensive*), founded by one of Italy's most famous chefs and cookbook writers, Angelo Parcucchi, is top notch; the menu changes often, but each dish is superb and often amazingly simple. Great desserts, especially the fruit flambée, and excellent wine list. *Closed Sun eve and Mon out of season.*

Also down by the sea at Fiumaretta, **Locanda delle Tamerici**, Via Litoranea 116, ✆ 0187 64262, ✉ 0187 64627 (*moderate rooms, restaurant very expensive*) has cosy, adorable, tranquil rooms by the sea and a romantic flower-filled garden; the restaurant rivals Angelo's for its lovely, flavour-enhanced seafood and vegetable dishes. A few days here on full board, unwinding by the sea, is one of the nicest possible cures for stress. *Closed Tues.*

Castelnuovo Magra ✉ 19030

People make special trips to dine at **Armanda**, Piazza Garibaldi 6, ✆ 0187 674 410 (*expensive–moderate*), where the famous speciality is stuffed lettuce in broth (*lattughe ripiene in brodo*), *cima*, an exquisite, delicate *torta* filled with zucchine and artichoke hearts, rabbit deboned and stuffed, and other authentic dishes. It's minute, so book. *Closed Wed.* For a wide selection of wines and tasty dishes to match them at Canale, the wine bar in an old, but still working mill, the **Mulino del Cibus**, ✆ 0187 676 102 (*moderate*) serves tasty food to match its bottles, whether you just feel like nibbling cheese and salami or need something more filling like lasagne or duck's breast in vinegar and honey. *Closed Mon.*

Sarzana ✉ 19038

★★★★**Al Sant'Andrea**, Aurelia 32, ✆ 0187 621 491, 🖷 0187 621 494 (*moderate*) is near the *autostrada*, comfortable and convenient. For an elegant meal, **Taverna Napoleone**, Via Mascardi 16, ✆ 0187 627 974 (*moderate*), housed in a restored stable, serves refined dishes based on ingredients from the garden (ravioli with radicchio, aubergine tart) with a few meat dishes thrown in. *Closed Wed.*

The Lunigiana

From Sarzana and La Spezia, the Val di Magra continues up through the rugged, chestnut-forested Lunigiana, the *entroterra* of ancient Luni that separates Liguria from Tuscany. It has traditionally been a tough nut to crack. The Romans found it a wild place, and even in the 7th century missionaries were still bashing revered ancient idols. Not long after, the first pilgrims and merchants were marching down the valley's Via Francigena to Rome, and by the early Middle Ages, castles of would-be rulers and toll-collecting gangsters were in place to make them pay for the privilege. In the early 1900s the Lunigiana was a stronghold of rural anarchism, and in 1944 its partisans made it one of the bigger free zones in the north.

Tourist Information

Pontrémoli: Piazza della Reppublica, ✆ 0187 831 180.

Aulla

Aulla grew up at the Lunigiana's hotly contested crossroads, guarding access into the Magra valley. The powerful, four-square 16th-century **Fortezza della Brunella** was built by the Genoese, who bought Aulla in 1543; Napoleon snatched it from them and handed it over to his sister Elisa in Lucca, and the province of Lucca has kept it ever since. The fortress now contains a small museum of natural history (*open daily 9–1, 3–6; adm*). Nearby are the citadels of two other rivals who fought for Aulla—the Bishop of Luni's **Caprigliola**, a fortified village still inaccessible to motor traffic (6km southwest on the

SS62) and the Malaspina's fortified hamlet of **Bibola** and romantically ruined **Ponzanello**, both due south of Aulla. The Malaspina also fortified the strategic road northeast to the pass, at **Licciana Nardi** and especially at **Bastia**, 4km further on.

North of Aulla, **Villafranca in Lunigiana** takes its name from its location on the Via Francigena; it offers the visitor two charming terracottas from the Della Robbia workshop in the 16th-century church of **San Francesco** and, in an old mill, an **Ethnographic Museum** (*open winter 9–1, 3–6, summer 9–12, 3–7; closed Mon; adm*) devoted to rural life in the Lunigiana, especially the chestnut industry. From Villafranca yet another mighty castle beckons up at **Bagnone**, 5km to the east.

Pontrémoli

Long, low-key, stretched out lazily along the shallow river Magra and the Torrente Verdi, Pontrémoli (pop. 10,200) is chief town of the Lunigiana and the northernmost in Tuscany. It wasn't always so peaceful: in the old days the quarrels between local Guelphs and Ghibellines were so vicious that in 1322 Castruccio Castracani built a fortress in the town centre, called *Cacciaguerra* ('Drive away war'), to keep the two parties apart until they made peace. Of this noble effort only the **Torre del Campanone** and what is now the campanile of the **Duomo** survive. The Duomo itself has a fine, ballroom interior, unusual for Tuscany, which rarely indulges in anything so frivolous. Over the Torrente Verdi, the church of **San Francesco** has a baroque entrance and contains a lovely polychrome relief of the Madonna and *bambino* attributed to Agostino di Duccio. Between the centre and the station the oval 18th-century church of **Nostra Donna** is another rare example of rococo that seeped over the frontier from Liguria.

Prehistoric Mysteries

Behind all these baubles, this hidden corner of Italy holds a genuine prehistoric mystery. Take the narrow medieval lanes above Pontrémoli up to the gloomy, 14th-century Castello del Piagnaro and its **Museo delle Statue-stele della Lunigiana** (*open summer 9–12, 4–7; Oct–May 9–12, 2–5, closed Mon; adm*). It holds over a score of large, carved statue steles made by the Celto-Ligurians or just plain old Ligurians, nearly all of which were discovered by accident. The steles, rather like menhirs with personality, depict stylized warriors with daggers or axes, and women with little knobbly breasts. The oldest (3000–2000 BC) have a U for a face and a head that is hardly distinguishable from the trunk; the middle period (2000–8th century BC) sport anvil heads and eyes; the last group (7th–2nd century BC) are mostly warriors, with a weapon in each hand, just as Virgil described the Gauls who invaded Lazio. The statue steles were often discovered near sources of water, and some scholars think they may have symbolized the heavens (the head), the earth (the arms and weapons) and the underworld (the lower third, buried in the ground). Similar statue steles turn up in southern Corsica, Languedoc, Portugal, Romania and the Crimea. Some of the steles had their heads knocked off, a sure sign that the pope's missionaries in the 8th century were doing their job. Curiously, in the nearby hamlet of

Vignol near Pontrémoli, a folk memory survives of the destruction of idols; during the patron saint's festival they make little wooden idols strangely similar to Pontrémoli's statue steles and burn them to celebrate the triumph over the pagans.

In 1471 the Virgin made an appearance a mile south of Pontrémoli, and to honour the spot the church of **Santissima Annunziata** was built with a lovely marble **Tempietto** by Jacopo Sansovino, a quattrocento fresco of the *Annunciation* by Luca Cambiaso, an elegant triptych of unknown hand or date, and some fun *trompe-l'œil* frescoes by a baroque painter from Cremona named Natali.

Where to Stay and Eating Out

Aulla ✉ 54011

A good central base in the region, the old-fashioned ★**Alpi Apuane di Malatesta** is in a former posthouse at Pallerone near Aulla, ✆ 0817 418 045, although rooms (*inexpensive*) are only a sideline to the fine restaurant (*moderate–inexpensive*), cosy in the winter with its fireplace. Specialities include wildfowl excellently prepared—pheasant, duck and pigeon, and, for big appetites, kid with polenta.

Also in Aulla is the sophisticated and refined **Il Rigoletto**, Quartiere Matteotti 29, ✆ 0187 409 879 (*expensive–moderate*) serving unusual and excellent food, such as salmon cooked with fennel and pear strudel with red wine sorbet and liquorice. *Closed Mon.*

Bagnone ✉ 54021

Up in fortified Bagnone, **I Fondi**, Via della Repubblica 26, ✆ 0187 429 086 (*inexpensive*) offers good, solid country cooking—trout, mushroom dishes, rabbit, stuffed cabbage, venison with polenta—amid simple Italian elegance.

Pontrémoli ✉ 54027

Pontrémoli is rich in good restaurants, and has two smart hotels, the new ★★★**Golf Hotel**, outside town in a pine wood, Via Pineta, ✆ 0187 831 573, 🖷 0187 831 591 (*moderate*), offering 90 very comfortable rooms, all with bath and TV; and the ★★★**Hotel Napoleon**, Piazza Italia 2B, ✆/🖷 0187 830 544 (*moderate*), with garage and modern rooms. When it's time to eat, there's the age-old **Da Bussé**, Piazza del Duomo 31, ✆ 0187 831 371 (*moderate*), featuring Pontrémoli's special pasta *testaroli*, roast meats, stuffed vegetables and other local dishes. *Closed Fri.* **La Romantica**, Piazza SS Annunziata 86, ✆ 0187 830 106, offers ravioli with basil and walnuts, artichoke or *porcini crocchette*, and a delicious selection of meat dishes (*moderate*). Another good bet in the centre, **Da Ferdinando**, Via San Gimignano, ✆ 0187 830 653 (*moderate–inexpensive*), is a little bistro in a 17th-century building, where you can dine on *testaroli* with pesto or boar *alla cacciatora*. *Closed Mon.*

c. 80,000 BC	First residents on the Riviera, in the Balzi Rossi caves
c. 5000 BC	Neolithic culture and technology reach Italy
c. 1800 BC	Celto-Ligurians begin to occupy the north
c. 900 BC	Arrival of Etruscans in Italy
753 BC	Legendary date of Rome's founding
390 BC	Rome sacked by Gauls
264–238 BC	First Punic War
236–222 BC	Romans capture Po Valley from Gauls; conquest complete up to the Rubicon
218–201 BC	Second Punic War; the Carthagians recruit the Ligurians to fight against Rome
177 BC	Romans found Luni
151–146 BC	Third Punic War and the destruction of Carthage
115–102 BC	Last Celtic raids on Italy
100 BC	Birth of Julius Caesar
59 BC	First Triumvirate formed: Caesar, Pompey and Crassus
51 BC	Caesar conquers Transalpine Gaul
50 BC	Caesar crosses the Rubicon and seizes Rome
44 BC	Caesar done in by friends
42–32 BC	Second Triumvirate: Octavian, Mark Antony and Lepidus
31 BC	Battle of Actium leaves Octavian sole ruler of the Empire
27 BC–AD 17	Octavian (now Augustus Caesar) rules Rome as Princeps
AD 42	St Peter comes to Rome
305	Diocletian's reforms turn the Empire into a bureaucratized despotism
330	Pagan temples closed by order of Emperor Constantine

Chronology

364	Final division of the Empire into eastern and western halves
402	Ravenna becomes capital of Western Empire
476	Western Empire ends when the Goth Odoacer is crowned King of Italy
493–514	Theodoric rules the west, mostly from Ravenna
540	Byzantines capture Ravenna and rule it through their Exarchs; they also control the coast of Liguria

568	Lombards invade Italy
590	Lombards become orthodox Christians
641	Lombards finally take the Riviera
800	Charlemagne crowned Emperor in Rome
901	First Saracens on the Riviera
962	Otto the Great occupies north Italy, and is crowned emperor at Rome
1075	Beginning of Investiture conflict between popes and emperors
1097	First Crusade: Genoa and other Ligurian seaports win their first trading concessions in the East
1099	Genoa becomes a *comune*
1167	To combat Emperor Barbarossa, cities in the north form Lombard League
1171	At Genoese instigation, the emperor of Constantinople arrests Venice's trading colony, 200,000 strong, and confiscates its goods. Doge declares war and leads Venice into one of its most humiliating defeats
1183	Treaty of Constance between Barbarossa and Lombard League
1204	Taking charge of the Fourth Crusade, the Venetians capture Constantinople
1261	Charles of Anjou invades Italy at behest of the Pope
1266	Charles defeats the last of the Hohenstaufens
1284	Genoa defeats Pisa at Meloria and becomes the chief sea power in the western Mediterranean
1298	Genoa defeats Venice at Curzola, sinking 65 out of the total fleet of 95 ships, and captures Marco Polo
1309	French Pope Clement V moves papacy to Avignon
1314	Dante completes the *Commedia*
1339	Genoa bars nobles from power and elects its first Doge, Simone Boccanegra
1348	The Black Death halves the population
1377	Papacy moves back to Rome once and for all
1380	Genoa defeated by Venice at Chioggia
1402	Death of Milan boss Gian Galeazzo Visconti leaves most of northern Italy up for grabs
1453	Mahomet II captures Constantinople
1492	A certain admiral from Genoa discovers the New World for Spain
1494	Italy invaded by Charles VIII of France
1495	Indecisive Battle of Fornovo; Italian armies, led by Venice, try to stop the French army of Charles VIII

1498	Vasco da Gama's voyage around the Horn
1519	Charles V elected Holy Roman Emperor
1522	Imperial army sacks Genoa
1527	Imperial army sacks Rome
1528	Andrea Doria sells Genoa's French allies down the river and puts the Republic of Genoa under the protection of Spain
1534	Founding of the Jesuits
1545–63	Council of Trent initiates reforms in the Catholic Church
1547	Fieschi conspiracy against Andrea Doria fails
1559	Treaty of Château-Cambrésis confirms Spanish control of Italy; Andrea Doria recaptures Corsica for Genoa
1571	Battle of Lepanto, great naval victory over the Turks in the Gulf of Corinth, won by the Holy League led by Spain and Venice
1657	Cholera rages along the Riviera
1684	Louis XIV bombards Genoa
1700–13	War of the Spanish Succession
1720	The Dukes of Savoy becomes the Kings of Piedmont-Sardinia
1746	Genoa occupied by Austrians during War of the Austrian Succession, but successfully kicks out the intruders
1768	Genoa sells Corsica to the king of France
1797	Napoleon changes the Republic of Genoa into the Republic of Liguria
1809–12	Napoleon imprisons Pope Pius VII in Savona
1815	Liguria annexed to the Piemonte
1848	Garibaldi and Mazzini run the Republic of Rome
1855	Giovanni Ruffini publishes *Doctor Antonio* in Edinburgh and excites British interest in the Riviera
1860	Garibaldi and his Thousand conquer Sicily and the Kingdom of Naples, leaving all of Italy, except for Rome and Venetia, unified under King Vittorio Emanuele II; Nice and western Liguria given to France
1869	Opening of Suez Canal
1887	Earthquake centred in Bussana damages many towns on the Riviera di Ponente
1915	Italy enters the First World War
1917	Military disaster at Caporetto
1918	Victory over Austria at Vittorio Veneto

1920	Treaty of Rapallo defines Italy's eastern frontiers
1925	Conversion of Italy to a Fascist dictatorship
1935	War against Ethiopia
1940	Italy enters the Second World War
1943	Nazis set up Mussolini in puppet government at Salò
1946	National referendum makes Italy a republic
1956	Italy becomes a charter member of the EU
1950s	Continuing 'economic miracle' integrates Italy more closely into Western Europe
1990	*Mani pulite* investigations begin in Milan, leading to the downfall of Italy's corrupt and Mafia-tainted political parties
1992	Columbus celebrations in Genoa
1999	Italy joins in the new Euro currency

Barzini, Luigi, *The Italians* (Atheneum, 1996). A perhaps too clever account of the Italians by an Italian journalist living in London in the 1960s, but one of the classics.

Burckhardt, Jacob, *The Civilisation of the Renaissance in Italy* (Phaidon, 1995). The classic on the subject (first published 1860), the mark against which scholars still level their poison arrows of revisionism.

Columbus, Christopher, *The Book of Prophecies Edited by Christopher Columbus* (University of California, 1996). When he returned from his Third Voyage in chains, the Admiral compiled this peculiar list of Biblical writings, prophecies and medieval theology in a manuscript, in the hopes of justifying himself and preserving his rights.

Hibbert, Christopher, *Garibaldi and his Enemies* (Penguin, 1987). The whole sorry tale, told entertainingly by a master.

De Madaraiga, Salvador, *Christopher Columbus* (Greenwood, 1979). Translated from Spanish, the intriguing if largely unsubstantiated theory that Columbus was Jewish.

Procacci, Giuliano, *History of the Italian People* (Penguin, sadly out of print). An in-depth view from the year 1000 to the present—also an introduction to the wit and subtlety of the best Italian scholarship.

Sardi, Roland, *Mazzini* (Praeger, 1996). New, full-length biography of Genoa's great revolutionary and an in-depth exploration of his precocious ideals.

Smith, Denis Mack, *Garibaldi: A Great Life in Brief* (Greenwood, 1982) and *Mazzini* (Yale, 1994). Biographies by one of the best authors on modern Italian history.

Tagliattini, Maurizio, *The Discovery of North America* (not yet published). Read his chapter 10 on Columbus on the web at *www.millersv.edu/~columbus/ tagliattini.html* .

Trevelyan, G.M., *Garibaldi and the Making of Italy* (Greenwood, 1982). Tales of the Risorgimento.

Wittkower, Rudolf, *Art and Architecture in Italy 1600–1750* (Pelican, 1992). The classic on Italian baroque; good for putting the Genoese in context.

Further Reading

Atrium: entrance court of a Roman house or early church

Badia: abbazia, an abbey or abbey church

Baldacchino: baldachin, a columned stone canopy above the altar of a church

Basilica: a rectangular building, usually divided into three aisles by rows of columns. In Rome this was the common form for law courts and other public buildings, and Roman Christians adapted it for their early churches

Calvary chapels: a series of outdoor chapels, usually on a hillside, that commemorate the stages of the Passion of Christ

Campanile: a bell tower

Camposanto: a cemetery

Cardo: transverse street of a Roman castrium-shaped city

Carrugi: narrow Ligurian alleys

Cartoon: the preliminary sketch for a fresco or tapestry

Caryatid: supporting pillar or column carved into a standing female form; male versions are called telamons

Castellari: ancient Ligurian fortified settlements, often on hilltops

Castrum: a Roman military camp, always nearly rectangular, with straight streets and gates at the cardinal points. Later the Romans founded or refounded cities in this form, and hundreds of these survive today

Cavea: the semicircle of seats in a classical theatre

Cenacolo: fresco of the Last Supper, often on the wall of a monastery refectory

Centro Storico: historic centre

Ciborium: a tabernacle; the word is often used for large, free-standing tabernacles, or in the sense of a baldacchino

Chiaroscuro: the arrangement or treatment of light and dark in a painting

Comune: commune, or commonwealth, referring to the governments of the free cities of the Middle Ages. Today it denotes any local government, from the *Comune di Roma* down to the smallest village

Condottiere: the leader of a band of mercenaries in late medieval and Renaissance times

Confraternity: a religious lay brotherhood, often serving as a neighbourhood mutual aid and burial society, or following some specific charitable work (Michelangelo, for example, belonged to one that cared for condemned prisoners in Rome)

Cortile: inner atrium or courtyard of a palace

Cupola: a dome

Decumanus: street of a Roman castrum-shaped city parallel to the longer axis: the central, main avenue was called the Decumanus Major

Duomo: cathedral

Entroterra: the Ligurian hinterland; each coastal town has its *entroterra*

Forum: the central square of a Roman town, with its most important temples and public buildings. The word means 'outside', as the original Roman Forum was outside the first city walls

Frantoio: olive press

Fresco: wall painting, the most important Italian medium of art since Etruscan times. It isn't easy: first the artist draws the sinopia (q.v.) on the wall. This is then covered with plaster, but only a little at a time, as the paint must be on the plaster before it dries. Leonardo da Vinci's endless attempts to find clever shortcuts ensured that little of his work would survive

Ghibellines: one of the two great medieval parties, the supporters of the Holy Roman Emperors

Gonfalon: the banner of a medieval free city; the gonfaloniere, or flag-bearer, was often the most important public official.

Grotesques: carved or painted faces used in Etruscan and later Roman decoration; Raphael and other artists rediscovered them in the 'grotto' of Nero's Golden House in Rome.

Guelphs (*see* Ghibellines): the other great political faction of medieval Italy, supporters of the Pope

Intarsia: work in inlaid wood or marble

Lungomare: seaside; also a name given to a coastal road

Monte di Pietà: municipal pawn shop

Narthex: the enclosed porch of a church

Palazzo: not just a palace, but any large, important building (though the word comes from the Imperial palatium on Rome's Palatine Hill)

Passeggiata: promenade

Piano: upper floor or storey in a building; *Piano Nobile*, the first floor

Pieve: a parish church, especially in the north

Architectural, Artistic and Historic Terms

Podestà: a mayor or governor from outside a *comune*, usually chosen by the emperor or overlord; sometimes a factionalized city would itself invite a *podestà* in for a period to sort itself out

Polyptych: an altarpiece composed of more than three panels

Predella: smaller paintings on panels below the main subject of a painted altarpiece

Presepio: a Christmas crib

Putti: flocks of plaster cherubs with rosy cheeks and bums that infested baroque Italy

Quadratura: *trompe l'oeil* architectural settings, popular in Mannerist and baroque time, and something of a speciality of artists from Bologna

Quattrocento: the 1400s—the Italian way of referring to centuries (duecento, trecento, quattrocento, cinquecento, etc.)

Risseu: a figurative black and white pebble mosaic, often in a sagrato of a Ligurian church or oratory

Rocca: a citadel

Sacra Conversazione: Madonna enthroned with saints

Sagrato: a specially marked holy area or *parvis* just outside a church

Scuola: the headquarters of a confraternity or guild, usually adjacent to a church

Sinopia: the layout of a fresco (q.v.), etched by the artist on the wall before the plaster is applied. Often these are works of art in their own right

Terra firma: Venice's mainland possessions

Thermae: Roman baths

Tondo: round relief, painting or terracotta

Transenna: marble screen separating the altar area from the rest of an early Christian church

Triptych: a painting, especially an altarpiece, in three sections

Trompe l'œil: art that uses perspective effects to deceive the eye—for example, to create the illusion of depth on a flat surface, or to make columns and arches painted on a wall seem real

Tympanum: the semicircular space, often bearing a painting or relief, above a portal

The fathers of modern Italian were Dante, Manzoni and television. Each had a part in creating a national language from an infinity of regional and local dialects; the Florentine Dante, the first to write in the vernacular, did much to put the Tuscan dialect in the foreground of Italian literature. Manzoni's revolutionary novel, *I Promessi Sposi*, heightened national consciousness by using an everyday language all could understand in the 19th century. Television in the last few decades is performing an even more spectacular linguistic unification; although the majority of Italians still speak a dialect at home, school and work, their TV idols insist on proper Italian.

Perhaps because they are so busy learning their own beautiful but grammatically complex language, Italians are not especially apt at learning others. English lessons, however, have been the rage for years, and at most hotels and restaurants there will be someone who speaks some English. In small towns and out-of-the-way places, finding an Anglophone may prove more difficult. The words and phrases below should help you out in most situations, but the ideal way to come to Italy is with some Italian under your belt; your visit will be richer, and you're much more likely to make some Italian friends.

Italian words are pronounced phonetically. Every vowel and consonant is sounded. Consonants are the same as in English, except the 'c' which, when followed by an 'e' or 'i', is pronounced like the English 'ch' (*cinque* thus becomes cheenquay). Italian 'g' is also soft before 'i' or 'e' as in *gira*, or jee-ra. 'H' is never sounded; 'z' is pronounced like 'ts'. The consonants 'sc' before the vowels 'i' or 'e' becomes like the English 'sh' as in 'sci', pronounced shee; 'ch' is pronouced like a 'k' as in Chianti, kee-an-tee; 'gn' as 'ny' in English (*bagno*, pronounced ban-yo); while 'gli' is pronounced like the middle of the word million (Castiglione, pronounced Ca-stee-lyon-ay).

Vowel pronunciation is: 'a' as in English father; 'e' when unstressed is pronounced like 'a' in fate as in *mele*, when stressed can be the same or like the 'e' in pet (*bello*); 'i' is like the 'i' in machine; 'o', like 'e', has two sounds, 'o' as in hope when unstressed (*tacchino*), and usually 'o' as in rock when stressed (*morte*); 'u' is pronounced like the 'u' in June.

The accent usually (but not always!) falls on the penultimate syllable. Also note that in the

Language

big northern cities, the informal way of addressing someone as you, *tu*, is widely used; the more formal *lei* or *voi* is commonly used in provincial districts.

Useful Words and Phrases

yes/no/maybe	*si/ no/ forse*	Good night	*Buona notte*
I don't know	*Non lo so*	Goodbye	*Arrivederla* (formal), *arrivederci, ciao* (informal)
I don't understand (Italian)	*Non capisco (italiano)*	What?/Who?/Where?	*Che?/Chi?/Dove?*
Does someone here speak English?	*C'è qualcuno qui che parla inglese?*	When?/Why?	*Quando?/Perché?*
Speak slowly	*Parla lentamente*	How?	*Come?*
Could you assist me?	*Potrebbe aiutarmi?*	How much?	*Quanto?*
Help!	*Aiuto!*	I am lost	*Mi sono smarrito*
Please	*Per favore*	I am hungry	*Ho fame*
Thank you (very much)	*(Molte) grazie*	I am thirsty	*Ho sete*
You're welcome	*Prego*	I am sleepy	*Ho sonno*
What do you call this in Italian?	*Come si chiama questo in italiano?*	I am sorry	*Mi dispiace*
It doesn't matter	*Non importa*	I am tired	*Sono stanco*
All right	*Va bene*	I am ill	*Mi sento male*
Excuse me	*Mi scusi*	Leave me alone	*Lasciami in pace*
Be careful!	*Attenzione!*	good	*buono/bravo*
Nothing	*Niente*	bad	*male/cattivo*
It is urgent!	*È urgente!*	It's all the same	*Fa lo stesso*
How are you?	*Come sta?*	fast	*rapido*
Well, and you?	*Bene, e lei?*	slow	*lento*
What is your name?	*Come si chiama?*	big	*grande*
Hello	*Salve* or *ciao* (both informal)	small	*piccolo*
		hot	*caldo*
Good morning	*Buongiorno* (formal hello)	cold	*freddo*
		up	*su*
Good afternoon, evening	*Buonasera* (also formal hello)	down	*giù*
		here	*qui*
		there	*lì*

Shopping, Service, Sightseeing

I would like...	*Vorrei...*	money	*soldi*
Where is/are...	*Dov'è/Dove sono...*	newspaper (foreign)	*giornale (straniero)*
How much is it?	*Quanto viene questo?*	pharmacy	*farmacia*
open	*aperto*	police station	*commissariato*
closed	*chiuso*	policeman	*poliziotto*
cheap/expensive	*a buon prezzo/caro*	post office	*ufficio postale*
bank	*banca*	sea	*mare*
beach	*spiaggia*	shop	*negozio*
bed	*letto*	room	*camera*
church	*chiesa*	tobacco shop	*tabaccaio*
entrance	*entrata*	WC	*toilette/bagno*
exit	*uscita*	men	*Signori/Uomini*
hospital	*ospedale*	women	*Signore/Donne*

Time

What time is it?	*Che ore sono?*	today	*oggi*
month	*mese*	yesterday	*ieri*
week	*settimana*	tomorrow	*domani*
day	*giorno*	soon	*fra poco*
morning	*mattina*	later	*dopo/più tardi*
afternoon	*pomeriggio*	It is too early	*È troppo presto*
evening	*sera*	It is too late	*È troppo tardi*

Days

Monday	*lunedì*	Friday	*venerdì*
Tuesday	*martedì*	Saturday	*sabato*
Wednesday	*mercoledì*	Sunday	*domenica*
Thursday	*giovedì*		

Numbers

one	*uno/una*	twenty	*venti*
two	*due*	twenty-one	*ventuno*
three	*tre*	twenty-two	*ventidue*
four	*quattro*	thirty	*trenta*
five	*cinque*	thirty-one	*trentuno*
six	*sei*	forty	*quaranta*
seven	*sette*	fifty	*cinquanta*
eight	*otto*	sixty	*sessanta*
nine	*nove*	seventy	*settanta*
ten	*dieci*	eighty	*ottanta*
eleven	*undici*	ninety	*novanta*
twelve	*dodici*	hundred	*cento*
thirteen	*tredici*	one hundred & one	*centouno*
fourteen	*quattordici*	two hundred	*duecento*
fifteen	*quindici*	one thousand	*mille*
sixteen	*sedici*	two thousand	*duemila*
seventeen	*diciassette*	million	*milione*
eighteen	*diciotto*	a thousand million	*miliardo*
nineteen	*diciannove*		

Transport

airport	*aeroporto*	port station	*stazione marittima*
automobile	*macchina*	railway station	*stazione ferroviaria*
bus/coach	*autobus/pullman*	seat (reserved)	*posto (prenotato)*
bus stop	*fermata*	ship	*nave*
customs	*dogana*	taxi	*tassì*
platform	*binario*	ticket	*biglietto*
port	*porto*	train	*treno*

Travel Directions

I want to go to...	*Desidero andare a...*	Have a good trip	*Buon viaggio!*
How can I get to...?	*Come posso andare a...?*	near	*vicino*
		far	*lontano*
Do you stop at...?	*Ferma a...?*	left	*sinistra*
Where is...?	*Dov'è...?*	right	*destra*
How far is it to...?	*Quanto siamo lontani da...?*	straight ahead	*sempre diritto*
		forward	*avanti*
When does the ... leave?	*A che ora parte ... ?*	backwards	*indietro*
What is the name of this station?	*Come si chiama questa stazione?*	north	*nord*
		south	*sud*
When does the next ... leave?	*Quando parte il prossimo...?*	east	*est/oriente*
From where does it leave?	*Da dove parte?*	west	*ovest/occidente*
		round the corner	*dietro l'angolo*
How long does the trip take...?	*Quanto tempo dura il viaggio?*	crossroads	*bivio*
		street/road	*strada*
How much is the fare?	*Quant'è il biglietto?*	square	*piazza*

Driving

bicycle	*bicicletta*	motorbike/scooter	*motocicletta/Vespa*
breakdown	*guasto* or *panne*	narrow	*stretto*
bridge	*ponte*	no parking	*sosta vietata*
car hire	*noleggio macchina*	parking	*parcheggio*
danger	*pericolo*	petrol/diesel	*benzina/gasolio*
driver	*guidatore*	slow down	*rallentare*
driving licence	*patente di guida*	speed	*velocità*
garage	*garage*	This doesn't work	*Questo non funziona*
map/town plan	*carta/pianta*	toll	*pedaggio*
mechanic	*meccanico*	Where is the road to...?	*Dov'è la strada per...?*

Italian Menu Vocabulary

Antipasti

These before-meal treats can include almost anything; among the most common are:

antipasto misto	mixed antipasto
bruschetta	garlic toast (sometimes with tomatoes)
carciofi (sott'olio)	artichokes (in oil)
crostini	liver pâté on toast
frutti di mare	seafood
funghi (trifolati)	mushrooms (with anchovies, garlic, and lemon)
gamberi ai fagioli	prawns (shrimps) with white beans
mozzarella (in carrozza)	cow or buffalo cheese (fried with bread in batter)
olive	olives
prosciutto (con melone)	raw ham (with melon)
salami	cured pork
salsicce	sausages

Minestre (Soups) and Pasta

These dishes are the principal typical first courses (*primi*) served throughout Italy.

agnolotti	ravioli with meat
cacciucco	spiced fish soup
cannelloni	meat and cheese rolled in pasta tubes
cappelletti	small ravioli, often in broth
crespelle	crêpes
fettuccine	long strips of pasta
frittata	omelette
gnocchi	potato dumplings
lasagne	sheets of pasta baked with meat and cheese sauce
minestra di verdura	thick vegetable soup
minestrone	soup with meat, vegetables, and pasta
orecchiette	ear-shaped pasta, often served with turnip greens
panzerotti	ravioli filled with mozzarella, anchovies, and egg
pappardelle alla lepre	pasta with hare sauce
pasta e fagioli	soup with beans, bacon, and tomatoes
pastina in brodo	tiny pasta in broth
penne all'arrabbiata	quill-shaped pasta with tomatoes and hot peppers
polenta	cake or pudding of corn semolina
risotto (alla milanese)	Italian rice (with stock, saffron and wine)
spaghetti all'amatriciana	with spicy sauce of salt pork, tomatoes, onions, and chilli
spaghetti alla bolognese	with ground meat, ham, mushrooms,etc
spaghetti alla carbonara	with bacon, eggs, and black pepper
spaghetti al pomodoro	with tomato sauce
spaghetti al sugo/ragù	with meat sauce
spaghetti alle vongole	with clam sauce
stracciatella	broth with eggs and cheese
sagliatelle	flat egg noodles
tortellini al pomodoro/panna/in brodo	pasta caps filled with meat and cheese, with tomato sauce/with cream/in broth
vermicelli	very thin spaghetti

Carne (Meat)

abbacchio	milk-fed lamb
agnello	lamb
anatra	duck
animelle	sweetbreads
arista	pork loin
arrosto misto	mixed roast meats
bistecca alla fiorentina	Florentine beef steak
bocconcini	veal mixed with ham and cheese and fried
bollito misto	stew of boiled meats
braciola	chop
brasato di manzo	braised beef with vegetables
bresaola	dried raw meat similar to ham
capretto	kid
capriolo	roebuck
carne di castrato/suino	mutton/pork

carpaccio	thin slices of raw beef served with a piquant sauce
cassoeula	winter stew with pork and cabbage
cervello (al burro nero)	brains (in black butter sauce)
cervo	venison
cinghiale	boar
coniglio	rabbit
cotoletta (alla milanese/alla bolognese)	veal cutlet (fried in breadcrumbs/with ham and cheese)
fagiano	pheasant
faraona (alla creta)	guinea fowl (in earthenware pot)
fegato alla veneziana	liver (usually of veal) with filling
lepre (in salmi)	hare (marinated in wine)
lombo di maiale	pork loin
lumache	snails
maiale (al latte)	pork (cooked in milk)
manzo	beef
ossobuco	braised veal knuckle with herbs
pancetta	rolled pork
pernice	partridge
petto di pollo	boned chicken breast
(alla fiorentina/bolognese/ sorpresa)	(fried in butter/with ham and cheese/ stuffed and deep fried)
piccione	pigeon
pizzaiola	beef steak with tomato and oregano sauce
pollo	chicken
(alla cacciatora/alla diavola/ alla Marengo)	(with tomatoes and mushrooms cooked in wine/grilled/ fried with tomatoes, garlic and wine)
polpette	meatballs
quaglie	quails
rane	frogs
rognoni	kidneys
saltimbocca	veal scallop with prosciutto and sage, cooked in wine and butter
scaloppine	thin slices of veal sautéed in butter
spezzatino	pieces of beef or veal, usually stewed
spiedino	meat on a skewer or stick
stufato	beef braised in white wine with vegetables
tacchino	turkey
trippa	tripe
uccelletti	small birds on a skewer
vitello	veal

Pesce (Fish)

acciughe or alici	anchovies
anguilla	eel
aragosta	lobster
aringa	herring
baccalà	dried salt cod
bonito	small tuna
branzino	sea bass
calamari	squid

cappe sante	scallops
cefalo	grey mullet
coda di rospo	angler fish
cozze	mussels
datteri di mare	razor (or date) mussels
dentice	dentex (perch-like fish)
dorato	gilt head
fritto misto	mixed fried delicacies, usually fish
gamberetto	shrimp
gamberi (di fiume)	prawns (crayfish)
granchio	crab
insalata di mare	seafood salad
lampreda	lamprey
merluzzo	cod
nasello	hake
orata	bream
ostriche	oysters
pescespada	swordfish
polipi/ polpi	octopus
pesce azzurro	various types of small fish
pesce di San Pietro	John Dory
rombo	turbot
sarde	sardines
seppie	cuttlefish
sgombro	mackerel
sogliola	sole
squadro	monkfish
tonno	tuna
triglia	red mullet (rouget)
trota	trout
trota salmonata	salmon trout
vongole	small clams
zuppa di pesce	mixed fish in sauce or stew

Contorni (Side Dishes, Vegetables)

asparagi (alla fiorentina)	asparagus (with fried eggs)
broccoli (calabrese, romana)	broccoli (green, spiral)
carciofi (alla giudia)	artichokes (deep fried)
cardi	cardoons, thistles
carote	carrots
cavolfiore	cauliflower
cavolo	cabbage
ceci	chickpeas
cetriolo	cucumber
cipolla	onion
fagioli	white beans
fagiolini	French (green) beans
fave	broad beans
finocchio	fennel
funghi (porcini)	mushrooms (boletus)

insalata (mista, verde)	salad (mixed, green)
lattuga	lettuce
lenticchie	lentils
melanzane (al forno)	aubergine/eggplant (filled and baked)
patate (fritte)	potatoes (fried)
peperoni	sweet peppers
peperonata	stewed peppers, onions, etc., similar to ratatouille
piselli (al prosciutto)	peas (with ham)
pomodoro (i)	tomato(es)
porri	leeks
radicchio	red chicory
radice	radish
rapa	turnip
sedano	celery
spinaci	spinach
verdure	greens
zucca	pumpkin
zucchini	courgettes

Formaggio (Cheese)

bel paese	a soft white cow's cheese
cacio/caciocavallo	pale yellow, often sharp cheese
fontina	rich cow's milk cheese
groviera	mild cheese (gruyère)
gorgonzola	soft blue cheese
parmigiano	Parmesan cheese
pecorino	sharp sheep's cheese
provolone	sharp, tangy cheese; dolce is less strong
stracchino	soft white cheese

Frutta (Fruit, Nuts)

albicocche	apricots
ananas	pineapple
arance	oranges
banane	bananas
cachi	persimmon
ciliege	cherries
cocomero	watermelon
composta di frutta	stewed fruit
datteri	dates
fichi	figs
fragole (con panna)	strawberries (with cream)
frutta di stagione	fruit in season
lamponi	raspberries
macedonia di frutta	fruit salad
mandarino	tangerine
mandorle	almonds
melagrana	pomegranate
mele	apples

melone	melon
mirtilli	bilberries
more	blackberries
nespola	medlar fruit
nocciole	hazelnuts
noci	walnuts
pera	pear
pesca	peach
pesca noce	nectarine
pinoli	pine nuts
pompelmo	grapefruit
prugna/susina	prune/plum
uva	grapes

Dolci (Desserts)

amaretti	macaroons
cannoli	crisp pastry tubes filled with ricotta, cream, chocolate or fruit
coppa gelato	assorted ice cream
crema caramella	caramel-topped custard
crostata	fruit flan
gelato (produzione propria)	ice-cream (homemade)
granita	flavoured ice, usually lemon or coffee
Monte Bianco	chestnut pudding with whipped cream
panettone	sponge cake with candied fruit and raisins
panforte	dense cake of chocolate, almonds and preserved fruit
Saint-Honoré	meringue cake
semifreddo	refrigerated cake
sorbetto	sorbet/sherbet
spumone	a soft ice cream
tiramisù	sponge fingers, mascarpone, coffee and chocolate
torrone	nougat
torta	cake, tart
torta millefoglie	layered pastry with custard cream
zabaglione	whipped eggs, sugar and Marsala wine, served hot
zuppa inglese	trifle

Bevande (Beverages)

acqua minerale con/senza gas	mineral water with/without fizz
aranciata	orange soda
birra (alla spina)	beer (draught)
caffè (freddo)	coffee (iced)
cioccolata (con panna)	chocolate (with cream)
gassosa	lemon-flavoured soda
latte	milk
limonata	lemon soda
succo di frutta	fruit juice
tè	tea
vino (rosso, bianco, rosato)	wine (red, white, rosé)

Cooking Terms, Miscellaneous

aceto (balsamico)	vinegar (balsamic)
affumicato	smoked
aglio	garlic
alla brace	on embers
bicchiere	glass
burro	butter
cacciagione	game
conto	bill
costoletta/cotoletta	chop
coltello	knife
cucchiaio	spoon
filetto	fillet
forchetta	fork
forno	oven
fritto	fried
ghiaccio	ice
griglia	grill
in bianco	without tomato
limone	lemon
magro	lean meat/or pasta without meat
marmellata	jam
menta	mint
miele	honey
mostarda	candied mustard sauce, eaten with boiled meats
olio	oil
pane (tostato)	bread (toasted)
panini	sandwiches
panna	cream
pepe	pepper
peperoncini	hot chilli peppers
piatto	plate
prezzemolo	parsley
ripieno	stuffed
rosmarino	rosemary
sale	salt
salmi	wine marinade
salsa	sauce
salvia	sage
senape	mustard
sartufi	truffles
tazza	cup
tavola	table
tovagliolo	napkin
tramezzini	finger sandwiches
umido	cooked in sauce
uovo	egg
zucchero	sugar

Main page references are in **bold**. Page references to maps are in *italics*.

Index

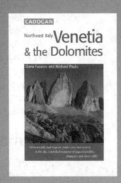
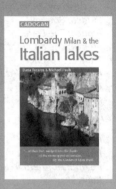

Also Available from Cadogan Guides...

Country Guides

Antarctica
Belize
Central Asia
China: The Silk Routes
Egypt
France: Southwest France;
    Dordogne, Lot & Bordeaux
France: Southwest France;
    Gascony & the Pyrenees
France: Brittany
France: The Loire
France: The South of France
France: Provence
France: the Côte d'Azur
Germany: Bavaria
India
India: South India
India: Goa
Ireland
Ireland: Southwest Ireland
Ireland: Northern Ireland
Italy
Italy: The Bay of Naples and Southern Italy
Italy: Lombardy, Milan and the Italian Lakes
Italy: Venetia and the Dolomites
Italy: Tuscany and Umbria
Japan
Morocco
Portugal
Portugal: The Algarve
Scotland
Scotland's Highlands and Islands
South Africa, Swaziland and Lesotho
Spain
Spain: Southern Spain
Spain: Northern Spain
Syria & Lebanon
Tunisia
Turkey
Western Turkey
Yucatán and Southern Mexico
Zimbabwe, Botswana and Namibia

City Guides

Amsterdam
Brussels, Bruges, Ghent & Antwerp
Edinburgh
Florence, Siena, Pisa & Lucca
Italy: Three Cities—Rome, Florence, Venice
Italy: Three Cities—Rome, Naples, Capri
Italy: Three Cities—Venice, Padua, Verona
Spain: Three Cities—Granada, Seville,
    Cordoba
London
Madrid
Manhattan
Moscow & St Petersburg
Paris
Prague
Rome
Venice

Island Guides

Caribbean and Bahamas
NE Caribbean; The Leeward Is.
SE Caribbean; The Windward Is.
Jamaica & the Caymans

Greek Islands
Crete
Mykonos, Santorini & the Cyclades
Rhodes & the Dodecanese
Corfu & the Ionian Islands

Madeira & Porto Santo
Malta
Sicily

Plus...

Southern Africa on the Wild Side
Bugs, Bites & Bowels
Travel by Cargo Ship
London Markets

Available from good bookshops or via, in the UK, **Grantham Book Services**, Isaac Newton Way, Alma Park Industrial Estate, Grantham NG31 9SD, ✆ (01476) 541 080, @ 541 061; and in North America from **The Globe Pequot Press**, 6, Business Park Road, Old Saybrook, Connecticut 06475-0833, ✆ (800) 243 0495, @ 820 2329.